South West France
and the Dordogne

South West France made-to-measure

South West France à la carte

South West France in detail

South West France made-to-measure

DÉGUSTATION ICI!

Of course, some people associate the Bordeaux region with only one thing – great wine. Look out for the 'dégustation' signs and try the local vintage during your holiday, whether at one of the smaller châteaux or one of the great wine-cellars of the region, such as Château Margaux. It's an essential part of any holiday to the region. See page 34 for more information.

A weekend
in Bordeaux

landscaped garden where you can linger for just long enough to gather your strength before setting out on the wine tour (p. 197), an excursion not to be missed! Spend as long as you need here; then, to test the effect of the wine on your balance, go and visit the battle cruiser *Colbert*, with its steep,

To get a feel for this prosperous regional capital, take a close look at the imposing façades lining the quays. The best place for this is from the Pont de Pierre, with its view of the Place de la Bourse (p. 201). From here you'll see the grand effect the burghers of Bordeaux were trying to achieve. To see the sort of houses they lived in, visit the Musée des Chartrons, in the heart of the wine-merchants' district (p. 198). It's a good neighbourhood for browsing, particularly in the antique shops, and the beautiful public park is only five minutes away. This is a lovely

narrow companionways (p. 200). You'll just have the time to take a look at the Rue Sainte-Catherine before the evening, when you can mingle with the student crowd in the cafés in the Place de la Victoire. The next day, turn up early at the flea market in the Saint-Michel district (p. 63), and you may unearth the mahogany wardrobe of your dreams. At La Tupina restaurant you can test the 'retour du marché' menu (p. 31). If you're not too full after your delicious meal, why not visit the Musée d'Art Contemporain, the CAPC (p. 198) or perhaps sample the rich regional history in the Musée d'Aquitaine? Take advantage of any fine weather by going down to the Quinconces pier (p. 197) and crossing the Gironde to visit the citadel town of Blaye, on the opposite side of the estuary. You'll come back with a bag of pralines and the memories of a unique landscape.

A weekend
on the Basque coast

Enjoy the sea air at Biarritz as you take a stroll and admire the beautiful villas are a reminder of the great days of La Belle Époque and the Basque style of the 1930s (p. 51). In the summer you can take a dip or simply wander along the wonderful beaches, watching the surfers and windsurfers as they skim the waves; they're here all year round. If you play golf,

Fishing boats in Saint-Jean-de-Luz

practice your swing at the Ilbarritz driving range (p. 250), otherwise, enjoy a long and relaxing session at the seawater treatment centre (thermes marins): choose from thalassotherapy, seaweed baths and massage (p. 248). After that, you ought to be fit enough to take a tour of Bayonne and treat yourself to a *makila* (p. 245). To feed your mind, take a visit to the Bonnat

Museum could be up your street. If you prefer to feed your stomach, discuss the finer points of curing ham at the Ibaïalde charcuterie and taste the chocolate at Cazenave (p. 244). Evening is a perfect time to sample *pintxos* (p. 244) in the bars on the river Nive. Early the next day, if you've booked in advance, leave Anglet and go fishing for sea-bream and John Dory (p. 106). Otherwise, take your time to explore the Basque coast right down to Hendaye. While in Bidart, treat yourself to a pair of made-to-measure espadrilles (p. 250). In Guéthary, you can see the famous Parlementia wave (p. 251) and, between Guéthary and Hendaye, admire the wonderful landscape, best viewed from the Corniche road that runs along the coast (p. 251). On the way, don't forget to visit the Château

d'Abbadie (or Abbadia, p. 251) and its lovely grounds. Leave time to stop in Saint-Jean-de-Luz to taste the macaroons (p. 253), a local speciality, and buy at least one set of Basque table linen (p. 254). You may even have enough time left for a boat trip on the *Marie-Rose* (p. 254).

Biarritz lighthouse

A weekend
Béarnais

You can't see Pau without taking the time to visit the chateau of Henri IV (p. 288), so start your visit there. Once you've learned about the king's baptism here in the Jurançon, you can head immediately for the Gan Cooperative (p. 292) to discover the great wines it has to offer. Continue the vineyard tour by dropping in to the Cinquau estate (p. 292) just to see how its wines compare with those of the Cooperative. Once you have tasted the difference, you can admire the lovely wooden structure of the Saint-Girons-de-Monein church (p. 293). Back in Pau, if it should rain, use it as an excuse to buy a genuine shepherd's umbrella (p. 291) and taste some delicious jams

the first to be opened in France (1856), which was founded by English officers; its Victorian clubhouse is very quaint (p. 107). Then visit the birthplace of Bernadotte, a native of Pau, who served under Napoleon and became King of Sweden (p. 290). Thanks to its lovely parks, you can see why Pau is called a garden city. Take in the atmosphere of old Pau in the Place Royale, then spend some time at the casino in

(p. 289). If there's time, why not watch a game of ninepins? This is a version of skittles or bowling from the Béarne which is enjoying a revival (p. 289). You might like to visit the Gelos stud farm, one of the Anglo-Arab breeding stables (p. 291). You can take some exercise on the Billère golf course,

the Parc Beaumont. You can then admire the view from the Boulevard des Pyrénées. Complete your trip to Pau by visiting the Beaux-Arts Museum, which contains works by Degas and Rubens (p. 289), unless, of course, you prefer to spend the day at the famous Pont-Long racecourse.

Four or five days in
the great vineyards

Before you arrive, be sure to make reservations. You'll only be allowed to visit the great wine-cellars (*chais*) of the Bordeaux region if you have booked in advance. Plan your tour well ahead, and don't try and do too much at once. Two châteaux a day should be the maximum. Why not start with the Médoc and the oriental touch of its Cos-d'Estournel (p. 205)? You should have time to visit Pichon-Longueville on the same day. Combine Château Mouton-Rothschild with Château Latour, and Beychevelle (for its beauty as well as its wine) with Château Margaux. Médoc is also worth seeing for its landscape and the rolling hills beside the river Gironde. Dream of crossing the Atlantic by ocean liner in Pauillac port where you can taste the local lamb (p. 206) and the noisettine sweets. Take another day to visit the

Applied Arts and Crafts of the Vineyards and Wine in the Château de Maucaillou, and the École du Bordeaux, at Cordeillan-Bages (p. 206), where you can see just how much you have learned about wine. Complete the trip with a visit to the Sauternes region: if you enter by La Brède, you'll then be able to meditate on *L'Esprit des lois* in Montesquieu's personal library when visiting his charming château (p. 193). Admire the legendary Château-Yquem and then the Château de Malle, with its lovely gardens (p. 192). If you get tired of vineyards, pop over to the Gulf of Saint-Pardon-de-Conques (p. 107) or go horseriding in the vineyards of the Sauternes district on a misty morning (p. 193). On your way back, stop at the Château de Belloc which grows rare and forgotten vegetables which you can sample and then take home in tins and jars (p. 187).

Four or five days in
the Lot-et-Garonne

Start in the north by visiting the plethora of *bastides* (walled towns), including Villeréal (p. 165), Monflanquin (p. 166) and Castillonnès (p. 169). At nearby Douzains, hire a pack-donkey to carry your children and luggage on a country walk (p. 164). Visit nearby Bonaguil, the last fortress château in France (p. 167), but don't leave before tasting a delicious, golden crispy local pie. On the second day, stock up on local food. There are some delicious specialities made with the prunes from the Duras region (p. 183), as well as fruit, vegetables, foie gras and other sweet and savoury preserves from Marmande (p. 181). On the

*Above: Villeréal market-hall
Below: the Clarens lake.*

third day, discover the Serres region, its walled towns and its prehistoric caves (p. 170). Hunt around Pujols for antiques and stock up on hazelnut oil (p. 169). Agen and its old town are worth seeing, and the children can enjoy themselves in the Walibi park (p. 175). Enter the town by the Montesquieu orchard, where you can sample some of the rare fruits of the region (p. 177). At Nérac, take a walk in the Garenne park then take a boat trip on the river Baïse (*see photo on the right*). You should just have time to raid

the chocolate shop (p. 225). Vianne, another walled town, has a glass-blowing industry, and in Casteljaloux, if the weather is fine, take a dip in Clarens lake or go mountain-biking. The great forest of Landes also awaits (p. 226). While in Landes you can visit a pigeon-loft and a breeding ranch for the *Course Landaise* (p. 226). Don't leave empty-handed, or with an empty stomach – taste the asparagus,

foie gras, duck or goose pre-serves and Floc de Gascogne liqueur in Mézin and Poudenas (p. 227). If you're in Moncra-beau on the first Sunday of August, push your way through the crowd to listen to the election of the King of the Liars: you're never too old to learn a thing or two (p. 227)!

A week
in Landes

Explore the Atlantic coast from north to south, starting with a visit to the lighthouse of Cordouan, off the Pointe de Grave, followed by a boat trip. Then admire the neo-Colonial villas in Soulac-sur-Mer (pp. 51 and 208). The next day, travel round the Arcachon basin by Gujan-Mestras (oyster capital of the region), visit the winter-villa quarter of Arcachon, and climb the incredible Pilat dune (p. 211). On the third day, spend time in the Born region (p. 214) which is full of attractions: the Petroleum Museum, the Hydroplane Museum, freshwater lakes, and the paper-mills of Mimizan. Spend the next day in Le Marensin, and take a boat trip on the 'tropical' current of the river Huchet, which is a unique experience. Hossegor beach has a pretty sea-front lined with 1930s houses (p. 51) for you to admire, and at Capbreton, its twin, you can take a boat trip (p. 240). Travelling through Hastingues and Peyrehorade, you'll pass along the flood meadows on the river Adour (p. 238). At Dax, a spa town, take the cure and pamper yourself (p. 237) or you could go to a bullfight, depending on the season. From here the winding lanes of the Chalosse will lead you to the foie gras capital, Montfort and to Pomarez, Mecca of the Landes bull-running.

Visit the bullfighting café and the bullrings. You may be lucky enough to see a real *Course Landaise* (p. 234). Taste the wines of Chalosse in Pouillon, play skittles in the villages, then go to Saint-Sever, where you can stock up on foie gras before admiring the illuminations depicting the Apocalypse (p. 232). You can also buy beautiful plates. If you're in the mood, taste the wines of Tursan or drink the spa waters of Eugénie-les-Bains (p. 231). If you still have time, you are close enough to Armagnac to be able to complete your tour of the Landes by tasting its famous brandy (pp. 42 and 228).

A week
in Périgord

Your first stop should be the birthplace of the famous writer Michel de Montaigne, Périgord's most famous son (p. 127). Then lose yourself in the primeval forests of the Double region (p. 124) before re-emerging in Ribérac to visit the local farms (p. 134) and admire the Romanesque

prehistory before diving into the pond of Saint-Estèphe (p. 145). On your third day, deep in heart of green Périgord, you'll be able to pan for gold at Jumilhac (p. 147). You can then learn about the underground fungus, known as the black diamond of the Périgord, at the Truffle Museum in Sorges, or if you like formal gardens, visit Hautefort (p. 142). Not far from there are the gorges of the Auvézère which can be toured by mountain-bike or on foot. After reflecting on the grave of a Patagonian king (p. 143), you can spend

you can admire the work of the artists of the Cro-Magnon period, painted some 30,000 years ago (p. 148)! Learn more about early mankind by visiting the Prehistory Museum (p. 149), the Préhisto-Parc and the Thot Museum (p. 151). You can then enjoy a day in Sarlat, starting early in the morning with the market (p. 155), this is also the time to go shopping for walnut oil (p. 156), copper (p. 153), foie gras and walnuts. The day before you leave, take a relaxing boat trip in Beynac (p. 160), and visit the Château de Marqueyssac and its gardens (p. 160). End with a tour of the Château de Castelnaud (p. 159) to leave a lasting impression of the valley of the Dordogne.

churches. Or, if you prefer, you can rent a bike and take the tour of the châteaux of the region (p. 135). Don't miss the Châteaux de Brantôme which should be approached from the river Dronne (p. 136). In Nontron, you can buy a knife, and make your first contact with

at least half a day wandering through the colourful streets of Périgueux (p. 138), which are at their most lively on market days. Prepare yourself for an orgy of prehistory on the fifth day because you're entering the oldest inhabited part of France. At Les Eyzies, Commarque and Montignac,

A fortnight in
Southern Aquitaine

After a couple of days in Bordeaux (p. 196), drive to the Côte d'Argent via the vineyards of Médoc. Make a point of visiting Pauillac, the regional capital (p. 206), on the left bank of the Gironde. From here, take a visit to the Cordouan lighthouse, off the Pointe de Grave (p. 208), a palace in the middle of the sea, and relax on one of the sandy beaches leading to the basin of Arcachon. This is a region known for its oysters as well as its mild winters. An excursion for day four is a visit to the Teich bird sanctuary, a paradise for migrating birds (p. 212), then

drive on to see the nature reserve of the Landes de Gascogne (p. 218). In the next two days, you'll have time to visit the three branches of the Ecomuseum of the Grande Lande, Marquèze, Luxey and Moustey, the latter in the heart of an immense pine forest. On day seven, take the cure at the spa town of Dax (p. 236), before moving to Biarritz (p. 246), gateway to

the Basque coast. Drive along the rocky coastline, until you get to Saint-Jean-de-Luz, the only port in the Basque region and the place where Louis XIV married (p.252). The next day, take the little train to the top of the Rhune, the highest peak in the Basque region, to admire the mountainscapes of the Basque country. It's a region of chillies and sweet peppers, black cherries, wine, pelota and games of strength (p. 74). Saint-Jean-Pied-de-Port, in the east, was capital of Lower Navarre, and on the pilgrimage route to Compostela. Continue on to the nearby Béarn district and explore its three wonderful valleys, Barétous, Aspe and Ossau (p. 284, 298 and 302). In terms of wildlife, look out for vultures hovering above you, and though you probably won't see any, the brown bears may be watching you. On day twelve, visit Pau,

birthplace of King Henri IV, and enjoy its château-museum, gardens and views of the Pyrenees (p. 288). Gan, just before Pau, is the place to taste the wines of the Jurançon, used to christen the future king (p. 292). Then travel northwards, across the Vic-Bilh, a district of châteaux (p. 296), the Tursan and its hills (p. 230). Stop and visit the medieval town of Labastide-d'Armagnac (p. 228), then Bazas and the gorges of the Ciron (p. 194), beside the Sauternes-Barsac vineyard, ending at the Château-Yquem (p. 192).

A fortnight in
Northern Aquitaine

T here's plenty to see and do in Bordeaux (p. 196). After you have visited its streets, museums and monuments, take a boat trip on the river Garonne to get a breath of fresh sea air, and discover the citadel of Blaye. Don't be intimidated by it: wander its narrow lanes, lined with hollyhocks (p. 114). On day four, take the road to Libourne (p. 116), a rather perilous route which will take you through the Côtes-de-Blaye and Côtes-de-Bourg vineyards. However, the best is yet to come, as you reach Saint-Émilion the next day (p. 120). Try to spend at least a day in this legendary town. In the Entre-Deux-Mers district (don't miss the Château de Vayres and the abbey of La Sauve-Majeur), see if you can glimpse the Mascaret, a tidal wave that regularly sweeps up the river Dordogne (p. 185). Reserve day five for exploring the château where Michel de Montaigne lived (p. 126) and for the wines of Bergerac. Walk through the town and visit the tobacco museum (p. 130). Continue on to Duras (p. 182) and Marmande (p. 180), where the local specialities are prunes and *cous farcis*.

Tour the Lot-et-Garonne with its walled towns and its farms and enjoy the impressive sight of the Château de Bonaguil (p. 167). You still have a few days left to explore the Dordogne. Between Trémolat (p. 132) and Monfort (p. 161), admire the fortresses (stop off at Beynac and Castelnaud and lunch in Domme) then make for Sarlat. You'll need a whole day for touring the town (p. 154). Drive on to Les Eyzies and follow the river Vézère to

Lascaux, where you can take the prehistoric tour (p. 148). For the last three days, enjoy the peace of green Périgord, Périgueux and its Saint-Front cathedral (p. 138). Stop at the Truffle Museum in Sorges, then go and see the goose and duck breeders at work, and stock up on foie gras (p. 146). After stopping at Brantôme (p. 136) and Mareuil (p. 135), travel through the Double forest (p. 124) to Montpon, where sturgeons are bred, following the Romanesque churches route of the Ribéracois.

Trémolat

South West France à la carte

A taste of
South West France 22

Markets and fairs

You will find the best country produce here, straight from the farm. The delicious foies gras are, of course, the focus of all attention at the *marchés au gras*.

Markets

1. **Agen (Sat.)** p. 175.
2. **Bazas (Sat.)** p. 194.
3. **Bordeaux (daily)** p. 197.
4. **Dax (Sat.)** p. 236.
5. **Lalinde (Thurs.)** p. 132.
6. **Marmande (Tues.–Sat.)** p. 180.
7. **Mauléon-Licharre (Tues., Sat.)** p. 273.
8. **Mont-de-Marsan (Sat.)** p. 222.
9. **Nay (Tues.)** p. 286.
10. **Périgueux (Sat.)** p. 138.
11. **Peyrehorade (Wed.)** p. 239.
12. **Ribérac (Fri.)** p. 134.
13. **Saint-Jean-Pied-de-Port (Mon.)** p. 268.
14. **Saint-Palais (Fri.)** p. 271.
15. **Sarlat (Wed., Sat.)** p. 155.

16. **Tardets (Mon. in July and Aug., every other Mon. out of season)** p. 275.
17. **Villeneuve-sur-Lot (Tues., Sat.)** p. 168.

Foie gras and cattle markets

㉓ Aire-sur-l'Adour: foie gras market (every Tues. from Nov. to Feb.) **p. 231.**

㉔ Bazas: Fête des Bœufs Gras (Thurs. before Shrove Tuesday) **p. 195.**

㉕ Brantôme: foie gras market (winter) **p. 136.**

㉖ Périgueux: foie gras market (Sat. and Wed., Nov. to March). **p. 138.**

㉗ Ribérac: foie gras fair (mid-Nov. to mid-March) **p. 134.**

Festivals

㉘ Brantôme: truffle market (winter) **p. 136.**

㉙ Duras: wine fair (end July) **p. 182.**

㉚ Espelette: pottok fair (Jan.) and chilli pepper festival (last Sun. in Oct.) **pp. 83 and 259.**

㉛ Issigeac: pumpkin fair (Nov.) and basketry fair (July) **p. 129.**

㉜ Laruns: cheese fair (1st Sun. in Oct.) **p. 305.**

㉝ La Latière: cattle fair (30 Apr. and 1 May) **p. 125.**

㉞ Penne d'Agenais: *Tourtière* fair (2nd weekend in July) **p. 173.**

㉟ Ribérac: walnut fair (Oct. and Nov.) **p. 134.**

㊱ Saint-Jean-de-Luz: tuna festival (early July) **p. 254.**

㊲ Varaignes: turkey fair (11 Nov.) and walnut fair (Feb.) **p. 145.**

Specialist markets

⑱ Bordeaux: organic market (Thurs.) **p. 202.**

⑲ Monpazier: cep market (August and Sept.) **p. 162.**

⑳ Sainte Alvère: truffle market (Mon., Dec. to March) **p. 19.**

㉑ Villeneuve-sur-Lot: organic market (Wed.) **p. 168.**

㉒ Villefranche-du-Périgord: cep market (Sept. or Oct., depending on availability) **pp. 18 and 163.**

The cep
the king of mushrooms, the mushroom of kings

The cep is in season from early September to 1 November. Its annual appearance is an occasion for great excitement. However, before dashing into the forest to pick them, connoisseurs keep an eye on their barometers and thermometers, since mild, humid weather means the crop will be particularly good.

The boletus

There are about fifteen varieties of edible boleti, fungi with pores instead of gills. The best are the cep of Bordeaux and the black-headed boletus, both of which, unlike other boleti, do not turn blue when bruised. The brown-capped cep, or penny bun mushroom, with its yellow pores and streaky stem, is firm, fleshy and fragrant. The black-headed boletus has a black cap and white flesh.

Picking the fungi

This has always been governed by tradition. Pick early in the morning if the moon is new. The earth should have been warmed in July and watered in August, and the wind should turn to the south. In some parts of France, however, the traditional rules of when to pick have been abandoned due to greed, and plantations and forests are raided in the depth of night, and the poached spoils sold in the markets. However, the forest is becoming ever better protected. Local landowners on whose land the ceps are found, defend them with signs and notices.

Villefranche market

Tons of ceps pass through the wholesale market of Ville-franche-du-Périgord. Because this market sets the rate in Périgord, the whole region bases its selling price on the wholesale prices in this walled town. Good fresh ceps in season are to be had in other markets, but they are so expensive that they are a rare tasty treat. Those on a tight budget can

savour the cep cooked in an omelette or served in a mouth-watering salad.

Choosing and preserving ceps

The smell of the mushroom should always be pleasant and the texture firm and worm-free. In Landes, however, some prefer the *papouns*, large, slightly soft specimens that will melt in a sauce or a *salmis*. Don't wash ceps under the tap, wipe them with a damp cloth or kitchen paper. The best way to preserve them is to keep them in a jar of olive oil. They can also be canned or frozen, though the flavour is never quite as good as when they are fresh.

The truffle
the black diamond of Périgord

The fact that truffles have been found outside prehistoric caves seems to prove that early man also enjoyed them. Their scarcity, subtle fragrance and flavour have ensured that truffles command the respect of gourmets.

Truffle-hunting
This usually takes place between November and March. There are several techniques to choose from. The truffle-fly technique requires the hunter to spot the insect hovering over the 'burnt patch' beneath which a truffle may lurk, and waiting for it to land at the place where it finds

the scent strongest. They then scrape the ground at that spot to see if there is a truffle underneath. Truffle-hunters also sometimes use a trained sow, which roots in the ground with her snout. But she has to be relieved of the truffles quickly before she can gobble them up! Or they can use a truffle-hound – thanks to their keen sense of smell, dogs can detect truffles. No specific breed is required, just a good nose and a good trainer should be enough!

Buying truffles
You can buy truffles in the markets. The largest truffle market in Périgord is the **Sainte-Alvère market** which is held on Monday mornings from December to March.

Before they are sold truffles are brushed, cleaned and graded. They remain fresh for about a week, but must be protected from the air (by immersing them in a glass of oil, for instance). To keep them for more than a week, you should freeze or sterilise them.

Don't get ripped off!
There are several varieties of truffles and prices vary a great deal. La Maison de la Truffe in Sorges (p. 147), will give you valuable advice.

Foie gras

France is the leading producer, consumer and exporter of processed foie gras, thanks to South West France, in which the regions of Périgord and Landes compete with each other. Many visitors find the idea of force-feeding geese and duck very distasteful, but foie gras is one of the great French delicacies and firmly entrenched in their cuisine. In comparison, the flavour of goose is finer and more delicate, that of the duck is more powerful and robust. It's all a matter of taste.

technique is a very ancient one that has been handed down from generation to generation. In fact, over-fattening is not a human invention. Geese and ducks overeat in the wild before they begin their great migrations, as the extra fat protects them from cold at high altitudes.

or three times a day with a purée of maize (or a 'ready-mix') that is very high in calories.

Modern times

The explosion in consumption has revolutionised production methods. Fattening time has shortened to 10 to 12 days for ducks, 15 to 16 days for geese. Birds over two months old are force-fed through a funnel two

The geese are getting fat...

Although the tradition of force-feeding geese and ducks has had its ups and downs, it's been retained throughout the centuries. Domesticated geese and ducks appear to have been introduced by the Roman legions, and they immediately took to the climate of South West France. From the fattened geese served at the royal table, to the fat used in preserving the flavour, it's clear that south of the Loire, the fattening

cooked and vacuum-packed should be meltingly soft and should be eaten in two or three weeks. Cooked foie gras has been sterilised; it is a preserve which, like wine, gets better with age. If you want to cook your own foie gras, you need to choose some good fresh liver. It should be pale in colour, devoid of blood vessels, marks, or stains and the flesh should be supple but not soft.

There's even a foie gras museum!

The farms of the South West which sell on a small scale will often welcome visitors. The breeding grounds and even the fattening process can be watched, when in season (i.e. not at the hottest time of year). For a better understanding of the subject, the Musée du Foie Gras at Souleilles, which is also a breeding farm, is the place to go (p. 173).

Their wings are clipped so that they do not use energy by flying in the fields. They are raised by the thousand until the age of 12 weeks for ducks (16 for geese): the bird's liver will then weigh more than 2 lb 4 oz (1 kg) for geese and 14 oz to 1 lb 9 oz (400 to 700 g) for ducks.

A lesson in labelling

A tin of real foie gras will be labelled 'foie gras entier'. This indicates a specific quality of

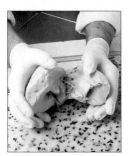

liver and the price will be commensurate with it. Goose foie gras costs between 800 and 1,000 F for 2lb 4oz (1 kg), duck foie gras between 600 and 700 F (there are twice as many duck as goose foies gras on the market). Block foie gras consists of pieces of liver which have been kneaded and emulsified. Beware of these, as the quality is not guaranteed. It's worth paying a little more to have a good quality product. Parfait de foie contains a maximum of 75% foie gras, while galantine, mousse or purée contain no more than 50%.

Keeping and cooking your foie gras

Fresh or raw foie gras can be kept for five or six days. It is uniform in colour, supple and firm. Semi-cooked foie gras can be kept in the refrigerator for about a month. Foie gras

HOW SHOULD IT BE EATEN ?

Cooked foie gras is best kept cool for a few hours before the meal, but it should be taken out of the refrigerator half an hour before it is eaten. The foie gras should be sliced with a thin-bladed knife which has been dipped in hot water, and wiped after each slice is cut. The foie gras is then eaten unadorned, with toast or crusty wholemeal bread. It goes well with a large number of wines, but purists generally drink a glass of Sauternes with it.

A taste of South West France

Foie gras, ham, walnut oil, and sturgeon caviar, these are a few of the ingredients used in the region's great gastronomic tradition. Your tastebuds will be in heaven!

Foies gras and confits

1. Laplume: *confit* of goose
   p. 176.
2. Marmande:
   confit of duck
   p. 181.
3. Mézin: foie gras
   p. 227.
4. Saint-Sever: foie gras
   p. 233.
5. Souleilles: foie gras
   p. 173.

Seafood

6. Biganos:
   sturgeon caviar
   p. 213.
7. Gujan-Mestras :
   oyster farm
   p. 212.
8. Montpon-Ménestérol :
   sturgeon caviar
   p. 125.

Drinks

9. Mézin: Floc de Gascogne
   p. 227.
10. Pays de Cize: cider
    p. 267.
11. Podensac: Lillet apéritif
    p. 190.
12. Saint-Jean-de-Luz :
    Izarra distillery
    p. 254.

Blaye 28
32
A10
N10
Libourne
Bordeaux ●
24
Garonne
11
6
Arcachon ● 7
A63
A660
Langon ●

N10
A63
18
Dax
30
Adour 4
Mont-de-Marsan ●

Biarritz ● 15 29
Bayonne
Saint-Jean-de-Luz 12
14
A64
19

St-Sébastien
Pau ● N117

Drinks
13
10 21
33
Oloron-Sainte-Marie
16

SPAIN
Pic d'Anie
8,216 ft
(2,504 m)
Tunnel du Somport
Pic du Midi d'Ossau
9,462 ft
(2,884 m)

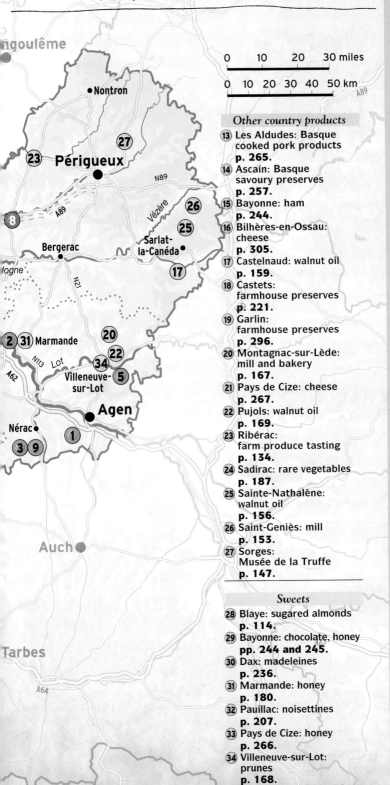

Other country products

⑬ **Les Aldudes: Basque cooked pork products** p. 265.

⑭ **Ascain: Basque savoury preserves** p. 257.

⑮ **Bayonne: ham** p. 244.

⑯ **Bilhères-en-Ossau: cheese** p. 305.

⑰ **Castelnaud: walnut oil** p. 159.

⑱ **Castets: farmhouse preserves** p. 221.

⑲ **Garlin: farmhouse preserves** p. 296.

⑳ **Montagnac-sur-Lède: mill and bakery** p. 167.

㉑ **Pays de Cize: cheese** p. 267.

㉒ **Pujols: walnut oil** p. 169.

㉓ **Ribérac: farm produce tasting** p. 134.

㉔ **Sadirac: rare vegetables** p. 187.

㉕ **Sainte-Nathalène: walnut oil** p. 156.

㉖ **Saint-Geniès: mill** p. 153.

㉗ **Sorges: Musée de la Truffe** p. 147.

Sweets

㉘ **Blaye: sugared almonds** p. 114.

㉙ **Bayonne: chocolate, honey** pp. 244 and 245.

㉚ **Dax: madeleines** p. 236.

㉛ **Marmande: honey** p. 180.

㉜ **Pauillac: noisettines** p. 207.

㉝ **Pays de Cize: honey** p. 266.

㉞ **Villeneuve-sur-Lot: prunes** p. 168.

Oysters

queens of Arcachon

The Arcachon basin is the realm of the oyster. The stakes which you can see sticking out of the water are covered in them. Oysters have been a favourite food since prehistoric times. If you are already an aficionado, you will probably know to avoid them during months without an 'r' in them (May to August), because then the oysters are fatty and milky as this is the time when they reproduce. They are best eaten with a squeeze of lemon juice added just before swallowing whole.

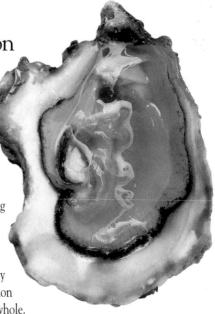

A Roman feast

Oysters have always been found in the Arcachon basin. In 55 BC, the Romans, who had just conquered Aquitaine, were already eating them raw. In the 4th C., the reputation of the local oysters had become so great that the Latin poet Ausonius, who was born in Bordeaux, regularly sent them to the Emperor Gratianus.

The introduction of oyster-farming

Until 1850, oysters were gathered from natural beds by dragging them or hand picking them. It was not until the second half of the 19th C., when they were being harvested to extinction, that oyster-farming was introduced. Victor Costes, a local man, successfully mastered oyster reproduction, and other farmers followed his lead. Today, 750 oyster-farmers farm more than 4,448 acres (1800 ha) of underwater concessions.

Three years to mature

An oyster begins as a spat, a microscopic larval form that floats in the water. This is captured by attracting it to a submerged tile to which it then clings. The following spring, it is detached and placed in a bed covered by a grille, to protect it from its predators, fish and crustaceans.

Ten months later, bunches of oysters are placed on raised supports. They are turned regularly to obtain an even shape and shell. In three years, the oyster is fully grown.

The benefits

Oysters have many nutritional virtues. Their fat, glucose and protein content is well balanced, and they contain a treasure: **iodine**, an element that is essential for a good metabolism. The fact that oysters are eaten alive means that their organic

components are at their most effective. However, never soak oysters in fresh water, they will begin to putrefy immediately. Keep them for a maximum of two or three days in a container in the refrigerator and discard any that are no longer swimming in their water.

Flat or hollow?

The oldest species cultivated is the *gravette*, a flat oyster which was ravaged by a disease in 1920, but which is making a comeback. The hollow oyster is more recent, having only arrived in the late 19th C., and it also had some health problems. In 1970, the so-called Portuguese oysters were wiped out by a virus. The variety thus disappearing in the same way that it had originally appeared – by accident, when a damaged Breton boat threw its cargo overboard. This oyster has been replaced by the giant Pacific oyster, *Ostreus gigas*, from Japan.

The oyster-farmer

Using a traditional wooden boat called a *pinasse*, the oyster-farmer works with the tides. He

OYSTERS ARCACHON-STYLE

(to serve 4)
Raw oysters, some hot *crépinettes*, a little bread and butter and a glass or two of white wine. That's the way the people of Arcachon like to eat their oysters. Allow a dozen oysters per person. Open them carefully then fry a dozen *crépinettes* (faggots that have been poached in white wine), or better still barbecue them. Eat them all together, with buttered rye bread. Accompany this feast with a dry white wine from Bordeaux. Truly wonderful!

spends over ten hours a day working hard, sometimes starting very early to catch the low tide. He then takes his tools, a fork, a rake and a harrow, and cultivates the land. He cleans the beds, removing mud and sand and checks the alignment of the stakes or poles and the grilles which keep out predators. At high tide he returns to his base.

Bayonne ham
an ancient pedigree

Ham was the subject of a prolonged dispute between the Béarnais and the Bayonnais. Salies-de-Béarn claimed to have discovered the virtues of salt as a preservative, while Bayonne considered that without its

contribution, ham could never have been sold. From the 16th C., ham was frequently given as a gift to important visitors. The ham is even lauded in literature. Rabelais describes his insatiable Grandgousier as 'happy to eat savoury foods and normally kept a good supply of Mayence and Bayonne hams'.

The art of preparing a real Bayonne ham

The charcutiers rub salt into the ham seven times in 15 days, then dry it suspended for seven to 12 months (as against three to six months for an ordinary ham). This is where the *fœhn*, the south wind that blows through the region, plays its part. To find out whether the ham is ready for sale, it needs to be pricked with a sliver of bone taken from a horse. Doing this, and sniffing the ham, will indicate whether it has been properly

dried. French law also takes an interest in ham. Since 1996, the letters I.G.P. (*Indication géographique protégée*) guarantee the origin of the ham.

The ham fair

You won't know which to try first out of all the appetising hams on display. Gourmets can rest assured; all are locally produced. The Bayonne ham fair has not deviated from tradition for five centuries. It is held at Easter-time on Maundy Thursday and Good Friday. On the other days of

the year, you can taste this delicious ham in Bayonne itself, in any of the many *bars à pintxos* (tapas bars, p. 244).

HAM WITH BASQUAISE SAUCE

Fry some green peppers in oil with finely sliced onion and garlic. Add some peeled and quartered tomatoes, a bouquet garni, salt, a pinch of powdered *piment d'espelette* (don't overdo it), and simmer, uncovered, on a very low heat for about an hour and a half. Lightly fry slices of Bayonne ham on both sides. Add a ladleful of the Basquaise sauce and a fried egg.

Walnuts
a Périgourdine from the Orient

The walnut tree originated in the Near East and was introduced to Europe in ancient times. The Romans called it *nux* and for them it symbolised marriage – because of the strong bond between its two shells – and fertility. There are some who claim that the French word *nuisible*, meaning 'harmful', is associated with the nut, because it is said to be harmful to rest under a walnut tree.

Its kingdom: the Dordogne

Although the walnut tree grows throughout France, the Dordogne is its favourite haunt. The Périgord walnut is part of the countryside. It falls from the sky on All Saints Day (1 November) from the tops of the lone, ageless walnut trees. The trees also supply a much sought-after wood, which is used to make furniture and the butts of guns.

Varieties for connoisseurs

There are several varieties of walnut, the most common of which is known as the *corne* (horn). This is oblong with a hard kernel and is enjoyed for its pale nut with a delicate flavour. The *marbot* has a rounder shell that breaks more easily. The kernel has a very good flavour. The *granjean* is known for its soft shell. If you are looking for the best value for money, stock up on walnuts in the local markets of Périgord in autumn when they are in season.

Walnut oil

The making of walnut oil is often a family secret. There is, however, a standard procedure used by all the manufacturers. The kernels are crushed in a mill and the pulp heated over a wooden fire until it reaches 122 °F (50 °C). It is then pressed to extract the precious liquid, but the skill of the professional is only revealed in the final taste. A good walnut oil should have a subtle fragrance. Dieticians recognise walnut oil as having an additional advantage, in that it's low in cholesterol.

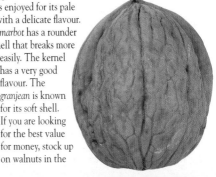

Where to eat

However hungry you are, you can be sure to find a restaurant serving the region's most delicious dishes. Addresses and descriptions are on pp. 30–33.

Gironde

① Arcins: Le Lion d'Or
② Bazas: Le Restaurant des Remparts
③ Bordeaux: Le Chapon Fin, La Tupina
④ Bouliac: Le Café de l'Ésperance
⑤ Le Porge: La Vieille Auberge

Landes

⑥ Eugénie-les-Bains: La Ferme aux Grives
⑦ Garein: Chez Suzon
⑧ Grenade-sur-Adour: Pain, Adour et fantaisie
⑨ Luxey: Le Relais de la Haute-Lande
⑩ Mazerolles: Auberge de la Pouillique
⑪ Uchacq-et-Parentis: Restaurant Didier Garbage

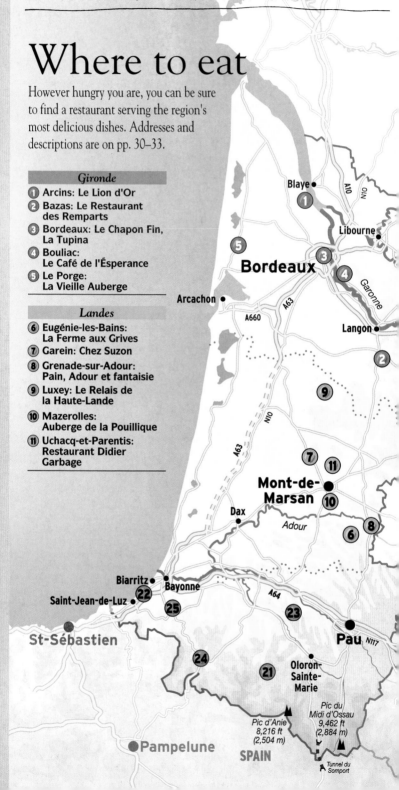

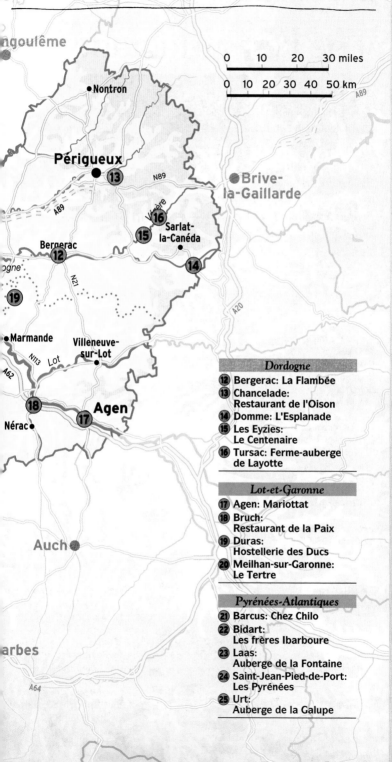

ngoulême

● Nontron

Périgueux ⑬

●Brive-
la-Gaillarde

⑯ Sarlat-
⑮ la-Canéda

Bergerac
⑫

⑭

⑲

●Marmande   Villeneuve-
sur-Lot

⑱   **Agen**
⑰

Nérac●

Auch●

arbes

Dordogne
⑫ Bergerac: La Flambée
⑬ Chancelade:
Restaurant de l'Oison
⑭ Domme: L'Esplanade
⑮ Les Eyzies:
Le Centenaire
⑯ Tursac: Ferme-auberge
de Layotte

Lot-et-Garonne
⑰ Agen: Mariottat
⑱ Bruch:
Restaurant de la Paix
⑲ Duras:
Hostellerie des Ducs
⑳ Meilhan-sur-Garonne:
Le Tertre

Pyrénées-Atlantiques
㉑ Barcus: Chez Chilo
㉒ Bidart:
Les frères Ibarboure
㉓ Laas:
Auberge de la Fontaine
㉔ Saint-Jean-Pied-de-Port:
Les Pyrénées
㉕ Urt:
Auberge de la Galupe

0   10   20   30 miles

0 10 20 30 40 50 km

The best restaurants

No matter where you go, your tour in South West France will be a gourmet's delight! This region is justly proud of its gastronomic prowess. There are wonderful traditional, innovative or classic restaurants to suit every budget all over the region. Here just a few examples for you to begin with.

Roland Mazère's nut cake

Dordogne

Bergerac
La Flambée
Route de Périgueux
☎ 05 53 57 52 33
Closed on Sun. evenings and Mon. out of season, and Jan.
Menus from 100 to 300 F.
On the outskirts of Bergerac, in a park with huge trees, taste local foods, especially the fish. The perch-pike, which should be accompanied by a white Bergerac, is unforgettable.

Chancelade
Restaurant de l'Oison
Avenue des Reynats
☎ 05 53 03 53 59
Closed Mon., Sat. for lunch and Sun. evenings from Nov. to Dec.
Closed 2 Jan. to 2 Mar.
Menus from 140 to 350 F.
The menu changes daily depending on availability and season, but it is always good, especially the fish. Near Périgueux.

Domme
L'Esplanade
☎ 05 53 28 31 41
Closed Mon. for lunch, and from Nov. to Feb.
Menus from 160 to 380 F.

Experience the happy combination of sole and ceps at l'Esplanade, which is famous for its local dishes as well as the view of the Domme and excellent service.

Les Eyzies
Le Centenaire
Rocher de la Penne
☎ 05 53 06 68 68
Closed Tue. for lunch as well as from Nov. to Apr.
Menus from 295 to 520 F.
Imaginative cooking. Ceps, confits, broad beans and chestnuts feature on the menu.

Tursac
Ferme-auberge de Layotte
Route de Périgueux
☎ 05 53 06 95 91
Closed Sun. evenings and Mon. in season as well as in Jan. and Feb.

Roland Mazère, whose restaurant is a stone's throw from the Prehistory museum at Les Eyzies

Open from Wed. evenings to Sun. lunch out of season.
Menu: 145 F.
An old farm in the forest with a beautiful arbour. For a set price there is a huge range of dishes to choose from. Not for those with a small appetite.

Gironde

Arcins
4 m (6 km) from Margaux
Le Lion d'Or
Place de la République
☎ 05 56 58 96 79
Closed Sun. and Mon. in Jul., and from 24 Dec. to 1 Jan.
Menu: 59 F.
A la carte: about 200 F.
Lamprey, herring, omelettes, ham – all depending on availability and season, but always just right in this excellent bistro in the vineyard.

Bazas
Le Restaurant des Remparts
49, Place de la Cathédrale (access from the Espace Mauvezin)
☎ 05 56 25 95 24
Closed Sun. evenings and Mon. (except Jul. and Aug.).
Menus from 70 to 210 F.

A beautiful setting on the ramparts and classic local dishes, such as Bazas beef, scallop salad with lemon, calf sweetbreads with prunes in Madeira sauce and, as a dessert, apple pie with vanilla icing.

Bordeaux

Le Chapon Fin
5, Rue Montesquieu
☎ **05 56 79 10 10**
Closed on Sun. and Mon.
Menus from 275 to 425 F. Bistro menu (very good value for money): 160 F (lunch only).
In this restaurant there's foie gras, game and local produce as well as caviar, lobster and scallops. In summer, be tempted by a lobster gazpacho, speciality of the chef, Francis Garcia.

La Tupina
6, Rue Porte-de-la-Monnaie
☎ **05 56 91 56 37**
Open daily.
Menus from 100 to 280 F.
Everyone in Bordeaux knows La Tupina and its chef, Jean-Pierre Xiradakis. This is a traditional restaurant serving authentic local dishes. Don't fail to taste the unmissable shoulder of Pauillac lamb and the juicy stuffed fowls that you can watch roasting in the hearth.

Francis Garcia, chef of the Chapon Fin, Bordeaux

Bouliac

Le Café de l'Espérance
10, Rue de l'Esplanade
☎ **05 56 20 52 16**
Closed on Sun., Mon., and Feb. to mid-Mar.
Menu: 160 F.
Small rooms with velvet banquettes, a summer arbour and a terrace: you'll immediately feel at ease in this charming village bistro where even potato wedges are cooked with care. Everything is simple and perfect, from the appetizers to the dessert sideboard.

Le Porge

La Vieille Auberge
15, Avenue de Bordeaux
☎ **05 56 26 50 40**
Closed Wed. and from end of Jan. to early Feb.
Menu from 130 to 300 F.
This is the place to eat after a day on the beach. Chicken in aspic, scallops layered in puff pastry with shallot butter, and claret: nourishing food after a day's surfing.

Duck ragoût concocted by Francis Garcia

La Ferme aux Grives restaurant at Eugénie-les-Bains.

Landes

Mazerolles

Auberge de la Pouillique
656, Chemin de la
Pouillique
☎ 05 58 75 22 97
Closed Sun. evening,
Mon. and 1–15 Sept.
Menus from 90 to 150 F
Here, traditional cooking
and innovative dishes live
together in harmony on the
menu: foie gras and *paupiettes
de magret* (breast of duck), and
barbecued peppers with pigs'
trotters. In winter, you can
enjoy your meal by the fireside
in this old country farm, or on
the terrace in summer, with a
view over the magnificent
grounds.

Eugénie-les-Bains

La Ferme aux Grives
☎ 05 58 51 19 08
Closed Mon. evening
and Tue. (except Jun. to
Sept.), and Jan. to
early Feb.
Menu: 195 F.
This restaurant is run by
Michel Guérard just like the
Prés d'Eugénie right next
door, but here you might
think yourself in an old cloak-
and-dagger film. The suckling
pig turns on the spit in the
fireplace, hams hang from the
ceiling and an inn table
groans with food. Drink a
musketeer's wine, a Turşan,
with this traditional repaşt.

Garein

Chez Suzon
21, Route de Peyrehorade
☎ 05 58 73 03 78
Closed Fri. evening and
one week in Jan.
Menus from 64 to 160 F.
After 6pm, the *belote* players
sit around the fire. The points
are more often counted in
Gascon than in French. Local
cooking at unbeatable prices.

Grenade-sur-l'Adour

Pain, Adour et Fantaisie
14-16, Place des Tilleuls
☎ 05 58 45 18 0
Closed Sun. evening,
Mon., Wed. lunch and
Feb. school holidays
*Menus from 165 F
(incl. wine and coffee) to
350 F (out of season)*
In this Landais restaurant,
Mediterranean flavours such
as olive oil, herbs and spices
enhance the local specialities.
The result is original, creative
cuisine, prepared by a talented
(and Mediterranean!) chef.

Luxey

**Le Relais de la
Haute-Lande**
☎ 05 58 08 02 30
Closed Sun. evenings
(except summer) and Mon.
Menus from 80 to 230 F.
A good place to eat in the
pine forests. *Salmis* and game
are on the menu, as well as sea
fish, such as the delicious *civet
de lotte au Pomerol* (monkfish).

Uchacq-et-Parentis

Restaurant Didier
Garbage
☎ 05 58 75 33 66
Closed Sun evenings and
Mon. except Jul. to Aug.
*Menus from 98 to 380 F
for the restaurant. 65 F
for the bistro, under the
same roof.*
Didier Garbage studied
cookery in China, which
explains some of his dishes
such as lacquered breast of
duck with Shanghai spices.
Try his gratin of scallops.

Lot-et-Garonne

Agen

Mariottat
25, Rue Louis Vivent
☎ 05 53 77 99 77
Closed Sun. evening, Sat.
lunch and Feb. school hols
Menus from 105 to 285 F.
A 19th-C. mansion in the
heart of Agen. The rooms
are lovely and there is a sunny
terrace. The cookery is
traditional but delightfully
light. Try the turbot with ceps
or the pigeon *salmis*.

Bruch

Restaurant de la Paix
Place de la Mairie
☎ 05 53 95 25 54
Closed Sat. and Sun.
evenings.

Menus from 70 to 120 F.
Simple, French provincial cooking. There's chicken in the pot, salt cod with potatoes and truffles and other firm favourites – all of them excellent.

Duras

Hostellerie des Ducs
Boulevard Jean-
Brisseau
☎ 05 53 83 74 58
Closed Sun. evening and Mon. out of season.
Menus from 90 to 295 F.
Pleasant decor and food that is balanced and exotic. Taste the Asian pear tart with foie gras. For dessert, there is Saint-Marcel, a rich chocolate cake served with mint custard.

Meilhan-
sur-Garonne

Le Tertre
Place du Tertre
☎ 05 53 94 30 28

Walnut and chestnut liqueurs from La Salamandre distillery at Sarlat

Closed Mon. and from 15 Jan. to 1 Feb.
Menus from 140 to 260 F.
This restaurant overlooking the Garonne is full of flowers. Foie gras fritters with caramel sauce, cabbage with oyster stuffing – creative cooking indeed! The genius of the South West is clearly in evidence.

Pyrénées-Atlantiques
Barcus

Chez Chilo
☎ 05 59 28 90 79
Closed Sun. evening and Mon. out of season, and Jan.
Menus from 120 to 350 F.
Off the beaten track in a quiet place, people come from afar to taste the traditional food. Milk-fed lamb and plaice take on a new, more Basque, flavour, which attracts the gourmets.

Bidart

Les Frères Ibarboure
Chemin Italienea
☎ 05 59 54 81 64
Closed Wed. and Sun. evenings (out of season) and Sun., 15 Nov. to 30 Nov. and 5 Jan. to 20 Jan.

Menus from 195 to 480 F.
One of the great restaurants of the Basque coast. They serve fish and seafood from near and far: you can even order Breton lobster. Nevertheless, Basque food predominates, though the reputation of this restaurant goes way beyond the frontiers of the Basque country.

Laas

Auberge
de la Fontaine
☎ 05 59 38 59 33
Closed Wed. out of season.

Menus from 90 to165 F.
Alain Darroze has made his restaurant into a preserve of South-West cuisine, whether the ingredients are from the farmyard, kitchen garden or the hunt. Try his *garbure*, stewed partridge or the sweetcorn stew.

Saint-Jean-Pied-
de-Port

Les Pyrénées
19, Place du Général-
de-Gaulle
☎ 05 59 37 10 75
Closed Mon. evening (from Nov. to March) and Tues. (from Nov. to Jun.). Closed in Jan. and from end Nov. to end Dec.
Menus from 250 to 550 F.
This is one of the most famous restaurants in the Basque country. The menu includes hare, wild mountain salmon and langoustines. Only the best ingredients are used and the preparation is impeccable.

Urt

Auberge de la Galupe
Place du Port
☎ 05 59 56 21 84
Closed Sun. evenings and Mon.
Menus from 245 to 550 F.
Come and taste the delights of the Ardour River, in a most beautiful setting close the old river port. You can feast on shad (herring), lamprey, pike and wild salmon, all prepared with great care and subtlety. Don't be put off by the name, the blood sausage is one of the chef's specialities.

Vineyards

Mellow or syrupy white wines, red wines with great bouquets:
the reputation of the wines from the South West is firmly established.
Visiting the cellars and châteaux is a great way to explore the region.

① *Côtes-de-Blaye,*
Côtes-de-Bourg

Maison des Vins de Blaye,
Maison du Vin at Bourg
pp. 114 and 115.

② *Médoc*

Châteaux Margaux,
Beychevelle,
Cos-d'Estournel,
Mouton-Rothschild,
Pichon-Longueville-Baron, Latour,
Musée des Arts et Métiers de la Vigne et du Vin
pp. 204–207.

③ *Bordeaux*

Vinorama,
L'Intendant,
Vinothèque
Musée des ,Chartrons
pp. 197 and 198.

④ *Coteaux-de-Garonne*

Maison du Pays de Saint-Macaire,
Le Château de Cadillac,
Cave Coopérative de Langoiran
pp. 189–191.

⑤ *Irouléguy*
Cave d'Irouléguy
p. 265.

⑥ *Béarn*

Domaine Lapeyre-Guilhemas,
Les Vignerons de Bellocq
pp. 276 and 277.

0   10   20   30 miles

0 10 20 30 40 50 km

⑫ Côtes-de-Brulhois

Coopérative de Goulens
p. 176.

⑬ Buzet

Cave des Vignerons
de Buzet,
Château Pierron
p. 226.

⑭ Sauternes

Château-Yquem,
Château de Malle
p. 192.

⑮ Côtes-du-Marmandais

Cave Coopérative
de Cocumont,
Cave Coopérative
de Beaupuy-Dupuy
p. 181.

⑯ Sept-Monts

Cave des Sept-Monts de
Monflanquin
p. 166.

⑰ Côtes-de-Duras

Maison du Vin at Duras,
Cave Coopérative
Berticot
p. 183.

⑱ Monbazillac

Château de Monbazillac
p. 128.

⑲ Entre-Deux-Mers

Maison des Bordeaux
et Bordeaux
Supérieurs,
Vinothèque at
Sauveterre-de-Guyenne,
Union des Producteurs
de Rauzan
pp. 184–187.

⑳ Pomerol, Fronsac, Saint-Émilion

Maison des Vins
at Fronsac,
Maison du Vin
de Saint-Émilion,
Maison du Vin
des Côtes-de-Castillon,
Train ride through the
great vineyards,
Le Cellier des Gourmets
pp. 117–123.

⑦ Jurançon

Cave des Producteurs
de Jurançon,
Domaine du Cinquau
p. 292.

⑧ Madiran

Château de Crouseilles
p. 297.

⑨ Tursan

Coopérative des
Vignerons du Tursan
p. 231.

⑩ Chalosse

Cave de Jean-Claude
Romain
p. 234.

⑪ Armagnac

Domaine d'Ognoas,
Écomusée de
l'Armagnac
p. 229.

Vineyards
the glory of the Bordeaux region

The vineyards of Bordeaux produce 650 million bottles of fine wine annually, a veritable ocean of reds, rosés and whites, harvested from 271,810 acres (110,000 ha) of the world's most famous vines. The climate of the Gironde, the diversity of soils, sub-soils and the mixture of grape varieties have made the district a premier wine producer since the 18th C. Today, nearly 8,000 châteaux and 57 appellations (A.O.C.) contribute to the reputation of the district.

The leading ones are Médoc, Graves, Côtes-de-Blaye, Saint-Émilion, Entre-Deux-Mers and Sauternes.

The location
The Bordeaux region is an excellent location that is very favourable for grape-growing. In the west, a plateau slopes gently down to the coast (Haut-Médoc and Médoc), and in the east there are rolling hills (333 to 434 ft (100 to 130 m), with deep valleys but no steep gradients or rugged ground. Two major rivers, the Garonne and the Dordogne, and many smaller ones, ensure that there is continuous, ideal irrigation.

History
It was the Bituriges, a tribe of Celtic warriors, who planted the first vines in the Bordeaux district, in the first century AD. Over a thousand years later, the marriage of Eleanor of Aquitaine to Henry II of England opened up the British market and later claret began to be exported as far afield as Holland and the West Indies. In the 18th C., innovations in the bottling of wine and sealing it with a cork, spread the fame of Bordeaux around the world.

What is an appellation ?
The word Appellation on a bottle of wine is a guarantee that the wine conforms to certain specified conditions of origin. Each Appellation has its own combination of grape varieties, soil conditions and climate that influence its wines. The Bordeaux vineyards now have 57 combinations of Appellations d'Origine Contrôlée (A.O.C.).

Grape varieties
Among the clarets, the favourite is Merlot, which is grown in more than one third

of the vineyards. It allows the wine to achieve a bouquet in the shortest possible time. Cabernet Sauvignon is slower to mature, since it is richer in tannins, and preferred on the left bank of the Garonne. Its cousin, Cabernet Franc, distills its finest aromas in the Libournais district. Of the white varieties, the smooth Sémillon is the star in the Sauternes district, while Sauvignon, famous for its sweetness, is a contrast to Muscadelle, with its powerful, musky scent.

The climate

The Bordeaux region enjoys an exceptionally temperate ocean climate, thanks to the influence of the Gulf Stream, which flows along the coast and increases the temperature. The vines derive maximum benefit, helped by the forest of the Landes which forms an effective protective screen against the ocean winds. However, there are occasional

spring frosts, and hail may fall at any time up to the harvest. The autumns are extremely beautiful and the winters are very mild.

The soils

The poor soil of the Bordeaux region actually helps the grapes to grow. On the left bank of the Garonne, pebbles, sand and gravel, washed down from the Pyrenees, absorb the heat which helps in the ripening process. On the right bank, down to the Dordogne, the clay and limestone soils retain the rainwater and allow the excess to flow deep down without drowning the roots. The trace minerals in the soil play an important role in the final taste of the wine.

Production

On average the Bordeaux vineyards produce 285,000,000 pts (5 million litres) of AOC wines a year. Claret (red wine) represents 80% of total production, and there are also dry white wines, sweet syrupy white wines, rosés and sparkling wines. Only 10% of production, turned out by more than 8,000 growers, is exported to the international market, and gives the whole region its world-famous reputation. These wines are called the **crus classés**.

SO MANY CHÂTEAUX!

In the Bordeaux district, the name of a fine wine is always preceded with the term 'château' to give it prestige. Château this, Château that... more often than not, it simply indicates a wine-producing estate rather than a stately home. This convention has existed for centuries and is simply associated with buildings suitable for the production and ageing of wine. Other terms used for wineries are *domaine*, *clos* or *cru*.

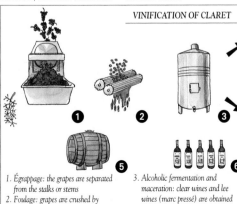

VINIFICATION OF CLARET

1. *Égrappage: the grapes are separated from the stalks or stems*
2. *Foulage: grapes are crushed by rollers*
3. *Alcoholic fermentation and maceration: clear wines and lee wines (marc pressé) are obtained*
4. *Malolactic fermentation: both these blended products are incubated at 64ºF-68ºF (18ºC-20ºC)*
5. *Wine transferred to oak casks*
6. *Bottling*

The great Sauternes
gold in a bottle

The Sauternes district is on the left bank of the Garonne, 25 miles (40 km) from Bordeaux. Its 3950 acres (1600 ha) produce the most prestigious of the sweet white wines of the Bordeaux region. Their golden colour and sweet, exotic fragrance make them ideal as an apéritif. The sweetness is actually the result of allowing the grapes to rot on the vine. Every year, bunches of grapes are left after the harvest has ended, and the resulting breakdown of substances produces the wonderful flavour.

The microclimate

The Sauternes district owes much to the Ciron, a tributary of the Garonne, which provides the moisture that is indispensable in the creation of the sweet wines. Its cold waters flow into the river causing the weather to change in the early autumn, by creating morning mists, which gradually disperse throughout the day in the heat of the late-summer sun. This creates the ideal combination of hot and cold conditions which cause the vine to rot.

Noble rot

Noble rot (*pourriture noble*) is the great secret of Sauternes wines. Unlike all other vines, when the grapes are ripe, they are not harvested immediately. They're left on the vine until they become overripe. In this condition, the flavour and sugars are more concentrated. When they're thoroughly spoiled by the action of the 'pourriture noble', and are a soggy mess, they are picked, one or two months after the rest of the harvest.

The harvest

Noble rot never develops uniformly, so during the harvest each bunch (and even each grape) is carefully examined individually so that

Château-Yquem

and harmonious 'mouth' developing into full and persistent flavours, all typical of a white Sauternes. Its alcohol content may exceed 15% and it's fruity and lively when young (less than 10 years old). But over time it develops a wonderful smoothness and can quite happily be left to mature for a century.

Classifications

At the 1855 Universal Exhibition in Paris, Napoleon III asked the syndicate of Bordeaux brokers to produce a classification for the wines of Sauternes-Barsac. Twenty-six grades were identified, including an *impérial* (and unrepeated) *premier cru supérieur*, the Château-Yquem. After this came the *premiers crus* and six *seconds crus*. These are the aristocrats of the sweet wines of Bordeaux. Together, they represent 50% of the vineyard but as much as 75% of the income. The price of a bottle starts at 100 F.

ADVICE ABOUT DRINKING WHITES

Contrary to widespread belief, Sauternes is not merely an apéritif or a dessert wine. It can also be served during a meal, if you avoid drinking it with very sweet or strong-tasting food. It is a perfect accompaniment to foie gras, fish in sauce, white meat, poultry, soft cheeses (try it with Roquefort) and sorbets or tarts. Sauternes should be drunk cold, between 46 and 50°F (8 and 10°C), but never with ice.

Grape varieties

There are three varieties which form the famous trio of white Bordeaux wines. Sémillon, which accounts for 70% of the crop, is grown for its ability to develop noble rot, its delicate fragrance, its juice and its full taste in the mouth. Sauvignon (25%) contributes its sugars and a note of freshness and vigour. Finally, Muscadelle (5%), a distinct variety, adds a hint of roundness and musky aromas.

The 'golden wines'

A golden colour; a bouquet of exotic fruits, honey, lime or acacia; nuances of almond and spices; a round

they can be picked at the best possible moment. There are therefore several harvests, lasting right into November, because no harvesting takes place in the rain; the precious grapes must be dry when picked. The yields are consequently very low. A single Sauternes vine will only produce a single glass of wine, while all the other varieties will produce about one bottle per vine!

A vineyard in Sauternes

The great Médocs
the gods of wine

M édoc, on the west bank of the Gironde, is a prestigious vineyard covering a narrow 50 mile (80 km) strip, 3 miles (5 km) wide. It is sun-drenched, protected from the sea winds by the forest of Landes and benefits from a microclimate that is particularly propitious for vine growing. In this 'middle ground', squeezed between two large bodies of water, the most famous red wines in the world are grown. Production amounts to 92 million bottles a year.

Appellations

The Médoc vineyard contains eight world-famous Appellations covering 37,065 acres (15,000 ha). The leaders are Médoc and Haut-Médoc representing 60% of the area and 55 million bottles a year. Next come the appellations of Saint-Estèphe, Margaux, Pauillac, Saint-Julien, Listrac and Moulis, of which 37 million bottles are produced annually. In all of them, the wine in its natural state (without the addition of sugar) must never have an alcohol content of less than 10%.

Grape varieties

Cabernet Sauvignon is the predominant variety grown in Médoc, because it benefits from the poor, stony soil in which the roots of the vine dig down as much as 67 feet (20 m) until they find the water they need. The stones absorb some of the heat of the day and release it again at night. In this type of soil, the grape develops exceptional qualities of longevity. In the cellars this is combined with other qualities from the traditional varieties with which they are blended, Merlot and Cabernet Franc.

The personality of the wines

In blends, the Cabernet Sauvignon variety predominates and moulds the character of the red wines of Médoc, producing their generous bouquet, balance, body, strength and lovely colour. It also gives the wines an exceptional capacity to age

production of white wines, since there are no Médoc whites. The reds are lighter in the south than in the north. The leading wine, since 1855, is the famous Château Haut-Brion, which is the only *premier cru classé* in this whole area of the Médoc Appellation. A bottle of Château Haut-Brion will cost a minimum of 40 F.

well. With age, the wines of the Médoc always increase in finesse and delicacy. These wines will keep for a very long time.

The hierarchy of the *grands crus*

Since 1855, the 60 most prestigious Bordeaux wines have been classified by quality. Wine-makers, at the instigation of Napoleon III, established this hierarchy in 1855. Five *premiers crus* are the undisputed leaders. These are Haut-Brion, Lafite, Latour, Margaux and, since 1973, Mouton-Rothschild. Sixty other châteaux are next, identified as second, third, fourth and fifth *crus*. A bottle of any of these will cost between 150 and 1,200 F).

The *crus bourgeois et artisans*

In 1932, five wine-brokers decided to classify the remaining wines of Médoc. They created the category of *crus bourgeois*. This denomination covers 420 estates and 50% of total production. Below them

are 330 small growers who meet the criteria recognised by the European Community in 1994 and who are allowed to call themselves *crus artisans* (11% of production). Finally, there are a thousand wine-makers, grouped into 13 cooperative cellars, who market harmonious blends of various areas of Médoc under brand names (17 % of production). A bottle should cost between 30 and 450 F.

Graves, cousins of Médoc

The Graves area is an extension of Médoc, extending south of Bordeaux for 31 miles (50 km), along the left bank of the Garonne. Soil and varieties are almost identical. The only differences are in the blending and

DRINKING THE WINES OF MÉDOC

The rule is to drink the youngest wine first, to be able to appreciate the better qualities of an older wine (The age of the *crus* is crucial in the case of a Médoc.) A recent Médoc, served at 59°F (15°C), should therefore precede an older bottle, left at room temperature for a few hours before serving at about 64°F (18°C). Never drink this wine with a vinaigrette-type sauce; it probably goes best with pork, veal or poultry, but can be drunk with any meat or a hearty vegetable dish.

Armagnac

I n the Middle Ages, Armagnac was considered to be a medicinal remedy but now it is called 'the milk of the elderly' by the old men of Landes who drink it every day. This is probably because the part of the vineyard that is in Landes produces the best, and most fruity, brandies.

An extensive vineyard

There is nowhere more Gascon than Armagnac. The vineyard is in the heart of Gascony, straddling three départements; Gers, the largest section, Landes and a part of Lot-et-Garonne, mostly around Nérac. There is Bas-Armagnac in the west, whose brandy is delicately perfumed; Armagnac-Thénarèze in the centre, whose brandies are more lively and strong; and Haut-Armagnac, which was developed in the last century to meet the increased demand but nowadays represents a very small proportion of the production.

A good traveller

Armagnac has always had a good press abroad. It has been exported to London and the Low Countries since the Middle Ages. The flattened shape of the bottle was, no doubt, due to the need to make it easy to export by boat to the Dutch. California soon opened its doors to Armagnac. Dashiell Hammett's sophisticated gangsters prefer it to Cognac, thus perpetuating the old French feud between the two types of brandy.

Metamorphosis in the still

When first made, the white wines of Armagnac are not particularly notable. They have the same rather low

degree of alcohol, between 8 and 10%. The grapes are harvested in October and are vinified in the traditional way. They are mainly Ugni-Blanc, Colombard, Folle Blanche and Baco Blanc. However, there are a few Armagnacs made with the old traditional varieties, such as la Clairette de Gascogne,

Jurançon Blanc, Mauzac, Le Graisse or Meslier Saint-François. The quality of the wine is transformed by distillation, a process that takes place between November and March. The still has to be a special type of Armagnac still, which received a royal patent in 1818 from Louis XVIII. The wine is distilled continuously, so by the time it leaves the copper boilers it has been transformed. The rather weak white wine has become a powerful and fragrant clear liquid up to 72°.

Ageing

As soon as it leaves the still, the brandy is transferred to huge 87 gallon (400 litre) oak casks whose new wood comes from the forests of Gascony or Limousin. Inside the cask, the complex chemistry of alcohol and wood gets to work. The brandy is gradually enriched with the odours of the new wood which also imparts an amber tint to the liquid. To complete the ageing process, the brandy is then transferred to older casks. At the same time, it reduces in quantity and mellows. The lost liquid

is the famous 'angels' share' which is the result of the natural evaporation process. In the last stage, the cellarer (*maître du chai*) blends it with other brandies of different ages. Or he may decide to leave the Armagnac to continue to its natural degree of ageing. This is usually how vintage Armagnacs are treated.

Bottling

Once bottled, distilled alcohol does not age further. The Armagnac retains its alcohol content – at least 40% – and its virtues are established. The flavours it acquires in the cask may be vanilla, candied fruit, prunes, violets, etc.

Serenity

The best way to appreciate Armagnac is in a snifter, warmed in the hand, after a hearty meal. However, it's an indispensable ingredient in making pâtisserie, for example the pastry from which a *tourtière* is made contains Armagnac which, along with orange flower water gives it the characteristic taste. It's also used in the barbaric practice of drowning *ortolans* in brandy before cooking them (p. 241). If taken before bed in small quantities, it makes an excellent sleeping draught and apparently sweetens the breath.

Villages and *bastides*

Bastides, walled towns, inherited from the Middle Ages, Basque villages clinging to the mountainsides, seaside resort towns: the architecture of South West France is as diverse as its geography.

Seaside resorts
1. Arcachon
   pp. 50 and 210.
2. Hossegor
   pp. 51 and 241.
3. Soulac-sur-Mer
   pp. 51 and 208.

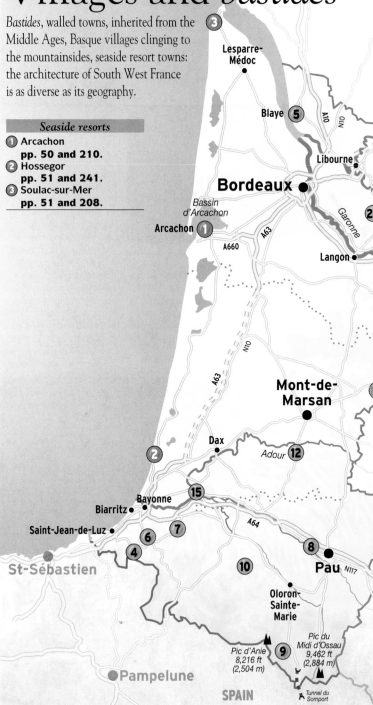

Lesparre-Médoc

Blaye ⑤

Libourne

Bordeaux

Langon

Bassin d'Arcachon

Arcachon ①

Garonne

A10

A63

A660

Mont-de-Marsan

Dax

Adour ⑫

②

⑮

Bayonne

Biarritz

Saint-Jean-de-Luz

St-Sébastien

⑥ ⑦

④

⑩

A64

⑧

Pau N117

Oloron-Sainte-Marie

Pic d'Anie
8,216 ft
(2,504 m)

⑨

Pic du Midi d'Ossau
9,462 ft
(2,884 m)

● Pampelune

SPAIN

Tunnel du Somport

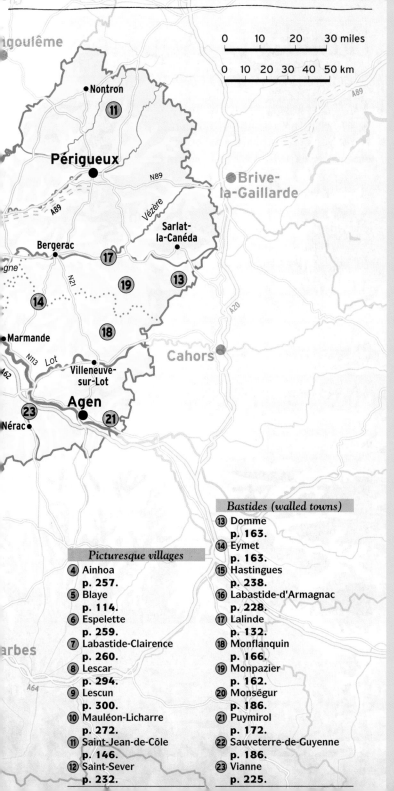

goulême

• Nontron

⑪

Périgueux

N89

•Brive-
la-Gaillarde

Vézère

Bergerac

Sarlat-
la-Canéda

⑰

A89

gne

N21

⑲

⑬

⑭

A20

⑱

• Marmande

N113   Lot

Cahors

462

Villeneuve-
sur-Lot

Agen

⑳

⑳

⑳

Nérac•

A64

arbes

Picturesque villages

④ Ainhoa
   p. 257.
⑤ Blaye
   p. 114.
⑥ Espelette
   p. 259.
⑦ Labastide-Clairence
   p. 260.
⑧ Lescar
   p. 294.
⑨ Lescun
   p. 300.
⑩ Mauléon-Licharre
   p. 272.
⑪ Saint-Jean-de-Côle
   p. 146.
⑫ Saint-Sever
   p. 232.

Bastides (walled towns)

⑬ Domme
   p. 163.
⑭ Eymet
   p. 163.
⑮ Hastingues
   p. 238.
⑯ Labastide-d'Armagnac
   p. 228.
⑰ Lalinde
   p. 132.
⑱ Monflanquin
   p. 166.
⑲ Monpazier
   p. 162.
⑳ Monségur
   p. 186.
㉑ Puymirol
   p. 172.
㉒ Sauveterre-de-Guyenne
   p. 186.
㉓ Vianne
   p. 225.

Bastides of Aquitaine
Medieval strongholds

I n 1152, Eleanor of Aquitaine married Henry II, who became King of England in 1154. The Duchy of Aquitaine was part of her dowry and was administered by the English, under the sovereignty of the King of France. The English and French were bitter rivals and each sought to consolidate their position. To keep the population loyal and extend their influence, they founded new fortified towns, all of which sprang up over a period of 30 years. These were the *bastides*.

The motives for their foundation

There were obvious political and military motives for founding the *bastides*, as well as demographic ones. The population of Aquitaine suddenly expanded in the 13th C.; some historians even claim that it tripled. The overpopulated country-side forced people in exile to the large towns, such as Bordeaux and Périgueux.

The creation of the *bastides* was designed to remedy the situation and introduced a colonisation phenomenon.

Profitable towns

The new towns, which had as many as 1,000 to 2,000 inhab-itants, made their founders rich. Fairs and markets proliferated, and were taxable. Furthermore, strangers passing through the *bastides* had to pay a circulation tax and anyone

passing goods through the town had to pay a toll. Finally, residents were often subject to fines by the courts.

Safety reasons

The *bastides* also contributed to improving the safety of the population in very troubled times. The roads were unsafe in the Middle Ages. There were highwaymen and bands of robbers who roamed the countryside, terrorising the

Monpazier

inhabitants and plundering isolated villages and farms. The people who had chosen to live in the *bastides* were better protected against these marauders.

Revealing names

The names of these rationally organised towns, often built on a **grid pattern**, can be a clue to their history or character. Villeneuve-sur-Lot reveals that it was a new town built on the river Lot, Monflanquin shows that the *bastide* was built on a mountainside, Villefranche was a town that had tax exemptions, and Beaumont was in a pretty setting.

A strict town plan

The layout of the *bastide* was not left to chance. There were no tortuous passages, the streets were built at right angles to each other and the intersections determined the plots of land allotted to the inhabitants (in general there were between 200 and 1,000 plots). The **place** (town square), which replaced the church as the traditional centre of the town, was the venue for fairs and festivals.

Produce from all over the region was sold here. The buildings around the square had arcades at ground level called *couverts* or *cornières*, which protected craftsmen and merchants from the sun and rain. After seven centuries of vicissitudes, and many ups and downs, the *bastides* of Aquitaine are very close-knit communities. Time has given a patina and richness to the various styles of architecture of the different periods.

Different plans

When the founder chose a site for a *bastide*, he would plant a stake bearing his arms and then comb the countryside to round up potential inhabitants for his new town. Surveyors would map out the contours, adapting the standard grid pattern of the *bastide* to the geometry of the landscape. The most common plan is a rectangle, as used in Monpazier and Vianne, but they can be oval or circular due to the topography, as in Monflanquin and Saint-Sardos, or elongated as in the case of the smaller and less important *bastides*, of which Beaumont and Lagruère are good examples.

DISCOVERING THE *BASTIDES* OF HAUT-AGENAIS

A one-day circular tour which leaves from Monflanquin, will take you on a journey of discovery through Monpazier, Beaumont, Issigeac and Villeréal. An Espace Bastide, opened in June 1997, explains the whole *bastide* phenomenon. Information at the Maison du Tourisme de Monflanquin, ☎ 05 53 36 40 19.

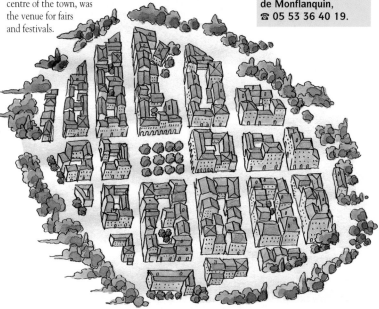

The Basque house
in white and red

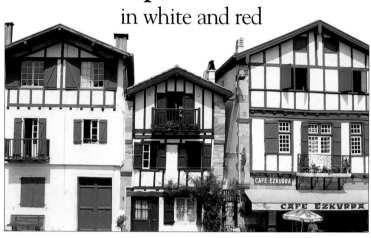

T he *etxe* is typical of all the villages in the Basque country. This country house exists in three versions, one for each province, *la maison labourdine, la maison navarraise* and *la maison souletine*. Built of wood or stone, with tiled or slate roofs and whitewashed walls with wooden half-timbering, they were the keystone of Basque social and family life.

Orientation

Basque houses never face west or northwest, as that's the direction from which rain and storms often come. They have wide frontages which generally face south or south-east so as to get the most sun. In the past, people lived in the southern part of the house and animals would occupy the northern part, at the back. The animals served as a buffer against the cold, a sort of central heating – and their smell and noise permeated the whole dwelling!

The inhabitants

The traditional Basque house is large as it has to accommodate not only the master and mistress of the house, but also the heir or heiress (the

eldest son or daughter), his or her spouse and their children. Generally, the brothers and sisters of the heir would also live there, but were forced to remain single. The role of the family home was so important that all its residents took the family name. Therefore the husband of the eldest daughter took his wife's name.

The social role

The Basque house was long a cornerstone of the Basque social and political system. It was a material manifestation of economic unity and power,

THE BASQUE HOUSE ● 49

EXILE OF THE YOUNGER CHILDREN

In the Basque country, the family home was automatically inherited by the eldest child. The younger sons and daughters were dispossessed and only had two options. They could either marry an heir or heiress, or place themselves in the service of their elders. In the mid-19th C., many of them emigrated to the United States or South America. Some won fame and fortune, like Paul Laxalt, who became an adviser to Ronald Reagan.

as represented by the extended family and its land and, until the 20th C., formed the basis of Basque law, invented by and for a rural society.

The layout

The house was divided into three main areas. In the centre, there was a living room which served as a workshop and delivery area through which fodder, destined for the loft, had to pass. The bedrooms, on either side of this room, housed an entire family, and the kitchen, the only place heated in winter, served as a communal room. When, as in some cases, the living quarters were on the first floor, the whole of the ground floor was used as farm buildings.

La maison labourdine

This wood and stone house is in typical Basque style. Many examples of it can be seen in the village of Aïnhoa. It is plastered a brilliant white and the front is decorated with wooden battens, usually painted red, but sometimes green or dark blue. The corners and lower parts reveal the stonework, and the large porch is open to the sun. The slightly sloping, asymetrical roof is covered in semi-circular tiles.

La maison navarraise

In this more austere style the house timbers are concealed. It generally consists of a single storey, with limewashed walls. Its windows are narrower than the door, which is always massive. Over the door, there is a Basque lintel which bears the names of the owners, the date of construction and often a religious verse or some symbolic designs. The roof is steeper and may be slate or tiled.

La maison souletine

The slate-covered roof has something in common with houses in the neighbouring Béarn district and is very pointed with four sides. It overhangs severe white walls devoid of decoration or inscription, except for window frames of Pyrenean marble. The houses are sober and solid and the walls are edged with ashlar or pebbles, to combat the mountain weather. The farm buildings are arranged in a square.

Houses by the sea
a hymn to the ocean climate

The exceptionally mild climate is worth sampling and you can take in the enchanting architecture, too. The town of Arcachon is the best example of 'resort architecture', evidence of an era when high society inhaled the sea air as protection against tuberculosis, and expressed their gratitude by building elaborate villas. Welcome to the celebrated Winter City.

A climatic resort

Arcachon's popularity grew with the introduction of sea-bathing in the mid-19th C., thanks to its mild winter climate (p. 210). As early as 1862, doctors were praising the benefits of the sea air, as being both a tonic and a sedative, as well as being full of the aroma of pinewoods. Above the summer city, a new type of resort opened, the Ville d'Hiver (the so-called Winter City), where the builders competed with each other to build the most impressive villas.

The Winter City

In the upper part of the town, where the temperature is always 5°F

Villa Brémontier in Arcachon

(3 °C) higher than it is on the beach, aristocrats and royalty built miniature palaces, surrounded by shady gardens of magnolias, palm trees, evergreen oaks and pine trees. For ten years, the Winter City was the favourite resort of wealthy invalids who were able to afford this winter paradise. In 1863, the Moorish-style casino (demolished in 1977) was erected in the centre, just like the cherry on a cake.

The idylls of Arcachon

The villas of Arcachon have witnessed many famous

romances, the most famous being in 1879 between King Alphonso XII of Spain and the Archduchess Marie-Christine of Austria. Although it was an arranged marriage which, in the event, turned out badly, their first official meeting at the Villa Athéna was love at first sight. They plighted their troth in the Park Pereire. In the 20th C. the Winter City saw the romances of Yvonne Printemps and Pierre Fresnay, Jane Fonda and Roger Vadim, Mireille Darc and Alain Delon, among others.

Villa San-Antonio at Hossegor

which had been so highly praised by famous writers, including Edmond Rostand. The most spectacular are the villas Adichats, Maya and San Antonio. The seafront, with its central square, offers many examples of this very stylised architecture.

Biarritz

All the classic styles of architecture are to be found here, including Art Nouveau, Art Deco, the so-called English style and the mock-Tudor, to say nothing of styles of no particular origin like the brainchild of a Chicago magnate, the villa Castel-Adour. There are lovely examples on the Avenue de l'Impératrice, but the style which is most typical of Biarritz is related to that of Hossegor. It was born in the 1930s, and was inspired by the Basque neo-regionalism of nearby Spain. The rooms are spacious, the roofs have

overhanging eaves and there are balconies and rounded windows. It's a very original style, which can be seen at the Villa Paz, at the Maison Basque in the Avenue Edouard-VII or at the Anglet town hall.

Soulac

North of Arcachon, Soulac was attracting wealthy residents of Bordeaux who wanted to try bathing in the sea as early as 1860 (p. 208). Large resort villas were built facing the ocean. Each was designed to hold a single family and all are built to the same plan, consisting of a kitchen and maid's bedroom at the back, combined living and dining room overlooking the street and bedrooms separated by a central corridor. The choice of brick and/or stone for building was often dictated by economy.

Villa Trocadéro in Arcachon

Hossegor

In the 1920s and 1930s, in the aftermath of World War I, a huge town-planning operation created a second generation of resort villas in Aquitaine, this time at Hossegor (p. 241). The villas were built by the golf course amid the pines, and adopted the 'Basque-Béarnais' style. They were occupied by wealthy patrons, many of them foreign, who came to experience the delights of the region

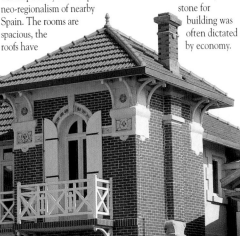

Typical example of seaside architecture at Soulac

Caves and legends

A visit to this region, which was the
cradle of humanity, gives you the
opportunity to take a fascinating journey
to see prehistoric remains and learn
about the traditional folklore.

Saint-Émilion
Monolithic church
and Ermitage cave
pp. 120 and 122.

Moustey
Musée des Croyances
Populaires
p. 219.

Escource
Healing springs
p. 215.

Aire-sur-l'Adour
Sainte-Quitterie
spring
p. 230.

Brassempouy
Musée de la Préhistoire.
p. 233.

Lestelle-Bétharram
Bétharram caves
p.286.

Sare
Caves
p. 257.

Isturitz et Oxocelhaya
Caves
p. 260.

Bidarray
Cave of the 'Saint-
qui-sue' (sweating saint)
p. 263.

Roncevaux
Site of a legendary
battle
pp. 267 and 269.

La-Pierre-Saint-Martin
Ravine
p. 284.

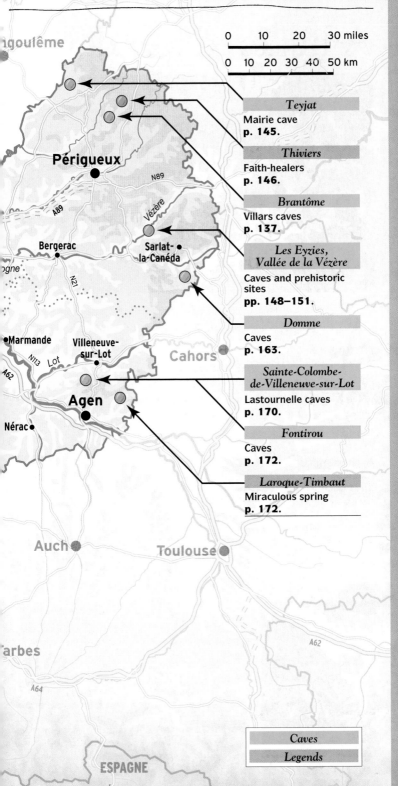

0   10   20   30 miles

0   10 20 30 40 50 km

Teyjat
Mairie cave
p. 145.

Thiviers
Faith-healers
p. 146.

Brantôme
Villars caves
p. 137.

Les Eyzies, Vallée de la Vézère
Caves and prehistoric sites
pp. 148–151.

Domme
Caves
p. 163.

Sainte-Colombe-de-Villeneuve-sur-Lot
Lastournelle caves
p. 170.

Fontirou
Caves
p. 172.

Laroque-Timbaut
Miraculous spring
p. 172.

ngoulême

Périgueux

N89

Vézère

A89

Bergerac

Sarlat-la-Canéda

ogne

Marmande

Villeneuve-sur-Lot

N21

Lot

Cahors

N113

A62

Agen

Nérac

Auch

Toulouse

arbes

A62

A64

ESPAGNE

Caves

Legends

A hundred feet down

Cave of Villars

Aquitaine has many subterranean features – potholes, caverns, grottos – and some are quite spectacular. They are beautiful in themselves, containing magnificent natural sculptures as well as cave paintings by Cro-Magnon man. Early humans found shelter in the caves in the cliffs, which protected them from the elements and wild animals. By painting the walls they have left wonderful records of what the Vézère valley was like, and it is now classified as a World Heritage Site.

Archeological excavations: high technology

The tools used for excavation may look very basic, but the work and research taking place is actually extremely advanced. Studying rock strata makes it possible to determine the position of each buried object, and

Canoeing down the Dordogne, the Vézère, or the Beune is a good way of discovering the great prehistorical sites

geologists then study the sediment deposits that surround it. Carbon 14 dating makes it possible to determine how much time has passed since the death of a living thing.

Cro-Magnon man

Cro-Magnon man was the direct ancestor of modern man, *Homo sapiens*. He

settled in the region 35,000 years ago in the Vézère valley. In 1868, excavations revealed fossilised human remains at Les Eyzies, where Cro-Magnon man lived. A study of the skeletons showed they were not much different from modern man. They tended to be tall with a long skull, straight forehead and firm chin.

Gouffre de Proumeyssac

STALACTITES AND STALAGMITES

 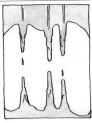 

Rainwater filters into the caves after seeping through layers of limestone. During this journey, it becomes loaded with calcium carbonate. As it drops from the ceiling of the cave, the water forms into stalactites, in which it deposits some of its mineral salts. Immediately below it, stalagmites are formed by the build up of the calcium carbonate deposited by droplets from the ceiling. Over time, stalactites and stalagmites eventually join up to form true columns

Cave paintings

Cro-Magnon man was the great artist of the Palaeolithic era. He drew, painted and sculpted. He reproduced on the walls of his caves what he had seen in nature, though his resources were limited. For light, he burned animal fat in lamps or torches and he extracted his colours from different soils. Manganese was used to obtain black, clay gave him brown, red and ochre. Caveman drew and painted with his fingers or animal-hair brushes.

Frescoes

Why is it necessary to leave prehistoric paintings in the dark? They have been preserved in the caves for thousands of years, but in only a few decades visitors have caused them to deteriorate. Heat, germs, and even our breath are causing the frescoes to melt like snow in the sun, and the extra carbon dioxide exhaled by visitors accelerates the rate of limestone deposits. Scientists have checked the 'health' of the painted caves and calculated the maximum number of visitors they can tolerate annually.

Little-known treasures?

About 40 Paleolithic sites containing paintings were discovered in a decade in Europe, of which about 20 are in France and about the same number in Spain. In Périgord and in the Pyrenees, many entrances were blocked by fallen boulders. The sophisticated technology of oil prospectors was used to increase the speed of excavation but each new cave is costly in terms of security and conservation.

Stalagmites and stalactites: natural decoration

Water filtering underground deposits the limestone with which it is laden, and this forms all sorts of accretions in mysterious shapes. The best known are the stalagmites and stalactites. Each droplet, forming on the ceiling before falling, deposits some of the calcite it contains. This becomes a stalactite. Other water droplets fall in the same place and gradually a mound builds up from the floor to form a stalagmite. When the two meet they form a column. Stalactites and stalagmites form extremely slowly, in the order of just over half an inch (1 cm) every century.

The Cave of Isturitz

Artists and kings

Whether South West France was the land
of their birth or their land of adoption,
the place to which they retired or a source
of inspiration, the residents of the region
have produced many great masterpieces
of art and literature.

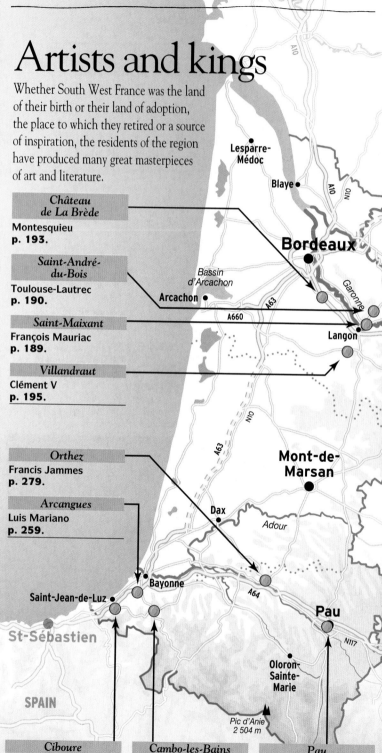

**Château
de La Brède**
Montesquieu
p. 193.

**Saint-André-
du-Bois**
Toulouse-Lautrec
p. 190.

Saint-Maixant
François Mauriac
p. 189.

Villandraut
Clément V
p. 195.

Orthez
Francis Jammes
p. 279.

Arcangues
Luis Mariano
p. 259.

Ciboure
Maurice Ravel
p. 251.

Cambo-les-Bains
Edmond Rostand
p. 258.

Pau
Henri IV and Bernadotte
pp. 288 and 290.

Lesparre-
Médoc

Blaye ●

Bordeaux

*Bassin
d'Arcachon*

Arcachon ●

A660

A63

Garonne

Langon

N10

A63

**Mont-de-
Marsan**

Dax

Adour

Bayonne

Saint-Jean-de-Luz ●

A64

St-Sébastien

Pau

N117

Oloron-
Sainte-
Marie

SPAIN

*Pic d'Anie
2 504 m*

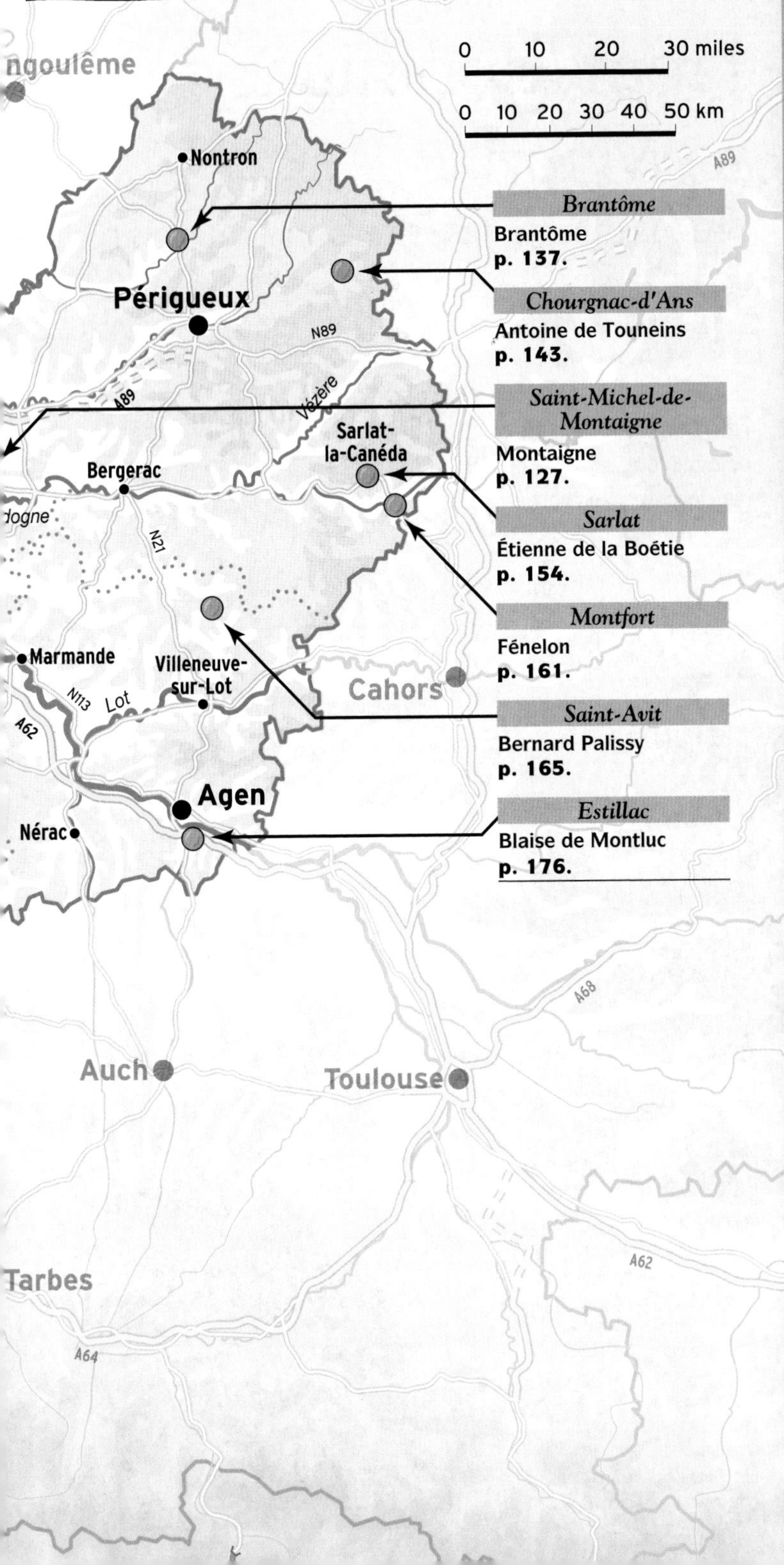

0   10   20   30 miles

0 10 20 30 40 50 km

ngoulême

● Nontron

Périgueux

N89

Vézère

A89

Bergerac

logne

N21

●Marmande

N113   Lot

Villeneuve-
sur-Lot

Agen

Nérac●

Cahors

Auch●

Toulouse●

A68

A62

A62

Tarbes

A64

Sarlat-
la-Canéda

A89

Brantôme

Brantôme
p. 137.

Chourgnac-d'Ans

Antoine de Touneins
p. 143.

Saint-Michel-de-
Montaigne

Montaigne
p. 127.

Sarlat

Étienne de la Boétie
p. 154.

Montfort

Fénelon
p. 161.

Saint-Avit

Bernard Palissy
p. 165.

Estillac

Blaise de Montluc
p. 176.

From Montaigne to Mauriac
the Aquitaine of writers and musicians

The Aquitaine of the north is the land of the three Ms, Montaigne, Montesquieu and Mauriac. All three great French writers were born here and local people remember them proudly. The composer Maurice Ravel, a Basque, came from the south, the poet Francis Jammes died there, and the author Edmond Rostand left a villa just as extraordinary as his writings.

Montaigne (1533-1592)

Michel de Montaigne was Mayor of Bordeaux from 1581 to 1585. The famous philosopher lived in the family home, which can still be seen on the Rue Fauré and his tomb lies in the hall of the former humanities faculty. Montaigne's château, where he was born and died, lies 78 miles (125 km) from Bordeaux, on the Dordogne river. It contains much of the writer's memorabilia, especially in the famous **tower** in which he liked to hide himself away to think and work (p. 127).

Montesquieu (1689-1755)

Montesquieu was born in the Château de La Brède, in the south of Bordeaux (p. 193). It is here that he wrote *De l'esprit des lois*. He worked in a Louis XIII-style room, his feet resting on the mantelpiece which still bears his footprint. He also stayed at the Château de Ramonnet (now called Château Charles-de-Montesquieu), which he inherited from his uncle, and where he produced much of the *Lettres persanes*.

Edmond Rostand (1868-1918)

Rostand settled in the Basque country on the advice of his doctor. In 1903, while taking the cure at Cambo-les-Bains, the author of *Cyrano de Bergerac* built a magnificent 'gingerbread' villa, the Villa Arnaga. It is here that he wrote *Chantecleer*, his last play, and died. The Villa Arnaga is at the entrance to Cambo (p. 258).

François Mauriac (1885-1970)

Mauriac was born in Bordeaux and was inspired by Aquitaine for several of his works. As an adult he lived at Malagar, an estate facing Sauternes. It has a magnificent view of the vineyards, the Garonne and the forest of Les Landes. It was the setting for his novel *The Knot of Vipers* (p. 189). But most of his work revolves around the village of Saint-Symphorien, near Bazas, where he spent his childhood.

Francis Jammes (1868-1938)

Jammes spent the last 17 years of his life at Hasparren in the Basque country. The French poet, whose works have been translated into many languages, left Orthez in 1921 following a fortunate inheritance. For the salvation of his soul, a pious local woman had chosen him as her heir because he was a Catholic writer, although she had never read a word he had written! Francis Jammes is buried in the village cemetery. See also the Maison de Francis Jammes, Hasparren, (p. 260).

Maurice Ravel

Maurice Ravel (1875-1937)

The composer of the famous *Bolero* was born in Ciboure, twin city of Saint-Jean-de-Luz (p. 251). His birthplace (12, Quai Ravel) and a high school (*lycée*) have carried his name since 1961. Every September, the Académie Internationale Maurice-Ravel organises a festival in his honour, even though his work bears no direct reference to his Basque origins (apart from certain rhythms and an unfinished concerto which he called *Zazpiat Bat*).

Stendhal, in his Journal of a Voyage *in the French Midi described the charms of Aquitaine at length*

AND THE KINGS...

Aquitaine has meted out some curious fates to its kings. First, because it included Navarre, a French kingdom which had long been independent, and whose capital was Pau. Marguerite de Navarre, Queen and author, wrote the *Heptameron*. Her grandson Henri IV, King of Navarre and leader of the Protestants, acceded to the throne of France by converting to Catholicism, hence his famous aphorism: 'Paris is worth a mass.' Bernadotte, a marshal under Napoleon, became king of Sweden (after becoming a Protestant!). Antoine de Touneins was not so lucky. In 1860, he was proclaimed King Orélie-Antoine 1 of Araucania by local tribes in Chile, but he did not reign for long. Expelled by the Chilean authorities, he died in Tourtoirac (p. 143).

Antiques and flea markets

There are many great bargains to be had in
the local markets, so have a browse. Useful
information and further comments
are on pages 62-63.

Gironde

1. Arcachon:
   antiques fair
2. Bordeaux: many fairs
   and flea markets
3. Le Teich:
   antiques fair
4. La Teste de Buch: antiques
   fair and flea market

Landes

5. Dax:
   flea market
6. Labastide-d'Armagnac:
   flea market
7. Mont-de-Marsan:
   flea market
8. Peyrehorade:
   antiques fair
9. Port-de-Lanne:
   Fête des Brocs

0   10   20   30 miles

0 10 20 30 40 50 km

ngoulême

⑪ Nontron

⑬   Périgueux

⑫   N89

Brive-la-Gaillarde

Vézère

Sarlat-la-Canéda

⑭

Bergerac

dogne

N21

⑰   ⑩   ⑮

Marmande   Villeneuve-sur-Lot

N113 Lot

A62   Agen

⑯

Nérac

Auch

Tarbes

A64

Dordogne

⑩ Monpazier: Antiquités-Brocante en Bastide

⑪ Nontron: antiques fair and flea market

⑫ Périgueux: antiques fair

⑬ Ribérac: Large flea market

⑭ Sarlat: Brocante d'Automne

⑮ Villefranche du Périgord: old book and manuscript fair, antiques fair

Lot-et-Garonne

⑯ Agen: flea market

⑰ Duras: Grand Rendez-vous Antiquités-Brocante

Pyrénées-Atlantiques

⑱ Ahetze: flea market

⑲ Anglet: flea market

⑳ Ascain: antiques fair and flea market

㉑ Bayonne: flea market

㉒ Cambo-les-Bains: antiques fair, flea market

㉓ Guéthary: flea market

㉔ Hendaye: antiques fair and flea market

㉕ Pau: antiques fair

㉖ Salies-de-Béarn: antiques fair

㉗ Soumoulou: antiques and flea market

A calendar of antiques and flea markets

Antique hunters will love the South West with its numerous antique- and flea markets. Before consulting the diary, remember the universal rules: get up very early, ideally before the stallholders get a chance to unpack; don't dress too elegantly, as this might put the prices up; and above all, rummage and poke about – the best items are often hidden from view! And don't forget that rain usually means fewer customers, so you might unearth even better bargains.

Dordogne

Monpazier
Antiquités-Brocante en Bastide
2nd weekend in August.

Nontron
Antiques fair and flea market
2nd weekend in November.

Périgueux
Périgueux-Ouest antiques fair
Thursday to Sunday of Ascension week (late May to early June).

Ribérac
Large flea market
3rd Saturday in August.

Sarlat
Brocante d'Automne
2nd or 3rd Sunday in October.

Villefranche-du-Périgord
Salon du livre ancien et des vieux papiers (book fair)
mid-July.
Antiques fair
End of August.

Brasserie des Antiquaires, in Bordeaux, held inside an old perfume flask factory

Gironde

Arcachon
Antiques fair
mid-August.

Bordeaux
Large flea market
late Nov. to early Dec.
Journées Nationales de la Brocante 'Automne'
October.
Journées Nationales de la Brocante 'Eté'
June.
Journées Nationales de la Brocante 'Printemps'
March.
Bordeaux antiques fair
early January.
Sud-Ouest antiques fair
late January to early February.

La Teste-de-Buch
Antiques fair and flea market
late July and late October.

Le Teich
Bassin d'Arcachon antiques fair
week of the 14th of July.

Lot-et-Garonne

Agen
Flea market
1st Mon. in February.
4th Monday in March.

WHERE TO HUNT IN BORDEAUX

Passage Saint-Michel, 14-15, Pl. Canteloup
☎ 05 56 92 14 76
Open Mon.–Sat.
9.30am–6.30pm,
Sun. 8.30am–2pm.
Saint-Michel is an antique-hunter's paradise. Haggling is all part of the fun. Rummage and poke, feel the goods, go round the square several times and you'll find that old oil lamp, hall mirror, or a child's wrought iron bed. You can no longer smell the vanilla and orange flower water which was once bottled here in the factory that occupied this huge building. Now there are 45 stallholders selling antiques and craft items, including furniture and house-hold goods.

Peyrehorade
Antiques fair
3rd weekend of January.

Port-de-Lanne
Fête des Brocs
14 and 15 August.

Pyrénées-Atlantiques

Ahetze
Flea market
3rd Sunday of the month.

Anglet
Flea market
2nd Sunday of the month.

Ascain
Antiques fair and flea market
late July.

Bayonne
Flea market
Every Friday morning,
Place Montaut.

Cambo-les-Bains
Antiques fair
mid-November.

Flea market
On Wednesday, Parc
Saint-Joseph or city
centre car park.

Guéthary
Flea market
Sat. morning, mid-June to
mid-September, Fronton.

Hendaye
Antiques fair and flea market
last weekend of February.
Flea market
4th Sunday of the month.

Pau
Antiques fair
early October.

Salies-de-Béarn
Antiques fair
Easter and late August.

Soumoulou
Antiques fair and flea market
1st Sunday of the month.

BORDEAUX LE VILLAGE NOTRE-DAME
61, Rue Notre-Dame
☎ 05 56 52 66 13.
Open daily, 10am–
12.30pm and 2–7pm;
Sun., Oct.–Apr.
2–7pm.

Le Village Notre-Dame will enchant antiques hunters. Once an old print works (16,150 sq feet/1,500 sq m), it has been converted into an antiques market with 15 stallholders. Information is available from antique dealers in the village, and you will have plenty of time to wander about. The village also organises practical courses on furniture restoration, upholstery, and other skills (from 1,500 F).

1st Mon. in June.
4th Mon. in
September.
2nd Mon. in December.

Duras
Grand rendez-vous
Antiquités-
Brocante
15 August.

Landes

Dax
Flea market
1st Thurs. of the month.

Labastide-d'Armagnac
Flea market
4th Sun. of the month.

Mont-de-Marsan
Flea market
1st Wednesday of
the month.

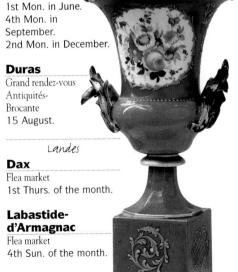

Traditional arts and crafts

This brief overview is designed to give you an insight into the traditional implements used by shepherds and wine growers, the secrets of the Basque beret and the local craft of knife-making.

Local artefacts

1. Bayonne: *palas* (pelota bats) **p. 242.**
2. Bellocq: *bourdon* (pilgrim's staff) **p. 277.**
3. Came: chair making **p. 270.**
4. Larressore: swordsticks **p. 259.**
5. Mauléon-Licharre: espadrilles **p. 272.**
6. Nay: sheep-bells **p. 287.**
7. Nontron: knives **p. 144.**
8. Oloron-Sainte-Marie: berets, Basque fabric **p. 283.**
9. Pau: shepherd's umbrellas **p. 291.**
10. Preignac: vine-growers' clogs **p. 192.**

Blaye ●

Libourne ●

Bordeaux ●

Bassin d'Arcachon

Arcachon ●

Langon ●

Mont-de-Marsan ●

Dax ●

Adour

Biarritz ●

Saint-Jean-de-Luz ●

Bayonne

St-Sébastien ●

Pau

Oloron-Sainte-Marie

Pic du Midi d'Ossau 9,462 ft (2,884 m)

Pic d'Anie 8,216 ft (2,504 m)

SPAIN

Tunnel du Somport

11. Saint-Étienne-d'Orthe: clogs **p. 239.**
12. Saint-Jean-Pied-de-Port: Basque fabric **p. 269.**
13. Saint-Palais: Basque fabric **p. 271.**
14. Ygos: espadrilles **p. 218.**

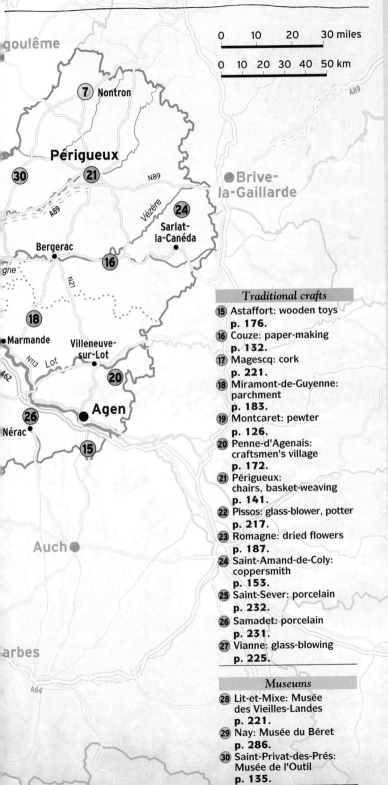

goulême

⑦ Nontron

Périgueux

③⓪　②①

N89

●Brive-
la-Gaillarde

Vézère

②④
Sarlat-
la-Canéda

A89

Bergerac

①⑥

gne

N21

①⑧

●Marmande

Villeneuve-
sur-Lot

Lot　②⓪

N113

462

Agen

②⑥

Nérac ●

①⑤

Auch ●

arbes

A64

0　10　20　30 miles

0　10　20　30　40　50 km

A89

Traditional crafts

⑮ Astaffort: wooden toys
p. 176.

⑯ Couze: paper-making
p. 132.

⑰ Magescq: cork
p. 221.

⑱ Miramont-de-Guyenne:
parchment
p. 183.

⑲ Montcaret: pewter
p. 126.

⑳ Penne-d'Agenais:
craftsmen's village
p. 172.

㉑ Périgueux:
chairs, basket-weaving
p. 141.

㉒ Pissos: glass-blower, potter
p. 217.

㉓ Romagne: dried flowers
p. 187.

㉔ Saint-Amand-de-Coly:
coppersmith
p. 153.

㉕ Saint-Sever: porcelain
p. 232.

㉖ Samadet: porcelain
p. 231.

㉗ Vianne: glass-blowing
p. 225.

Museums

㉘ Lit-et-Mixe: Musée
des Vieilles-Landes
p. 221.

㉙ Nay: Musée du Béret
p. 286.

㉚ Saint-Privat-des-Prés:
Musée de l'Outil
p. 135.

Basque and Landais furniture

furniture from the fields

Rustic furniture can still be seen in some farmhouses in the Basque country or in Landes. The furniture is easily adapted, thanks to its multi-purpose design. This authentic style is now very much in vogue, due to the popularity of natural materials and nostalgia for country life. Each region of France had distinctive furniture styles, only the materials used and the decoration vary. The heavily carved wood of Basque furniture contrasts with the plain Landes style.

The Basque house interior

The kitchen of a Basque house also serves as the living-room, so it contains all the important furniture, such as the dresser, the chest, the table and benches, the draining-board, the clock and, by the fireplace, the *zūzūlū*, a three-seater bench, with a folding shelf. The bedroom, often on the floor above, usually contains one or more beds, a few chairs and a bedside table covered with a cloth or *taouline*, for toilet articles.

Which wood?

Basque furniture is generally sturdy and made to last. A variety of woods are used, depending on the district. In Labourd, oak and walnut are favourites, in lower Navarre, cherrywood, applewood, pearwood, chestnut and walnut are also used. In Soule, it is mainly oak. A chest of drawers or wardrobe may be made of several different kinds of wood.

Kitchen utensils

These have become **decorative objects** and antiques and are highly sought after. Typical Basque utensils include the *herrade*, the container that women sometimes carried on their heads for bringing water from the pump or well. The *coutchet* was a narrow, long-handled spoon, used for ladling out water from these containers. You will also see a wide selection of tinware, pewter, pottery, earthenware, faience and wooden utensils such as wooden whisks for making sauces or whipping egg whites.

The dresser

This is a very important item of furniture in the Basque country, as important as it is in Brittany. Usually made of walnut, which turns almost black when it is heavily varnished, the dresser is most often used for storage. It has a large, engraved wrought iron lock and the decoration, often carved in the wood, consists of geometric patterns, religious motifs or vegetables and flowers.

The chests of Chalosse

They are usually called *mankas*. They have a false drawer which hides a kneading-trough which is revealed by lifting up the top of the chest. Chalosse style is influenced by that of Béarn. As elsewhere in the South-West, decoration consists of the Maltese cross, symbol of the peoples who spoke the *langue d'oc*, round or oval decorative shapes called *galettes* and fan-shapes.

In Landes: two styles for two districts

In the Marensin, pine is the favoured wood for furniture. This so-called 'wood of the poor' has a golden patina and a variety of shades.

In Chalosse, the richest region, craftsmen preferred to use walnut, cherrywood or other fruitwood. The furniture is plain with few decorations but it is carefully proportioned.

Incidental furnishings of Landes: simplicity

Furniture is plain in the farmhouses. There are rustic larders with wooden lattice doors (rather in the Spanish tradition). A salt-cellar (*chaise à sel*) was put by the fireplace in order to protect this precious ingredient from humidity. The *bacherey* is a drainer for draining crockery. It is rarely made of pine, more often of willow, elm, ash or acacia. Sideboards were extremely plain and were more utilitarian than decorative.

Came, the chair-making village

Came is a little village in the Basque country which is famous for its furniture, especially chairs. On visiting the workshops, you will find craftsmen who still turn wood into its traditional shapes.

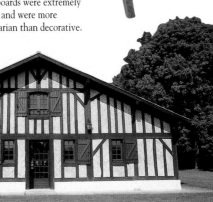

Linen and fabrics

More than 500 families of weavers lived in the Basque country until the mid-19th C. Fabric was manufactured because flax was grown on small holdings. The women spun the linen thread and the men did the weaving. Today, this woven cloth makes a great souvenir to bring home: the red- and blue-striped cloth is an elegant addition to any table.

For oxen and humans

In the 19th C. two types of fabric were woven here. The first was a thick cloth called *marregue*, which was used to make blankets for oxen. These protected the oxen from flies while they were ploughing the fields. The second fabric had a finer weave and was used for clothing, sheets and tablecloths.

The story of the stripes

Where does the idea of the blue threads in the weft of the fabric come from? Some people believe that it resembles the prayer shawls which Jews wear in their religious ceremonies (many Jews fleeing from Spain and Portugal found refuge in Navarre in the late Middle Ages). The seven stripes that represent the seven Basque

provinces (four French, three Spanish) developed much later, in the 19th C., when new dyes were invented.

The most simple explanation is that there was plenty of blue dye around because woad was produced in Toulouse and Lauragais for export via Sète and Bayonne, and this natural dye did not run. The stripes were used only to define the sizes of the cloths destined for different sizes of table.

A period of decline

Although there are so many unknowns in the origins of this craft, it is thought that it began to flourish from the 16th C., especially when tables were always laid with cloths on feast days. Basque weaving continued to flourish until the second half of the 19th C. It then felt the full force of the Industrial

Revolution and competition with English and American cotton goods. A few weavers reacted by establishing mills in the valleys of Soule and

Béarn, where the necessary hydraulic power was available for running the looms on steam and later electricity.

The beret: more Béarnais than Basque

The beret as a head-covering worn by the shepherds of Aquitaine, is first mentioned in a text from Landes, dating from 1461: 'similarly, any beret-seller who places his berets on the market…'. But

contrary to appearances, the beret does not originate from either Landes or the Basque country, it is from Béarn!

The shepherd's beret

The beret served to protect shepherds from the sun, the cold and the rain. In the Middle Ages, they were knitted from sheep's wool. Four large boxwood knitting needles were used and the berets were shaped over the knee. They were then washed and beaten in warm, soapy water to give them their felted look. The beret first gained popularity in the 18th C.,

and was adopted as part of the uniform by the French army in the late 19th C. Some foreign armies adopted it in the early 20th C.

Basque beret?

The beret has always been made exclusively in Béarn, but it acquired its Basque label thanks to tourists in the early 20th C., who thought it amusing to wear it in the streets of Biarritz! This acceptance into the smart set at the most

fashionable seaside resort propelled the beret to the height of fashion and the beret was forever associated with the Basque country. Making berets is no easy task. At least **13 operations** are required to obtain this woolen 'pancake'. It is knitted from a single thread 1,660 ft (500 m) long into a circle of wool and the ends are drawn together to form the bottom of the hat. It is then 'tortured'. The woollen circle is beaten with a hammer in a barrel of soapy water, which makes it shrink, become thicker and felts the wool. It is then dyed, dried, scraped, shaved (with an electric razor!), ironed, and finally the leather rim is sewn on.

Festivals and feast-days

Traditional gatherings of shepherds,
trials of strength and public holidays:
Aquitaine enjoys a good celebration.

Music

1. Aiguillon: jazz **p. 178.**
2. Bayonne: Jazz aux Remparts **p. 244.**
3. Monflanquin: Music in Guyenne **p. 166.**
4. Monpazier: Festival du Périgord pourpre **p. 162.**
5. Monségur: 24- Heures du Swing **p. 186.**
6. Oloron-Sainte-Marie: jazz festival **p. 282.**
7. Orthe district: Nuits d'été en pays d'Orthe **p. 238.**
8. Ribérac: music and lyrics in Ribéracois **p. 134.**
9. Saint-Amand-de-Coly: Festival de Musique du Périgord Noir **p. 153.**
10. Villeneuve-sur-Lot: jazz **p. 169.**

Pelota and 'Force Basque'

11. Saint-Étienne-de-Baïgorry : Force Basque. **p. 265.**
12. Saint-Jean-Pied-de-Port : pelota. **p. 268.**
13. Saint-Palais : pelota and Force Basque Festival **p. 271.**

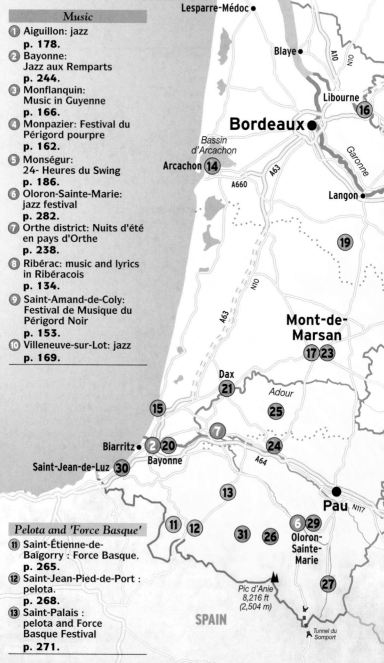

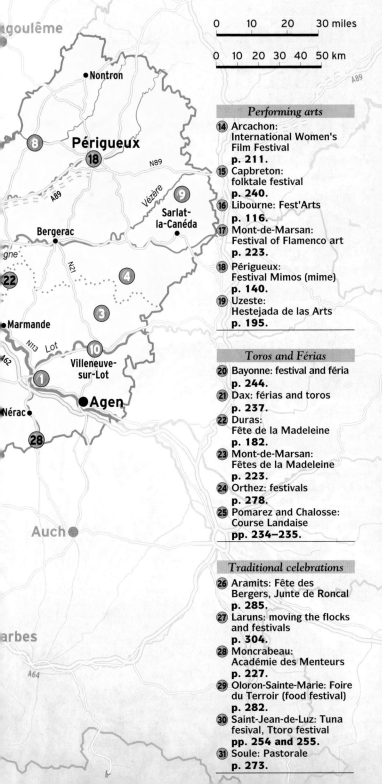

0   10   20   30 miles

0   10   20   30   40   50 km

Performing arts

⑭ Arcachon:
International Women's
Film Festival
p. 211.

⑮ Capbreton:
folktale festival
p. 240.

⑯ Libourne: Fest'Arts
p. 116.

⑰ Mont-de-Marsan:
Festival of Flamenco art
p. 223.

⑱ Périgueux:
Festival Mimos (mime)
p. 140.

⑲ Uzeste:
Hestejada de las Arts
p. 195.

Toros and Férias

⑳ Bayonne: festival and féria
p. 244.

㉑ Dax: férias and toros
p. 237.

㉒ Duras:
Fête de la Madeleine
p. 182.

㉓ Mont-de-Marsan:
Fêtes de la Madeleine
p. 223.

㉔ Orthez: festivals
p. 278.

㉕ Pomarez and Chalosse:
Course Landaise
pp. 234–235.

Traditional celebrations

㉖ Aramits: Fête des
Bergers, Junte de Roncal
p. 285.

㉗ Laruns: moving the flocks
and festivals
p. 304.

㉘ Moncrabeau:
Académie des Menteurs
p. 227.

㉙ Oloron-Sainte-Marie: Foire
du Terroir (food festival)
p. 282.

㉚ Saint-Jean-de-Luz: Tuna
fesival, Ttoro festival
pp. 254 and 255.

㉛ Soule: Pastorale
p. 273.

Bull-running and bullfighting

A cow stands in the centre of the arena, and an *écarteur* stands facing her. This is *La Course Landaise*, a cousin of the bullfight, or *corrida*, from which it takes its inspiration, and is very popular in South West France. Of course, not everyone agrees with bull-fighting. For the French it is an honourable and traditional pursuit, whereas the average holiday-maker may find the brutal reality unappealing.

The step-aside

The feet-together leap

as well as taking daring running, twisting leaps over the animal. Some *écarteurs* go as far as tying their feet together or leaping with their feet held together inside a beret! The skill is then in jumping with the small of the back as close as possible to the animal's horns. Courage, agility, precision and grace are rewarded by enthusiastic applause.

Course Landaise

It began in 1850, at the same time as the Spanish bullfight came to France. The ancient practice of releasing bulls to run through the streets was changed: bulls were replaced by cows and the *écarteur* came on the scene. At the same time, the *écarteurs* formed themselves into a *cuadrilla*, breeding farms became *ganaderias* and the cows acquired Spanish-sounding names.

No killing

Unlike the *corrida*, bulls are not allowed to fight here. Only cows have access to the ring and they always come out **alive**. The principle is simple. An *écarteur* stands facing the cow, in the centre of the arena, his back arched. He calls the cow and teases her to provoke her into

charging, and, at the very last moment, he steps aside. To prevent an accident, the horns of the animal are 'buffered' and its head held in a forward position by means of a rope in order to prevent any side-swipes.

The art of the *écarteur*

The whole success of the show depends on the agility of the *écarteur* who uses the classic step-aside manoeuvre,

The cows

Bred on special farms called *ganaderias*, they are kept apart from dairy cows and are from the same breed as Spanish fighting bulls. They tolerate the man who looks after them for three years, but once in the bullring, if the same man were to face them, they would charge!

The angel leap

THE *BANDAS*

Bullfighting or bull-running never take place without the accompaniment of *bandas*. These musicians consists of a group of 20 to 40 young people, often from local schools of music, who enliven the streets of the villages. Their repertoire has a Basque or Navarrian inspiration, but may drift into jazz riffs or South American music. As an experience, try following a *banda* for a whole night, in Dax, Aire-sur-l'Adour or Bayonne. It will be a night to remember!

Some champion cows have long careers (10 to 15 years) because, through experience, they learn their opponents' side-stepping moves and other avoiding tactics and the game becomes a true battle of wits.

The *corrida*

The *corrida* has been practised in Spain since the 18th C., and arrived in France in 1850. The rules are immutable. During a *corrida*, six *toros* (bulls) are fought in turn by three matadors. In the ring, the matadors are assisted by three *toreros* on foot (the *peones*) and two on horseback (the *picadores*), who prepare the bull for the master and protect him should it prove necessary.

The personality of the bull

The *toro* is the only animal who marks out the space it wants for itself, in which it will tolerate no intrusion. It identifies the red cape of the toreador as a trespasser and is determined to attack it. The bullfighter must therefore lure the animal and exploit its strength, speed and aggression in order to make it understand that it is not the master. The bull is exhausted in the struggle, and eventually concedes, is vanquished and dies.

Bullfights in three parts

The *corrida* is always divided into three parts (*tercios*). First there is the *tercio de vara* (sticking), during which the mounted *picador* weakens the animal. Then comes the *tercio de banderillas*, when the *banderilleros* anger the beast by sticking long, brightly-coloured lances in its back, and then there is the *tercio de muleta*, reserved for the matador, who subdues the bull using his small red cape (*muleta*). At the end the bull is killed.

Pelota and *Force Basque*

games of strength

Pelota is played all over the Basque country. Briefly, it consists of hitting a ball against a wall before it bounces twice. Every village has a *fronton* (pelota wall) or a *trinquet* (covered wall) and the games can be fast and furious!

chistera was born. It is used to catch the ball and, thanks to its curved shape, throws it back with increased force. The success of this version has produced a number of variations on the game, the latest of which is the *cesta punta*.

The ball can travel at up to 185 mph (300 km/h), as it is hurled back and forth! The *cesta punta* ('basket point', in Spanish) requires prolonged and strenuous effort, and only the fittest can compete.

Bare-handed

This is the most demanding version. In pelota, the hard ball is hit with the flat of the hand. The palms of the professionals are often covered in calluses making their hands look deformed.

La *pala*

This is a bat, a little like a table-tennis bat but made of solid wood. It sends back the ball with a loud clap. Thanks to its weight (1 lb 5 oz to 1 lb 7 oz (600 to 700 g) and its size (20 in long by 4 in wide (50 cm x 10 cm), it can only be used by experienced players.

The *chistera*

One day in 1857, Jean Dithurbide, a child from Saint-Pée-sur-Nivelle, had the novel idea of catching the ball in a fruit basket. That is how the wicker

The *cesta punta*

This is the most dangerous

version of the game. It is played in *frontons* (open air courts) with three walls, called *jaï-alaï*. The hardness of the ball and the use of a large *chistera* make wearing a helmet essential.

The grounds

Pelota is played in a *fronton* or a *trinquet*. A *fronton* is in the open air, and consists of a stone wall 67 feet (20 m), wide in front of a court up to 100 to 300 feet (30 to 90 m) long enabling the players to move about freely. The *fronton* is always in the centre of the village. The *trinquet* is a covered area measuring 93 by 30 feet (28 m by 9 m), closed in by four walls.

The spectators sit in two galleries, on the

La *soka-tira*

This is the tug-of-war, the highlight of the games. Two teams of eight men each pull on the rope and to win, one side must drag the other at least 13 feet (4 m). Teams complete in five categories depending

A RETURN TO THE OLYMPIC GAMES?

Prior to 1904, Basque tug-of-war (*soka-tira*) was an olympic sport. Basque teams are now working to get this trial of strength reinstated in the most prestigious of all sporting events. There has been a world championship in tug-of-war since 1970.

left and at the back and are protected by a net. At the *fronton*, physical strength is essential. At the *trinquet*, the rebounds against the walls give the game speed, and the resonance of the court gives an impression great power and strength.

Force Basque

Every year, champions compete in these games, which were originally based on farm labouring tasks. Foreign spectators are tolerated if they are discreet. The Basques hate it when their competitors are treated little better than circus animals.

Lasto Altsari

Aizkolari

on the combined weight of the team. Before the tug-of-war begins, each man is weighed on scales. The categories are: 1232, 1320, 1408 and 1584 lb (560, 600, 640, 680 and 720 kg).

Carrying and lifting trials

The milk-churn trial consists of running the furthest distance with a milk-churn weighing 88 lb (40 kg) in each hand. The sack race is a relay race in teams of three. The sack of maize carried by the runners weighs 187 lb (85 kg)! In the cart trial competitors

must turn a cart weighing 836 lb (380 kg) on its axis, using only their hands, for as long as possible. In the raising the stone event, contestants have a choice of either raising a large stone block weighing 550 to 319 lb (250 to 320 kg) as many times as possible, or of rolling a round stone, weighing 220 lb (100 kg) around their necks.

Training

A contender cannot just decide to take part in a *Force Basque*. The best of them undergo the rigorous training of a professional athlete, including footwork, exercise and trials of strength. But the psychological aspect is of prime importance, they need to learn how to 'suffer in front of an audience'. They must stay true to the maxim *Zazpi ahalak*, 'do the maximum'!

Industrial and scientific sites

Whether you want to take flying lessons, visit a printer, look at the stars from an observatory or see horses on a stud farm, South West France has something for everyone.

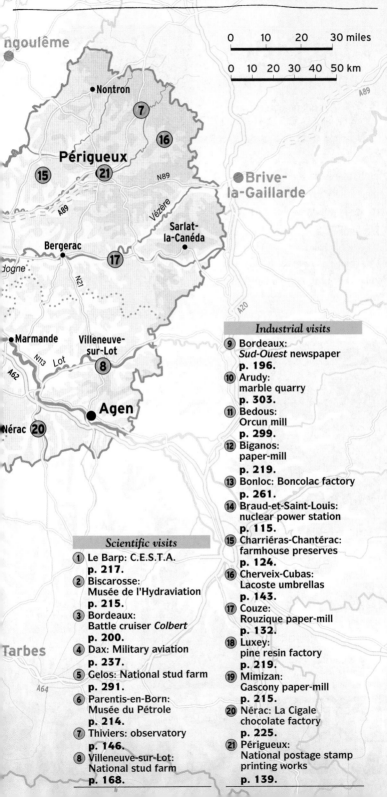

ngoulême

●Nontron

⑦

⑯

Périgueux

⑮ ㉑

N89

●Brive-
la-Gaillarde

A89

Vézère

Sarlat-
la-Canéda

Bergerac

⑰

dogne

A89

N21

A20

●Marmande

Villeneuve-
sur-Lot

⑧

N113 *Lot*

A62

Agen

●Nérac ⑳

Tarbes

A64

Industrial visits

⑨ Bordeaux:
Sud-Ouest newspaper
p. 196.
⑩ Arudy:
marble quarry
p. 303.
⑪ Bedous:
Orcun mill
p. 299.
⑫ Biganos:
paper-mill
p. 219.
⑬ Bonloc: Boncolac factory
p. 261.
⑭ Braud-et-Saint-Louis:
nuclear power station
p. 115.
⑮ Charriéras-Chantérac:
farmhouse preserves
p. 124.
⑯ Cherveix-Cubas:
Lacoste umbrellas
p. 143.
⑰ Couze:
Rouzique paper-mill
p. 132.
⑱ Luxey:
pine resin factory
p. 219.
⑲ Mimizan:
Gascony paper-mill
p. 215.
⑳ Nérac: La Cigale
chocolate factory
p. 225.
㉑ Périgueux:
National postage stamp
printing works
p. 139.

Scientific visits

① Le Barp: C.E.S.T.A.
p. 217.
② Biscarosse:
Musée de l'Hydraviation
p. 215.
③ Bordeaux:
Battle cruiser *Colbert*
p. 200.
④ Dax: Military aviation
p. 237.
⑤ Gelos: National stud farm
p. 291.
⑥ Parentis-en-Born:
Musée du Pétrole
p. 214.
⑦ Thiviers: observatory
p. 146.
⑧ Villeneuve-sur-Lot:
National stud farm
p. 168.

0   10   20   30 miles

0   10 20 30 40 50 km

The pine
from resin to paper

When a pine in the forest of Landes is 50 years old, it is ready for felling. Once felled, it is made into paper pulp, planks, boards, beams, panelling, furniture, flooring, and so on. For 30 years, forest timber production from Landes has increased steadily. However, in this immense reserve, 4,590,950,000 cubic feet (130 million cubic m) of trees, resin collection has now been abandoned.

Timber-felling

The diameter of the trunk determines the way in which the timber will be used when a tree is felled. It is immediately cut into lengths of 6 feet (2 m) for 'pulp wood' (for paper or chipboard), from 8 to 9 feet (2.4 m to 2.7 m) for woodworking (carpentry, flooring, panelling, crates) and lengths of 10 feet (3 m) for joists and beams. Once graded, the logs are loaded on a truck with a capacity of 1,413 to 1,766 cu ft (40 to 50 cu m) and sent to a saw mill or paper-mill.

Woodworking wood

The wood used for woodworking represents an average of 65% of the production. It may be sawn or unwound. Sawn wood is generally destined to be

made into flooring, panels or mouldings. Unwinding involves slicing the wood into very thin sheets, using a procedure similar to sharpening a pencil. Thsews thin slices are then made into plywood sheets by sticking them together and putting them through a press.

Pulp wood

Pulp wood is also called 'industrial wood'. It cannot be sawn because it is too thin. It generally comes from clearings and is sent to be made into paper or cardboard. There are currently four paper-mills in Aquitaine. Facture, in Gironde and Mimizan, in Les Landes, produce craft paper for wrappings. Tartas, in Chalosse, makes cellulose paper, toilet paper, paper tissues and disposable nappies (diapers). The Condat factory, in the Dordogne, specialises in printing paper and notepaper.

The panels

Pulp wood can also be made into chipboard or fibreboard

(MDF). In the first instance, it is chopped into small fragments which are glued together then piled on top of each other and put through a heavy press. In the case of fibreboard, the wood is defibred and the fibres are collected,

laminated and pressed to make very strong panels.

Resin collection

The pines which produced the resin for which the Landes forest was once famous, have become very rare. Resin collection, known in French as *gemmage*, is now a marginal activity. Competition from chemical substitutes has caused this traditional occupa-

tion to disappear. Until 1950, it was the principal source of income in what was then a rather underdeveloped region. Only a single factory still exists in Aquitaine which uses real pine resin to produce household cleaning products.

Good qualities and defects

'Could do better'. The timber of Landes has excellent intrinsic qualities but the trees have a major defect, the curving of the trunk, which means it cannot be used in long, straight lengths. Intensive research is being conducted

into forestry in order to actively improve the quality of the seedlings by genetic manipulation, and the foresters try to ensure that there are clearings and plenty of space between the trees so that they can reach the light without having to twist their trunks.

THE WORK OF A FORESTER

The people of Landes love their forest and are devoted to the trees. They constantly wander through the timber plantations to make sure that deer have not damaged the saplings, to see whether the latest storm has brought down a large pine tree, or to make an axe mark on the trees to be felled. When a forester plants timber, he knows that his son or grandson will be felling the pines 40 years later, whereas in the past, the trees stood for 100 years or more before dying of old age.

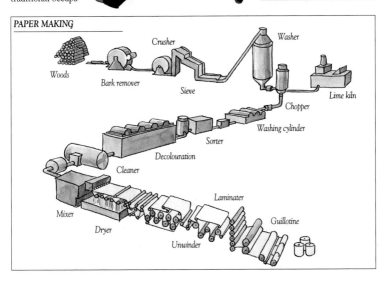

PAPER MAKING

Woods — Bark remover — Crusher — Sieve — Washer — Lime kiln — Chopper — Washing cylinder — Sorter — Decolouration — Cleaner — Mixer — Dryer — Unwinder — Laminater — Guillotine

Nature, gardens and wildlife

Learn about the local flora and fauna while you're out for a drive, on a visit, or hiking and walking in South West France.

Parks and gardens

1. Bayonne:
   botanical gardens
   p. 245.
2. Beynac:
   Marqueyssac gardens
   p. 160.
3. Bordeaux:
   Parc de Bourran
   p. 198.
4. Dax: Parc du Sarrat
   p. 237.
5. Eyrignac:
   gardens of the château
   p. 152.
6. Hendaye: grounds of
   the Château d'Abbadie
   p. 251.
7. Le-Temple-sur-Lot:
   water-garden
   p. 172.

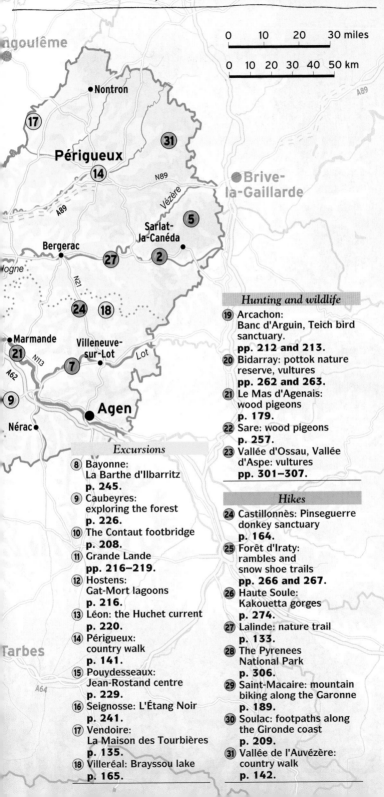

ngoulême

●Nontron

17

Périgueux

14

31

N89

●**Brive-la-Gaillarde**

Vézère

A89

Bergerac

Sarlat-
la-Canéda

5

2

27

ogne

24   18

●**Marmande**

Villeneuve-sur-Lot

21

Lot

N113

7

9

Agen

●**Nérac**

Tarbes

A64

Excursions

⑧ Bayonne:
La Barthe d'Ilbarritz
p. 245.
⑨ Caubeyres:
exploring the forest
p. 226.
⑩ The Contaut footbridge
p. 208.
⑪ Grande Lande
pp. 216–219.
⑫ Hostens:
Gat-Mort lagoons
p. 216.
⑬ Léon: the Huchet current
p. 220.
⑭ Périgueux:
country walk
p. 141.
⑮ Pouydesseaux:
Jean-Rostand centre
p. 229.
⑯ Seignosse: L'Étang Noir
p. 241.
⑰ Vendoire:
La Maison des Tourbières
p. 135.
⑱ Villeréal: Brayssou lake
p. 165.

Hunting and wildlife

⑲ Arcachon:
Banc d'Arguin, Teich bird
sanctuary.
pp. 212 and 213.
⑳ Bidarray: pottok nature
reserve, vultures
pp. 262 and 263.
㉑ Le Mas d'Agenais:
wood pigeons
p. 179.
㉒ Sare: wood pigeons
p. 257.
㉓ Vallée d'Ossau, Vallée
d'Aspe: vultures
pp. 301–307.

Hikes

㉔ Castillonnès: Pinseguerre
donkey sanctuary
p. 164.
㉕ Forêt d'Iraty:
rambles and
snow shoe trails
pp. 266 and 267.
㉖ Haute Soule:
Kakouetta gorges
p. 274.
㉗ Lalinde: nature trail
p. 133.
㉘ The Pyrenees
National Park
p. 306.
㉙ Saint-Macaire: mountain
biking along the Garonne
p. 189.
㉚ Soulac: footpaths along
the Gironde coast
p. 209.
㉛ Vallée de l'Auvézère:
country walk
p. 142.

The pottok
a throwback

The name is pronounced 'potiok'. This sturdy 'little horse' (the literal translation) is the Basque workhorse *par excellence*. Unfortunately, it is on the verge of extinction, the number of thoroughbreds now being as few as 200 animals. There is a general movement in the Basque country to preserve and protect this authentic descendant of the prehistoric horse.

A very special build

The pottok is described thus 'it measures an average 12½ hands (1.25 m) at the withers, the coat is bay or black, the head massive, the ears small and mobile, the neck short and the back long. Its long, dry legs end in small hooves that are very tough, especially adapted for the mountains. Its abundant mane and tail are never curly'. Seen from afar, it looks like a little horse, but up close it looks more like a big pony. In both cases, its gentleness and hairy, sturdy build attract attention.

Why is the pottok disappearing?

There are two main reasons: firstly, the massive destruction of its natural habitat, which has been happening for the last 30 years, but above all the large-scale unplanned crossbreeding with larger breeds. As a result, at horse fairs one can find animals that are small like the pottok, but have the bulky shape of a carthorse, to say nothing of their colour, which really

offends the purists. These are only used for horsemeat and have nothing in common with the original animal.

The coat colour mutation

Many horses described as pottoks today have a piebald (patchy) coat. These are not true pottoks, but descendants of a mutation which emerged in 1935, and which has continued to develop ever since. To attract buyers from circuses in the 1950s, and to meet the requirements of the

pony clubs in the 1970s, there were far too many cross breedings with Spanish horses (whose bloodline had already been diluted by breeding with horses of indeterminate origin brought from America).

The pottok on the big screen

In order to see what a pottok once looked like, go and see the film *Ramuntcho*, made in 1936 by René Barbéris. Alongside Louis Jouvet, the lead

rigorously matched the detailed standard of the original pottok, irrefutable proof of its good health at the time.

A controversial future

There is some controversy over the future of the pottok. In the Basque country the school of thought which rejects the unplanned crosses is opposed by another which claims that the breed has been improved by multiple crossings. These breeders were supported in the past by the smugglers who used the pottok to cross the Spanish border illegally. They needed an animal that was as dark as possible, so that they would not be seen at night in the forest. This meets the requirements of the purists, since black was the original colour of the pottok…

The pottok fair

Whether thoroughbreds or cross breeds, the pottoks have their own fair. It is held at Espelette twice a year, in November and January (on the last Tuesday and first Wednesday of the month).

Now protected

All that remain today are 150 mares of the original breed in the French Basque country. These are descendants of horses of the Magdalenian period (14,000 to 7,000 years BC). In 1994, Michel Laforêt, a pottok enthusiast, opened a protected reserve for them in Bidarray. He nurtures the breed on a 81½ acre (33 ha) estate in the mountains, which has links with several breeders in the region. The stud farm is open to the public (in summer only). The aim is to restore the purity of the breed and return it to its original environment (p. 262).

actor, you can see 47 of these small horses on the Rhune mountains west of the Basque country. Of these horses, 42

Shepherds
mountain-dwellers

More than ever before, shepherding is a thriving occupation in the Pyrenees. About a hundred people settle in the mountains every year, and 20% of them are under 35 years of age. Although living conditions have improved, the shepherds scrupulously respect the ancestral traditions, handed down over a period of 5,000 years.

Transhumance
Every year, around the middle of May, the shepherd heads for the mountains with his herd of black-headed Manex ewes, which is a sturdy breed. This is called the *Transhumance*. The shepherd will have been watching the sky for a month to check that the snow is retreating from the pastures, and must decide the precise day on which to undertake the annual journey. The Sunday before Palm Sunday is the ritual day of the 'shepherds' count'. The shepherds gather to establish shared rules for the coming season.

Sheep-bells
Around 10 May, the animals realise that they will soon be leaving, because bells are fixed around their necks, each with its own pitch. The bells play a very special role. They provide general and specific information about how the flock are doing. The shepherd's experienced ear enables him to discern the absence of even one of his ewes in this familiar daily concert. Individually, the bells also indicate the age and sex of the ewes.

Departure
At about 4am on the day of the *Transhumance*, when the night is at its coldest, the flocks start on their way, waking the villages through which they pass with the sound of their bells. The strongest ewes lead the flock (of about a thousand sheep) and the shepherd, his donkey and his dog follow at the rear.

CHEESE-MAKING

1. Curdling the milk

2. Cutting the curd

3. Mashing and heating

4. Moulding and pressing

5. Salting

6. Ageing

and break up the curd. When the milk dries up, in mid-July, the shepherd spends all his time working with the cheese, which must be turned at least once a day while it is ageing, and the flock is often left unattended.

SLEEPING IN SPAIN

In the Cize valley, near Saint-Jean-Pied-de-Port, the pastures have no frontiers. Ewes can wander into Spain whenever they wish. Ever since the Treaty of the Pyrenees was signed in 1837, French shepherds are entitled to let their animals graze on the Spanish side of the mountain, on condition that they return to France at nightfall. Very recently, they were even granted permission to spend the night there, thanks to a new agreement between the département of Pyrénées-Atlantiques and Navarre, in Spain.

The journey will last for one day at the most, although it is more and more frequently being made by truck. Upon arrival, the quality of the grazing is ample reward for the exhausting journey.

The *olha*

The *olha* is a traditional shepherd's hut. It's small in size (about 20 ft by 20 ft (6 m by 6 m), and consists of a main room, the *atzia*, with a hearth for cooking and cheese-making, a few mattresses and stools, a cauldron and a few utensils. The other room (*gasnategia*) is used for storing and ageing the cheeses. The huts are shared, so that several shepherds can take their turn in watching the flocks.

Modern times

The living conditions of shepherds are changing. Their huts are now being built of modern materials and equipped with all mod cons: shower, toilet, electricity, etc. Fewer and

fewer of them lead the austere existence of their elders, some of them no longer take their sheep into the mountains or make their own cheeses, but are content to sell their milk to the cheese factory in the valley and go home every night.

Cheese-making

Cheese-making in the summer pastures is still practised by half the shepherds in their mountain huts. The process is long and involved and they spend several hours a day working on it. They milk the ewes morning and evening (each time for two or three hours), filter the milk, heat it

Wood pigeon hunting
a long tradition

Every year, the men of the South West spend a month or so waiting for the ring-doves or wood pigeons. From the end of September onwards, when the great migration southward begins, they get ready to intercept the birds. Pigeon hunting is an obsession, known locally as 'the blue disease', as the hunters constantly scan the blue sky in which the birds appear, until the last days of October.

The wood pigeon route

The birds never change their route. Every year they travel through the same places. About 4.5 million of them converge on Spain and North Africa and take the lowest route through the Pyrenees, at the western end of the range. The hunters position themselves in the valleys which lie just before the lowest mountain passes and shoot about one third of the migrating birds.

Approach or ambush

The most 'sporting' technique, which has no fixed position, is practised in the most inaccessible and wild places. Hunters have to march for a whole day through ravines in the hope of getting close enough to shoot the few birds which have stopped to drink or to eat beech mast. This is the technique used by most local landowners.

Hunting from hides or pigeon huts (*palombières*)

This technique is most frequently used in northern Aquitaine. The hunters take up their position in huts or hides (*palombières*) which are either at ground level or in the tree-tops. Since shooting a bird in flight is prohibited, this position makes it possible to attract distant birds in flight and take a better shot at those which have landed. These huts contain trained pigeons called *appeaux*

which are used as decoys to attract the birds to make them settle within range.

Netting the birds

This traditional form of hunting does not use firearms and is practised in a group, in the mountain passes of the Pyrenees. A beater is stationed in a treetop and throws down

feathered decoys as the birds approach. The wood pigeons think they are being attacked by a hawk so they make for the ground and continue on

their way by hedge-hopping. At that moment, the *xatarrak* (men in the heights) wave pieces of white cloth to direct the flight towards the *pantières* (nets) which the netters then throw over the wood pigeons.

The origins of bird-netting

One day a shepherd at Roncevaux, near the Ibaneta pass, saw a flight of wood pigeons overhead. He picked up a flat stone and threw it at the migrating birds. The wood pigeons thought the stone was a hawk and stayed close to the ground as they flew over the pass. The shepherd was surprised and did the same thing with the next flight, obtaining the same result. A monk from the nearby abbey, observing the scene, had the idea of installing vertical nets at the place where the flights passed and thus invented hunting with a net.

Hunting in flight

Wooden hides among the ferns are used in this form of hunting. These are built at regular intervals on the peaks and passes. The positions in the passes are auctioned every three years to hunters who are allowed to shoot at birds in flight as soon as they have crossed the summits. During

the main migrations (19th to 20th October), the pass echoes to the sound of gunfire.

SALMIS OF WOOD PIGEON
Allow one wood pigeon per person. Roast the birds until they are just tender. Cut them up, separating legs, wings and breasts, keeping them warm in a covered pan. Meanwhile, sauté some onions and shallots in butter until brown. Add some red wine, a little Armagnac, the carcasses of the birds and a bouquet garni. Season with salt and pepper and allow to simmer for about 90 minutes. Pound the carcasses, press the sauce through a sieve and pour over the birds. Cover the pan and cook gently for a few more minurtes. Serve on croûtons fried in butter.

Bears and vultures
lords of the Pyrenees

Honey and hibernation are the two favourite pursuits of the brown bears of the Pyrenees. They indulge in them in the beech forests and on the rocky slopes of the mountains at altitudes of 5,000 ft (1500 m). Solitary creatures, bears rarely venture out during the day and so are seldom seen. The other lords of the mountains are the fawn vultures, which glide effortlessly over the snowy peaks.

The brown bear

The brown bear is found in the valleys of Aspe and Ossau. Only six bears are known to live on the French side of the border and just two on the Spanish side. Bears are omnivorous. Plants represent three quarters of their diet, but they also enjoy insects, rodents and even sheep.

Solitary animals, they are good climbers and are mainly nocturnal. The female only produces cubs every second year.

Vital statistics

The female bear weighs between 143 and 484 lb (65 to 220 kg) and the male between 176 and 660 lb (80 and 300 kg). Around 40 in (1 m) on all fours, they generally live until the age of 20. Their hearing and sense of smell are very sharp, detecting the slightest sounds in the forest and scents from more than 6 miles (10 km) away! On the other hand, they have poor eyesight. Bears are excessively cautious and move very silently.

A protected species

At the beginning of the 20th C., there were more than 200 bears in France. By 1950, 70 were left, but there are less than 10 living today in the

Pyrenees. Their disappearance is due to poisoning and poaching. Legal protection came into force in 1981, but was too late. However, people's attitudes have now changed and every effort is being made to conserve the bear today.

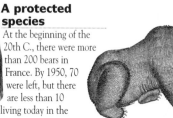

Can the bear be saved?

A team of scientists, local politicians and hunters have been working to reintroduce the brown bear. Three bears were imported from Slovenia and released in the Haute-Garonne in 1996 and 1997, which will hopefully breed over the next three or four years. The objective is to bring the brown bear back to the mountains of Béarn and succeed in revitalising the region by attracting 'ecological tourism'.

The fawn vulture

The fawn vulture lives in the Pays Basque and Béarn. It was once a common sight, but today fewer than 200 breeding pairs remain, in a few colonies. It flies in the daytime at an altitude of between 5,000 and 6,600 ft (1,500 and 2,000 m), and has a wingspan of 8 ft 4 in to 9 ft (2.50 m to 2.80 m). The vulture feeds exclusively on carrion and is recognisable by its small bare head on a long

neck with a ruff at the base and a thick grey, hooked beak. It lives in hollows in the cliffs.

The gravedigger

The fawn vulture does not venture far from flocks of sheep, as it preys on those that fall ill. Thanks to its extraordinarily sharp eyesight, it can spot corpses up to 13 miles (20 km) away and it indulges in feeding frenzies with its fellow birds. A vulture can eat a third of its own weight (4½ lb/2 kg) at a time and with its fellows can devour the carcass of a ewe in less than an hour!

A ghoulish bird

The image of the fawn vulture is associated with death. It is seen circling in the air above corpses. But without it, carrion would pollute the mountain streams and spread contagious diseases. Its hooked beak enables it to pick a carcass clean in a very short time. It was threatened with extinction in the 1960s, but the population is currently on the increase, encouraged by hunters and shepherds.

BEAR FESTIVALS
For several villages in the Pyrenees, February is the month for festivals involving the bear. In these man is seen to conquer the bear, who is often portrayed threatening the virginity of young girls! These festivals are an adaptation of an old pagan ritual, when, after a mock battle, a bear (a man dressed

in a bearskin) is brought to the centre of the village and 'killed' by the chief hunter who appropriates its strength and wins the gratitude of the ladies.

Watery pursuits

A refreshing dip is always possible thanks to the many lakes, rivers and beaches of South West France: swimming, sea-water therapy or kayaking – it's up to you!

The sea and the coast

1. Arcachon:
   walks round the Basin
   p. 213.
2. Contis:
   the Contis current
   p. 221.
3. Lacanau:
   water sports
   p. 208.
4. Pointe de Grave:
   Cordouan lighthouse
   p. 208.
5. Saint-Jean-de-Luz:
   sea trips
   p. 254.
6. Soustons-Port-d'Albret:
   water sports centre
   p. 220.

Blaye 21

Libourne

Bordeaux

Bassin d'Arcachon

Arcachon 1

A660

Langon

11

34

33

Mont-de-Marsan

Dax

Adour

19

6

31

32

Biarritz
Bayonne

A64

17

Saint-Jean-de-Luz 5

24

12

Pau

N117

St-Sébastien

Oloron-Sainte-Marie 14

29

SPAIN

Pic d'Anie
8,216 ft
(2,504 m)

Pic du Midi d'Ossau
9,462 ft
(2,884 m)

Tunnel du Somport

Pampelune

Garonne

A10

N10

A63

A63

4

30

3

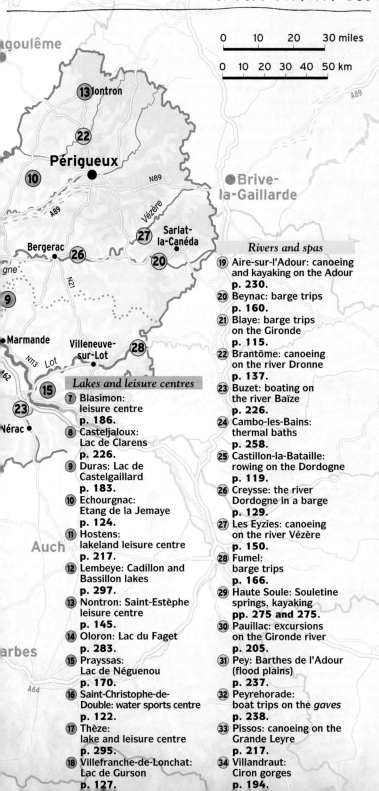

goulême

⑬ Nontron

㉒

Périgueux

⑩

N89

●Brive-la-Gaillarde

Vézère

A89

㉗ Sarlat-la-Canéda

Bergerac ㉖

⑳

gne

N21

⑨

●Marmande

N113 *Lot*

62

Villeneuve-sur-Lot ㉘

⑮

㉓

Nérac ●

Auch

arbes

A64

0   10   20   30 miles

0 10 20 30 40 50 km

A89

Lakes and leisure centres

⑦ Blasimon:
leisure centre
p. 186.

⑧ Casteljaloux:
Lac de Clarens
p. 226.

⑨ Duras: Lac de
Castelgaillard
p. 183.

⑩ Echourgnac:
Etang de la Jemaye
p. 124.

⑪ Hostens:
lakeland leisure centre
p. 217.

⑫ Lembeye: Cadillon and
Bassillon lakes
p. 297.

⑬ Nontron: Saint-Estèphe
leisure centre
p. 145.

⑭ Oloron: Lac du Faget
p. 283.

⑮ Prayssas:
Lac de Néguenou
p. 170.

⑯ Saint-Christophe-de-
Double: water sports centre
p. 122.

⑰ Thèze:
lake and leisure centre
p. 295.

⑱ Villefranche-de-Lonchat:
Lac de Gurson
p. 127.

Rivers and spas

⑲ Aire-sur-l'Adour: canoeing
and kayaking on the Adour
p. 230.

⑳ Beynac: barge trips
p. 160.

㉑ Blaye: barge trips
on the Gironde
p. 115.

㉒ Brantôme: canoeing
on the river Dronne
p. 137.

㉓ Buzet: boating on
the river Baïze
p. 226.

㉔ Cambo-les-Bains:
thermal baths
p. 258.

㉕ Castillon-la-Bataille:
rowing on the Dordogne
p. 119.

㉖ Creysse: the river
Dordogne in a barge
p. 129.

㉗ Les Eyzies: canoeing
on the river Vézère
p. 150.

㉘ Fumel:
barge trips
p. 166.

㉙ Haute Soule: Souletine
springs, kayaking
pp. 275 and 275.

㉚ Pauillac: excursions
on the Gironde river
p. 205.

㉛ Pey: Barthes de l'Adour
(flood plains)
p. 237.

㉜ Peyrehorade:
boat trips on the *gaves*
p. 238.

㉝ Pissos: canoeing on the
Grande Leyre
p. 217.

㉞ Villandraut:
Ciron gorges
p. 194.

Spas and seawater treatments

the benefits of water

Although the Romans were familiar with the benefits of water (as can be seen from the remains of Roman baths) spa treatments only became popular in France in the 19th C. Today, French doctors still prescribe water cures for their patients. There are many hot springs in the region, offering a wide range of therapeutic applications to treat rheumatics, skin diseases, gynaecological problems, respiratory diseases, growth problems, stress, tobacco addiction, etc. Seawater treatment, a newer therapy, uses the benefits of seabathing and the seaside climate to improve health and morale.

The aptly-named Eaux-Bonnes and Eaux-Chaudes,

Their waters, full of chlorine, sulphur and sodium, are used for treating respiratory infections (p. 305). Eaux-Bonnes is at the entrance to the Sourde Gorges and 5 miles (8 km) from the ski resort of Gourette. Eaux-Chaudes treats respiratory afflictions and rheumatism. It is situated beside a lake, the *lac national*, above the right bank of the Gave d'Ossau.

Dax

The sulphurous and chlorinated waters of Dax are recommended for the treatment of rheumatism. The resort has devised a specific treatment, called *péloïde*, a hot mud made from the alluvial soil of Adour, aged for 6 months with very hot spring water. Its pain-relieving effect can last for a year. Dax is also recommended for sufferers of varicose veins (p. 236).

Cambo-les-Bains: a little oxygen

The waters here are rich in calcium, magnesium and iron. They successfully tackle inflammation of the joints. Treatments include specifically directed showers, followed by applications of mud and turpentine, all of which help to relieve pain in the joints. Cambo-les-Bains is also famous for its benefits to the respiratory system (p. 258).

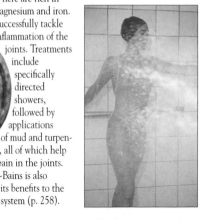

SHORT-STAY PACKAGES

Seawater treatment (*thalassothérapie*) is popular on the Basque coast and modern facilities can be found at Hendaye, Saint-Jean-de-Luz (p. 255) and Biarritz (p. 248). Even if you don't want to take a course of treatments lasting several days, most of the establishments offer a full-day or half-day session. The only formality is that you must take a medical examination before indulging in the wonderfully relaxing treatment.

Salies-de-Béarn

The waters are sulphurous and have a higher salt content than seawater (seven times more salty). They have the effect of healing wounds and alleviating pain. The resort is recommended for gynaecological and rheumatological disorders (p. 276).

Water, water everywhere!

As part of the cure you have to drink plenty of water, so you'll have to say goodbye to alcoholic beverages for a time. Fans of the power shower will

be particularly envigorated by some of the treatments involving needle-sharp jets of water. There are also shower massages available which are said to tone and relax the body. Other treatments simply involve extremely hot baths and swimming several lengths of the pool!

Seawater treatments: emphasis on general health

Accompanied by sea air, these are part of the philosophy of well-being. Rest, massage and showers take up most of the day for those taking the cure. The client is there to forget stress and worry, to be pampered and to rest. The choice of centre depends only on budgetary constraints and taste.

A vast choice

There are seawater treatments designed for the mother-to-be

as well as the young mother. Before the birth, there is a programme to help her prepare for the happy event, and, after the birth, she can take a cure with the baby (dieting, exercise, aquarobics, workouts) to help get her back in shape. Stressed-out people can choose the anti-stress programme with massage and shiatsu, and for those with chronic back pain there is a special course involving bathing, massages, specific treatments and suitable exercises to help take the pain away .

Rivers of the Dordogne

The Dronne, the Isle and the Dordogne itself cross Périgord from east to west. They all rise in the Massif Central before flowing through Aquitaine to the sea, whilst the Vézère prefers to merge with the Dordogne at Limeuil. The Dropt, in the far south, is a capricious little river, which joins the Lot-et-Garonne after bathing the *bastides* of Aquitaine in water. To the north, the Bandiat swings lazily round Nontron before flowing into the Charentes.

The water-mills

The waters of the rivers of Périgord have largely been harnessed by man. The Bigaroque mill on the Dordogne was recorded in the 12th C., while at Brantôme on the Dronne there is the magnificent, boat-shaped mill of the Lord of Bourdeilles. The proliferation of these mills on the Dordogne, the Dronne, the Isle, the Vézère and their tributaries prove how much commercial activity took place on the rivers and how busy they were.

River boats

Ever since the Middle Ages, river boats permitted and promoted trade in the valleys and enriched the local merchants. As a result, many occupations flourished by the river, including boatbuilders, coopers, ropemakers, paper-makers and blacksmiths. In those days, local produce was sent from Bergerac to Bordeaux and from there the merchandise continued on its way to England, Portugal or Holland.

Gabares, ancestors of the *péniche*

The *gabare* was a sailing barge (*see illustration on right*) with a flat bottom and a very small draught to enable it to pass through shallow waters. The largest of these barges measured up to 83 ft (25 m). When travelling upriver, they were towed by oxen or horses but genuine horse power eventually gave way to the mororised kind when the

outboard motor took over in 1920. They were eventually replaced by *péniches*.

No pleasure cruise

Trips downriver were often very dangerous. There were difficult stretches to negotiate, eddies, whirlpools and the famous *mascaret*, a tidal wave. The boatmen greeted with relief the opening of the side-canal at Lalinde, a 9-mile (15 km) stretch of water. The canal is divided into three sections by two locks. However, it was only used for 30 years or so after it was opened in 1841, because of increasing competition from the railways. .

When rivers teemed with fish

The days are long gone when a local decree forbade masters giving their servants salmon to eat more than three times a week! It was a happy time when the Dordogne river was brimming with fish. Since the 19th C., the dams that have been built almost everywhere have stopped the fish migrating. Fish-ladders had to be created (at Bergerac, and Mauzas) to enable the shad and other fish to swim upriver, but unfortunately these measures were insufficient to repopulate the Dordogne (at Tuilières, the fish are taken up in a lift in order to cross the 40 ft (12m) high dam).

Active rivers for anglers

There are still 65 fishermen (or rather, that's all that is left) who spread their nets and wet their hoop-nets (in the Dordogne). Although the rivers of Périgord no longer feed the population, they are nevertheless far from being deserted. **Amateur anglers** get plenty of pleasure from the river. About 30,000 of them fish for pike, perch-pike, tench, eels and even lamprey (*see below*).

When rivers teem with canoes

There are hundreds, even thousands, who invade the waters of the Dordogne, the Dronne, the Vézère, the Isle and their tributaries. Local commerce soon realised that much could be made of the river and its environs. People wanting to canoe or kayak are now able to hire a boat at all the major sites, making the sport available to all. The rivers of the Dordogne, once bustling with industry, are today busy with **pleasure boats**.

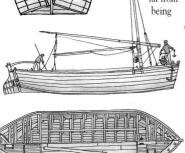

The lamprey (above) and the eel

Surfing
gliding over the waves

On the Silver Coast, as soon as a promising wave appears on the horizon, the surfers are ready for it. The sport came to France from the United States, and has become extremely popular in Aquitaine. From the small or medium-sized waves of Les Landes to the huge breakers of the Basque country, it is practised all year round, whether the seabed is sandy or rocky.

Recognition

In 1980, surfing received official recognition in France with the organisation of the first **European amateur championships,** held at Biarritz and Hossegor. A very inspired young surfer, Tom Curren, emerged as the star and has since won the professional championship three times. The commercial enterprise quickly followed, when surfboard manufacturers opened workshops at Saint-Jean-de-Luz and Biarritz.

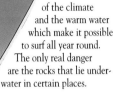

A stormy ocean

The powerful temperament of the Atlantic Ocean gives the Basque coast the best waves in Europe. There is a swell from the north-west which creates huge rollers that crash onto the shore, some as high as 13 ft (4 m). Other attractions for the surfer are the mildness of the climate and the warm water which make it possible to surf all year round. The only real danger are the rocks that lie underwater in certain places.

Catching the wave

Surfers get to know the best beaches and the kinds of waves they are likely to encounter. Beach-breakers form where the bottom is sandy and reef-breakers form over underwater rocks. All surfers aspire to a long run in to shore, so a good wave is a long one, extending for some 300 to 400 yards (200 to 300m). Waves that form further out to sea are usually for the experienced only. If you don't surf yourself, just stay and watch – a long run on a large wave is absolutely spectacular.

How to get in touch with the wave

The surfer attaches the surfboard to his ankle with a long, flexible line and swims out into open water, lying on the board and using his hands as paddles. He then waits for the right moment. Having chosen his wave, he turns towards the shore, keeping ahead of the wave,

and stands up on the surfboard, keeping as close as possible to the hollow of the wave. Having caught his wave he tries to ride it in to the shore.

The surfing movements

Here's how to recognise (and perform?) the four basic surfing movements: the *roller-coaster*, a turn on the top of the wave, the *bottom-turn*, at the foot of the wave, *riding the crest* and finally, the *tube* where the surfer dives through a hollow roller. With practice, the surfer learns to move from one to the other and keep abreast of the wave for as long as possible, as well as surfing in the hollow (*the curl*), before it breaks.

Variations

Beginners generally practice on a *body-board* (or *morey*), adapted for those who are only able to surf for a few days a year. The board, nicknamed a 'rusk' (*biscotte*), is short and the surfer wears flippers. Champions, on the other hand, use a specially long board, which is less manoeuvrable and more stable. The *skimboard* is an oval board which makes it possible to surf between two waves.

THE CHAMPIONSHIPS

In France, the heats for the professional world surfing championships are held in Biarritz, Hossegor and Lacanau. They take place between 15 July and 15 October. It is worth watching the ever more spectacular performances of the great champions. Don't forget your binoculars and if you plan on taking photographs you will need a telephoto lens of at least 300 mm.

The dunes
still moving

One grain of sand, then another, then another… make a dune. A dune subjected to a gust of wind, then another gust… starts to move. But when grass, a rush and then a shrub start to grow on it, it slows down and even stops. It could almost be said that a battle between man and nature takes place on the beach, with man employing a very elaborate botanical strategy, to counterbalance the dune.

The speed of the dune

A dune is capable of moving completely in the space of a few weeks, or of growing very large

water holds the grains of sand together. So if its growth is to be stopped, one can take advantage of wet weather

Wind →

Ocean

Movement of a dune

in the space of a few years. A famous example is the dune at Pilat, south of Arcachon. It first formed in the 18th C., and by 1855 it was 116 ft (35 m) high. It has been growing unimpeded and is now nearly 600 ft (180 m) high! It was planted with trees and sold by the state to its present owners, who are trying to control it, but it is still advancing by 13 ft (4 m) a year!

The strategy

A dune can be stabilised when it is wet. The phenomenon is familiar to anyone who has ever built a sand-castle. A mass of wet sand is stable because the

when it is compact and stable, and cover it with plants that grow very rapidly before it gets the chance to move again.

The attackers

The best attackers are grasses, because they reproduce very rapidly. They can colonise large dunes in the space of a few months. An additional advantage is that they resist being temporarily buried by sand due to gusts of wind. The most frequently used species are marram-grass, which is very popular, and a type of oat called *Elymus*.

Tuft of marram-grass

The second wave

Once the 'skin' of the dune has been more or less fixed, other greenery can be planted. These plants grow on the decomposing leaves of the grasses and develop

THE LOVELY SEA-LILY

It's not easy being a lovely plant whose job it is to stabilise the sand dunes by the sea. The sea-lily knows all about it. This lively plant with a very efficient bulb never goes unnoticed. It has lovely trumpet-shaped white

flowers, about 4 in (10 cm) long, which are so attractive that they are inevitably picked or savagely uprooted (which means the sand dunes can run wild again). What's needed is a plant to stabilise the sand-dunes that's not so attractive!

subterranean roots which block the dune's movement deep down. These plants must be resistant to the intense heat on the surface of the dune, where it can get hot enough to fry an egg. The most effective are the carnation, the wild rose, the rush and the arbutus.

Insects of the dunes

As the flora invades a seashore dune, the insects follow. Wasps and flies have amazing abilities as miners. They manage to dig deep tunnels and passages in the moving sand, in which to conceal their eggs or larvae. The warmth and stability of the temperature beneath the surface makes the dune a perfect insect incubator.

Animals

The rabbits come out on the dunes at night. It's understandable that animals who live in the sand spend most of the day underground, waiting for the temperature to drop before emerging. The rabbit, a famous burrower, is not the only animal to do this. Ducks who live by the sea also like to nest in sandy hollows. These include the Belon sheldrakes, locally known as *oies-renards* (fox-geese), nest in hollows in the sand.

Reparatory surgery

There are esthetic ideals that are applied to sand dunes. They should have a stable form, have the longer side facing the sea, with an aerodynamic profile at the rear. A dune that is deformed (by the swell or by human intervention) is difficult to control, so it needs a helping hand to reform. Wind-breakers are arranged at right-angles to the wind which is then forced to drop the sand wherever there is an absence of wind. In extreme cases, earth-moving equipment may have to be used to reshape the dune and to prevent it from toppling.

The Pilat Dune

Zoos, aquariums and leisure parks

Would you be brave enough to face the vultures and brown bears of the Pyrenees? If you would prefer a peaceful meeting with these animals, there are many zoos, aquariums and bird sanctuaries for you and your family to visit. Don't forget the leisure parks as well!

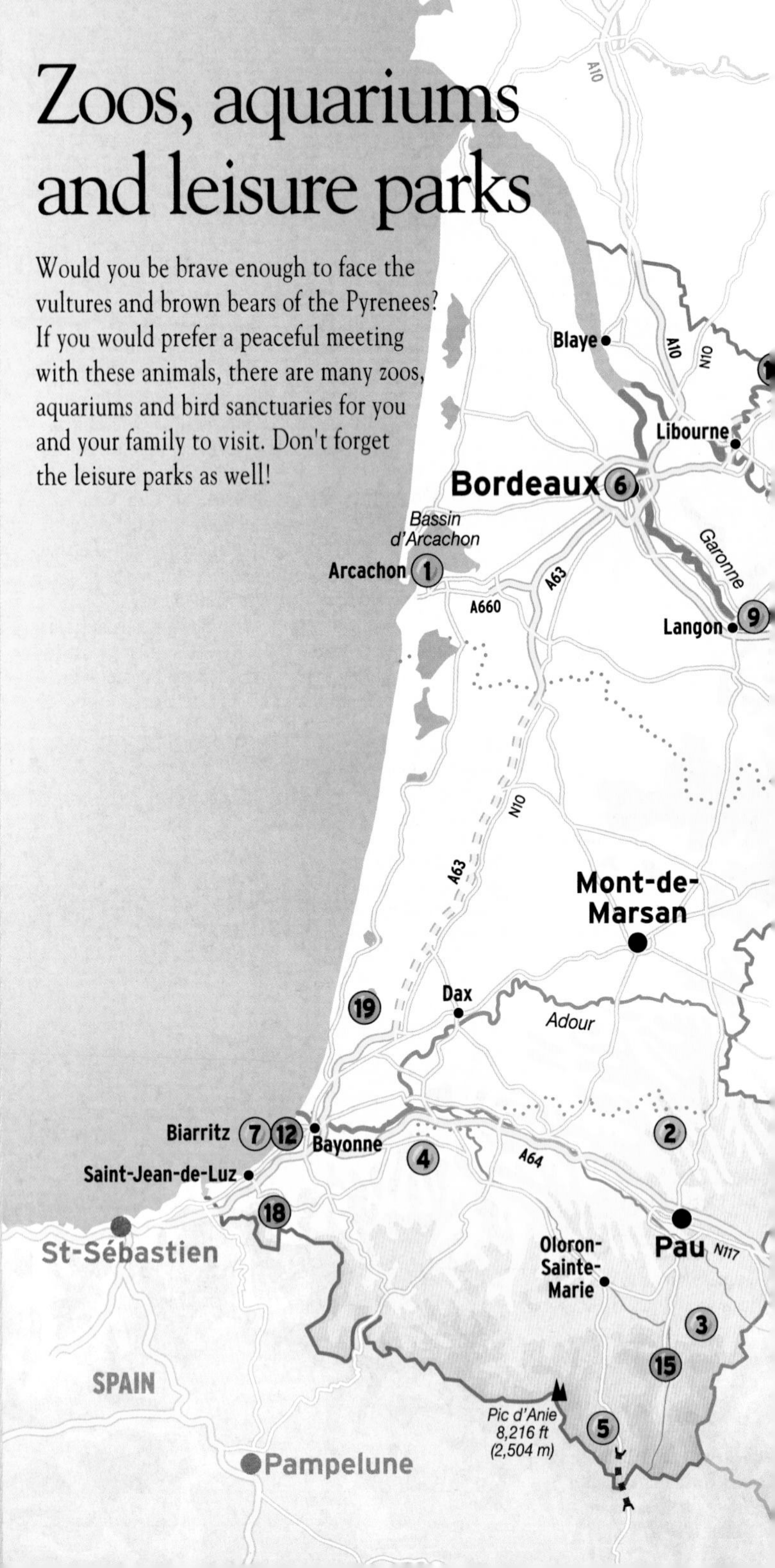

Blaye

Libourne

Bordeaux ⑥

Bassin d'Arcachon

Arcachon ①

A660

A63

Garonne

Langon ⑨

A10

N10

N10

A63

N10

Mont-de-Marsan

Dax

Adour

⑲

Biarritz ⑦⑫ **Bayonne**

Saint-Jean-de-Luz

④

A64

②

⑱

St-Sébastien

Oloron-Sainte-Marie

Pau N117

③

⑮

SPAIN

Pic d'Anie 8,216 ft (2,504 m)

⑤

Pampelune

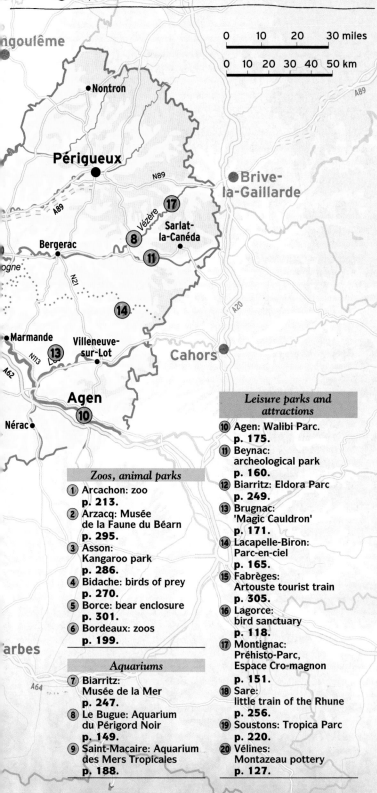

ngoulême

●Nontron

Périgueux

N89

●Brive-
la-Gaillarde

A89

Vézère

⑰

**Sarlat-
la-Canéda**

Bergerac

⑧

A89

ogne

⑪

N21

⑭

A20

●Marmande

N113

⑬

**Villeneuve-
sur-Lot**

Cahors

A62

Nérac●

Agen

⑩

arbes

A64

Zoos, animal parks

① Arcachon: zoo
p. 213.
② Arzacq: Musée
de la Faune du Béarn
p. 295.
③ Asson:
Kangaroo park
p. 286.
④ Bidache: birds of prey
p. 270.
⑤ Borce: bear enclosure
p. 301.
⑥ Bordeaux: zoos
p. 199.

Aquariums

⑦ Biarritz:
Musée de la Mer
p. 247.
⑧ Le Bugue: Aquarium
du Périgord Noir
p. 149.
⑨ Saint-Macaire: Aquarium
des Mers Tropicales
p. 188.

*Leisure parks and
attractions*

⑩ Agen: Walibi Parc.
p. 175.
⑪ Beynac:
archeological park
p. 160.
⑫ Biarritz: Eldora Parc
p. 249.
⑬ Brugnac:
'Magic Cauldron'
p. 171.
⑭ Lacapelle-Biron:
Parc-en-ciel
p. 165.
⑮ Fabrèges:
Artouste tourist train
p. 305.
⑯ Lagorce:
bird sanctuary
p. 118.
⑰ Montignac:
Préhisto-Parc,
Espace Cro-magnon
p. 151.
⑱ Sare:
little train of the Rhune
p. 256.
⑲ Soustons: Tropica Parc
p. 220.
⑳ Vélines:
Montazeau pottery
p. 127.

Sporting activities

South West France is a paradise for sporty holidaymakers! Surfing, skiing, rafting, hang-gliding; there's something for every taste (addresses and advice, pp. 104–107). For walks and hikes, see the map on pp. 80–81 and for water sports see the map on pp. 90–91.

Golf courses (18 holes)

(1) **Barbaste**
   p. 107.
(2) **Billère**
   pp. 7 and 107.
(3) **Biscarosse**
   p. 107.
(4) **Casteljaloux**
   pp. 107 and 226.
(5) **Hossegor**
   p. 241.
(6) **Ilbarritz: golf driving range**
   pp. 107 and 250.
(7) **Mont-de-Marsan**
   pp. 107 and 223.
(8) **Le Pian-Médoc**
   pp. 107 and 207.
(9) **Saint-Pardon-de-Conques**
   p. 107.

Lesparre-Médoc

Blaye ●

A10

N10

Libourne ●

Bordeaux ●

Bassin d'Arcachon

Arcachon ●

Garonne

A63

A660

Langon ●

Mont-de-Marsan

Dax ●

Adour

Biarritz ●
Bayonne ●
Saint-Jean-de-Luz ●

A64

Pau ●

N117

Oloron-Sainte-Marie

St-Sébastien ●

SPAIN

● Pampelune

| 0 | 10 | 20 | 30 miles |

| 0 | 10 | 20 | 30 | 40 | 50 km |

Water sports

⑲ Anglet: sea fishing
p. 107.
⑳ Sanguinet:
water sports
p. 214.
㉑ Castillon-la-Bataille:
rowing
p. 119.
㉒ Dordogne: angling
p. 161.
㉓ Vézère and Dordogne:
canoeing and fishing
pp. 150 and 161.
㉔ Hossegor:
water sports
p. 241.
㉕ Hourtin-Carcans:
water sports
p. 105.
㉖ Lacanau: surfing
p. 208.
㉗ Léon: water sports
pp. 105 and 220.
㉘ Navarrenx:
salmon fishing, rafting
p. 281.
㉙ Oloron: water sports.
p. 283.
㉚ Orthez : water-skiing
p. 279.
㉛ Parentis: water sports
pp. 105 and 214.
㉜ Soustons: bodyboarding,
surfing, skimboarding
p. 220.
㉝ La Teste-de-Buch: sailing
p. 105.
㉞ Vallée d'Ossau: rafting
p. 304.

Rambling, horse-riding, mountain-biking

⑩ Arbus: pony trekking
in Jurançon
p. 293.
⑪ Casteljaloux: biking
p. 226.
⑫ Hostens: biking
p. 217.
⑬ Saint-Christophe-de-
Double: biking
p. 122.
⑭ Sauternais: horse-riding
p. 193.
⑮ Soulac: biking
p. 209.
⑯ Vallée d'Aspe:
rambling, biking
p. 300.
⑰ Vallée du Barétous: biking
p. 107.
⑱ Vallée d'Ossau: biking
p. 304.

Mountain sports

㉟ Artouste-Fabrèges: skiing
p. 106.
㊱ Forêt d'Iraty: cross-country
pp. 106 and 266.
㊲ Gourette: skiing
p. 105.
㊳ La Pierre-Saint-Martin:
skiing, potholing
p. 285.
㊴ Vallée d'Aspe: hang-
gliding, deltaplaning
p. 301.
㊵ Vallée d'Ossau: skiing
pp. 105 and 305.

Sports in Aquitaine

Long stretches of open country, beaches as far as the eye can see, mountains in which to climb, hike or bike, Pyrenean streams – the South West is a sporting paradise.

Surfing and body-boarding

You think you'll be happy just swimming, but after watching surfers teasing the waves you'll want to try it for yourself. There are plenty of surfing schools to teach the basics. There are two essential names to remember: the label E.F.S., or École Française de Surf, awarded by the F.F.S. (Fédération Française de Surf), guarantees that the training and advice given are under the auspices of the F.F.S. The Federation is based at Hossegor ☎ 05 58 43 55 88. If surfing looks too risky, try a body-board (p. 97). You won't have to try and stand up on the board, but you do need to know how to swim and to like the waves. Don't forget the ocean can be dangerous for bathers and surfers. Always use a beach with a lifeguard, especially if you are a beginner.

Sea-side sport

From the Pointe de Grave to the Basque coast, Aquitaine has some of the loveliest sandy beaches in the whole of Europe, stretching for an almost uninterrupted 144 miles (230 km) between the Gironde estuary and the mouth of the Adour. The Côte d'Argent (Silver coast) is a paradise for swimmers and water sports enthusiasts and its string of seaside resorts offer swimming in the summer, an exceptionally mild climate in winter, and the breakers loved by surfers throughout the year.

Nature on horseback

Riders, close your eyes ... no tarmac, no cars, not even a pedestrian! A path stretches into the distance, bordered by ferns. Sunlight plays on the pine trees and the wind rustles the branches. You loosen your grip on the reins, a slight pressure with a riding boot and your horse gallops off into the ride of your dreams! But the place actually exists, it's that large green patch on the map, Les Landes forest. You can have other dreams too. Going hiking in the early morning when the sun pierces the mist over the Sauternes vineyard. Or the mountains – imagine yourself on the smugglers' route, with sure-footed, sturdy mounts, riding right up to the gateway of the canyons and sierras of Aragon! The bridle paths are open to all riders, experienced or beginners. To choose your route, there's an organisation which provides guides, instructors, hosts and so on and offers a dozen different pony-trekking packages for Aquitaine (Landes, Gironde, Pyrénées-Atlantiques): courses, excursions and treks: ADEL, 21 Cours de l'Intendance, 33 000 Bordeaux ☎ 05 56 51 05 62.

Golf

Aquitaine is the doyenne of golfing in France. In 1856, a British garrison chose the climate and landscape of Pau in order to build the first golf course on the 'continent'. Since then, some of the great golf course architects have left their mark on Aquitaine. There are no fewer than 50 quality golf courses today (see box on p. 107). For touring golfers, there is a Golf Pass system which makes it possible for a player to use several associated golf courses. For information in Gironde, Comité Départemental du Tourisme, ☎ 05 56 52 61 40; in Biarritz and Landes, Association Golf Côte Basque-Sud Landes ☎ 05 58 48 54 65.

Sailing and windsurfing

This coast is not always hospitable for sailing and there are only three coastal resorts that are called 'sailing centres' (*Station Voile*) a title granted by the Fédération Française de Voile. They are La Teste-de-Buch, Arcachon and Hendaye. However, there are lakes in Landes and Gironde where you go windsurfing or sailing. These are Hourtin-Carcans, Lacanau, Cazaux, Sanguinet, Biscarosse and Parentis, Aureilhan, Léon, Souston and Hossegor. Adults and children alike can sail in perfect safety, thanks to the numerous yachting clubs.

Winter sports

The Pyrenees are the sunniest mountain range in France and the perfect place for winter sports. For instance, Gourette, 5 miles (8 km) from Eaux Bonnes, at the bottom of an imposing *cirque*, has 30 ski runs, of between 4,666 and 8,000 ft (1,400 and 2,400 m) with a superb view of the Vallée d'Ossau.

Nor are cross-country skiers forgotten; at the Aubisque pass there are 12½ miles (20 km) of pistes. Artouste-Fabrèges, at the edge of the Pyrenees National Park, is a nature reserve. In summer you can watch mountain goats, but in winter it's a paradise for cross-country skiers. The resort also has 13 alpine skiing pistes. You can also ski in the Vallée de Barétous, La Pierre-Saint-Martin. This is where long treks on snowshoes are possible, giving your holiday a taste of the Frozen North. At Issarbe, 3¾ miles (6 km) from La Pierre-Saint-Martin, and in the Forêt d'Iraty in the Basque country there are 26 miles (42 km) of cross-country and snowshoe routes. The same is true of Somport, with 15½ miles (25 km) of routes through the heart of the Pyrenees National Park. For everything you need to know about winter sports, contact La Maison des Pyrénées, 6 Rue Vital Carles, 33 000 Bordeaux ☎ 05 56 44 05 65.

Canoeing, kayaking, white-water rafting

Aquitaine is a land of streams, rivers and torrents. That's why lovers of canoeing, kayaking, white-water rafting, as well as those who like to row in more peaceful currents, are so often found here. There's plenty of white water in Périgord, on the Dordogne and the Vézère, or in the Pyrenean mountain streams. The local sports club will know every navigable waterway. Lists are available at all the tourism offices in the département.

Sport fishing: from trout to sharks

Oceans, rivers, mountain streams, torrents and lakes – there's a complete range. From surf-casting on the coast to fly-fishing in the lakes among snow-covered peaks, there are carp, trout, black bass, salmon, gilthead bream, tuna, and even sharks. A paradise for fly-fishermen (p. 273), the wild brown trout is the queen of the Pyrenean mountain waters. Its average weight is a pound (425 g), an exceptional size! The Gave d'Oloron is one of the best salmon rivers in France: the world salmon fishing championships are held at Navarrenx (p. 281). As for sea fishing, you can chase tuna and shark on the high seas with professional fishermen in Arcachon (p. 211). For a calmer

excursion, in search of gilthead bream, John Dory, conger or wolf-fish you can enjoy a day's sea fishing in coastal waters off Arcachon (excursions are organised by Anglet Nautique ☎ 05 59 63 51 91). As for anglers who enjoy surf-casting, normally seen on the beaches with their long rods stuck in the sand, they should concentrate on fishing at night or very early in the morning as these are the best periods for the catch.

By bicycle

Cycle paths, footpaths and other types of designated path are plentiful and cycling or mountain-biking are ideal ways to explore the interior. See the *bastides* of Agenais, châteaux of Périgord, Basque villages, Chalosse, the Landes forest or the coastal paths. There is something for every taste and every level of athleticism. The most ambitious cyclists can take on the mountain and explore the Barétous Valley, 156 miles (250 km) of signposted routes (a topographical guide is available at the Arette Tourist Office ☎ 05 59 88 95 38) in the Ossau Valley (a topo-graphical guide is available at the Valley Tourist Office).

Pelote Basque (pelota)

Every village in the Basque country has a *fronton* or a *trinquet*, if not both, for playing Pelota (p. 74). If you want to learn to play the game, you will need a teacher. Two addresses for lessons are: Luzean in Saint-Jean-de-Luz (p. 253) and Jean-Luc Chrisostome in Bayonne, ☎ 05 59 64 02 81.

OUR SELECTION OF GOLF COURSES

Golf du Médoc, Le Pian-Médoc
☎ 05 56 70 11 90
Golf des Graves et du Sauternais, Saint-Pardon-de-Conques
☎ 05 56 62 25 43
Golf d'Albret, Barbaste
☎ 05 53 65 53 69
Golf de Casteljaloux, Casteljaloux
☎ 05 53 93 51 60
Pau Golf Club, Billère
☎ 05 59 13 18 56
Scottish Golf d'Aubertin, Aubertin
☎ 05 59 82 70 69
Golf de Biscarosse
☎ 05 58 09 84 93
Golf de Mont-de-Marsan
☎ 05 58 75 63 05
Golf de Moliets
☎ 05 58 48 54 65
Ilbarritz – Golf school, Bidart
☎ 05 59 43 81 30
Makila Golf Club, Bassussarry
☎ 05 59 58 42 42

New things to try

Those who want to try new experiences, sports enthusiasts and those who like adventure will find some ideas here for new activities or skills to try, and will soon discover the diverse opportunities on offer in the region.

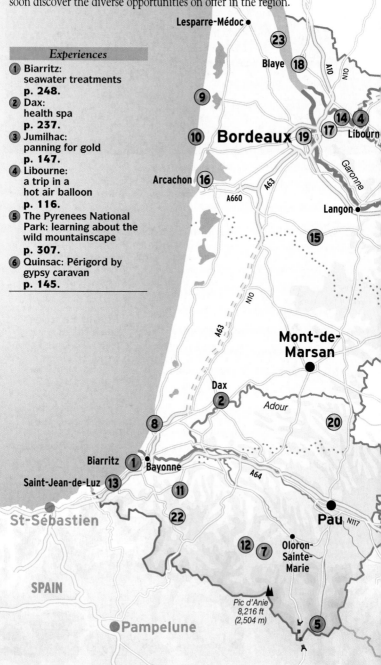

Experiences

(1) **Biarritz:**
seawater treatments
p. 248.

(2) **Dax:**
health spa
p. 237.

(3) **Jumilhac:**
panning for gold
p. 147.

(4) **Libourne:**
a trip in a
hot air balloon
p. 116.

(5) **The Pyrenees National
Park:** learning about the
wild mountainscape
p. 307.

(6) **Quinsac:** Périgord by
gypsy caravan
p. 145.

Lesparre-Médoc ●

(23)

Blaye (18)

(9)

(14) (4)
(10) **Bordeaux** (19) (17) Libourn

Garonne

Arcachon (16)

Langon ●

(15)

**Mont-de-
Marsan**
●

Dax
(2)

Adour

(20)

(8)

Biarritz (1) ● Bayonne

Saint-Jean-de-Luz (13)

(11)

St-Sébastien

(22)

Pau N117

(12) (7) Oloron-
Sainte-
Marie

SPAIN

Pic d'Anie
8,216 ft
(2,504 m)
(5)

● Pampelune

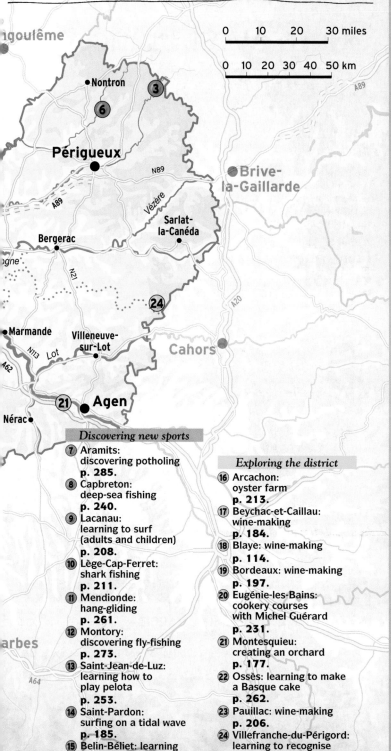

0   10   20   30 miles

0 10 20 30 40 50 km

A89

gouleme

● Nontron

③

⑥

Périgueux ●

N89

●Brive-la-Gaillarde

A89

A89

Vézère

Sarlat-la-Canéda ●

Bergerac ●

ogne

N21

②④

A20

● Marmande

Villeneuve-sur-Lot ●

Cahors ●

N113 Lot

A62

②① **Agen** ●

Nérac ●

Discovering new sports

⑦ Aramits:
discovering potholing
p. 285.

⑧ Capbreton:
deep-sea fishing
p. 240.

⑨ Lacanau:
learning to surf
(adults and children)
p. 208.

⑩ Lège-Cap-Ferret:
shark fishing
p. 211.

⑪ Mendionde:
hang-gliding
p. 261.

⑫ Montory:
discovering fly-fishing
p. 273.

⑬ Saint-Jean-de-Luz:
learning how to
play pelota
p. 253.

⑭ Saint-Pardon:
surfing on a tidal wave
p. 185.

⑮ Belin-Béliet: learning
to walk on stilts
p. 217.

Exploring the district

⑯ Arcachon:
oyster farm
p. 213.

⑰ Beychac-et-Caillau:
wine-making
p. 184.

⑱ Blaye: wine-making
p. 114.

⑲ Bordeaux: wine-making
p. 197.

⑳ Eugénie-les-Bains:
cookery courses
with Michel Guérard
p. 231.

②① Montesquieu:
creating an orchard
p. 177.

②② Ossès: learning to make
a Basque cake
p. 262.

②③ Pauillac: wine-making
p. 206.

②④ Villefranche-du-Périgord:
learning to recognise
mushrooms
p. 163.

arbes

A64

South West France in detail

South West France in detail

On the following pages, you can find details of the most interesting places to visit in South West France. For easy reference, the region has been divided into zones. A colour code will allow you to find the area you are looking for at a glance.

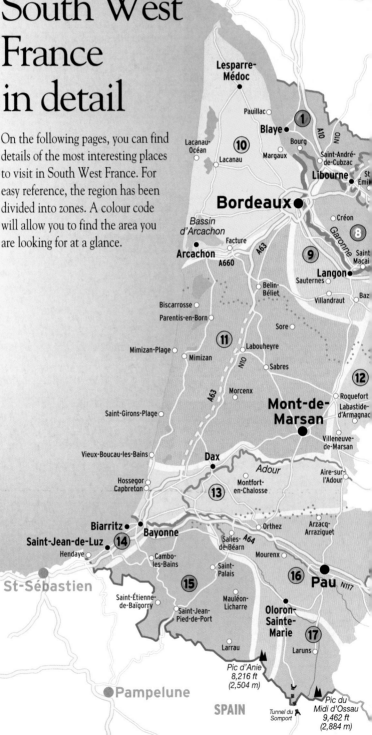

Lesparre-Médoc

Pauillac

Blaye (1)

Bourg

Lacanau-Océan

(10)

Margaux

Saint-André-de-Cubzac

Lacanau

Libourne

St Émi

Bordeaux ●

Créon

Bassin d'Arcachon

Garonne

(8)

Facture

Arcachon

A63

(9)

Saint Maca

A660

Langon ●

Sauternes

Belin-Béliet

Villandraut

Baz

Biscarrosse

Parentis-en-Born

Sore

(11)

Labouheyre

Mimizan-Plage

Mimizan

(12)

Sabres

● Roquefort

A63

Morcenx

Labastide-d'Armagnac

Saint-Girons-Plage

Mont-de-Marsan

Villeneuve-de-Marsan

Vieux-Boucau-les-Bains

Dax

Adour

Aire-sur-l'Adour

Hossegor Capbreton

(13)

Montfort-en-Chalosse

Orthez

Arzacq-Arraziguet

Biarritz ●

Bayonne

Saint-Jean-de-Luz (14)

Salies-de-Béarn

A64

Hendaye

Mourenx

Cambo-les-Bains

Saint-Palais

(16)

Pau ●

St-Sébastien

(15)

N117

Saint-Étienne-de-Baïgorry

Mauléon-Licharre

Saint-Jean-Pied-de-Port

Oloron-Sainte-Marie

(17)

Larrau

Laruns

Pic d'Anie 8,216 ft (2,504 m)

● **Pampelune**

SPAIN

Tunnel du Somport

Pic du Midi d'Ossau 9,462 ft (2,884 m)

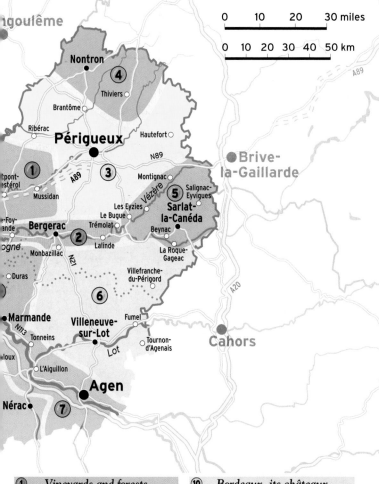

0   10   20   30 miles

0   10   20   30   40   50 km

The Blaye and Bourg districts sentinel towns

The Blaye and Bourg districts, although close to Bordeaux, are not well-known. North of Saintonge and bordered in the east by Pays Gabaye, where the *langue d'oc* meets the *langue d'oil*, they are, however, neither geographially nor historically linked. The magnificent citadel of Blaye dominates the Gironde estuary. It has given its name to a delightful wine, as has Bourg, which sits on the banks of the Dordogne.

Between the two, the roads are dotted with hamlets, villages, vines and châteaux, which offer many prospects for exploration.

perfectly preserved. Enter through the Porte Royale by car, or the Porte Dauphine on foot, to discover a whole town The citadel covers almost half a mile (1 km) with chapel, cloisters and houses with flower gardens. A little **tourist train** takes

Blaye
The citadel
☎ 05 57 42 12 09
Open daily. 24 hours a day.
Free admission.
This masterpiece of 17th-C. military architecture is

you round the citadel. (☎ 05 56 23 02 87 or 06 08 60 80 91. Daily in summer except Thurs. afternoon. Admission charge). On the way, buy a bag of 'pralines'; the famous sweets were invented here by the chef to the Maréchal de Plessis-Praslin in the17th C. (Pâtisserie Brégier, 15, Cours de la République, ☎ 05 57 42 09 76, 22 F for 3¹/₂ oz (100 g).

Les Côtes-de-Blaye
Maison des Vins de Blaye, 11, Cours Vauban
☎ 05 57 42 91 19
Open Mon.–Sat., 8.30am–noon and 2–6pm. *Free admission.*

These local dry red and white wines can be bottled quite young and age well. The Maison des Vins will help you with your choice and give you some tips for other excursions in the region. **Free introductions** and **wine-tastings** are organised in July and August (Tues., Wed. and Thurs. at 6.45pm). Booking is required.

A trip on the *Deux frères*

From July to October
Book at the Blaye or Bourg Tourist Offices
This part of the estuary is called the Corniche Fleurie. Why not man the tiller on the only sailing-barge left on the Gironde, the *Deux frères*, sailing from Blaye to

The Côtes-de-Bourg are brightly-coloured, strong, red wines, full of vigour, that improve with age.

The Maison du Vin lies in the **magnificent setting** of a garden which overlooks the Dordogne river. In the vaulted cellar they will answer any questions you may have about this vineyard and the delicious wine it produces. There are more than 80 different Côtes-de-Bourg to choose from.

Spotcheck
C2

Things to do

Visit a nuclear power station
Cross the estuary in a sailing-barge
Fishing in the estuary
Côtes-de-Blaye wine
Côtes-de-Bourg wine

Within easy reach

Bordeaux, approx. 15½ miles (25 km) S, p. 196.

Tourist Offices

Blaye: ☎ 05 57 42 12 09
Bourg: ☎ 05 57 68 31 76

Bourg. After a crossing of about 3 hours, you'll land at Bourg where you can climb the cliff to the Citadel and the Terrasse du District to appreciate the wonderful view: the peninsula that you can see below is the Bec d'Ambès.

Bourg
Maison du Vin

Place de l'Éperon
☎ 05 57 94 80 20
Open daily. 15 July–15 Sept., 10am–13pm and 2.30–7pm; out of season, Mon.–Fri., 10am to noon and 2–5pm.
Free admission.

Braud-et-Saint-Louis
Nuclear power station

8 miles(13 km) N of Blaye
☎ 05 57 33 30 30
Visits by appointment, daily except Sun. and bank holidays.
Free admission.
French people often visit nuclear power stations, and now you can as well. After visiting the power station, carry on to see the pretty ports of Callonges and Vitrezay where the estuary fishing fleets are based. You can then try the shrimp cooked in aniseed.

FISHING IN THE ESTUARY

A piece of advice: ask the local fisher-men what fish to eat and how to cook it. Locally, lamprey and shad are only caught in April and May, so don't go looking for them in August! Lamprey is often eaten stewed with the white parts of leeks, while shad is grilled over vine tendrils like the other estuary fish (eels, plaice, mullet). To find the best *crevettes* (prawns) of the Gironde, go straight to the fishermen in the villages near the river, along the Corniche road and around Saint-Ciers-sur-Gironde.

Libourne

L ibourne stands at the point where the river Isle flows into the Dordogne, and is a former English *bastide* (fortified town). The cargoes of Saint-Émilion and Pomerol were sent down-river by barge to Bordeaux from this junction. The town remains an important centre of the wine trade because it is surrounded by such noble vineyards as Pomerol, Lalande, Fronsac, and Canon.

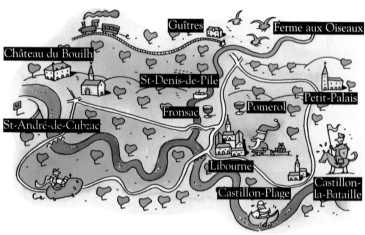

Guîtres

Ferme aux Oiseaux

Château du Bouilh

St-Denis-de-Pile

Petit-Palais

Fronsac

Pomerol

St-André-de-Cubzac

Libourne

Castillon-Plage

Castillon-la-Bataille

Libourne, the *bastide*

Libourne has retained the Tour du Grand-Port, some of the town walls, and old houses from its days as a fortified town. The Place Abel-Surchamp, surrounded by arcaded Renaissance houses is typical of the main square of a *bastide*. It gets busy on the market days: Tuesdays, Fridays, and especially Sundays. For three days in the second half of August, the streets of Libourne fill with acrobats, musicians, jugglers, storytellers and clowns for the Fest'Arts, the street entertainers' festival. ☎ 05 57 51 15 04.

The town hall

This former 15th-C. residence contains an archaeological museum and the Musée des Beaux-Arts, a fine-art museum which has a room dedicated to the work of René Prince-teau, a painter of animals and friend of Toulouse-Lautrec. The municipal library in the same building, houses the *Livre velu*, a manuscript written in 1476, which traces the history of the town and is bound in calf skin.

Tour du Grand-Port

A balloon ride

Lambert Voyages, 84, Rue Montesquieu ☎ 05 57 25 98 10

A ride in a hot-air balloon is a wonderful way to discover the *bastides*, the great châteaux and vineyards of the district. The flight lasts from one to two hours. Available all year round, weather permitting, book first (1 to 4 people, approximately 900 F per person).

The Pomerol vineyard

1 mile (2 km) of N of Libourne

This is one of the smallest vineyards in the Bordeaux district, 2½ miles long by 2 miles wide (4 km by 3 km). The wine produced is recognisable by its subtle odour of truffles. The soil contains iron oxide which gives the wine its delicious fragrance. Of all the Pomerols, Château Pétrus is the best-known and the most expensive. Each of the 40 vineyards is well signposted and can be visited: l'Évangile, Trotanoy, Vieux-Château-Certan. The price of a bottle of Pomerol ranges from 80 F to tens of thousands of francs.

SANTA CLAUS LANDS AT LIBOURNE

It's the magic of Christmas. Did you know that all the letters in France addressed to Father Christmas are sent to Libourne? They are not discarded but forwarded to this sorting office where a team of around 60 people take on the delightful, but delicate, task of replying to all the children. You can even go and visit to watch the sorting process.

Fronsac
Maison des Vins

1 mile (2 km) from Libourne
☎ 05 57 51 80 51
Open, 10.30am–noon and 2–6pm.
Free admission.

The capital of Fronsac wines is built around its Romanesque church, overlooking a vineyard which has existed for a thousand years. From the top

Spotcheck
C2

Gironde

Things to do

The markets of Libourne
Fest'Arts
Hot-air balloon flight
The wine route
A cruise on the River Isle
Rowing on the Dordogne

With children

La Ferme aux Oiseaux

Within easy reach

Bordeaux, 15 miles (24 km) W, p. 196.

Tourist Office

Libourne:
☎ 05 57 51 15 04

of the mount (253 feet/76 m), the view of Libourne and the rivers Dordogne and Isle is magnificent. The Fronsac red wines are powerful and their colour distinctive. Sample them at the Maison des Vins from April to September; you can taste a different château-bottled wine daily (there are about 70). Direct sales from 35 F a bottle.

Saint-André-de-Cubzac
Birthplace of Jacques Cousteau

12½ miles (20 km) from Libourne

This village is the birthplace of Commander Jacques Cousteau, and is also worth a detour for its 12th-C. church, in the shape of a Latin cross. It was fortified in the 14th C., and the choir and nave were rebuilt at the same time. The terrace of the Coteau de Montalon (½ mile; 1 km), has a lovely view of the vineyards (with an orientation guide). There is also a sign to mark the 45th parallel which passes through here.

Château du Bouilh

3 miles (5 km) N of Saint-André-de-Cubzac
☎ 05 57 43 01 45
Open 1 July–1 Oct., Thur., Sat., Sun., and public holidays, 2.30–6.30pm.
Admisison charge.
This eleganr residence is an example of late 18th-C taste in the Bordeaux district. It was built by Victor Louis, architect of the Grand-Théâtre in Bordeaux.

Saint-Denis-de-Pile

Cruising down the Isle

6 miles (10 km) N of Libourne
Maison de l'Isle
☎ 05 57 55 44 30
Open mid-April–June and Sept.–mid-Oct., on Sun.; July–Aug., daily. Leave 3pm, stop in Guîtres, arrival at 5pm in Coutras and in Saint-Denis-de-Pile at 7pm. Or leave 3.30pm from Coutras, stop at Abzac and return to Coutras around 7.30pm.
Admission charge.
Leave your car and take to the water. This cruise on the Isle lasts for half a day and is an unusual way of exploring the towns of Guîtres and Coutras.

Guîtres

The scenic route by train

9 miles (15 km) N of Libourne
☎ 05 57 69 10 69
Sun. and public holidays, 1 May–31 Oct.; Sat., 14 July–31 Aug. Leave from Guîtres 3.30pm.
Admission charge.
This town used to be a stop on the pilgrimage route to the tomb of St James (Santiago de Compostela). The ancient church, part of a Benedictine abbey, was started in 1080, but only completed in the 15th C. The nave has one of the most beautiful wooden gothic ceilings in Aquitaine. Take the **train touristique** from Guîtres to Marcenais, pulled by a locomotive built in 1924. Top speed is only 19 m.p.h. (30 km/h), leaving you plenty of time to see the countryside. The trip covers about 9 miles (15 km) and lasts three-quarters of an hour.

Organ recital

Église de Guîtres
☎ 05 51 69 10 34
Every Monday in July and August there are free organ recitals at 5pm in the ancient Benedictine abbey church. There are also recitals with paid admission on Fridays at 9pm. The organ is often accompanied by an orchestra.

Lagorce

La Ferme aux Oiseaux

16 miles (25 km) N of Libourne
Bird sanctuary
☎ 05 57 49 13 02
Open daily 9am–7.30pm.
Admission charge.
A bird-collector opened this sanctuary in the 1970s. He turned his hobby into a profitable occupation and now has over 200 species of birds in an area covering 10 acres (4 ha). There are all kinds of exotic birds, including waxbills, ostriches, cockatoos and ibises. They are acclimatised and breed successfully here. Some of the birds are kept in aviaries, others fly freely in parks under a covering of netting.

The Dordogne is perfect for trying your skills at canoeing or kayaking

Castillon-la-Bataille
Down the Dordogne
11 miles (18 km) SE of Libourne
Rowing Club, Quai André-Duranton
☎ 05 57 40 23 68
Closed 24 Dec.–3 Jan.

Between Castillon and Sainte-Foy-la-Grande, the Dordogne river runs through 12½ miles (20 km) of protected country-side. It is a lovely trip and a perfect opportunity to try your hand at rowing. Children over 8 years old are welcome pro-vided they can swim. Beginners are taught by the licensed professionals of the Fédération Française des Sociétés d'Aviron. The 'rowing board', an unsink-able rowing skiff, can be hired for one hour (50 F), half a day (150 F), or even longer (ask for details). *For Castillon, see also pp. 122 and 123.*

Petit-Palais
Romanesque church
16 miles (25 km) from Castillon-la-Bataille

This is one of the loveliest Romanesque churches in the départe-ment. It stands in a cemetery and has a richly decorated façade.

THE LAMPREY, A GREAT DELICACY

The lamprey is an extraordinary creature. It is a parasite which attaches itself to other fishes and sucks their blood with its nozzle-like mouth. The lamprey is as long as an eel, but thicker, and can reach a weight of 4lb 8oz (2 kg). The fish, popular in the Middle Ages, is now rare and expensive and is caught in eel-pots. In recent years, the lamprey has been fetching 180 F for 2lb 4oz (1 kg) in the local markets. Its prepara-tion is best left to experts. Try it in a stew with leeks and a sauce made from its own juices and red wine.

Saint-Émilion
hill of a thousand vintages

The village of Saint-Émilion is one of the most famous sights in the Bordeaux district. It's small enough to be seen in an afternoon, but is at its best in the early morning or early evening. The medieval layout of its pretty cobbled streets, churches, and the golden coloured stone is enhanced by the wonderful light. In addition to its famous wine, Saint-Émilion has a less well-known speciality: the macaroon, which you should try if you can.

Great walls

You'll find the entrance to the walls if you take the road from Libourne. This section of wall is 67 ft (20 m) high and 83 ft (25 m) long. It was once part of a Dominican convent.

Monolithic church and catacombs

Place des Créneaux
☎ 05 57 55 28 28
Open daily, 10am–noon and 2–5.45pm (5pm Nov–March; 6.30pm July–Aug.). Tours daily, every 45 minutes.
The Tourist Office occupies the Doyenné, once the cannon's refectory and dormi-

tory, which you have to pass through to visit the monolithic church, the chapel of La Trinité, the cloister of the collegiate church and the

catacombs. The church (guided tours only) was dug out of a rock, a Herculean task performed from the 9th to the 12th C., and has three naves, separated by imposing pillars.

Collegiate church

Open daily,
10am–6.30pm.
Free admission.
This is now the parish church of Saint-Émilion, as the mono-lithic church was seen as being too austere by the canons. Go through the Tourist Office to get to the lovely cloister.

The marketplace

The bustle of the Sunday morning market can be observed from a café terrace

while drinking a glass of wine or enjoying an ice cream. The square itself is surrounded by walls and rocks, and a steep ramp leads to the Rue du Clocher and the Place des Créneaux. Take it; the view of the square and the church is wonderful.

The Saint-Émilion macaroon

Try this melting macaroon! Its recipe, made from almonds, sugar and egg whites, dates from 1620! You can buy macaroons at **Blanchet** (9, Rue Guadet), a traditional bakery founded in the 1930s, or at **Mouliérac** (Tertre de la

Tente), where the bakery and shop are on the same premises (30 F for a pack of 24).

The jury of Saint-Émilion

The jury (*jurade*), a medieval institution, was revived in 1948. It controls the quality of production, storage and barrels of the famous vintage. Traditionally, twice a year, in the autumn for the start of the

harvest and in spring, jurors wearing their red robes edged with ermine gather in the monlithic church to decide whether the previous harvest can receive the Saint-Émilion seal of approval. Each wine-maker submits a sample for the scrutiny of the jury.

La Maison du Vin de Saint-Émilion
Place Pierre-Meyrat
☎ 05 57 55 50 55
Open daily, 9.30am–12.30pm and 2–6.30pm. In Aug., 9am–7pm.
Free admission.
Wines of the appellation are sold at whatever price the estate decides. La Maison du Vin offers you the opportunity to educate your palate with Saint-Émilion wines, in order to better appreciate them. A bottle of Saint-Émilion starts at 36 F, the *grands crus* sell for 50 to 90 F, the *grands crus classés* for more than 100 F, and the *premiers grands crus classés*, from 300 F.

Spotcheck
D3

Gironde

Things to do
The Sunday market
Walking and mountain-biking
Swimming and windsurfing
Visiting the vineyards
The train ride through the vineyards
Écomusée du Libournais

With children
The Castillon historic pageant

Within easy reach
Montaigne country, p. 126, Entre-deux-Mers, p. 184.

Tourist Office
Saint-Émilion:
☎ 05 57 55 28 28

VISITING THE VINE-YARDS: TOURING AND WINE-TASTING

You can get plenty of information at the Tourist Office. The hardiest tourists can wander through the vineyards on foot. The Tourist Office also rents bicycles by the day (90 F) and half-day (60 F), and can suggest tours such as those taking in the valleys or Romanesque churches. You can also go by car and take a guide with you who will show you the best sights. Whatever way you choose to tour the vineyards of Saint-Émilion, the owners of the châteaux and estates will give you a warm and hearty welcome.

In the vicinity

The Ermitage cave: faith and legend and sorcery

This is where Saint Émilion, who was a hermit, found refuge. A spring, whose virtues are now legendary, flows from here. According to the legend, young girls are sure to marry within the year if, when they

throw two pins into the water, they fall into the shape of a cross. Then all they have to do is sit in the so-called 'saint's armchair' (made of two stones), to guarantee their fertility. Whether you believe the legend or not, the waters are said to have curative powers for rheumatism and eye diseases.

The forest and the water

24 miles (38 km)
from Saint-Émilion
Centre Nautique et de Loisirs Saint-Christophe-de-Double
☎ 05 57 69 51 11
The forest waits to be explored on foot, on horseback or by mountain-bike (signposted paths). Or you might prefer to swim or windsurf on the lake at this water sports centre.

The beach at Sainte-Terre

Approx. 6 miles (10 km)
from Saint-Émilion
Centre de loisirs
☎ 05 57 47 13 65
You can swim in the Dordogne (lifeguard on duty 15 June to 15 Sept.) and practice archery on the shore at Sainte-Terre.

Castillon-la-Bataille

6 miles (10 km)
from Saint-Émilion
**Maison du Vin des Côtes-de-Castillon,
6, Allée de la République**
☎ 05 57 40 00 88
Open Mon.–Fri., 8.30am–12.30pm and 2–5pm.
July–Aug., Mon.–Sat., 8.30am–12.30pm and 2–7pm.
Free admission.
The village name recalls a battle that once took place here, which is commemorated with a pageant. It has been very hard for its wine to get a separate appellation so close to Saint-Émilion! Yet the Côtes-de-

Castillon are gradually gaining ground on their famous neighbour and are becoming popular, especially as they offer excellent value at between 30 F and 50 F a bottle.

The battle of Castillon

Association La Bataille, Belvès-de-Castillon
☎ 05 57 40 14 53
Show: mid-July to mid-Aug., around 10pm.
Admission charge.
This *son et lumière* show is one of the most famous in France, rivalling the famous Puy-du-Fou in the Vendée. The event attracts 25,000 spectators every year. The reconstruction of the Battle of Castillon is performed by the inhabitants (500 actors, 50 of them on horseback!). *For Castillon, see also p.119.*

The vineyards of Saint-Émilion

Saint-Émilion is inseparable from its vineyards which according to the legend, date back to Roman times. They flourished from the 13th C. and today are among the most famous vineyards in the world They cover 13,343 acres (5,400 ha), distributed between nine communes with very different types of soil. The foremost is on limestone slopes, those producing *vin ordinaire* are on the plain which runs down to the river Dordogne.

The train through the great vineyards

☎ 05 57 51 13 76
1 June–31 Oct., departure every 45 min., from 10.30am until 6.30pm.
Admission charge.
Departing from a station near the collegiate church, the little train tours through the vineyards taking 35 minutes (with commentary). You can get off along the way and get back on next time it comes round. The vineyards have two *premiers grands crus* classified in category A, Ausone and Cheval-Blanc. These are very good and very expensive! There are ten Châteaux *premiers grands crus* category B and 72 Châteaux *grands crus classés* and also two other categories, Saint-Émilion *grands crus* and Saint-Émilion. These last two classifications,

A USEFUL ADDRESS FOR BARGAIN-HUNTERS
Le Cellier des Gourmets
Drive past the Coopérative de Saint-Émilion, turn left, the cross the railway line.
☎ 05 57 74 46 92
Open Mon.–Sat., 8.30am–noon and 2–5.45pm.
You can buy Saint-Émilion here at reasonable prices. Le Cellier des Gourmets sells wine by the demijohn from 9.90 F for 1¾ pints (1l), but we particularly recommend the wine at 21.50 F for 1¾ pints (1l). Decant it into bottles and let it age for a few years. With a little patience you will have an excellent wine.

based on the reputation of the various estates, can be changed by decree every ten years.

❀ Montagne, museum and vineyards

2½ miles (4 km) N of Saint-Émilion
Écomusée du Libournais
☎ 05 57 74 56 89
Open daily 10am–noon and 2–6pm. Closed 20 Dec.–10 Jan.
Admission charge.
Improve your knowledge of the area in this well-designed museum. The local history is illustrated with photographs, old documents and tools, and there's a film of contemporary life and new innovations. End the day in a more active way by taking a 2½ mile (4 km) walk through the vineyards.

La Double and Le Landais, la Petite Sologne

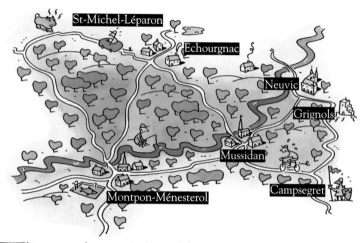

St-Michel-Léparon

Échourgnac

Neuvic

Grignols

Mussidan

Campsegret

Montpon-Ménesterol

This region is known as La Petite Sologne. It is steeped in legends and was once considered dangerous due to the wolves and wild boar that roamed its forests. It still has an air of mystery. Mussidan, in the heart of the region, makes an excellent stopping-point and base for trips to the numerous châteaux of the Landais.

Échourgnac

La Double cottages

Ferme du Parcot, just outside the village
☎ 05 53 81 99 28
Open daily, July–Aug., 2.30–7.30pm: on Sun., May–June and Sept., 2.30–5.30.
Admission charge.
Just past Échourgnac, the Ferme du Parcot, with its 123 acre (50 ha) park, demonstrates the traditional peasant cottage of the area, known as La Double. The simple, functional buildings are often built of local stone.

Grand Étang de la Jemaye
4½ miles (7 km) N of Échourgnac

This is a large pond, or small lake, with a beach in the heart of the forest. If you swim here on a hot day, you can watch dragonflies. Anglers should bring their fishing rods. After a swim, you can take an open carriage ride through the wooded avenues, from the Ferme Équestre de St-Rémy-sur-Lidoire. ☎ 05 53 82 49 04.

Have a go!
Conserves Fermières de Charriéras-Chantérac
☎ 05 53 82 61 23
Open Mon.–Sat., guided tours, 8am to 7pm.
Free admission.
Foies gras, truffled pâtés, breast of duck stuffed with duck liver – at the Charriéras farm you will be taught the techniques of preparing, seasoning and

cooking these delicacies.
If you visit the farm between
1 Sept. and 15 June, you can
watch the fattening of the
birds. There are **tastings** and
produce for sale.

La Latière cattle fair

Most of the time there is
nothing to see here, just a
clearing deep in the forest,
beside the D 38 (3¾ miles
(6 km) from Saint-Aulaye)
with a few empty sheds. But it
all changes on 30 April and
1 May when the Foire de la
Latière is held. You can check
out the cattle, have a drink
and watch people haggling in
the huge crowds.

Mussidan

❀ Craft workshops and distillery

**Le Musée des Arts et
Traditions Populaires
1-2, Rue Raoul-Grassin
☎ 05 53 81 23 55**
Open daily., 1 June–15
Sept., Sat., Sun. and
public holidays, 1 Oct.–
30 Nov. and 1 March–
31 May. Tours at 10am,
2.30pm and 4.30pm.

STURGEON
Sturgeon only reach
maturity between 5 and
7 years of age. The
males are good to eat
and the females pro-
duce Périgord caviar
which has an excellent
flavour. The grains are
smaller than those of
Russian or Iranian
caviar but they are
firm and stay separate.
Prices are high, though
– 5,400 F for 7 oz
(200 g) – but tin sizes
start at 1 oz (30 g).
Pisciculture Estudor:
Montpon-Ménestérol,
☎ 05 53 80 61 10.

Admission charge.
These collections were
assembled by Dr Voulgre in
a **Périgord charterhouse**.
There is a typical 19th-C.
middle class interior and craft
workshops (cooper, cobbler
and blacksmith). The barn
contains a collection of
agricultural equipment and
wooden La Double houses
have been erected in the
park. Take a detour through
Villamblard to admire the
magnificent brass vats of
the **Distillerie Reymond**.
This old firm, established in
1834, makes excellent
brandies, fruits preserved in
brandy and liqueurs.
☎ 05 53 81 90 01.

Neuvic

Château de Mellet

*7½ miles (12 km)
NE of Mussidan*
☎ 05 53 80 86 65
Open daily, July–Aug.,
1.30–7pm. Sept.–June
1.30–6pm (6.30pm
Sept.–Oct.).
Admission charge.
This listed 16th–
18th-C. château
contains rooms
of different
styles: large,
vaulted Great
Halls, King
Henry IV's bed-
chamber, the
Room of Diana,
the elegant Salon…
Its **huge botanical
gardens** cover 14¼ acres
(6 ha) and include 1,200
species of trees from all

Spotcheck
D2-E2

Dordogne

Things to do
Swimming and fishing
A ride in an open carriage
Guided tour of a farm

Within easy reach
*Montaigne country,
p. 126,
Bergerac, p. 130,
Ribérac, p. 134.*

Tourist Office
**Mussidan:
☎ 05 53 81 73 87**

over the world. Among them
are magical scarecrows, created
by children from the Institut
Médico-Éducatif du Château.

Grignols

The fortress

*3¾ miles (6 km)
E of Neuvic*
This fortress, dating from the
Middle Ages, once guarded
the road between Périgueux
and Bordeaux. It was destroyed
by the Prince de Condé in
1652. Its ramparts still dominate the village, but visitors
are not admitted in the
restored fortress itself.
The village has an old
covered market and
a handsome half-
timbered
house.

Montaigne country
between Périgord and Gironde

Montaigne country is for those who want to get off the beaten track. It stretches west from the frontiers of le Double and the Landes to the slopes of the Libourne and the Dordogne river. The view enjoyed by the philosopher, Michel de Montaigne, is much the same today. With the exception of the Lac de Gurson, a 27 acre (11 ha) artificial lake with a leisure centre, the landscape has hardly changed at all.

Vélines

Les Jardins de Sardy
☎ 05 53 27 51 45
Open daily, July–Sept., 11am–7pm; Sat., Sun., and public holidays, Apr.–June and Oct., 11am–7pm; by appointment on weekdays.
Admission charge.
This English-style landscape garden was created in the 1950s (*picture above*) in the grounds of an 18th-C. house and a 17th-C dovecote. Enjoy a wander through the rockery and shrubbery to the goldfish pond which keeps the area cool and fresh in summer. There's a café (cold food at lunchtime), with a delightful **view** over the river Dordogne, so it's perfect for picnics.

Montcaret

Gallo-Roman luxury
☎ 05 53 58 50 18
Open daily, Apr.–Sept., 9am–noon and 2–6pm; July–Aug., 9am–1pm and 2–7pm; 1 Oct.–31 March, 10am–noon and 2–4pm. Guided tours.
Admission charge.
The village has retained traces of its numerous occupants (Gauls, Visigoths and other barbarians). The vestiges of a Gallo-Roman villa and baths, built in the first century AD,

are the highlights of the visit. Admire the beautiful mosaics and the remarkable central heating system.

Pewter workshop
Le Bourg, Tête Noire
☎ 05 53 58 67 08
Open Mon.–Sat., 9am–noon and 2–7pm.
Free admission.
A pewter-smith born a few centuries ago would not feel out of place in Gérard Lasserre's workshop. He works in a little room into which the

L'ATELIER AUX ANIMAUX

Parc et Poterie de Montazeau
3¾ miles (6 km) from Vélines
☎ 05 53 61 29 84.
Open daily, 2–7pm.
Admission charge.
Let your children meet some animals their own size. There are dwarf donkeys and goats, llamas and nandus (a type of ostrich), deer and kangaroos. You can go inside the enclosures and touch the animals. There is a nursery for all the baby animals, and you will find those little bundles of fur hard to resist! Adults can go and see the display of pottery (egg-cup 35 F, wine jug 150 F, small gratin dish 135 F).

sunlight streams, beside the main road from Bordeaux to Bergerac. He barely has space for the showcase displaying copies of chandeliers, teapots, chargers, etc. (corkscrew 90 F, coaster 160 F). You can also bring him items to be mended or restored.

Saint-Michel-de-Montaigne
Château de Montaigne
☎ 05 53 58 63 93
Open Wed.–Sun., March–May and Nov.–Dec, 10am–noon and 2–5.30pm. June, Sept., Oct., 10am–noon and 2–6.30pm. Open daily July–Aug., 10am–6.30pm.
Admission charge.
Michel de Montaigne, the most famous inhabitant of Périgord, lived in a lovely château, surrounded by vineyards. Unfortunately, it was destroyed by fire in the 19th C., and was rebuilt in neo-Renaissance style. Luckily, the round tower, the author's library and study, escaped the fire. Don't forget to visit the neighbouring Château de Mathecoulon, which belonged to Montaigne's brother.

Carsac-de-Gurson
The lion and the leopard
1½ miles (2 km) E of Villefranche-de-Lonchat
The Romanesque church which dominates the village is dedicated to Eleanor, Duchess of Aquitaine and Queen of England, represented by the leopard of England and the lion of Aquitaine on the façade. There is a sculpted portico and a small cemetery. On the way to Villefranche-de-Lonchat, stop at Grappe de Gurson; this cooperative sells white, red and rosé wines.

Château de Mathecoulon, Carsac-de-Gurson

Spotcheck
D3

Dordogne

Things to do
Les jardins de Sardy
Visit a pewter workshop

With children
Lac de Gurson leisure centre
L'atelier aux animaux

Within easy reach
Saint-Émilion, p. 120,
Double and Landais, p. 124.

Tourist Office
Saint-Michel-de-Montaigne:
☎ 05 53 73 29 62

MUSÉE

Villefranche-de-Lonchat
The *bastide* and its lake
6½ miles (10 km) N of Saint-Michel-de-Montaigne
Musée d'Histoire Locale
☎ 05 53 80 77 25
Open all year round by appointment (Town Hall).
Admission charge.
This *bastide* once guarded the area between the river Isle in the north, the river Dordogne in the south and the slopes of Castillon in the west. It has a ruined 14th-C. château and a museum of local history. The nearby Lac de Gurson (27 acres; 11 ha) has a leisure centre with a flume 360 feet (108 m) long! (Base de Loisirs de Gurson, ☎ 05 53 80 77 57).

Monbazillac
the wine route

The route through the vineyards, dotted with pretty houses and ancient wine-cellars, allows you to stop as the fancy takes you, depending on what you want to see or which wine you want to taste. The vineyards of the Bergerac district cover more than 24,710 acres (10,000 ha) along the valley of the Dordogne, east of Bergerac itself. The best vintages include Côtes-de-Montravel, Pécharmant and Monbazillac.

The château

Monbazillac

4½ miles (7 km)
S of Bergerac
☎ 05 53 61 52 52
Open daily, June–Sept., 10am–12.30pm and 2–7.30pm (10am–7.30pm July–Aug.); out of season by appointment. *Admission charge.*
The château, with its cone-shaped roofs and four large round towers, contains two museums, the Musée des Arts et Traditions Populaires (which contains lovely Périgord furniture and documents on the history of Protestantism) and a small Musée des Vins (the visit is followed by a tasting). There is also a **view** of the vineyards of Bergerac.

Châteaux on the hilltops

Saussignac and Gageac

9½ miles (15 km)
W of Bergerac
Saussignac is surrounded by a vineyard which makes sweet white wines and strong reds, the Côtes-de-Saussignac. The château of the dukes of Lauzun stands on the hilltop opposite the Château de Gageac. Both châteaux are now private property, and can only be admired from the outside.

The mellow slopes

Lamothe-Montravel

25 miles (40 km)
W of Bergerac
This pretty little village is surrounded by slopes covered by one of the best vineyards in the valley of the Dordogne (the Montravel wines are sweet white wines). Montravel is also famous because the battle of Castillon (1453), which ended the Hundred Years War, took place 2 miles (3 km) from here. If you want to walk along the banks of the Dordogne, take the little road leading to Saint-Seurin-de-Prats.

Pécharmant
La Colline de Pécharmant
Château de Tiregand
☎ 05 53 23 21 08
Open Mon–Sat.,
8am–noon and 2–6pm.
Free admission.
The hill of Pécharmant (*péch*
means 'summit'), north-east of
Bergerac, produces full-bodied
red wines (approx. 741 acres
(300 ha) which are, according
to the experts, similar to the
red wines of Saint-Émilion.
Stop at the **Château de
Tiregand** to see its formal
gardens and fascinating
17th-C. wine-store (visits
by appointment, tastings
and sales: 44 F a bottle).

Issigeac
Pumpkin capital of France
*SE of the Monbazillac
vineyards*
This lovely medieval town has
little shops and half-timbered
houses with wattle-and-daub
frontages. Most noteworthy
houses are La Maison des
Dîmes and La Maison des
Têtes. The town prospered
in the 14th C. and was the
summer residence of the
bishops of Sarlat. The handsome Château des Évêques
(1660) was built by François
de Salignac, bishop of Sarlat.
In November, the **Foire au
potirons et aux cucurbitacées**
(pumpkin fair) is held in the
vault of the Bishop's room. In
July, the **Foire de la vannerie**,
a basketry fair, is held here.

Creysse
Bella Riva
☎ 05 53 23 20 45
Open daily June–Sept.,
10am–6pm: out of sea-
son, w/end and public
holidays, 10am–6pm.
Admission charge.

At the
Barbas site in
Creysse, thousands
of flint tools and
weapons have been unearthed
by teams of archaeologists.
An interesting exhibition
explains how flint is worked
into various cutting tools and
implements. Have a go at
being a caveman and try making your own
flint tool! Then why not take
a trip on the *Rivière Espérance*,
an old sailing-barge which
will take you down the

Spotcheck
E3

Dordogne

Things to do
The wine route
The Musée des Vins
Basketry fair at Issigeac
Discovering flint tools

Within easy reach
*Double and Landais,
p. 124.*

Tourist Office
Bergerac: ☎ 05 53 57 03 11

MONBAZILLAC
The vineyard covers
7,413 acres (3,000 ha)
and five villages.
It produces a
golden, syrupy
white
wine which
owes its
high sugar
content to
the famous
'noble rot'
(*pourriture
noble*) (see
pp. 38 and
39, Sauternes).
Monbazillac is a
stable wine that ages
well. It goes extremely
well with foie gras and
desserts. It's
regaining its
reputation
thanks to
manual
harvesting
and
smaller
yields.

Bergerac
or the ghost of Cyrano

Once the capital of French Protestantism, Bergerac's prosperity is based on the river Dordogne, as can be seen from the old town built around its port. Today this bustling little town, at the gateway to the Bordeaux district, has two major advantages:

it's the capital of French tobacco-growing, and it lies amid some prestigious vineyards, such as Bergerac, Montravel, Pécharmant, Rosette, Saussignac and Monbazillac.

which will take you back into Bergerac's glorious past.

Tobacco flower

A town, a river

Musée Ethnographique du Vin, de la Tonnellerie et de la Batellerie
5, Rue des Conférences
☎ **05 53 57 80 92**
Open Tues.–Sat., 10am–noon and 2–5.30pm:
Sun., 2.30–6.30pm.
Closed Sat. afternoons and Sun. from mid-Nov. to mid-March
Admission charge.
Bergerac was one of the major French ports in the 18th and 19th C. thanks to its shipping, cooperage, tobacco and wine. The museum in this 18th-C. wood-framed building displays objects linked to the town's activities, and has models, objects and photographs

Memorable river trips

Departures from the old port, Quai Salvette
☎ **05 53 24 58 80**
Open daily from Easter to 1 Nov. (public holiday).
Admission charge.
Travelling on a **sailing-barge** along the Dordogne river is

the most delightful way to discover Bergerac. A guide will explain the history of the river traffic. The trip takes you into a nature reserve where, depending on the season, you can see herons, kites, cormorants and terrapins.

THE TOBACCO CAPITAL

Maison Peyrarède, corner of the Rue des Rois-de-France
☎ 05 53 63 04 13
Open Tues–Fri., 10am–noon and 2–6pm, Sat. 10am–noon and 2–5pm; Sun. 2.30–6.30pm.
Admission charge.

The tobacco museum is housed in the Maison Peyrarède, a mansion built in 1604. The museum is unique in France, carefully explaining and charting the history of this plant brought back from the New World by Jean Nicot. Contrary to the anti-smoking campaigns of today, tobacco was originally used as a medicine to treat migraines! There are lovely collections of tobacco-jars, tobacco-pouches and carved pipes and you can find out how tobacco was used in Africa.

The old town: the myth of Cyrano
Tourist Office
☎ 05 53 57 03 11
Guided tours at 11am in July and Aug.

The town was very prosperous in the 16th C. and boasts several half-timbered houses (Rue d'Albret, Rue Saint-James, Rue des Fontaines). Walk down to the Dordogne through the Place Pélissière,

which has been beautifully renovated. The church of Saint-Jacques, entirely rebuilt in the 17th C., can be found *en route* to the Place de la Myrpe, where there is a statue of Cyrano de Bergerac. This famous French poet was not a native of Bergerac, as some believe, but was actually a Parisian. The locals, however, continue to perpetuate the myth.

Wine and jazz in the cloister
La Maison des Vins, Rue des Récollets
☎ 05 53 63 57 55
Open daily May–June, 10am–12.30pm and 1–6pm; June–mid-Oct., 10am–1pm and 2–7pm.
Free admission.

The Maison des Vins is the headquarters of the Council of Wine Makers of the Bergerac Region. You are welcome to come and taste their wines, which can be

Spotcheck
E3

Dordogne

Things to do
Trips on a sailing-barge
Tobacco museum
Jazz concerts
Art and antiques market

Within easy reach
Double and Landais, 15½ miles (25 km) N, p. 124.

Tourist Office
Bergerac: ☎ 05 53 57 03 11

purchased on the spot. In addition to the wine-making laboratory, it contains the beautiful **17th-C. Cloister des Récollets**, where jazz concerts are held every Wednesday in summer at 6pm (free admission). Do not miss the **arts and antiques market**, held all year round on the 1st Sunday of each month in front of the Maison des Vins.

The Cloister des Récollets

Trémolat

he landscape changes imperceptibly between Bergerac and Limeuil. The steep right bank of the Dordogne has narrow strips of land squeezed between the river and the hillsides. The left bank has flat plains which are devoted to the cultivation of tobacco and maize. Upstream from Lalinde, the Dordogne is picturesque with its pebble beaches and hairpin bends known as *cingles*. Here and there, defensive châteaux are a reminder of the strategic importance of the river.

A film set
If you saw the film, *Le Boucher* (1969), by Chabrol, the main square will look familiar as it was used as the main location. Trémolat is also famous for the the lookout post of Rocamadour, overlooking one of the loveliest bends in the river, known as the *Cingle de Trémolat*. The panoramic view is magnificent.

Trémolat

Touring the farms
☎ 05 53 22 77 38

Open every Tues., July–Aug. Tour starts 3pm. *Free admission.* This is an excellent idea if you want to learn more about life in this district, which is rich in a variety of farming trades. Any Tuesday in summer, you can meet Laurent Colet in front of the Grenier de Trémolat (with your car). He will take you to visit farms, goose-breeders, bee-keepers and basket-weavers. To end the tour, you'll be invited into his home to taste different kinds of delicious *confits* of duck.

Down the river Dordogne

Lalinde, the *bastide* which burned
5½ miles (9 km) W of Trémolat
This English *bastide*, built in the 13th C., was largely destroyed by fire in 1914. It has a lively Thursday **market** and a 14th-C. governor's house.

Some of the fortifications still remain and there's a **garden** leading down to the water, opposite the main square.

Couze, the paper-making town
2 miles (3 km) from Lalinde
Moulin de Rouzique
☎ 05 53 24 36 16
Open mid-June–mid-Sept., 10am–noon and 2.30–6.30pm; mid-Sept.–mid-Oct., 2.30–6.30pm; by appointment for the rest of the year.

The Moulin de Rouzique

Château de Lanquais

Spotcheck

E3

Dordogne

Things to do

Tour of the farms
Visit to a paper-mill
A nature walk

Within easy reach

*Les Eyzies, 6¼ miles
(10 km) NE, p. 148.*

Tourist Office

Trémolat:
☎ 05 53 22 89 33

Admission charge.
There have been a dozen paper-mills along the banks of the Couze since the 16th C. The paper-makers made paper for the Dutch. Reams of paper were shipped with the wines of Bergerac and Monbazillac, and were sent to Holland via Bordeaux. The **Moulin de Rouzique** can be visited and you can buy watercolour paper from 20 F, as well as writing paper, envelopes, etc. At the **Musée du Filigrane**, visitors can make their own paper.

Moulin de Larroque
☎ 05 53 61 01 75
Open Mon.–Fri.,
9am–noon and 2–5.30pm.
Free admission.
This is one of the few mills in France where paper is still hand-made. The sheets are drawn out of the pulp then laid on felt before being pressed and dried. Georges Duchêne offers the passing enthusiast embossed paper, writing paper, sketchbooks, etc. Business cards cost 90 F, a photo album costs 80 F, a watercolour sketchbook 90 F.

❀ Lanquais, the château of a beautiful spy

*1½ miles (2 km)
from Couze*
☎ 05 53 61 24 24
Open daily, exc. Tues.,
Sept.–June, 10.30am–
noon and 2.30–
6.30pm. Oct.–Apr.,
afternoons only.
Admission charge.
The history of this medieval château, with a Renaissance wing, is linked to that of Isabelle de Limeul, spy and confidante of Catherine de Medici. She became pregnant and was banished to the Château de Lanquais, with her husband, Scipion Sardini.

Saint-Capraise-de-Lalinde, from the locks to the forest

*2 miles (3 km)
from Lanquais*
This village between the Dordogne and the hills is traversed by a canal, a main road, a railway and even the river which runs beside it. Downstream at Tuilières, the side-canal ends in a series of locks. The lock-keepers cottages (of which two remain) are very picturesque. Climb up to the forest to explore Liorac-sur-Louvre and its 17th-C. houses.

A NATURE WALK

A two hour walk of 4½ miles (7 km) along a nature path will allow you to take full advantage of the lovely views, as well as admiring the flora and fauna along the banks of the Dordogne. You leave from the port of Mauzac, next to Lalinde, 18½ miles (30 km) north of Bergerac. The road is signposted in red and white on a yellow background. There are green lizards, black kites and wild flowers. You walk along a cliff then descend to the ruins of the 12th–15th-C. fortress of Milhac.

Ribérac and the Dronne valley

churches on the defensive

The Ribérac district, west of Périgord, is an area of transition and the gateway to the Charente. The rolling hills are irrigated by a pretty river, the Dronne, and there are elegant Romanesque churches with cupolas; so many, indeed, that you could do a whole tour of them.

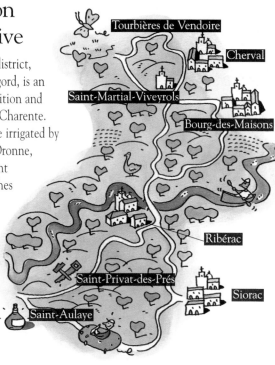

Tourbières de Vendoire

Cherval

Saint-Martial-Viveyrols

Bourg-des-Maisons

Ribérac

Saint-Privat-des-Prés

Siorac

Saint-Aulaye

Markets and fairs in Ribérac

The administrative capital of the district has a sizeable British community and on market days you may hear more English spoken than the native patois. You can attend the **traditional market** every Friday, Place du Palais

de Justice, the little **farmer's market** (Tues. mornings from May to September), Place de la Liberté, the **foies gras fairs** (mid-November to mid-March) and the **walnut fairs** (October and November), both Place J.-Débonnière. The third Saturday of August is traditionally reserved for **antiques**. In July and August, there is also the **Festival Musiques et Paroles en Ribéracois**, whose eclecticism is as great as its quality. Every kind of music can be heard from classical music to jazz.

Visit a farm

Every Tues., July–Aug. Meet at the Tourist Office (☎ 05 53 90 03 10). You

will be taken to one of the numerous farms in the district to see the calves, cows, pigs, hen-houses and horses. A farmhouse snack is then served. The visit is free but there is a charge for the optional snack, which is enormous.

In the land of churches with cupolas

The Romanesque churches of the Ribérac district are typically topped with cupolas. Some are fortresses with crenellations and loopholes, showing they were used for defence by the inhabitants. They include Saint-Martial-Viveyrols, Bourg-des-Maisons, Cherval and Siorac.

❀ MUSÉE DU COGNAC ET DU VIN

Saint-Aulaye
☎ **05 53 90 81 33**
Open daily except
Mon., July–Aug.,
3–5pm; Sept.–June
on Sat. 3–5pm;
closed in Feb.
Admission charge.
If you are nostalgic
for old crafts, and you
like brandy and wine,
visit this museum,
inside an old wine-
store and barn. The
work of the vine-
grower, wine-maker
and cooper are
explained, and you can
see many of the tools
of the trade, including
a still and an 18th-C.
grape-press. There is
also a realistic recon-
struction of a typical
merchant's shop of
the period.

Nearby
Musée de l'Outil et de la Vie au Village

*7 miles (11 km)
S of Ribérac*
Saint-Privat-des-Prés
☎ **05 53 91 22 87**
(Town Hall).
Open daily except Mon.
July–Aug., 3–6pm;
out of season, phone
for an appointment.
Admission charge.
Reconstructed in a period
street, all the crafts once
practised in La Double can be

seen in this museum dedicated to tools and village life.
You can watch glass-makers,
a cooper and a carpenter at
work. Carpentry tools, posters,
and prints are all on offer in
this street full of nostalgia!

❀ The peat-bogs of Vendoire

*9½ miles (15 km)
N. of Vendoire*
La Maison des Tourbières
☎ **05 53 90 79 56**
Open daily 1 May–30
Sept., 10am–7pm; Sun.,
April–Oct., 10am–6pm;
out of season, by appointment. *Admission free,
charge for guides*
Today, peat-bogs are no longer
worked, but the guided tour
(about 2 hours) will enable
you to discover and experience a unique environment,
alive with rare flora and fauna.
Take your binoculars and
watch the butterflies, dragonflies and birds which inhabit
these amazing marshes.

Château de Mareuil

*12½ miles (20 km)
NW of Brantôme*
☎ **05 53 60 74 13**
Open daily, July–Sept.,
10am–noon and
2.30–6.30pm; out of
season, 2–6.30pm.
Admission charge.

Spotcheck
D2

Dordogne

Things to do

Market and fairs
Music festival
Visit a farm
Visit the caves of Cluzeaux
La Maison des Tourbières
Musée du Cognac et du Vin

Within easy reach

*Double and Landais, 15.6
miles (25 km) S, p. 124.*

Tourist Office

Ribérac: ☎ 05 53 90 03 10

This former fortress once
defended one of the four
baronies of Périgord. It was
later converted into a lovely
Renaissance château. You
can tour the châteaux of the
district by bicycle (there are
about 15 around Mareuil, a
25-mile/40 km run). Tourist
Office: ☎ 05 53 60 99 85.

Les Cluzeaux

*2 miles (3 km) from the
Château de Mareuil*
**Saint-Pardoux-
de-Mareuil**
☎ **05 53 60 99 85**
(Tourist Office)
You can organise guided tours
of these caves which were
carved out of the limestone
rocks and inhabited by people
in the Middle Ages. It's hard
to imagine life in this underground dwelling, which
consists of rooms, very low
corridors (you have to bend
to get through them) and
vertical shafts.

Château de Mareuil

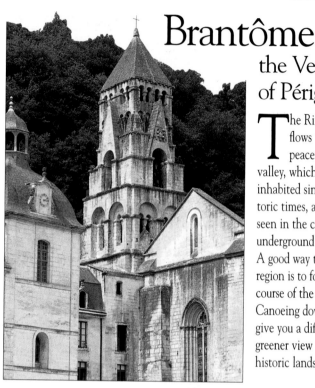

Brantôme
the Venice of Périgord

The River Dronne flows through a peaceful little valley, which has been inhabited since prehistoric times, as can be seen in the caves and underground shelters. A good way to see the region is to follow the course of the river. Canoeing down it will give you a different, greener view of this historic landscape.

Medieval Brantôme

The 'Venice of Périgord' is worth a detour. The town is dominated by a four-storey tower, built on a rock 40 feet (12 m) high, and lies deep in the valley of the Dronne. The elbow-shaped bridge, guarded by a Renaissance pavillion, leads to the **Monks' Garden**, which, with its 16th-C. seats, is a pleasant place for a walk. The Tourist Office organises a tour of the cave-dwellings in the abbey (all year round except 3 weeks in January).

Life in Brantôme

There are plenty of footbridges you can use to enter this town surrounded by water. A short walk takes you to the gothic and Renaissance houses, the vestiges of the ramparts and antique shops. If you like shopping for food, there's a **local market** every Friday morning in winter and on Tuesday morning in summer at the **farmer's market** the famous **truffle and foies gras markets** are held.

Château of the eldest son: Bourdeilles...

5 miles (8 km)
S of Brantôme
☎ 05 53 03 73 36
Open daily, July–Aug., 10am–noon; rest of the year, open daily exc. Tues., 10am–12.30pm and 1.30–5.30pm (to 7pm Apr.–June and Sept.–Oct.) Closed 3–25 Jan.
Admission charge.

This impressive château was the home of one of the four barons of Périgord. It was built by André de Bourdeille, the eldest son, who had it all: an inherited fortune, estates, honours and above all, a very beautiful wife. It is she who drew up the plans for the château and Pierre, André's younger brother, admired her.

The elbow-shaped bridge

The 16th C. Château de Puyguilhem is 5½ miles (9 km) E of Brantôme

Spotcheck
E1

Dordogne

Things to do
Fairs and markets in
Brantôme
Villars caves
Canoeing on the Dronne

Within easy reach
*Nontron, 13¾ miles
(22 km) N, p. 144,
Thiviers, 16¼ miles
(26 km) NE, p. 146.*

Tourist Office
Brantôme:
☎ 05 53 05 80 52

Pierre had to leave to seek his fortune at court, and was given the income from the Abbey of Brantôme, whose name he took as a *nom de plume*.

... and the younger son: Richemont
*4½ miles (7 km)
NW of Brantôme*
☎ 05 53 05 72 81
Open daily, July–Aug., 10am–noon and 2–6pm.
Admission charge.
Pierre de Bourdeille, the younger son, returned home at the age of 40. He built this ideal gentleman's residence on a hill. He had travelled and fought many battles, in the service of the king of Spain as well as three kings of France who all appreciated his lively storytelling. He had charm and an easy wit, but a fall from a horse put a stop to his adventuring. He chose to put pen to paper, writing memoirs (true and false), stories of women and brave soldiers. Signing himself 'Brantôme', he gained fame as the author of *Dames galantes*. Visit both châteaux and decide whether you prefer that of the millionaire or the author.

Grottes de Villars
*8 miles (13 km) NE of
Brantôme*
☎ 05 53 54 82 36
Open Apr., 2–6pm; June, Sept., 10am–noon and 2–7pm. July and Aug., 10am–7pm.
Admission charge.

CANOEING ON THE DRONNE
**The Dronne is particularly lovely for boating. Energetic folk can leave from Saint-Pardoux, the rest from Quinsac. The trip towards Brantôme (9½ miles/15 km) is delightful, the landscape changing constantly. The arrival in the heart of Brantôme is magical, the town with its mullioned windows and window-boxes, is reflected in the water. Continuing on your way, the next stop is Bourdeilles. There is a steep cliff, topped by the château. The Dronne is tamed in this way right down to Tocane. Then you have to make your way back.
Brantôme Canoës
☎ 05 53 05 77 24.
Allo Canoës
☎ 05 53 06 31 85.**

Take the time to stop at Villars. The abbey of Boschaud is a haven of peace, far from the major tourist route. It was founded in 1154 and became one of the four Cistercian abbeys of Périgord. Today, its ruins can be visited (the remaining walls are being restored) in a lovely **green setting**. If you are interested in prehistory, make a detour to visit the **caves of Villars**. The caves were discovered in 1953 and they contain stalactites and stalagmites as well as traces of our distant ancestors who left wonderful drawings of horses, including the *Little Blue Galloping Horse*.

Périgueux
capital of White Périgord

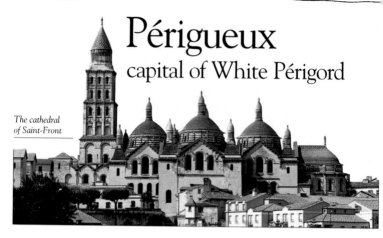

The cathedral
of Saint-Front

Périgeux, capital of the Dordogne, is a well-restored city. A visit will take you through four eras – prehistory, the Gallo-Roman era, the Middle Ages and the Renaissance. The town is best visited in two sessions: start with the Gallo-Roman district, then see the medieval town. If you want to keep only one memory of Périgueux, choose the market: it's a Saturday morning ritual. You will find all the produce from the surrounding market-gardens, and hear lots of local patois, the local accent and some *bons mots*.

The markets

In the Place du Coderc you can buy poultry, cheese, vegetables and fruit direct from the farms around Périgueux every day. If you want the ingredients to make a salad, this is the place to find them. The **marché au gras** (foie gras market) is held in the Place Saint-Louis on Saturday and Wednesday mornings, from November to March. The truffle-growers and hunters also sell their wares here, so get up early if you want to snap up the best buys.

POSTAGE STAMP CAPITAL

In 1970, the national postage stamp printing works moved to Périgueux. It produces all the postage stamps for France and certain foreign countries. The craft, art and industry involved in producing postage stamps is fascinating. Less poetic, perhaps, are all the road-tax disks and stamp duty stamps which are also printed here. The printing works can only be visited on Wednesday mornings, 9–11.30am, and you must book in advance. ☎ 05 53 03 17 00, (all year round except July and August). *Free admission.*

In the days of the Romans

Tour de Vésone and Jardin des Arènes, Quartier de la Cité
Free admission.
When the Romans established the city on the right bank of the river Isle, they named it after a Roman goddess, Vesunna. The 80 feet (24 m) high Tour de Vésone is all that remains of a temple which was probably dedicated to the goddess, the protecting divinity of the town. It was built in the 2nd C., and gives some idea of the Roman city which had temples, aqueducts and theatres. The 1st-C. theatre

in the gardens of the Arena could hold 20,000 spectators and was one of the largest in Gaul. If you want to know more about the Roman presence here, visit the Musée du Périgord.

Saint-Étienne-de-la-Cité

Until 1669, this was the cathedral of Périgueux. It is elegant and restrained but has been badly treated during the course of its history: several cupolas and the bell-tower have been removed. Look at the **Château Barrière**, next door. The castle keep is 12th C. and the adjacent building dates from the Renaissance.

The Puy-Saint-Front district

This district is surrounded by ancient walls and is a trip back into the Middle Ages. The **Tour Mataguerre** is the only survivor of the 28 towers which lined the walls which were 5,000 feet (1,500 m) long. Wandering through the narrow lanes, you will see the most picturesque side of Périgueux, including the mansions in the Rue Aubergerie and the Rue Limogeanne, now pedestrianised. If you push open a door or two in the Rue de la Sagesse, you will see some handsome staircases. It's well worth stopping for a drink at one of the cafés that line the little squares, such as those in the Place Saint-Louis.

Spotcheck
E2

Dordogne

Things to do

The farmers' markets
Walking by the canal
Trip on a sailing-barge
International mime festival
Discovering old crafts
The national postage stamp printing works

Within easy reach

Double and Landais, p. 124,
Les Éyzies, p. 148.

Tourist Office

Périgueux:
☎ 05 53 53 10 63

La Maison des Consuls

There are many lovely houses on the quayside in old Périgueux, such as La Maison des Consuls (c. 1475). Further along is a little wattle and daub construction, which once straddled the river. It is incorrectly known as the old mill (*Vieux Moulin*), but in fact, was once the grain-store of the monks of the chapter of Saint-Front.

The sweet delights of Périgueux

Philippon-Lavaud,
2, Rue Taillefer
☎ 05 53 53 40 48
Open Mon. afternoon–
Sat., 9am–noon and
2–7pm.

Philippon-Lavaud is probably the best sweet shop in the whole of Périgeux. Its specialities include the **croquant du Périgord,** a delicious confection of two shells of nougatine enclosing a layer of chocolate, flavoured with cognac and almonds. They cost 40 F for 3½ oz (100 g). Try the other delicacies of Périgord – truffles, wild mushrooms and walnuts – all made out of chocolate

(34 F for 3½ oz/100 g). Indulge yourself, after all, you are on holiday.

A walk by the canal

Making the Isle navigable was a long-term project, which began in the Middle Ages, but the diversion canal and its river port were not inaugurated until 1837. Today, walkers and joggers can take one of the three paths between the river and the canal, which are from ½ to 2½ miles (1 to 4 km) long.

The cathedral of Saint-Front

This imposing edifice seems to dominate the town. Is the style Périgourdine or Byzantine? This medieval cathedral has an unusual oriental influence in a land of Romanesque churches. It's in the shape of a Greek cross and its curved roof is typical of the Eastern Rite churches. The cathedral as it stands today was almost completely rebuilt in the 19th C. by the architect who later produced the plans for the Sacré-Cœur basilica in Montmartre, Paris.

Musée du Périgord

Cours Tourny
☎ 05 53 06 40 70
Open Mon.–Fri.,
Apr.–Sept., 11am–6pm;
w/end, 1–6pm. Out of
season by appointment.
Admission charge.

This museum was originally opened to display the Gallo-Roman antiquities of ancient Vésone. However, it has since become one of the most important prehistory museums in France, enriched by the accumulation of the historical treasures of the region. More exotically, it has an important section on ethnographic art.

Festival of Mime

Festival International du Mime
First fortnight of August (8 days)
☎ 05 53 53 18 71

Sad, expressive clowns – but all of them mute. This unique festival is inspired by mime on stage, in life, in the circus and in silent films. The Festival Mimos is all about the language of gestures and expressions. It is diverse and fascinating, with lots of performances and courses to teach mime. There are indoor as well as outdoor events.

Seeing Périgueux by barge

☎ 05 53 53 10 63 (Tourist Office).

From Easter to Oct., departures daily, every hour between 10am and 6pm. Ticket office and departure Quai de l'Isle. *Admission charge.*

Weigh anchor for a while and sail down the Isle, to recuperate after exploring the town! Take time to relax

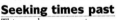

and discover Périgueux from the river in a *gabarre* (barge). There's a guide so you can learn about the history of the city and all the best sights.

Seeking times past

This wood-turner continues to make chairs as they were made in days gone by; his workshop smells of fresh wood (Place du Marché-au-Bois and 20 Rue Limogeanne, two entrances). By the Isle, a basket-weaver uses willow to to make objects such as cradles and storage baskets (33, Boulevard Georges-Saumande, ☎ 05 53 08 70 84). These would make great souvenirs of your holiday.

Nearby

Abbaye de Chancelade

3½ miles (6 km) NW of Périgueux

The abbey of Chancelade was founded in the 12th C. and is hidden near Périgueux in a magnificent setting . The buildings form a quadrangle around a central courtyard. You can see the huge vat in which monks made wine.

The abbey complex with its stables, dwelling-house (inhabited by de Bourdeilles or by the abbot). The Romanesque abbey-church and the chapel of Saint-Jean are really worth a detour.

COUNTRY WALK
Just 8½ miles (14 km) (3 hour walk) will take your away from the tourists. You leave from the Abbey of Chancelade and follow the two yellow arrows. You'll arrive at the village of Maines and continue to Les Andrivaux through the forest around the lake of Bétoux. This village was a headquarters of the Knights Templar from the 12th to the 14th C. From here, you walk through the woods to the Château des Brunies. This is where Jean Valjean took a detour in *Les Misérables*. Return to the abbey via Landes and Terrassonie.

Merlande priory

3½ miles (6 km) NW of Chancelade

This small 12th-C. foundation of the monks of the Chancelade is hidden deep in the forest of Feytaud. The chapel is fortified and its sculpted capitals, carved out of the thickness of the walls, depict a whole bestiary of strange monsters and frightening creatures. The prior's house and the overgrown cemetery in the shrubbery make this a very moving place.

Hautefort and the Auvézère valley

If you prefer landscapes and beautiful views to the standard cultural attractions and tourist sights, then the Auvézère is made for you. This is a neglected corner of the Dordogne, where the pale walls of

Périgord mingle with the dark roofs of Limousin. The area was once famous for its forges, when Périgord supplied the kingdom of France with more than 10% of its iron. Some smithies are still in operation, adding to the interest of the district.

Magnificent Hautefort

☎ 05 53 50 51 23
Open daily, April–Oct., 9.30–noon and 2–6pm; out of season, open on Sun. Closed 15 Dec.–15 Jan. *Admission charge.*
One of the loveliest châteaux in Périgord was nearly demolished by a terrible fire in 1968, but it was carefully restored by its owner with aid from the government. Today, Hautefort stands proudly on a limestone mount 770 ft (231 m) high and is clearly visible from afar. A few rooms survived with their original furniture and their 16th- and 17th-C. Flemish tapestries. Don't leave without visiting the **formal gardens** and the superb 99 acre (40 ha) **park** (Admission charge).

A walk through the gorges of the Auvézère

Your first trip should be to the Pervendoux mill. At Génis, take the Auvézère tour road to the Moulin de Pervendoux. The mill stands next to a bridge leading to the gorges and the walk will show you hairpin bends in the river.

The second route is to the Auvézère waterfalls. At Saint-Mesmin (behind the church), take the path that leads to the river, and walk for 15 minutes among the fragrant undergrowth. Follow the GR 646 to reach the waterfall

of Saut-Ruban. A *relais nature* field centre now occupies the 17th-C. presbytery and offers many kinds of sporting activities, including mountain biking, canoeing and kayaking and rock-climbing.

Excideuil

At the Thursday market

9½ miles (15 km) from Hautefort

Thursday morning, market day, is very busy. The town has some lovely old houses, in the Rue des Cendres, for example. A walk through the streets of Excideuil will take you to the Rue Jean-Jaurès, where you can admire the collection of coffee grinders in an antique dealer's window. Stop at **Leroy** (Avenue Gambetta) to try the macaroons or at **Conangle** (Place Bugeaud) for the cakes.

The château

The fortress of the viscounts of Limoges (*see picture below*), stands on a hill. Due to its strategic position, it was attacked many times. Two imposing castle keeps and a

LACOSTE PARAPLUIES

Cherveix-Cubas
2 miles (3 km) N of Hautefort
☎ 05 53 50 42 60
Open Mon.–Sat. Daily visits at 11am and 3pm in July and Aug. *Free guided tours of the factory*

Lacoste has been making umbrellas since the 1930s (among others, the green crocodile brand). They come in all colours and styles. You can buy your perfect umbrella here and only pay factory prices for it.

double curtain-wall are adequate proof of its turbulent past. Two gatehouses which were added in the 16th C. provide a surprising image of a château divided into two parts, of which only the public parts may be visited.

Tourtoirac and Chourgnac-d'Ans

The king of Patagonia

4 miles (6,5 km) W of Hautefort

Antoine de Touneins, a young man from Périgord, changed his unspectacular life as a lawyer because of his desire to become a king. In 1850, vacant thrones were rare, so he sought out one a long way from his native Dordogne. He found what he was looking for in southern Chile and Argentina, where he was

Spotcheck
F2

Dordogne

Things to do

Auvézère gorges
Relias nature activity centre
Excideuil market

Within easy reach

Thiviers, 15½ miles (25 km) N, p. 146, Causses and Vézère, 15½ miles (25 km) S, p. 152.

Tourist Office

Excideuil: ☎ 05 53 62 95 56

crowned king by the native Indians. Orélie-Antoine I did not rule Patagonia for long. He was banished by the Chileans and died in 1878. His grave is in the village cemetery and not far away, at Chourgnac-d'Ans, the family exhibits his crown in the tiny Musée des Rois d'Araucanie ☎ 05 53 51 12 76 (Open daily except Tues., 10.30am–noon and 2.30–5.30pm).

Nontron
the oldest knife in France

Far from the beaten tourist track, Nontron has been a well-kept secret. Make the journey and you won't be disappointed. Each turning reveals either a village, a bridge with a lovely view, a château or a prehistoric cave. This is the aptly-named Green Périgord: you may find yourself wondering why there are so many cars parked beside the forest after it has been raining. The simple answer is that this is cep (wild mushroom) country.

Childhood delights
Musée des Poupées et Jeux d'antan
☎ 05 53 56 20 80
Open daily, June–Sept., 10am–7pm; March–May, Oct. and public holidays, daily except Tues., 2.30– 6pm.
Admission charge.
The town, with its ramparts and ancient streets, has an old-fashioned charm. This museum of dolls and games from the past is housed in the 18th-C. château.

Boutique Hermès
Route de Piégut
☎ 05 53 60 86 21
Open Tues.–Fri., 8.30am –noon and 2–6pm; Mon. and Sat., afternoons only.
This former Adidas factory has been converted into a luxury goods workshop since the Hermès company opened its porcelain decorating workshop in the former trainer factory (saving hundreds of jobs). It is worthwhile visiting the factory outlet shop as porcelain firsts and seconds are sold at a 50% reduction.

The Nontron knife
33, Rue Carnot
☎ 05 53 56 01 55
Open daily, 9am–noon and 2–7pm; out of season, closed Sun. and Mon. morning.
This is the star of the town, the forerunner of all the penknives and folding knives. You'll recognise the knife from its pale boxwood handle, engraved with a black V. Miniature knives are hidden inside walnut or even hazelnut shells. The skill of the craftsmen of Nontron is famous, and the tradition dates back to the 15th C. The firm of Laguiole now owns the Nontron cutlers.

PÉRIGORD
BY GYPSY CARAVAN
Leave from Quinsac: Beauvignière
☎ 05 53 35 50 24
(Comité Départemental du Tourisme).
In high season, a gypsy caravan costs 4,500 F a week to hire. Don't indulge in one of these unusual methods of transport if you are in a hurry! An average distance covered is 10 miles (15 km) a day. You will find lots of *relais* on your route, which is mapped out for you. A unique way of discovering Périgord at the pace of a plodding carthorse.

A master glassmaker
3¹/₂ miles (6 km) W of Nontron
Louis Martin, La Cabane
☎ 05 53 56 16 98
Louis Martin created the logo of the Aquitaine region at the entrance of the county hall for the Bordeaux region. He is responsible for the revival of the art of stained glass in France. You can watch him at work here.

Teyjat
Prehistory in the countryside
6¹/₂ miles (10 km) N.-W. of Nontron
☎ 05 53 06 90 80
Open July–Aug., Sat., 10am–5pm, booking only.
Admission charge.
The cave of La Mairie made this little village famous. It's a long way from the best-known prehistoric sites but has about 40 high quality drawings, dating from the Upper Magdalenian period (10,000 BC). A limited number of visits are organised

on weekdays in the summer . Those who prefer life in the present can try the karting track which also runs training courses. ☎ 05 53 56 36 11.

Saint-Estèphe
Leisure centre
3¹/₂ miles (6 km) N of Nontron
☎ 05 53 56 18 31
Free admission.
This 57-acre (23 ha) pond has amenities for bathing, angling, pedalos, windsurfing and other attractions in the height of summer. Nearby, there is the Roc Branlant, a giant stone which which rocks up and down. Just below it, you'll see a tumble of eroded boulders known as the Devil's Rosary (*le chapelet du Diable*).

Varaignes
Love of tradition
9¹/₂ miles (15 km) W of Nontron
In this medieval village built on a hillside, it's the villagers themselves who have restored the feudal château (*see below*).

Spotcheck
E1

Dordogne

Things to do
Visit a glass-making workshop
Périgord by gypsy caravan

With children
The doll and games museum
Saint-Estèphe leisure centre
Karting track

Within easy reach
Brantôme, 13¹/₂ miles (22 km) S, p. 136.

Tourist Office
Nontron:
☎ 05 53 56 25 50

It contains the Musée des Arts et Traditions Populaires, including a weaver's workshop which makes Charentais cloth, ☎ 05 53 56 35 76. The **walnut fair** and the Mill Day in February, the weaver's market at Whitsun, and the **turkey fair** on 11 November (which has nearly 10,000 visitors) bring this little village to life.

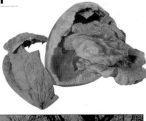

Thiviers
truffles and foie gras

The colours given to the districts of Périgord are based on the predominant colour of the landscape. The route from Thiviers to Jumilhac takes you to Green Périgord where there are lots of oak woods, chestnut groves and lush meadows. Another route via Saint-Jean-de-Côle and Sorges takes you to White Périgord.

The Foie Gras Museum
Place Foch
☎ **05 53 55 12 50 (Tourist Office).**
Open in summer, Mon.–Sat., 9am–6pm, Sun., 9am–noon: the rest of the year, 10am–noon and 3–6pm.
Admission charge.
The place where Jean-Paul Sartre spent his childhood is one of the capitals of foie gras. Its **foie gras markets** attract gourmets on winter Saturdays and there is even a Foie Gras Museum, so that visitors can experience the full flavour of the area and learn all about its favourite product.

Faith healers of all kinds
In Périgord, the old beliefs live on and there are dozens of faith healers who still operate here. They have inherited secrets and skills from the past which are said to get rid of warts and put dislocated joints back into position. A prelate (not recognised by the Catholic clergy) is open for business between Thiviers and La Coquille. He is said to cure illnesses of the soul and the body. Although he has been prosecuted, his followers have not abandoned him.

Nantheuil
A shower of stars
½ mile (1 km) E of Thiviers
End of June to end of Sept., every Friday evening.
☎ **05 53 55 21 95 or 05 53 62 08 08**
Admission charge.
Eclipses, comets, stars – the sky is full of splendour in summer. The Amicale Laïque de Thiviers brings both visitors and astronomers to the observatory of Périgord at Les Courtigeauds to scan the night sky with its 17 in (450 mm) telescope.

Saint-Jean-de-Côle
Château de la Marthonie
4½ miles (7 km) W of Thiviers

☎ 05 53 62 30 25
Open 1 July–31 Aug.,
10am–noon and
2–6.30pm.
Admission charge.
The ochre-coloured houses and
brown roof tiles makes this
one of the prettiest villages in
Périgord. On the square there's
a Romanesque church, a
Renaissance priory, a market-
hall and the 15th- and 16th-C.
Château de la Marthonie (*see
opposite page below*). Cross the
little humpback bridge to see
the church and cloister.

Saint-Paul-la-Roche
Local foods
*9½ miles (15 km)
NE of Thiviers*

☎ 05 53 62 50 01
Before the exit to La Coquille,
you can slake your thirst and
enjoy a taste of delicious
local cheese at the first house
on the right. Go and visit
Dominique Bost. He makes
refreshing, home-made apple
juice costing 12 F for 1½
pints (1 litre) and wonderful
goat's milk cheese (7.50 F a
portion).

Sorges
The capital of the truffle
*9½ miles (15 km)
S of Thiviers*
Musée de la Truffe
☎ 05 53 05 90 11
Open July-Aug.,
9.30am–noon and
2.30–6.30pm; for
the rest of the year,
10am–noon and
2–5pm: closed Mon.
Admission charge.
The truffle museum was not

Spotcheck
E1

Dordogne

Things to do
The Foie Gras Museum
Discovering the stars
The Jumilhac gold mine
The Truffle Museum

Within easy reach
*Brantôme, 16¼ miles
(26 km) SW, p. 136.
Vallée de l'Auvézère 15.6
miles (25 km) S, p. 142.*

Tourist Office
Thiviers: ☎ 05 53 55 12 50

opened in Sorges by accident.
Truffles grew here by the ton
at the beginning of the last
century, though only a few
hundred pounds are harvested
today. The museum uses
various media to convey the
information (including slide
shows and cartoons) and not
only tells you how to select
and eat your truffles, but
also supplies a list of truffle
restaurants for you to try.
There is also a 2-mile (3 km)
walk through a nearby truffle
ground (p. 19).

THE GOLD RUSH
Musée de l'Or, Jumilhac
*12 miles (19 km)
NW of Thiviers*
☎ 05 53 52 55 43
Open daily, mid-June–
mid-Sept., 10.30am–
12.30pm and 2.30–
6.30pm; Sun. and public
holidays, mid-Apr.–mid-
June and mid-Sept.–mid-
Oct., 3–6pm (informa-
tion at the Tourist Office).
Admission charge.
**Turn yourself into a
gold prospector! There's**
gold in the earth of
Jumilhac. One mine is
operational and can be
visited by appointment.
(Mines du Bourneix,
☎ 05 55 09 31 00).
Half-day lessons in
panning for gold in the
river are organised
every summer (informa-
tion at the Tourist
Office). But before going
off to make your for-
tune, learn more about
it at the Musée de l'Or
(gold museum), in the
cellars of the château.

Les Eyzies and the Vézère valley

land of the caveman

L es Eyzies and the Vézère valley contain more than 100 prehistoric sites. A tour of them will take you back 400,000 years in human history. To prevent sensory overload, begin at the very informative Musée des Eyzies. Early humans found caves and natural shelters in the cliffs of the Vézère valley to protect themselves from the cold and dangerous animals, and for this reason Les Eyzies-de-Tayac-Sireuil has become the world capital of prehistory in the centre of the so-called 'Valley of Early Man'.

Map labels: Lascaux I · Lascaux II · La Madeleine · La Roque Saint-Christophe · Commarque · Château de Beynac · Le Bugue · Bara-Bahau · Les Eyzies-de-Tayac · Grottes de Font-de-Gaume/Combarelles · Village du Bournat · Proumeyssac

---

Les Eyzies-de-Tayac-Sireuil

Prehistoric beginnings

28 miles (45 km) SE of Périgueux

The village stretches along a cliff in which there are caves about half-way up. This is where prehistoric science was born, thanks to the excavations which began in 1863. The capital of prehistory is packed with visitors in summer but don't let this deter you.

Grotte de Font-de-Gaume

At the exit from Les Eyzies to Sarlat
☎ 05 53 06 90 80
Open daily exc. Wed., Nov.–Feb., 10.am–noon and 2–5pm; Apr.–Sept., 9am–noon and 2–6pm; Oct. and March, 9.30am–noon and 2–5.30pm. Only 200 visitors a day allowed, book several days in advance. *Admission charge.*

This corridor-shaped cave 400 ft (120 m) long, was inhabited by Cro-Magnon man who painted and engraved a wonderful frieze of bison and other animals in a series of different poses and groups. Instruments measuring the humidity and a limit on the number of visitors help protect the drawings made by our ancestors.

Grotte des Combarelles

☎ 05 53 06 90 80
Same times as Grotte de Font-de-Gaume, by appointment.

Only 60 visitors a day.
Admission charge.
Tickets sold at Font-de-Gaume.
This 'art gallery' exhibits pictures of mammoths, bison, horses and mountain-goats. At the back of the cave, there are nearly 300 figures in a space 233 ft (70 m) wide. You can even see a few human faces.

National Museum of Prehistory
Château de Tayac
☎ 05 53 06 45 45

Open daily exc. Tues., July–Aug., 9.30–7pm; for the rest of the year, 9.30am–noon and 2–6pm (5pm from mid-Nov.–mid-March).
Admission charge.
This museum situated in an old 13th-C. fort, is guarded by a statue representing Primitive Man. The display

cases exhibit artefacts that he carelessly discarded. The collection is magnificent; this is the largest museum of prehistory in the world. It's extremely informative, educational and is an absolute must for any visitor to the so-called 'Valley of Early Man'.

Commarque
A ramble through the ruins
4½ miles (7 km)
E of Les Eyzies
If you like wandering through romantic landscapes, visit the Château de Commarque (12th C.), which was once heavily fortified. The ruins are beautifully maintained. The Château de Laussel (15th and 16th C.) is also in good condition. At its feet lie the prehistoric remains of Laussel where the famous *Horned Venus* was found. There is a plaster cast of it in the Musée des Eyzies.

Le Bugue
Aquarium du Périgord Noir
6½ miles (10 km) SW of Les Eyzies
☎ 05 53 07 10 74
Open daily, Feb.–March and Oct.–mid-Nov., 10am–5pm; April–May and Sept., 10am–noon; June–Aug., 9am–7pm (open at night Jul.–Aug.).
Admission charge.
The open air aquarium is spectacular. As you walk through glass tunnels, you

Spotcheck
F2

Dordogne

Things to do
Caves and prehistoric sites
National Museum of Prehistory
The village of Bournat
The ravine of Proumeyssac
Canoeing down the Vézère

With children
The Aquarium of Black Périgord

Within easy reach
Trémolat, 6½ miles (10 km) SW, p. 132.

Tourist Office
Les Eyzies-de-Tayac-Sireuil:
☎ 05 53 06 97 05

have the impression of moving among shoals of fish in the rivers of Périgord, France and Europe. There's a breeding centre in a laboratory which is also surrounded by glass.

✿ The village of Bournat
☎ 05 53 08 41 99
Open all year round except Jan.; May–Sept., 10am–7pm; Oct.–April., 10am–5pm.
Admission charge.
Go back in time and discover the simple life of a village in Périgord a hundred years ago. All the old occupations are demonstrated by artisans, the

tools are genuine museum pieces and the sets (with characters in action) are very lifelike. See the nut-grinder, the still and the bread oven.

Grotte de Bara-Bahau
Route de Bergerac
☎ 05 53 07 44 58
Open daily, July–Aug., 9am–7pm; Sept.–Dec., 10am–noon and 2–5pm; Feb.–June, 10am–noon and 2–5.30pm.
Admission charge.
In the *langue d'oc*, the word *bara-bahau* imitates a man falling or an avalanche of rocks. This is a gallery 394 feet long (120 m) in which cave-bears hibernated and left deep claw-marks. The very soft rock also enabled early man to carve animals as well as mysterious signs and symbols.

Gouffre de Proumeyssac
2 miles (3 km) S of Le Bugue
☎ 05 53 07 27 47

Open daily, July–Aug., 9am–7pm; Sept., Oct., March–May, 9.30am–noon and 2–5.30pm; Nov., Dec., and Feb., 2–5pm; visit lasts 45 min.
Admission charge.

If you like excitement, try descending into this ravine, 173 ft (52 m) deep, in a four-person cage (book in advance). The more cautious may prefer to use the access tunnel to explore this under-ground chamber decorated with ochre and white stalactites and stalagmites.

La Roque Saint-Christophe

The troglodyte caves
6½ miles (10 km) NE of Les Eyzies
☎ 05 53 50 70 45
Open daily, 10am–6.30pm in season (7pm July–Aug.); for the rest of the year, 11am–5pm.
Admission charge.
This is the largest collection of inhabited caves in Europe, carved into a towering cliff 267 ft (80 m) high which dominates the valley of the Vézère. A hundred cavities in five layers, one above the other, reveal the level of human occupation over several thousands of years.

CANOEING DOWN THE VÉZÈRE
**Bases de la FFCK, Les Eyzies
(at the road bridge)**
☎ 05 53 06 92 92.
**Loisirs Évasion, Les Eyzies
15, Av. du Cingle**
☎ 05 53 06 92 64.

The cliff served as a place of refuge in turbulent times and could hold up to 1,500 people. It is easy to climb as far as the fourth level, 115 ft (35 m) above the river.

The Magdalenians
☎ 05 53 06 92 49
Open daily, July–Aug., 9.30am–7pm: out of season, 10am–6pm.
Admission charge.
At the foot of the cliff, which contains caves that were inhabited until the mid-20th C., there is the prehistoric deposit which gave its name to a very specific era, the Magdalenian era (15,000 to 10,000 BC.). The artefacts discovered in the caves are displayed in the Museum of Les Eyzies, and visitors are invited to take the footpath to explore one of the clefts in the rock, on the face of the cliff.

Tursac

Le Préhisto-Parc
3½ miles (6 km) NE of Les Eyzies
☎ 05 53 50 73 19

Canoeing centres flour-ish along the Vézère, which is not surprising as it is the best way of discovering the 'Valley of Early Man'. The roads are hot and dusty; paddle gently down-stream and relax between trips. You can choose an excursion lasting two hours (60 F), half a day (160 F) or a whole day (260 F). The prices given are for two-person canoes.

DISCOVERING LASCAUX II

Montignac-Lascaux
*15½ miles (25 km)
NE of Les Eyzies*
☎ 05 53 51 96 23
Open daily exc. Mon.,
end Jan.–March and
Oct.–Dec., 10am–
12.30pm and 2–6pm;
daily Apr.–Sept., 9am–
7pm. *Admission charge.*
12 September, 1940
was a great day in the
study of prehistory.
Four boys looking for
their dog, wandered into
a cave and discovered
amazing coloured rock
paintings, over 15,000
years old. Montignac-
Lascaux immediately
became known as the
'prehistoric Sistine
Chapel'. But the find has
been a victim of its own
success, in spite of the
many precautionary
measures taken, such as
air conditioning, low
lights etc. Over a million

visitors between 1948
and 1963 came close to
destroying the paintings,
and the cave was there-
fore closed to the public.
A lifesize reconstruction
makes it possible for
people to enjoy this

masterpiece. Two of the
chambers have been
copied in this way. The
ticket also covers the
Thiot prehistory park.

Le Thot

Espace Cro-Magnon

*13½ miles (22 km)
NE of Les Eyzies*
☎ 05 53 50 70 44
Open daily, Apr.–Sept.,
10am–7pm; Oct.–2 Jan
and 25 Jan.–March,
daily exc. Mon.,
10am–12.30pm and
1.30–5.30pm.
Admission charge.
An indispensable
accompaniment
to a visit to
Lascaux, this
place deserves
at least half a
day of your time.
Several panels of the
reconstructed cave
paintings here are good
facsimiles of the galleries
not reproduced at
Lascaux II. The Espace
Cro-Magnon also
reconstructs scenes from
daily life in prehistoric
times and has a little zoo
inhabited by the direct
descendants of prehistoric
animals – deer, bison,
roebuck and horses.

Open March–11 Nov.,
10am–6pm.
Admission charge.
If you have had your
fill of caves, you can
go on a family
outing and get some
fresh air, while
still keeping a
prehistoric theme.
Throughout this
park you'll find
life-size tableaux,
each one the
re-creation of a
scene in the life
of Neanderthal
and Cro-Magnon
man. The setting,
the animals and the
people are all based
on the very latest
discoveries made by
archaeologists. The park
was designed by a palaeon-
tologist, so it's very accurate.
Children will love it.

Les Causses and la Vézère

the land of Jacquou le Croquant

Jacquou le Croquant is the hero of a Périgord myth, the story of a boy who revolted against the tyranny of the local overlords, and is set in the Barade forest. You can follow the footsteps of Jacquou and walk through the forest to the Château de l'Herm, chosen by Eugénie le Roy to serve as the Count of Nansac's den.

[Illustrated map showing: Rastignac, Losse, Saint-Armand-de-Coly, Saint-Geniès, Salignac-Eyvigues, Eyrignac]

former home of the de Salignac de la Mothe-Fénelon family. Hardly anything remains of the original 11th-C. citadel, but the château was rebuilt in the 15th and 17th C., and is magnificent. An **old-fashioned fair** is held here in early August.

Salignac-Eyvigues
A fair at the château
12 miles (19 km) NW of Sarlat
Tourist Office
☎ 05 53 28 81 93
Open daily except Tues., July–Aug., 10.30am–noon and 2–6pm.
Admission charge.
The château stands on a limestone outcrop and is the

Eyrignac
An old garden restored
☎ 05 53 28 99 71
Open daily, 1 April–31 May, 10am–noon and 2–7pm: June–Sept., 9.30am–7pm; Oct.–Mar., 10.30am–12.30pm and 2.30pm until nightfall.
Admission charge.
The neglected 18th-C. gardens were restored to their former

glory by the father of the present owner. They show signs of various influences: French in the the flower-beds in front of the 17th-C. manor house, Italian in the various shapes and settings and English in the touch of fantasy.

Saint-Geniès
Typical Périgord village and mill
10 miles (16 km)
N of Sarlat

This is a typical Périgord village with its château and its cottages with stone-tiled roofs huddled next to a Romanesque church with a fortified bell-tower. The Gothic chapel of Cheylard has lovely 14th-C. frescoes of the life of Christ and the saints. If you like freshly baked **old-fashioned bread**, take a trip to La Coste mill (1½ miles (2 km) from Saint-Geniès), one of the last working water-mills. It mills wheat using flint grinding stones. On Friday and Saturday evenings you can buy organic or wholemeal bread at 16 to 18 F for 2 lb 4 oz (1 kg). ☎ 05 53 28 96 64. Visits to the mill daily, except Sun.).

Saint-Amand-de-Coly
The warrior church
15½ miles (25 km)
N of Sarlat

The abbey-church is monumental in comparison with the size of the village. This fortified religious building, which is a lovely yellow colour, is the most surprising in Périgord. The church was turned into a fortress in the 14th C., as can be seen from the impressive castle keep with its defence room that is now used for concerts organised by the Festival de

Musique du Périgord Noir which brings enthusiasts from all over Europe.

The coppersmith
Le Bourg
☎ 05 53 51 66 48
Open Mon.–Fri., 8am–noon and 2–6.30pm (7pm in season).

At Saint-Amand-de-Coly, everyone can hear when the coppersmith is at work. He hammers his copper and brass by hand, forming the sheets of metal into saucepans, fish-kettles and preserving pans (casserole-saucepan, about 385 F; frying pan, 7 in (18 cm), 510 F). **Alain Lagorsse** sells at local fairs and festivals and has a stall in the Sarlat market on Saturday.

Losse
Renaissance château
17 miles (27 km)
NW of Sarlat
☎ 05 53 50 80 08
Open Apr., May and Sept., daily 10am–12.30pm and 1.30–5pm; June–Aug., daily 10am–7pm.
Admission charge.

This medieval fortress, built on a sheer cliff overlooking the Vézère, was transformed into an elegant château in the 16th C. (*see photo below*). A handsome flight of stone steps leads to the Renaissance building and the apartments are

Spotcheck
F2

Dordogne

Things to do
Fairs and festivals
The gardens of Eyrignac
La Coste mill
Visit a coppersmith

Within easy reach
Vallée de l'Auvézère, p. 142.

Tourist Office
Salignac-Eyvigues:
☎ 05 53 28 81 93

CHÂTEAU DE L'HERM
Rouffignac,
Tourist Office
☎ 05 53 51 66 48
The remains of the Château de l'Herm (16th C.) nestle in the Forêt Barade, scene of the mythical adventures of Jacquou. Legend has it that in protest against injustice and poverty, the tenant farmers, lead by Jacquou, attacked the castle of the ferocious count of Nansac and burned it down. Cross the moat to the remaining tower and monumental staircase. The château can be visited in summer during the restoration work.

beautifully furnished with 16th-C. furniture. The château is sometimes used for performances and events, such as the Montignac **Festival de folklore** in July.

Sarlat

Sarlat is an exceptional town and by far the most important tourist attraction in Périgord. This jewel of medieval architecture offers you a trip into the past. There are sculpted gable-ends, mullioned windows, roofs of stone tiles and walls of pale yellow limestone, making the town a classic example of urban architecture of the 15th and 17th C. The town, once surrounded by a wall, has retained its heart-shaped layout, although it is bisected by the busy shopping street Rue de la République (or the Traverse). The town is particularly crowded in summer, so that there is hardly room to move in the streets. It's better to visit out of season.

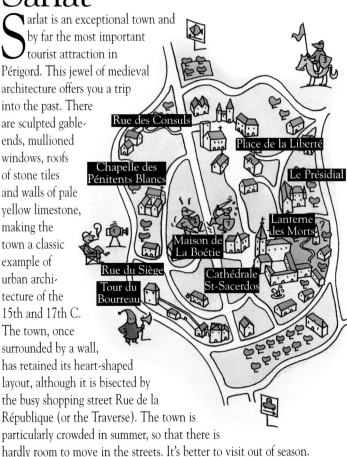

Rue des Consuls

Place de la Liberté

Chapelle des Pénitents Blancs

Le Présidial

Lanterne des Morts

Maison de La Boétie

Rue du Siège

Cathédrale St-Sacerdos

Tour du Bourreau

Maison de La Boétie

Three listed buildings face the former archbishopric and the cathedral of Saint-Sacerdos. The most beautiful is the Maison de La Boétie. This is where Sarlat's most famous son was born in 1530: Étienne de La Boétie was a friend of Montaigne. The house is used for exhibitions in summer.

La Lanterne des Morts

Leaving the chapel of the Pénitents-Bleus (in pure Romanesque style) go through the

courtyard of the Fontaines et des Chanoines. A passageway will lead you into the Jardin des Enfeux which is guarded by the Lanterne des Morts. This 12th-C. tower, topped by a cone-shaped roof, is said by some to commemorate the visit by Saint Bernard in 1147, while others believe it was a funerary chapel, but no one is certain. From the landscaped garden next to the tower there is a lovely view of the cathedral and various courtyards.

The Présidial and its surroundings

Nos 2 and 4 of the Rue d'Albusse are a triple gatehouse housing an exhibition about General Fournier-Sarlovèze. The Hôtel de Grerel in the corner of the Rue Salamandre and the Hôtel de Génis at 6 Rue du Présidial are also worth a look. The Présidial, the court established by Henri II in 1552, has two loggia windows topped by a turret and a façade covered with Viriginia creeper. It is now an antique shop.

Place de la Liberté

This handsome square is lined with old buildings with arcades on the ground floor,

many of which are now used as cafés and shops selling local produce. It has been used as a location for many films shot in Périgord and is the centre of the Festival des Jeux du Théâtre. The 16th-C. hotel Chassaing is one of the loveliest buildings. From the end of July to early August, Sarlat hosts a theatre festival at which the French classics

are performed. The Tourist Office is housed in the Hôtel de Vienne, a little Renaissance château.

The market, the pulse of the town

The **market**, held in the square on Wednesday mornings and Saturdays, is unfortunately the victim of its own success and in summer is jampacked by 10am.

So be brave, get up with the lark and experience this market where people come to browse as much as to bargain. At the right time of year you'll find ceps, foie gras and the mythical truffle, but be vigilant: some vendors profit from innocent tourists by selling them dubious merchandise. If you like truffles, learn to distinguish between good ones and bad ones (see p. 19).

Rue des Consuls

This was once the main road in which the gentry lived. The houses vie with each other for your attention. At no. 9 in the little **Place des Oies**, is the 15th-C. **Hôtel de Vassal** which is certainly the most picturesque residence in the town. The **Hôtel de Plamon** now contains the recently-opened Musée du Sarladais. It faces the Fontaine Sainte-Marie and the 15th-C. **Hôtel de Mirandol**. The **Hôtel Tapinois-de-Betou** has a wooden staircase which you should try to catch a glimpse of, if you are passing.

Geese *by the sculptor Lalanne*

Spotcheck
F3

Dordogne

Things to do

The market at Sarlat
Moulin de la Tour

Within easy reach

*Bastides du Périgord,
p. 162.*

Tourist Office

Sarlat:
☎ 05 53 31 45 45

The salamander

You will often come across this little lizard in the city of Sarlat. This is because it

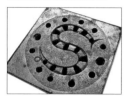

symbolized the reign of King François I (1515–1547). In the 15th C., the seal of Sarlat carried an 'S' surmounted by three fleur-de-lys. In 1523, the 'S' was replaced by the salamander on the arms of the city in order to mark its allegiance and loyalty to the king of France.

Rue du Siège

This street consists of a row of old houses, including, at the corner of the Rue des Trois-Conils, the 17th-C. Hôtel de Cerval. The Rue du

Siège runs close to the ramparts, topped with the Tour du Bourreau. Further on, in the Rue des Trois-Conils, no. 2 used to be a house of ill repute. However, on a more serious note, take a look at the Hôtel de Marsac, with its 15th-C. tower and attractive spiral staircase. Before you return to the Traverse, venture down the passage into the Place Liarsou.

The chapel of the Pénitents-Blancs

A 15th-C. half-timbered building in the Rue des Armes seems to occupy the whole street. Take the Rue de la Charité to the picturesque Rue Jean-Jacques-Rousseau via the baroque chapel of the Pénitents-Blancs which houses the Musée d'Art Sacré (17th-C. portico). After visiting the 17th-C. Hôtel Monmeja, the 17th-C. convent of Sainte-Claire with its turret with corbels, take the Rue de La-Boétie and admire the lovely little garden at the junction of these two streets.

Jardin du Plantier

A lovely place for a rest. It's cool and pleasant to linger here, while admiring the lovely view over the rooftops of Sarlat.

Sainte-Nathalène

The Moulin de la Tour

5½ miles (9 km) from Sarlat
☎ 05 53 59 22 08
Visit to the factory every Fri., Oct.–March, 9am– noon and 2–6.30pm; Apr.–June and Sept., every Wed. and Fri.; July–Aug., every Mon., Wed., Fri., Sat. (afternoons).

STUDIOS IN THE OPEN AIR

The cinema has a important place in the Sarlat district. More than 30 French films have been made in the capital of Black Périgord, making it the third most popular film location in the country, after Paris and Nice. Lights, camera, action!

Admission charge.
This tour will introduce you to one of the last craftsmen making authentic nut oils by hand. Jean-Pierre Bordier and his wife continue to make oil the old-fashioned way in their lovely 16th-C. mill. If you feel tempted to buy a bottle, the delicious walnut, hazelnut or almond oil will make your salads and stir-fries taste really exquisite and are also an aid to digestion.

ADVICE TO GOURMETS: BEWARE OF FAST FOOD!
When you visit Périgord in general, and Sarlat, in particular, you expect to be served good foie gras, confit and local wines. But if you're a tourist, beware of mouth-watering signs, especially in summer. Remember that good foie gras is expensive and set menus at less than 100 F probably have nothing miraculous about them.

Saint-André-d'Allas

The *bories* of Le Breuil

3 miles (5 km) W of Sarlat

On the road to Les Eyzies, the hamlet of Le Breuil Eyzies has one of the best collections of *bories* (drystone shepherds' huts) in Périgord. These flat-stone constructions are circular and are built using no mortar and their stone-tiled vaulted roofs are conical in shape. The examples found here are superbly preserved and there are several dozen of them, in groups of two or three. Used mainly as temporary shelters, sheepfolds or huts, they are evidence of an ancient pastoral civilisation which remains shrouded in mystery.

Puymartin

The haunted château

3½ miles (6 km) from Sarlat, Route des Eyzies
☎ 05 53 59 29 97
Open daily, Apr.–Oct., 10am–noon and 2–6.30pm.
Admission charge.

This is one of the very few haunted châteaux in Périgord. Some claim to have seen the ghost of a woman walking on the ramparts. Apparently her jealous husband walled her up here many centuries ago. However, you can rest assured that you won't find anything frightening on a daytime visit to the château!

However, you *can* be sure of seeing some lovely furniture, and a little bedroom whose walls are completely covered with 17th-C. paintings of mythological subjects.

The Dordogne valley
fortified châteaux

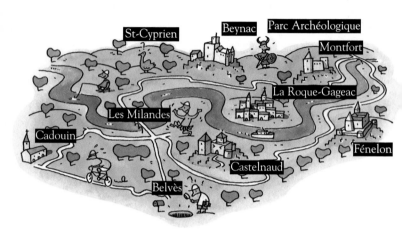

St-Cyprien · Beynac · Parc Archéologique · Montfort · La Roque-Gageac · Les Milandes · Cadouin · Castelnaud · Fénelon · Belvès

T he valley of the Dordogne in southern Périgord is a district of rivers, lovely views and châteaux. If you look up from the Dordogne river, you will see castles towering above the wooded banks on either side, making use of the high cliffs to establish their defensive positions.

Cadouin
Abbey and hall
☎ 05 53 63 36 28
Open daily, July–Aug., 10am–7pm. Phone for opening times out of season.
The village is famous for its 12th-C. Cistercian abbey. The cloister is a masterpiece

of flamboyant Gothic style and is beautifully preserved. The abbey was an important pilgrimage centre because it had the privilege of owning a relic of the Sindon (shroud) of Christ (see below). The convent also has a penny-farthing bicycle museum. Don't leave Cadouin without taking a look at the village **market hall** which has impressive stone pillars (*photo left*).

A holy shroud
The relic is in a vase near to the lance that pierced Jesus' side. A priest brought it back to France from the First Crusade (1096–1099). The sacred piece of linen was deposited at Cadouin in the 16th C. For centuries, thousands of pilgrims revered it,

but in 1933, it was subjected to expert examination and was found to be a fake. As a final irony, it bore 11th-C. Moslem inscriptions giving praise to Allah!

Belvès
The troglodyte caves
☎ 05 53 29 10 20
Rooms open daily, 15 June–15 Sept., 10.30am–noon and 3–7pm; guided tours by appointment. *Admission charge.*
This pretty medieval village with Gothic and Renaissance houses and gardens full of flowerbeds, stands on a rocky outcrop. The cellars are honeycombed with caves which were inhabited during

Spotcheck
E3-F3

Dordogne

Things to do

The troglodyte caves
The Campagnac goose farm
The walnut museum
Fishing in the Dordogne

Within easy reach

*Bastides de Périgord,
p. 162.*

Tourist Office

Beynac: ☎ 05 53 29 43 08

the Middle Ages (seven rooms have been restored).

Saint-Cyprien
The goose village

This is a typical village of the Sarlat district, with old houses and an animated **market** on Sunday mornings. About a mile (1.5 km) from Saint-Cyprien, Marc and Marcelle Boureau breed geese. If you are not disturbed by the

fattening process, you can view it at 2pm or 8.30pm (in spring and autumn). Mme Boureau also makes *confits* which cost 147 F for a 6 oz (170 g) can of goose foie gras (Ferme de Campagnac, ☎ 05 53 29 26 03).

Les Milandes
Château des Milandes

☎ 05 53 59 31 21
Open daily, June–Aug., 9am–noon; Apr., May and Sept., 10am–6pm; March, Oct.,–mid-Nov., 10am–noon and 2–5pm.
Admission charge.
It was in this 15th–19-C. château that Josephine Baker set up her 'world village' in the 1950s to raise children of different nationalities whom

she had adopted. The 18 acre (7 ha) park slopes down to the Dordogne river and has beautiful formal gardens. Part of the château is dedicated to the life of the artists, and another contains a museum of falconry (with demonstrations of birds of prey in full flight).

Castelnaud
The château

☎ 05 53 31 30 00
Open daily March–Apr., Oct.–mid-Nov. and school holidays, 10am–6pm; May, June and Sept., 10am–7pm; 9am–8pm in July–Aug.; mid-Nov.– Feb., 2–5pm (exc. Sat.).
Admission charge.
This magnificent château dominates the Dordogne and overlooks one of the loveliest landscapes in the valley. One's eye is immediately drawn to Beynac, its rival. The two fortresses confronted each other throughout the Middle Ages. The château houses a

museum tracing the history of the wars. In the summer you can watch a show of weapon-handling (in the afternoons), and attend historical recon-structions (evenings).

The Écomusée of Périgord Walnuts

Ferme de Vielcroze
☎ 05 53 59 69 63
Open April–Oct., 10am–7pm.
Admission charge.

Do you know what a *tricot* is? It's a little mallet used by the walnut harvesters to break open the walnuts. To learn all there is to know about the walnut, its cultivation, varieties and the use of walnut wood, visit this museum. The walk through the walnut grove lasts an hour. You can buy a variety of products made from walnut as well as other woods.

Beynac
The ochre château
☎ 05 53 29 50 40
Open daily, 15 Mar.–15 Nov., 10am–5pm (6.30pm in summer). All visitors get a guided tour, exc. at 12.15pm when entry is free with a booklet; 1 Dec. –14 March, 11.30am– 4.30pm (not guided). *Admission charge.*
The enormous mass of the splendid 12th-C. château clings to the clifftop like an eagle's nest (*see photo below*) and dominates the town.

A TRIP ON A BARGE
Beynac
☎ 05 53 28 51 15
Apr.–Oct., 10am–6pm, departure every 30 min. in season (every hour out of season).
Admission charge (mornings free for children under 12).
Embark at the end of the car park. The trip lasts about 50 minutes. The barge sails up the Dordogne towards Castelnaud, and offers another way of discovering the delights of the river.

You'll have to leave your car and climb up through the village to admire the magnificent view from the château. Opposite stands the château de **Fayrac** and behind it that of **Castelnaud**.

Lives of the ancient Gauls
Le Parc Archéologique
☎ 05 53 29 51 28
Open daily exc. Sat., 1 July–15 Sept., 10am– 7pm. *Admission charge.*

This theme park shows how the ancient Gauls lived thousands of years ago. Houses of wattle and daub, hand-tools, barns, the forge – everything here is lifesize. Children will find learning about history this way more interesting than reading their textbooks!

Marqueyssac
Château and park
☎ 05 53 31 36 36
Open daily May, June, Sept., 10am–7pm: July–Oct., 9am–8pm; Oct.–mid-May. and mid-Feb–April, 10am–6pm; mid-Nov–mid-Feb., 2–5pm. *Admission charge.*
The château faces Castelnaud in one of the most beautiful spots in Black Périgord, overlooking the road which runs beside the Dordogne.
The 15th-C. round tower and 17th-C. gatehouse

are extremely beautiful, as are the magnificent **gardens** designed by a pupil of Le Nôtre. They cover 54 acres (22 ha), with 3½ miles (6 km) of avenues and a view over the whole valley. The château is not open to visitors.

sunset the village is lit up and the stones take on a golden glow. As you climb the cliff you'll encounter an exotic garden, something totally unexpected. Thanks to the microclimate of La Roque-Gageac, there are palm-trees as well as cactuses, orange trees and oleanders.

Montfort

Château de Montfort

☎ 05 53 28 33 11
Daily visits to the park and the ramparts, July–Aug., 10am–7pm; June–Oct., 10am–noon and 2–6pm. *Admission charge.*
Montfort has been destroyed

is one of the most famous in the Dordogne valley.

✿ Château de Fénelon

☎ 05 53 29 81 45
Open daily, 9.30am–7pm June–Sept.; 10am–noon and 2–6pm rest of the year. *Admission charge.*
This château, begun in the 14th C. and completed in the 17th C., displays the severity of a medieval fortress, with its double curtain-wall, and the harmony of a Renaissance home. The stone tiling of the roof is superb. Part of the château interior can be visited.

FISHING IN THE DORDOGNE

The Fédération de la Dordogne pour la Pêche et la Protection du Milieu Aquatique, 2, Rue Antoine-Gadaud, Périgueux ☎ 05 53 53 44 21
With its two rivers, the Dordogne and the Vézère, its 2,500 miles (4,000 km) of waterways and its eight municipal ponds, the valley is an angler's paradise. But be sure to fish at dawn. There are so many people canoeing and generally messing about in boats that the fish are frightened away later in the day. You must buy a fishing permit (about 183 F from tackle shops) and don't try and sell your catch or you will be liable to a fine of between 1,000 F and 10,000 F.

La Roque-Gageac

The exotic garden

☎ 05 53 29 17 01 (Tourist Office).
Guided tour.
The houses are squeezed between the river and the steep cliff. At sunrise and

and rebuilt several times and it still stands thanks to its 19th-C. restoration. The Montfort meander

Château de Montfort

Bastides of Périgord

a war-torn past

The *bastides* were fortified towns built by kings in areas where they felt their rule was under threat. These new towns were designed to guard, control and work the land. Built in a grid pattern, with a central arcaded square and a fortified church, they

were surrounded by curtain-walls and gates. The town no longer centred around the church, but the public square in which the market was held.

Monpazier

The *bastide*

28 miles (45 km) SE of Bergerac
Information at the Tourist Office.
Open daily, June–Sept., 10.30am–5pm; Oct.–May, by appointment.
This *bastide* was founded in 1284 by King Edward I of England to colonise the regions between Agenais and Périgord. Try and see everything: the market-hall, the church of Saint-Dominique, the gates to the town, the 32 historic monuments. From the end of July to the beginning of August, the region holds the **Festival de musique du Périgord pourpre**. Don't miss the **cep market**, held every day from 3pm in Aug. and Sept. in the market hall.

Biron

Château de Biron

5 miles (8 km) S of Monpazier
☎ **05 53 63 13 39**
Open daily, July–Aug., except Mon., 10am–noon and 1.30–5.30pm (until 7pm Apr.–June and Sept.–1 Nov.). Closed 3–25 Jan.

Admission charge.
Contemporary art exhibition in July–Aug. The château (*see photo below*) was begun in the 12th C. and continued expanding over the centuries. It comprises a group of buildings of very different styles built by 14 generations of the Biron family. The village which surrounds the château has preserved some magnificent Renaissance houses.

A MUSHROOMING WEEKEND

Villefranche-du-Périgord.
You may know how to spot ceps in the market, but it's much more fun to find them in the wild. Learn here in the woods on a 'Connaissance des Champignons' weekend organised by the Comité Départemental du Tourisme (☎ 05 53 35 50 05) in summer and autumn. The weekend with accommodation costs around 1,300 F.

Domme

The acropolis of Black Périgord

6½ miles (10 km) S of Sarlat

This *bastide* was built on a clifftop by the French king Philippe le Hardi in 1281. Its lanes are lined with **ochre-coloured houses** (Maison des Gouverneurs, Place de la Halle). Take a walk on the ramparts to the Del-Bos gate, the Combe gate and the Tours gate, which was used as a prison by the Templar Knights. Past the church, the terrace of La Barre offers a **magnificent view** from Beynac to Castelnaud.

The Domme caves

Place de la Halle
☎ 05 53 31 71 00
(Tourist Office)
Open daily, July–Aug., 10am–7pm: 1 April–30 June and 1 Sept.–mid-Nov., 10am–noon and 2–6pm; mid-Nov–Apr. and school holidays. *Admission charge.*

The caves lie under the town and there's an entrance in the old market-hall. You'll feel the cold amidst the stalactites even in summer. A lift, which some say has disfigured the cliff, gives a **spectacular view** of the valley. On leaving the caves, don't take the Promenade du Jubilé if you suffer from vertigo, the view is startling!

Eymet

A British colony

12½ miles (20 km) S of Bergerac

This pretty *bastide* was built in the 13th C. by the French to oppose the numerous *bastides* which had been built in the region by the English. Ironically, it is now home to a colony of British people. Is it the charm of the town (with its lovely square) or the reasonable price of the houses that attracts the British here? At any event, they are here and they have even started a cricket club. If you like **antiques**, there's a market in the Place d'Eymet on the 3rd Sunday in July.

Spotcheck

E3-F3

Dordogne

Things to do

Music festival
The cep market
Antiques in Eymet
Chestnut museum
Mushrooming weekend
The Domme caves

Within easy reach

Sarlat, p. 154,
Valley of the Dordogne,
p. 158.

Tourist Office

Monpazier:
☎ 05 53 22 68 59

Villefranche-du-Périgord

Chestnuts and wild mushrooms

12½ miles (20 km) E of Monpazier
☎ 05 53 29 98 37

In season, open daily exc. Sun. and Mon. afternoon, 9.30am–12.30pm and 3–6.30pm; out of season, open daily exc. Weds., Sun. afternoon and Mon. afternoon, 9.30am–noon and 3–6pm. *Admission charge for the museum.*

This *bastide* is surrounded by oak and chestnut **forests** and is famous for its **cep market** (in the market-hall). It also has a museum of chestnuts and mushrooms which also has varying displays featuring the uses for chestnut wood.

Bastides and châteaux of Agenais

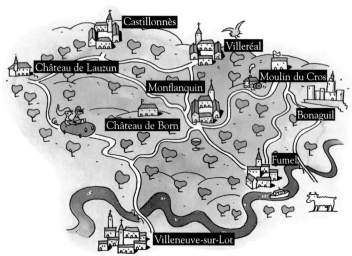

Castillonnès

Villeréal

Château de Lauzun

Monflanquin

Moulin du Cros

Château de Born

Bonaguil

Fumel

Villeneuve-sur-Lot

The *bastides* of Agenais have remained unchanged for centuries and are reminiscent of the era when the region was fought over interminably by the English and French. Alphonse de Poitiers, the counts of Toulouse and the kings of England founded most of the *bastides*. This trip through Black Périgord will enable you to explore wonderfully preserved *bastides*. You can also taste the local plums and the regional wines.

Lauzun

The young Gascon

7½ miles (12 km)
W of Castillonnès
☎ 05 53 94 18 89
Open daily, 11 July–
22 Aug, 10am–noon
and 2–6pm
Admission charge.
The village entered history when a young Gascon became a celebrated courtier at the court of Louis XIV, and was made a marshal of France and a duke. Only the Renaissance wing of the château is open to the public.

Castillonnès

Guarding the Dropt

The *bastide* dominates the Dropt valley. From the **promenade de la Mouthe** on the ramparts there's a quite beautiful **view** of the valley.

Donkey sanctuary

2 miles (3 km) from Castillonnès
Asinerie de Pinseguerre Douzains
☎ 05 53 36 92 35
By appointment only.
Donkeys are said to be stubborn and insist on having their own way. In fact, they simply have character. Pay them a visit at this stud farm and tour the surrounding area

THE SAILING-BARGE

The *gabare*, a sailing-barge which is the ancestor of the modern barge, the *péniche*, has a flat bottom and was used for carrying cargo on the river. In the 17th C. its use expanded when Colbert, minister to Louis XIV, ordered the Lot to be made navigable. The river crosses Quercy at Cahors then merges with the Garonne and it was an important route, but the dangerous river bed could only be negotiated by the flat-bottomed *gabares* (pp. 94 and 95).

Villeréal, has retained its 14th-C. market hall and fortified church. The Maison de Campagne, a nature museum, displays the flora and fauna of the region. The Brayssou lake (2½ miles/4 km away) is home to migrating birds and has an observatory and a lovely walk around the lake (4 miles/6.5 km).

Spotcheck
D3-E3

Lot-et-Garonne

Things to do

The Maison de Campagne
Bird sanctuary
A trip through plum country
Fairs, festivals and medieval days
Visit to a family bakery
The wines of Haut Agenais

With children

Donkey rides
Parc-en-ciel

Tourist Office

Monflanquin:
☎ 05 53 36 40 19

in a donkey-cart, unless you prefer to look around under your own steam. Donkeys have long been domesticated and used as beasts of burden, as well as delighting children by giving them rides.

Villeréal
Nature town
8 miles (13 km) E of Castillonnès
☎ 05 53 36 09 65
Open Mon.–Fri. 10am–noon and 2–5pm, by appointment. *Guided tour (free for under-16s) of the* bastide, *can be combined with a visit to the Maison de Campagne.*

Saint-Avit
Musée Bernard-Palissy
9½ miles (15 km) E. of Villeréal
☎ 05 53 40 98 22
Open daily, Jun.–Oct. and the rest of the year by appointment.
Bernard Palissy, who was born in Saint-Avit, burned his own furniture in an attempt to discover the secret of firing ceramics. He went on to become a respected ceramicist. This little museum is dedicated to him.

Lacapelle-Biron
Parc-en-ciel
1 mile (2 km) NE of Saint-Avit
☎ 05 53 71 84 58
Open Apr.–beginning Nov., daily, 10am–7pm; Nov.–March, public holidays.
Animals, games, Noah's farm, there's plenty in this park to amuse those aged between three and 14 years. If it's very hot, in July or August, you can dive into the Lougratte lake between Castillonnès and Cancon, on the N 21.

Marsal

Maison de la Vie Rurale

2½ miles (4 km) S of Monflanquin

☎ 05 53 41 90 19

Open daily, July–Aug., 3–7pm; Sat. and Sun., June–Sept., 3–7pm. *Admission charge.*

A chance to learn a little about country life. You can discover how prunes are made from plums and see the *fournial* (the room where the plums are dried

the river: a giant carp 60 in (1.50 m) long, or some grey herons.

in ovens), as well as learn how different kinds of tiles are made. You can also take a walk through the orchard containing more than 120 trees or a stroll along the banks of the river.

Fumel

Barge trips

La gabare fuméloise

☎ 05 53 71 13 70

Guided tours, daily, May–Sept; out of season, by appointment. *Admission charge.*

The first stop is the Fumel dam. The trip continues via the old industrial port of Condat, near the fortified mill of Garrigues, then the *gabare* passes the vineyards of Cahors eventually reaching the foundry and château of Fumel, overlooking the Lot. If you look carefully, you may see one of the inhabitants of

Monflanquin

An air of Tuscany

10½ miles (17 km) W of Fumel

The prettiest *bastide* in Lot-et-Garonne was founded in the 13th C. high up, and with a **superb view**. Although it has lost its ramparts and covered market, you can still admire the central square and surrounding houses as well as

the house of the Black Prince. There's always something happening at Monflanquin. There's an antiques fair on 13 and 14 July, a Festival of Music in Guyenne (2nd fortnight in July), Festival de la Tragédie (August), Journées Médiévales (August) and in December, the gargantuan Foire de la Saint-André.

Cave des Sept-Monts

Z. A. C. Mondésir Abattoir

☎ 05 53 36 33 40

Open Mon. afternoon–Sat., 9am–noon and 3–6.30pm. *Admission charge.*

The first vines were grown here in the Gallo-Roman period on the slopes of upper Agenais. The cellar of the Seven Mounts (Mondésir, Monflanquin, Monségur, Montagnac, Montaut, Monsempron, Mongahus) promotes the wines of the Agenais. The reds should be drunk when young (though they will keep for 4 to 6 years), and deserve to be better known. Expect to pay 16 to 27 F a bottle.

Montagnac-sur-Lède
Moulin du Cros

4½ miles (7 km) E of Monflanquin

☎ 05 53 36 44 78

Open July–Aug., Tues. and Thurs., 3–6pm; Mon., Wed., Fri., by appointment for groups. *Admission charge.*
Learn about the history of bread in this family bakery. Six generations of the Caumières family have been millers and bakers since 1833, always in this 16th-C mill. It has two restored millstones. The visit concludes with a **tasting** of breads flavoured with nuts, bacon, Gruyère cheese and poppyseed (for sale at around 10 F for 9 oz (250 g)).

Sauveterre-la-Lémance
Musée Laurent-Coulonges

9½ miles (15 km) N of Fumel

☎ 05 53 40 68 81
(Town Hall)

Open July–Aug., Mon., 8.30am–12.30pm; Tues.–Fri., 8.30am–12.30pm and 2.30–6.30pm (6pm Fri.). *Free admission.*
This pretty village is at the gates of Quercy and

Périgord. Prehistoric sites have been discovered in the commune, which suggest a new prehistoric culture, which has been dubbed 'sauveterrien'. A little museum in the town hall contains the archaeological finds.

Bonaguil
Château

5 miles (8 km) NE of Fumel

☎ 05 53 71 90 33

Guided tours, daily, June–Aug., 10am–6pm; Feb.–May, Sept.–Nov., 10.30am–noon and 2.30–5pm. Illuminations every evening 1 June–30 Sept., until midnight. *Admission charge.*
This impressive edifice, with its 13 towers, measures 1,166 ft (350 m) around and was the last fortified castle to be built in France (*see below*), at the end of the 15th C. by Béranger de Roquefeuil. He wanted to build a citadel that could not be captured by the English or the king of France. No one took up his challenge and the citadel was never besieged. There is an **ornithological museum** ½ mile (1 km) from the château (☎ 05 53 71 30 45, open daily

THE BEST GÂTEAU IN THE WORLD!

Odette Salesse, Bonaguil,
2 miles (1.5 km) from château (signposted 'Tourtières').

☎ 05 53 40 63 13
Demonstrations in July–Aug, daily; in winter, Thurs. and Fri. Closed Jan. and Feb.
The *tourtière* was the favourite dessert of nobles and kings in the region. It is made with pastry, apples and spirits and was traditionally eaten during the Carnival, like crêpes, in Britanny. In summer tourtières fairs attract visitors from all over the region and the local pastry-cooks spend a lot of time making these delicious apple gâteaux. Take the advice of the locals: 'A good foie gras, a *tourtière* and white wine!' From 40 F.

June–Sept., 2.30–6pm; July–Aug., 10am–7pm. admission charge).

Villeneuve-sur-Lot

How can one mention Villeneuve-sur-Lot without mentioning its speciality, the prune? However, Villeneuve is also known for another fruit, the hazelnut. Local delicacies apart, the region was heavily involved in the long conflict between English and French. Villeneuve-sur-Lot, built by the brother of St Louis, was in the front line of the battle between the French and the English and was one of the most powerful *bastides* in the South West.

Place La Fayette

This square is surrounded by several lovely 17th- and 18th-C. half-timbered houses. Visit it on **market days**, Tuesday and Saturday (Wednesday morning is the organic market day), when the stalls are overflowing with wonderful fruit and vegetables.

The church of Sainte-Catherine

The ancient Gothic church was in danger of subsidence, so it was replaced by a Romano-Byzantine edifice, the first stone of which was laid in 1898. The result is grandiose and original. The old 15th- and 16th-C. stained glass windows have been preserved in the side-chapels, 23 windows which are unique in Aquitaine.

La Tour de Paris

This is one of the four gates to the *bastide*. The town was built on a plain, but compensated for its position by having high look-out posts. You can visit the interior (guardroom and prison) which is now used as an exhibition hall. You might also enjoy a walk through such streets as the Rue de Paris.

La Boutique du Pruneau

11, Porte de Paris
☎ 05 53 70 02 75
Open Mon.–Sun. morning, 9am–noon and 2–7.30pm.
All sorts of sweetmeats made with prunes, of course. Sugar-plums can be found anywhere, but the Boutique du Pruneau, a traditional firm, has every type of sugar-plum imaginable (stuffed prunes: 14 F for 3½ oz (100 g). You can also buy vintage armagnac (from 196 F a bottle).

The National Stud

Rue de Bordeaux
☎ 05 53 70 00 91
Open Mon.–Fri., 2–6.30pm by appointment
Free admission.
The Villeneuve stud farm has about 40 thoroughbred and working stallions. There are

the aristocrats of the race course as well as provincial horses from Brittany, Percherons and Comtois carthorses. They can only be visited in the afternoon.

Jazz in Villeneuve
☎ 05 53 36 70 16
Admission charge.
Around the 14 July, Villeneuve starts to sound more like Louisiana with its traditional jazz festival. Strains of the traditional music from the bayous (zydeco) mix with Cajun music, and for four days it's New Orleans on the Lot.

(10 km/h). Electric boats can be hired on the banks of the Lot at the Ponton l'Aviron.

A trip on the Lot
Information from Tourist Office
☎ 05 53 36 17 30
You don't need to row or water-ski or race boats on the water, just go for a relaxing family outing (4–5 pers.) at a steady 6¼ mph.

SALADE GASCONNE
Choose a mixture of salad greens (chicory, curly endive, radicchio, dandelion). Combine them with thinly sliced hearts and gizzards of confit of duck, slivers of cooked duck breast or dried, smoked duck breast. Add a few cubes of toast and season with hazelnut oil, juice of ½ a lemon, salt and pepper.

Pujols
Art and antiques
2 miles (3 km) S of Villeneuve
This pretty medieval village (*see photo below*) overlooks the Lot valley. The Sunday morning **antiques market** is held in the old wooden market hall (from March to November). In summer many artists come here to exhibit and you can view their paintings whilst you browse among the antique dealers. (Antiques fair, 2nd fortnight in July).

Hazelnut farm
1½ miles (2½ km) of Pujols, towards Bias
Ferme de Vidalou
☎ 05 53 70 21 55
If you have a taste for nuts, take a visit to this farm. Its speciality is the hazelnut, from which hazelnut oil is made. A single drop improves the flavour of grilled fish or cheese and it can also be used as a seasoning for salads (48 F for 9 fl oz (25 cl).

Spotcheck
E4

Lot-et-Garonne

Things to do
Markets and sugar-plums
Visit to a stud farm
Jazz at Villeneuve
Antique fair at Pujols
Visit to a hazelnut farm

With children
A boat trip on the Lot

Within easy reach
Agen, p. 174,
Aiguillon, p. 178.

Tourist Office
Villeneuve-sur-Lot:
☎ 05 53 36 17 30

Serres

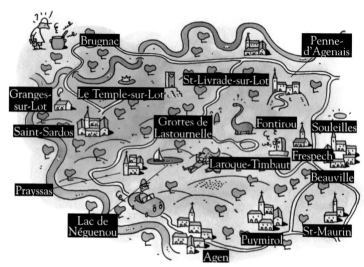

The Serres district stretches between the rivers Lot and Garonne. Some believe that the word *serre*, which means the claw of a bird of prey, refers to the rocky terrain. Others believe the word comes from the ancient language, *langue d'oc*. The many churches and abbeys are evidence of the pious nature of the inhabitants, who are also known for their hospitality.

Lac de Néguenou
2½ miles (4 km) from Prayssas
☎ 05 53 95 00 67
Open from May to Sept.
Admission charge.
In summer this is a popular place to meet due to its beach and a range of facilities, including a flume, pedalos and water-bicycles, as well as angling, mountain-biking and walking. The

little valley of the Masse, the river which feeds this 17 acre (7 ha) lake, has retained its natural charm and has banks lined with poplars.

Prayssas
Fresh fruit market
9½ miles (15 km) NW of Agen
The capital of the Serres district, this is a pretty *bastide* with an important fruit market. Its sunny slopes are famous for their peaches, apples, pears and grapes. These are celebrated at the **fruit fair**, held from the end of August to the beginning of September.

Sainte-Colombe-de-Villeneuve-sur-Lot
The caves of Lastournelle
6¼ miles (10 km) from Villeneuve-sur-Lot
☎ 05 53 40 08 09
Open daily, July–Aug., 10am–noon, 2–7pm; the rest of the year and Sun. by appointment.
Admission charge.
These natural caves contain wonderful formations of stalagmites and stalactites more than 25 million years old. Seven chambers can be

visited, including the very beautiful chamber of Columns.

Sainte-Livrade-sur-Lot
Richard the Lionheart's Tower
6¼ miles (10 km) from Villeneuve-sur-Lot
This quiet little town on the banks of the Lot is a plum-growing centre like Villeneuve-sur-Lot. The church has an astonishing Romanesque stone apse with radiating chapels. Visit the Tower of Richard the Lionheart, a tall brick tower which is all that remains of the fortifications. The little *bastide* of Monclar, 5 miles (8 km) to the north is at an altitude of 623 ft (187 m) and is worth visiting for the magnificent view.

Brugnac
The 'magic cauldron'
15½ miles (25 km) W of Villeneuve-sur-Lot
☎ 05 53 88 80 77
Open daily, July–Aug. 10am-noon and 3–6pm, and at 3pm on Sun; out of season, daily from 3pm.
Admission charge.
This 'Chaudron Magique' isn't a witches' cauldron and there's no danger of falling in. It's the cauldron in which the mohair of 250 angora goats from the farm is dyed. There are other animals, including angora rabbits, baby goats you can bottle-feed and, if you feel

like it, you can milk the goats and make your own cheese. The shop (open daily., from 10am to 7pm) sells sweaters, socks, etc., all in mohair, of course.

Granges-sur-Lot
❀ From fresh plum to prune
2 miles (3 km) W of Temple-sur-Lot
Musée du Pruneau Gourmand
☎ 05 53 84 00 69
Open all year round Mon.–Sat., 9am–noon and 2–7pm; Sun. and public holidays, 3–7pm.

Spotcheck
E4

Lot-et-Garonne

Things to do
The Néguenou lake
The caves of Lastournelle
The water-garden
Gourmet plum museum
The caves of Fontirou
Foie gras museum

With children
The 'magic cauldron'

Within easy reach
Agen, p. 174,
Aiguillon, p. 178,
Marmande, p. 180.

Tourist Office
Penne-d'Agenais:
☎ 05 53 41 37 80
Villeneuve-sur-Lot:
☎ 05 53 36 17 30

Admission charge.
Here you can learn about all the stages in processing plums to make them into prunes. Your patience will be rewarded by a tasting of old-fashioned sugar-plums, oven-dried plums and those soaked in armagnac or spirits, stuffed or chocolate coated. The shop sells prunes in brandy (73 F for 1¼ pt (70 cl), and stuffed prunes (61 F for 10½ oz (300 g).

THE WATER-GARDEN

La Tour Marliac, Le Temple-sur-Lot
10 miles (16 km) W of Villeneuve-sur-Lot
☎ 05 53 01 08 05
Shop open 15 March–31 Oct., 9am–6pm.
Tours May–Sept. *Admission charge.*
This historic collection of water-lilies is a family business. In 1870, an ancestor of the present owner, Joseph Latour-Marliac, brought water-lilies from all over the world and created the world's first nursery dedicated to the plant. If you like flowers, you'll love this collection which contains 140 varieties of water-lily.

Castella
Caves of Fontirou

7½ miles (12 km) S of Villeneuve-sur-Lot
☎ 05 53 41 73 97
Open daily, June–Aug., 10am–12.30pm and 2–6pm; Apr.–May and 1 Sept.–15 Sept., 2–5.30pm. Open Sun., Oct. and All Saints Day school holidays if weather permits.
Admission charge.
In the height of summer, the 40-minute tour of the caves – which have a temperature of 57°F (14°C) – is very refreshing. The seven chambers are full of limestone accretions tinted ochre by clay deposits. In one of them traces of the animal bones from the Tertiary Era can still be seen.

Penne-d'Agenais
Craftsman's village

5 miles (8 km) E of Villeneuve-sur-Lot
This village was once called Penne-la-Sanglante ('Penne the Bloody') because of the massacres that occurred here. It is a hilltop medieval village whose streets (Rue de Ferracap, Place Paul-Froment) are lined with corbelled, half-timbered houses. Many craftspeople have chosen to live here.

Laroque-Timbaut
Miraculous water

8½ miles (14 km) S of Penne-d'Agenais
Deep in the valley of Saint-Germain you'll find a church and a fountain. There's a legend that says the fountain has miraculous healing powers, as it cured the army of

the French hero, Roland. Since then it has been used for drinking water and pilgrims visit the chapel every year on 28 May. Don't miss the 12th-C. market-hall and the little Rue du Lô.

Puymirol
The impregnable *bastide*

8½ miles (14 km) S of Laroque-Timbaut
This *bastide*, founded in 1246 by the counts of Toulouse, was reputed to be impregnable. Today it's easy enough to enter: just take the Rue Royale. Admire the 13th-C. porch of the church of Notre-Dame-de-Grand-Castel. The main square has retained its well. There's a wonderful view from the town's ramparts. They stretch for 1¼ miles (2 km)

and from them you'll see many medieval rooftops, turrets and towers.

Saint-Maurin
Musée de la Vie Agricole et Artisanale

6½ miles (10 km) E of Puymirol
☎ 05 53 95 31 25
Open daily except Tues., July–Aug., 3–7pm; by appointment out of season. *Admission charge.*
This pretty village nestles in a little valley by a lake. The central square is surrounded by half-timbered houses and

has a central well, a market-hall and the remains of an abbey belonging to the Cluniac order. It is the perfect setting for the museum of agricultural life and crafts which has been set up here. You can see all the elements of village life, a carpenter's workshop, wood-turning lathe and ploughing implements.

Beauville and Frespech
Fortified *bastide* and village

6½ miles (10 km) N of Saint-Maurin
The *bastide* of Beauville dominates the valley of the Petite-Séoune with its imposing stature. A circular tour reveals its rich past. The

fortified village of Frespech retains the vestiges of its ancient gates. The church dates from the 11th C. and the apse is tiled with stone tiles. The old houses have mullioned windows and turrets.

TOURTIÈRE FAIR

2nd weekend in July. Each year, the serious brotherhood, the Confrérie de la Tourtière, meets in Penne d'Agenais to honour this famous gâteau of the Basque country. Saturday evening is spent performing traditional Basque dances. The following day, the jury awards the prize for the best *tourtière*, and crowns the lucky winner, who must swear to eat the gâteau as often as possible. The ceremony concludes with a procession through the village streets and festivities in the Place de la Mairie.

A tasty museum

Musée du foie gras, Souilles, near Frespech
☎ 05 53 41 23 24
Open daily, mid-June–mid-Sept, 10am–7pm. Closed in January. Guided tours. *Admission charge.*
This museum teaches you all you need to know about foie gras: its history from antiquity to the present day, and the production line which turns the unfortunate duck into a delicacy (see pp. 20 and 21). This museum is also a farm where all the ingredients are reared, grown and

processed, from the plantation of the oaks under which truffles are found, to meadows for rearing the ducks, the abattoir, etc. The result can be tasted in the form of foies gras, cassoulets with duck flamed in armagnac, and confits of duck with ceps. You can buy semi-cooked foie gras from the shop here for 160 F for 6 oz (180 g).

Saint-Sardos
A historic site

12½ miles (20 km) W of Villeneuve-sur-Lot
It's here that the Hundred Years War began. The English invaded and destroyed this *bastide* founded in 1323 by the monks of Saint-Sardos. The governor of the *bastide* (representing the king of France) was hanged. In retaliation, Charles IV of France sent an army into the South West in 1324 to destroy the English.

Frespech

Agen and Brulhois
Romanesque art

Agen is a very old city, half-way between Bordeaux and Toulouse. It's particularly famous for its prunes and rugby. As the capital of an essentially rural *département*, Agen entered the modern age relatively late and undertook 10 years of major rehabilitation. The old town has been revived thanks to tourism and the youthful impetus of its 2000 students. The châteaux and *bastides* in the area and the opportunity to taste Côtes-de-Brulhois wine make Agen a useful base for excursions.

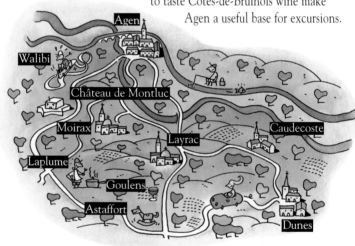

Le Quartier des Cornières

This has been the city's shopping district since the 13th C. There are arcades in the Rue des Cornières and the Place des Laitiers. This area of half-timbered and decorative brick houses

contains several listed buildings, including the 14th-C. Maison du Sénéchal in the Rue du Puits-du-Saumon, and the Hôtel Amblard in the Rue Floirac.

Prunes and sugar-plums

Confiserie Boisson, 20, Rue Grande-Horloge
☎ 05 53 66 20 61
Open Mon.–Sat., 9.30am–noon and 2–7pm. *Admission free.*
M. Boisson presents a slide-show about the plum, its history and transformation into the prune. Then you can taste and buy his wares (prunes in Armagnac: 92 F for 18 fl oz (50 cl), chocolate

coated prunes: 9 F each, pépites gasconnes: 6 F each, galets de Garonne: 80 F for 2.2 lbs (1 kg).

WALIBI, OH OUI !

Roquefort
*2½ miles (4 km)
S of Agen. Autoroute
A 62, exit Agen 7.*
☎ **05 53 96 58 32**
Open daily, 7 July–Aug.,
10am–7pm; Wed., Sat.,
Sun. and public holidays,
May–8 June, 10am–
6pm; daily, 9 June–
1 Sept., 10am–6pm;
Sat., Sun. and 8 Sept.,
2–26 Sept., 10am–6pm.
*Admission charge, free for children under
39 inches (1m) tall!*

Walibi is an amusement park with the emphasis on water. Take a change of clothes, as you're sure to get wet, and wear comfortable shoes. There are family rides (the Ladybird, the Water Maze), and roller-coaster rides for the more daring (the Boomerang: four tail-spins and two loop-the-loops at 56 miles/h/90 km/h). You can take a break by watching the sea-lions and musical fountains.

Le Musée Municipale des Beaux-Arts

**Place du
Docteur-Esquirol**
☎ **05 53 69 47 23**
Open daily except Tues.,
May–Sept., 10am–6pm;
in winter: 10am–5pm.
Admission charge.
This is one of the finest museums in the South West and is the pride of Agen. It's installed in the magnificent setting of four 16th- and 17th-C. mansions. The tour begins in the courtyard and leads you to a spiral staircase, then through some vaults. You'll also see a lovely Venus, porcelain including items from the school of Bernard-Palissy, who lived locally, and five paintings by Goya.

The 'Bull'

The mating of the shad
At night in June and July, the shad assemble in the river. Suddenly, there is a furious thrashing in the water, known here as a 'bull'. The shad are mating and the water seems

to boil for a few seconds. The first 'bull' of the evening has a stimulating effect and it's often followed by as many as a hundred matings in 15 minutes, turning the whole of the Garonne into a seething mass. It's a curiosity which some lucky night strollers will be able to see from the Passage footbridge (fishing is forbidden, naturally). To learn more about this extraordinary fish of the South West, visit the Exposition de la Frayère, 22, Rue Garonne, Le Passage, ☎ 05 53 87 67 21. Open Wed., Thurs. and 1st Sun. of the month, 2–5.45pm.

The Beauville quarter of old Agen

These handsome houses with corbels date from the 16 C. If the 13th-C. church of the Jacobins could speak it would tell you about the ceremony in which Philippe le Hardi restored the Agen district to England. It would also explain how it served as the headquarters of the Huguenots

Spotcheck

E4

Lot-et-Garonne

Things to do

The prune shop and exhibition
The Gravier gardens
Tasting Côtes-de-Brulhois
Tasting local foods
Learning how to can fruit
Visit to a metal sculptor's workshop

With children

Walibi, oh oui! theme park

Within easy reach

*Villeneuve-sur-Lot, p. 168,
Pays-des-Serres, p. 170,
Nérac, p. 224.*

Tourist Office

Agen:
☎ **05 53 47 36 09**

when Agen was captured in 1561, before it was turned into a prison during the Reign of Terror in the midst of the French Revolution.

The Gravier gardens

This esplanade was once an island in the Garonne but, in the 18th C., a branch of the river was diverted. It makes a pleasant **walk** beside the Garonne, and is busy during the **market** held here on Saturday mornings. There's a lovely view of the canal-bridge, a spectacular

The Gravier gardens

feat of engineering. Built in 1839, it has 23 arches and a span of 1,670 feet (500 m).

Le Brulhois

This little district south of Agen between Gers and Tarn-et-Garonne was once heavily wooded. It is famous for its wine, the Côtes-de-Brulhois. The *bastides*, churches and châteaux make it an interesting district to visit.

Nearby
The Château de Montluc

(7 km) SW of Agen
Estillac
☎ 05 53 67 81 83
Admission to the park, guided tour of the château by appointment.

Captain Blaise de Montluc, a marshal of France (1500-1577), retired here to write his *Commentaires* which Henri IV described as 'the soldier's breviary'. The bastions which he added to this 13th-C. château simply add to its quaint charm.

Les Côtes-de-Brulhois

Coopérative de Goulens
☎ 05 53 87 01 65
Open July–Aug., 8am–8pm; the rest of the year 8am–noon and 2–6pm, closed Sun.
Free admission.

This local wine has long been famous and was much prized during the Hundred Years War. It's a *vin de pays* which, depending on the year, can be aged for eight or ten years. It has a lively taste and quite a high alcohol content (12%).

You can visit the wine-cellars of Coopérative de Goulens, and taste and buy the wine. The prices are reasonable, from 14.50 F to 23 F a bottle.

Laplume: church and cassoulet

Ferme de Carolis
☎ 05 53 95 10 92
Open daily, 9am–9pm.
Admission free.

The Renaissance church (1511–1541) has a bell-tower which is square at the base and octagonal at the top, and is worth a visit. If you're more interested in food try the **Ferme de Carolis** where you'll find all the local produce that you'd expect in this area: cassoulet (70 F for 4 pers.), confits, *cous farcis*, and goose with Agen prunes (100 F approx. for 4 pers.).

Wooden toys and games

10½ miles
(17 km) SE of Agen
La Clotte, Marlène and André Weber, Astaffort
☎ 05 53 67 10 87
Tours daily, by appointment. Shop open Mon.–Fri., 9am–7pm; Sun. 1–7pm.
You can always stop at Astaffort in the hope of glimpsing its most famous inhabitant, Francis Cabrel (the town's singing mayor!).

Make sure, however, you visit the wood workshop. It's like wandering into the workshop where Pinocchio was made. There are toys in beech, oak and walnut which seem to come to life in the studio and can be bought in the shop. A magnificent rocking-horse

(1,200 F) stands proudly beside puzzles, clocks and lamp-stands. Difficult to resist.

you should visit Caudecoste, a real treasure and a legacy of the Hundred Years War.

Montesquieu
The fruit cannery
10½ miles (17 km) from Agen, before Bruch
Conservatoire Végétal d'Aquitaine
Domaine de Barolle
☎ **05 53 95 21 13**
Open Mon.–Fri. 9am–noon and 1.30–5.30pm; out of season, Mon.–Sat. *Admission charge.*
This extraordinary repository of rare plants has a 44½ acre (18 ha) orchard which contains 1,500 fruit trees, mainly local varieties from the South West such as the *gros museau de lièvre blanc* or the *pay bou* apples. If you have green

Caudecoste
Beautiful *bastides*
15½ miles (25 km) SE of Agen
If you're interested in the *bastides* of Lot-et-Garonne

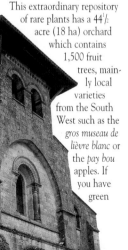

fingers, the owners run courses in creating an orchard, grafting and pruning (one-day course, from 185 F to 370 F).

THE ART OF METALWORKING
Serge Carvalho, Route de Caudecoste, Layrac
☎ **05 53 67 00 48**
Guided tour Sat. morning, by appointment during the week. At the southern exit from Agen if you are in a car, you'll see on the roundabout Serge Carvalho's monumental sculpture *The Myth of Sisyphus*. Continue on to Layrac, where the artist has his studio. Watch him work copper, bronze and ferrous metals. There's a variety of hand-made metal objects on sale. A pair of fire-dogs will cost around 800 F, 600 F for a lamp and 500 F for a candlestick.

Aiguillon and Tonneins

A iguillon is a pleasant little town, a useful base for excursions. It was once famous for royal celebrations, held in its 18th-C. château, and now also boasts pretty half-timbered houses. If you are anti-smoking, however, avoid Tonneins, as it is the capital of cigarette manufacture in France.

The Lot, the Garonne and the Canal all run through this region and it's pleasant to see the landscape from the water.

Jazz

Aiguillon is a quiet little town but it comes alive on market days, Tuesday and Friday mornings. It's at its busiest during the last weekend in July when there's a four-day festival of jazz. Every type of jazz is featured here, from blues to afro, trad to modern. For information ☎ 05 53 88 20 20.

Clairac
The life of the monk

5 miles (8 km) from Tonneins
☎ 05 53 79 34 81
Open daily 1 Apr.– 1 Nov., 10am-6pm;
out of season, Wed., Sat., Sun., school and public holidays, 10am–6pm.
Admission charge.
The Ente plum and tobacco were both cultivated by the Benedictine monks of Clairac Abbey. Today you can see 15 tableaux consisting of 250 **automata** that depict what their monastic life was like. Even if the children aren't too interested in the life of a monk, they'll love the automata and the **Magic Forest** (☎ 05 53 84 27 54, admission charge). There is also a train museum for railway enthusiasts, young or old (Musée du Train, ☎ 05 53 88 04 30, admission charge).

Tonneins
Capital of the Gauloise cigarette

½ mile (1 km) from Tonneins
Processing and packing tobacco.

WOOD PIGEON HUNTING

When the wood pigeons fly overhead, the action begins for thousands of local inhabitants, the 2,500 hides dotted throughout the forest come alive. They need to be operational for the start of the hunting season in October and November. The modest hides of branches and ferns are turned into the command posts of an army at war. Everything is ready for the pigeons flying over-head – traps, nets for throwing and platforms for the hunters and their rifles (see pp. 86 and 87).

☎ 05 53 88 33 20
Open Mon.–Thurs.,
7am–noon and 2–5pm,
Fri. morning.
Free admission for groups only.
This is where the growers deliver their tobacco leaves for processing. The harvest is fermented, then beaten. A ten-minute film traces the cultivation and marketing of the leaf. The tobacco is then sent to a cigarette factory, such as the Tonneins factory, where it is cut, blended and made into cigarettes.

Miniature museum

**Le Royaume de la Miniature et de la Collection,
3, Boulevard Charles de Gaulle**
☎ 05 53 79 22 79
Open daily July–Aug.,
9am–noon and 2–6pm;
out of season by appointment.
This museum was created for children, but parents too

will be reminded of their own first toys with a touch of nostalgia. Exhibits include electric cars and yesterday's pedal cars, aeroplane models and antique wooden toys, while the walls display superb antique enamelled plaques. During the Whitsun holiday weekend Tonneins hosts a vintage car rally.

The Garonne story

**Exposition A Garonna,
Quai de la Barre**
☎ 05 53 88 28 58
By appointment only for groups and individuals.
This exhibition, set up in the old royal Manufacture des Tabacs, focuses entirely on the great river: its flora and fauna, its ports and industries (fishing, hemp rope-making) as well as shipwrecks, irrigation, leisure navigation etc. Models of 18th- and 19th-C. ships, prints and videos depict the life and wealth of the Garonne river. They tell the story of its past and point to its future.

- - - - - - - - - - - - - - - - - -

Le Mas d'Agenais
The Rembrandt painting
*9¹⁄₃ miles (15 km)
S of Marmande*
Église Saint-Vincent
This is a wonderful surprise. This lovely Romanesque church, set deep in Lot-et-Garonne, contains *Christ on the Cross* by the Dutch Old Master Rembrandt. It was painted in 1631, and was one of a series of seven, of which the other six are in the Milan Pinacoteca.

Wood pigeons in the forest of Mas d'Agenais
La Palombière
☎ 05 53 79 47 14
Open daily July-Aug.,

Spotcheck
D4

Lot-et-Garonne

Things to do

Jazz festival
Le Royaume de la Miniature et de la Collection
Garonne exhibition
Learning about wood pigeons

With children

The automata of the Magic Forest

Within easy reach

*Villeneuve-sur-Lot, p. 168,
Marmande, p. 180,
Nérac, p. 224.*

Tourist Office

Aiguillon:
☎ 05 53 79 62 58
Tonneins: ☎ 05 53 79 22 79

10am–6pm; May, June and Sept., 2–6pm; guided tours for groups only by appointment. *Admission charge.*
The French are great hunters of many different kinds of wildlife and birds are no exception. Wood pigeons are hunted throughout this part of France. A visit to this centre explains all you need to know about the bird, its way of life and migratory habits, as well as the habits of the huntsman.

Marmande

Welcome to tomato country. Farming and wine-making are also of prime importance to the economy of Marmande. In the spring, the region is one big orchard in bloom. Tourism is well developed and there are lots of farms and small factories who welcome visitors to sample and buy their products. Take advantage of this to try out some local delicacies.

Old Marmande
Musée Albert-Marzelles, Rue Abel-Boyé
☎ 05 53 64 42 04
Open Tues.–Fri., 3–6pm; Sat., 10am–noon and 3–6pm; Sun., 3–6pm (exc. July–Aug.).
Free admission.
The main attraction of the tomato capital is the old district which contains all the cultural riches of the town (around the Place des Neufs-Fontaines). Visit the chapel of Saint-Benoît, the late 13th-C. church of Notre-Dame and its cloister, and the old houses in the Rue Labat. The Musée Albert-Marzelles contains works by local painters and collections of furniture and pottery. Temporary exhibitions take place regularly. Timetable at the Tourist Office.

Song festival
Festival lyrique en Marmandais
☎ 05 53 89 68 75
The Festival Lyrique takes place in the second fortnight in August. There are performances of opera, operetta, bel canto, and other types of song.

Gourmet Marmande
Épicerie Grandcoing, 39, Rue du Fougard
Tues.–Sat., 7am–1pm
At the hearty of the city, an old restored covered market houses the true embassy of all the flavours of South West France. Wines and spirits have their own place in the market, foies gras have theirs. Above all, don't leave Marmande without stocking up on fresh vegetables and fruit. For a really good grocer's try **Grandcoing** (39, Rue du Fougard).

Beyssac

In the land of honey
N of Marmande
Le Moulin du Télégraphe, Jean-Claude Saint-Marc
☎ 05 53 64 33 71
Weekend tours.
Free admission.
Six hundred beehives cover the slopes above Marmande. The owner of this old mill (1770) has opened a bee-keeping exhibition. You'll find flavoured honeys and delicious sweets, as well as a sweet mead, made from honey and alcohol (15°),

THE CÔTES-DU-MARMANDAIS,
WINES OF CHARACTER

These wines are very much appreciated by connoisseurs. There are 3,459 acres (1,400 ha) of vineyards along both sides of the Garonne. The red wines have a strong personality. The grape varieties used (Merlot, Cabernet Franc and Cabernet Sauvignon) contribute different qualities, such as adaptability, finesse and roundness, a fruity palate, bouquet and body. The white wines (the Sauvignon grape variety) are dry and very fruity.

Cave Coopérative de Cocumont, Vieille Église, ☎ 05 53 94 50 21. Visits and tasting from 18,50 F to 47.50 F a bottle.

Cave Coopérative de Beaupuy-Dupuy, ☎ 05 53 76 05 10. Visits and tasting from 11 F to 49 F a bottle.

Spotcheck
D3

Lot-et-Garonne

Things to do

Festival Lyrique in the Marmande
Gastronomic tourism
Côtes-du-Marmandais wine

Within easy reach

Aiguillon, 17½ miles (28 km) SE., p. 178, Le pays d'Albret, p. 224.

Tourist Office

Marmande:
☎ 05 53 64 44 44

a favourite drink in the days of the Gauls. To see the mill, take a detour through Gontaud-de-Nogaret (6¼ miles/10 km south of Marmande). Phone first to book (☎ 05 53 83 47 78), and then you'll be able to see the huge 53 ft (16 m) sails of the Moulin de Gibra in action (*see below, right*).

Mauvezin-sur-Gupie
Delicious foie gras
4½ miles (7 km) N of Marmande
Jacques Mathieu's Farm, Peyre-en-Haut
☎ 05 53 94 25 31
Open all year round, by appointment.
Duck is prepared here in every way possible, in a *confit*, as fresh foie gras, half-cooked, and tinned. You can see where the ducks are bred. If you're interested in French cuisine, try asking the owner for some advice, or even the odd recipe.

🦆 Musée des Conserves Gourmandes
☎ 05 53 94 20 48
Open daily except Sun. morning in season, 10am–noon and 3–7pm; Mon.–Fri. out of season, 8am–noon and 2–6pm. *Admission charge.*
The museum exhibits come

from a time before European health standards existed. The ways our ancestors used to preserve food may horrify you today. However, it's a very instructive museum, and it can make your mouth water at times. Fortunately, there's a shop selling the house specialities (foie gras, duck breast, etc.) for those who cannot resist the temptation.

Duras
a château and a vineyard

The lovely landscape makes a trip through the Duras district irresistible and perhaps inspired the French writer Marguerite Duras to take the name of the town as her pen-name. Very much a centre for local food specialities; the delicious and lavish produce is the delight of gourmets who also appreciate the local wine, Côtes-de-Duras. Add to this a cooling dip in the Lac de Castelgaillard and an afternoon lazing on the beach, and your holiday cocktail is ready.

✿ The Château-Museum
☎ 05 53 83 77 32
Open daily, 10am–7pm, 1 June–30 Sept.; Apr., May, 10am–noon and 2–7pm; Oct. and winter holidays, 10am–noon and 2–6pm; from Nov. to March, 2–6pm.
Admission charge.

The château of Duras was once a stronghold on the frontier of Guyenne, which was at that time in English hands. It lay abandoned for a long time but has now been restored, thanks to the local community. The guides may enliven your visit with touches of humour but are quite serious when they tell you that the water in the well is 4% alcohol, thanks to the surrounding vineyards! The many rooms contain a variety of exhibits, including period costumes, all of which relate to daily life at the château, and its history.

Local festivals
St. John's Day (mid-summer) in June, is celebrated by dancing around a bonfire.

Another festival, (La Fête de la Madeleine) is held on the third weekend in July. It lasts for four days and culminates on the Monday evening with fireworks, *son et lumière* and illumination of the château. Duras takes on a Spanish air with its *bandas* (musical bands) and *tapas* bars. Local foods and crafts are sold on Saturday and Sunday evenings (wine fair).

CÔTES-DE-DURAS, THE PAINTER'S PALETTE

This little 4,940 acre (2,000 ha) vineyard consists of several family properties. Using several grape varieties it produces wine which ranges in colour from golden-yellow to raspberry pink, and from pale red to deep purplish-red.
**Maison du Vin, 47120 Duras,
☎ 05 53 83 81 88**
(regional showcase).
**Cave-Coopérative Berticot,
Route de Sainte-Foy-la-Grande,
☎ 05 53 83 71 12.**

Musée Vivant
du Parchemin
et de l'Enluminure
Miramont-de-Guyenne
☎ 05 53 20 75 55
Open daily Apr.–Sept.,
3–6pm; July–Aug.,

10am–noon and 3–6pm;
out of season, Sun.,
school holidays, 3–6pm.
Admission charge.
In this unusual museum you can see parchment being made, from the initial treatment of the goat- or sheepskin through to the final product. The inks and colours are made from natural animal, vegetable and mineral extracts. After a demonstration of Gothic calligraphy, you can try it yourself with a goose quill pen. The parchment costs between 500 F and 3,000 F for a plain or decorated sheet!

Saint-Sernin
Lac de
Castelgaillard
*3¾ miles (6 km)
N of Duras*
A pretty village with a lovely 25 acre (10 ha) lake. Perfect for a dip, it has many facilities. Castelgaillard tourist complex (☎ 05 53 94 78 74).

Balayssagues
Local produce
*3¼ miles (5 km)
W of Duras*
**Danielle and Alain
Laroumagne, Baignac
☎ 05 53 83 77 59**

Spotcheck
D3

Lot-et-Garonne

Things to do
Local festivals
Lac de Castelgaillard
Tasting local foods
The living parchment museum
Côtes-de-Duras wine

Within easy reach
*Montaigne country,
p. 126.*

Tourist Office
Duras:
☎ 05 53 83 63 06

Open daily, 8am–8pm. This plum-grower will offer you a warm welcome. After showing you the plum-picking machinery, the grading system and the oven for drying the plums into prunes, he will serve you white wine and cakes, and show you the specialities of the house, including prune paste, chocolate coated prunes and truffles in plum brandy. Around 12 F for a pot of prune cream, 38 F for 7 oz (200 g) of prune paste (with nuts and chocolate) and 16 F for 1 lb 2 oz (500 g) of naturally preserved plums (without chemical preservatives).

Entre-Deux-Mers
a vineyard between two rivers

This is the region where one of France's most famous white wines is produced: a dry, fragrant white which is an excellent accompaniment to the oysters of the Arcachon basin. The area is bounded by the Garonne and the Dordogne, its name deriving from the tidal wave which sweeps up both these rivers. Take your pilgrim's staff (you're on the route to Santiago de Compostela) and explore the churches, *bastides* and châteaux.

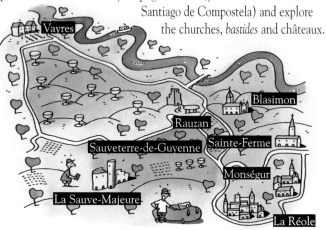

Vayres
Blasimon
Rauzan
Sauveterre-de-Guyenne
Sainte-Ferme
Monségur
La Sauve-Majeure
La Réole

Beychac-et-Caillau

A lesson on wine and the history of the vineyards

9¹⁄₂ miles (15 km) E of Bordeaux

Maison des Bordeaux et Bordeaux Supérieurs, N 89, exit no 5 near Beychac

☎ **05 57 97 19 20**

Open Mon.–Fri. 9am–noon and 1.30–5pm; Sat., June–Sept., 10am–5pm

Admission charge.

For a good grounding in wine tasting, stop here at the Maison des Bordeaux. It's as though all the châteaux were opening their wine-cellars to you and giving you the benefit of their knowledge. There's no need to feel intimidated, the welcome is warm and you can taste selected wines and buy them at estate prices plus 2 F. You'll also be given excellent advice on planning a wine tour to suit your tastes.

Vayres

The château

15¹⁄₂ miles (25 km) W of Bordeaux

☎ **05 57 84 96 58**

Open daily July–15 Sept., 2–6pm; Guided tours: 3pm, 4pm, 5pm, March–June and Oct., Sun. and public holidays.

Château de Vayres

Admission charge.
This fortress was converted
into a baroque palace in the
16th C. and overlooks the
Dordogne. A **monumental
flight of steps** leads to formal
gardens that extend down to
the river.

Les Graves-de-Vayres

**Maison du Vin,
Place du Générale-de-Gaulle
☎ 05 57 74 86 42**
It's the pure gravel or clay and
silica soils which have given
their name to this appellation.
These are red and white wines
(there are more whites than
reds) and you can taste them
at the Maison du Vin (about
25 F a bottle).

La Sauve-Majeure
A stone bible
*12¹/₂ miles (20 km)
S of Vayres*
☎ 05 56 23 01 55
Open daily Oct.–May,
10am–12.30pm and
2.30–5.30pm (6pm on
Sun.); June–Sept.,
10am–6.30pm, free tour
with booklet. *Admission
charge to museum.*
The abbey was founded in
1079, and was one of the
largest in the South West.
Although now

SURFING ON THE MASCARET

**Saint-Pardon, near
Vayres.**
This tidal wave sweeps
up the Dordogne daily
and can reach a height
of 5 ft (1.50 m). The
most skillful surfers can
ride it for some 900
yards (800 m). The
best spot is at the port
of Saint-Pardon, near
Vayres. To find out the
time of the Mascaret,
phone the Café du Port
(**☎ 05 57 74 85 98**)
and watch it from the
terrace.

in ruins, the well-preserved,
sculpted capitals decorated
with lively scenes such as
Daniel in the lions' den,
Samson, a bestiary, vices and
passions, good and evil etc,
are still visible. There's a
magnificent view
of the whole area
from the top of
the bell-tower .

Spotcheck
C3-D3

Gironde

Things to do
**La Maison des Bordeaux
Surfing the Mascaret
The farm-park
La Réole museums
Fairs and markets of
Monségur
Twenty-four hours of
swing
La Vinothèque at
Sauveterre
Swimming and cycling**

Within easy reach
*Saint-Émilion, p. 120,
Pays de Montaigne,
p. 126,
Sauternais, p. 192.*

Tourist Offices
**Sauveterre-de-Guyenne:
☎ 05 56 71 53 45
La Réole:
☎ 05 56 61 13 55**

La Réole
The barges and the market
*11¹/₂ miles (18 km)
E of Langon*
La Réole was once a flourishing river port, but the **gabares**
(barges) are now used to carry
tourists. However, the quayside is not deserted because
the **Saturday morning market**
is still held here. Ask for a
map of the town from the
Tourist Office (3, Pl. de la
Libération), to search out the
corbelled houses, the oldest
town hall in France, the
church of Saint-Pierre

La Réole

and the convent buildings, ending at the imposing fortress of Quate-Sos.

❀ The museums of La Réole
19, Av. Gabriel-Chaine
☎ 05 56 61 29 25
Open daily 15 June–
15 Sept., 10am–6pm; out of season, Wed.–Sat. and school holidays, 2–6pm, and Sun., 10am–6pm (1–6pm Dec.–March).
Admission charge.
The treasures contained in its four museums – automobile, agriculture, railway and military – would be reason

280 sq m of glass) however, dates from the 19th C. At the time, the trade in prunes was flourishing and the Monségur market was very active. Today, the market is held in the hall on Fridays. There are two **foie gras fairs** and a **flower market**. The *bastide* is closed on the first weekend of July .

Sauveterre-de-Guyenne
The Vinothèque
(14 km) N of La Réole
☎ 05 56 71 61 28
Open Tues.–Sat.,
9am–noon and 3–7pm;
open Sun. in season.

is considered to be a jewel of Romanesque art. North of it, you will pass the **Moulin de Labarthe**, built by the monks of the abbey in the 14th C.

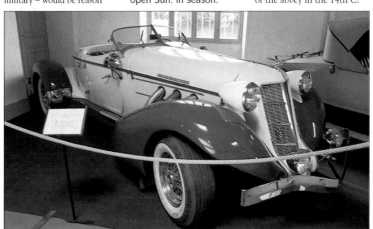

enough to visit La Réole. You'll find vintage cars such as a 1901 De Dion-Bouton, a Bugatti and a Packard; beautiful old classic American cars, with fine lines and sumptuous upholstery; racing cars which look too frail and unprotected for their great speeds, and even very old vintage cars that ran on steam (c. 1895), as well as agricultural machinery and tractors.

Monségur
An English *bastide*
8 miles (13 km)
NE of La Réole
This *bastide* was founded by the English in 1265. The large market-hall (3,000 sq ft;

Another *bastide*, typically English in style, with four fortified gates and a square. The Vinothèque, which is located right in the centre of the *bastide*, is a showcase of wines of Sauveterre (tastings).

The abbey of Blasimon
4 miles (6¹/₂ km) from Sauveterre-de-Guyenne
The abbey, nestling deep in a valley, has a portico which

Blasimon leisure centre
☎ 05 56 71 55 62
15 June–15 Sept.
After your journey into the past, relax in the bathing area at Blasimon where you can also rent a bicycle. If you want to taste the wine of Entre-Deux-Mers (approx. 20 F a bottle), the wine-makers of Guyenne will be ready to help you (the route is signposted, **☎ 05 56 71 55 28**).

Saint-Ferme

*7¹/₂ miles (12 km) E of
Sauveterre-de-Guyenne*
☎ 05 56 61 69 92
Open daily except Tues.,
15 June–19 Sept,
10am–noon and 2–7pm;
out of season, Wed.–Sat.,
9am–noon and 2–5pm.
Admission charge.
The abbey, founded in the
11th C., stands in the centre
of the village. On its capitals
you can admire scenes from
the Old and New Testaments,
David and Goliath, the Washing of the Feet, etc.

Rauzan
Le Château des Duras

*6¹/₂ miles (10 km) N of
Sauveterre-de-Guyenne*
☎ 05 53 83 77 32
Open daily June–Sept.,
10am–7pm; Oct. and
school holidays, 10am–
noon and 2–6pm; Nov.–
March, 2–6pm; Apr.–May,
10am–noon and 2–7pm.
Admission charge.
Rauzan and its surroundings is
a particularly romantic area
of dolmens and old churches
(the chapel of Notre-Dame-
de-Bonne-Nouvelle). This
large village is dominated by
the impressive ruins of the
Château des Duras, a fortress
built between the 13th and
15th C. The 100 ft (30 m)
high castle keep has arrow slits
and the walls are thick enough

to contain a spiral staircase.
To taste or buy wine, try the
the Union des Producteurs de
Rauzan ☎ 05 57 84 13 22.

Romagne
Dried flowers

*5 miles (8 km)
W of Rauzan*
La Chèvre
☎ 05 56 23 65 09
July-Aug., daily except
Mon. 2.30–6.30pm;
Sept.–June, by appoint-
ment.
This shop is dedicated to the
art of dried flower arranging.
Crab apples, gourds, bunches
of flowers, grasses, corn cobs
etc are dried and then mixed
into beautiful arrangements
by Jocelyne Riffaud. You can
also wander through the fields
of flowers which grow all over
the valley.

Sadirac
The farm-park: 'heirloom' vegetables

*5 miles (8 km) W
of La-Sauve-Majeure*
Château de Belloc
☎ 05 56 30 62 00
Open daily, 15 Apr.–
25 Dec., 2–6pm;
shop open Mon.–Fri.,
8.30am–5.30pm.
Admission charge.
In the past local
gardeners grew
Jerusalem artichokes,
melon-squash and other
vegetables, many of which
have been forgotten today.

The farm-park run by Bernard
Lafon is dedicated to saving
rare vegetables. If you're not
too familiar with these unusual
vegetables, try a slice of nettle
quiche or the Jerusalem
artichoke pancake. You can
also buy jam (32.50 F), and
jars of preserved nettles
(37.50 F) in the shop.

THE ORCHIDS OF ENTRE-DEUX-MERS

There's no need to go
to the tropics to find
orchids! About forty
species of these
extraordinary flowers
grow in Entre-Deux-
Mers, and especially in
the Dropt Valley. The
oval-leafed *Listera*,
which has a greenish
flower, loves the damp
meadows. The *Ophrys*
orchid is really quite
extraordinary. By some
miracle of nature, it
grows to resemble
the insect it is trying
to attract, and changes
shape according to
whether it's a butterfly,
a bee, a spider or
an insect.

Langoiran

Rions

Cadillac

Malromé

Loupiac

Ste-Croix-du-Mont

Ste-Foy-la-Longue

Podensac

St-Macaire

Malagar

The slopes of the Garonne

The landscape of the slopes of the Garonne is subject to the influences of both the land and the sea. The fishermen's huts on its banks are surrounded by the vines that cover the slopes. In the north, the red wines give way to semi-dry or sweet white wines and then to syrupy wines such as Cadillac, Loupiac and Sainte-Croix-du-Mont.

Saint-Macaire

Aquarium des Mers Tropicales

Place du Général-de Gaulle
☎ 05 56 63 05 62
Open daily (exc. Mon. out of season) 10am–7pm.
Admission charge.
Believe it or not, these tropical fish swim about in a medieval cellar! Thanks to the magic of technology, you can discover the fabulous inhabitants of coral reefs from opposite ends of the earth. There are turtles and even piranhas. Children will love it.

✿ The river and canal

Mountain bikes for hire, Cycles Garbay
1, Cours de la République
☎ 05 56 63 28 08
All year round, Tues.–Sat., 8.30am–noon and 2–7pm.
If you like cycling, but have little sense of direction, take the signposted path (yellow arrows) which follows the Garonne from Saint-Macaire. It leads to a bridge across to the other bank at Castets-en-Dorthe (approx. 3¾ miles (6 km); and the Canal de la Garonne. By following the yellow or green signs you'll enjoy some lovely walks or rides. You can also visit the Maison du Pays de Saint-Macaire, nearby.

Les Côtes-de-Saint-Macaire

Maison du pays de Saint-Macaire,
8, Rue du Canton
☎ 05 56 63 32 14
Open daily, July–Aug.; all year round for groups by appointment.
Admission charge.
This region extends the production of Côtes-de-Bordeaux,

a sweet white wine, towards the south. Learn about these delicious wines at the Maison du Pays where there's a slide show and a tasting. In July and August, you can take organised walks for the day, or guided tours of Saint-Macaire, including the wine storage-cellars (*chais*) and meeting the wine-makers themselves.

Saint-Maixant
The Maison de Mauriac

2 miles (3 km) NW. of Saint-Macaire
☎ 05 57 98 17 17
Open daily except Tues., May–Sept., 10am–noon and 2–6pm; out of season, phone for details.
The property has changed little since the death of François Mauriac, the writer, in 1970. The terrace and the old lime tree in the courtyard

VERDELAIS	2
St GERMAIN DE G.	6

| Château Malromé | |
| Toulouse Lautrec | |

| Domaine de Malagar | |

remain just as he would have known them. The Regional Council of Aquitaine took over the estate in 1985 and opened it to the public. The François-Mauriac Centre, housed in the neighbouring wine-cellars, displays documents and souvenirs of the life of the writer.

Sainte-Foy-la-Longue
The local nectar: sweet honey

6½ miles (10 km) NE of Saint-Macaire
Le Peydoucet, Ferme Apicole
☎ 05 56 76 45 85
By appointment only.
Learn about the life-cycle of the bee at this beekeeping farm. A hive with a glass

Spotcheck
C3-D3

Gironde

Things to do

Bicycle trips along the Garonne
Maison du Pays de Saint-Macaire
Visit to a bee-keeper
Cruise on the Garonne

With children

Tropical aquarium

Within easy reach

Sauternais, 6½ miles (10 km) S, p. 192,
Bazas, 12½ miles (20 km) SE, p. 194,
Bordeaux, 19 miles (30 km) NW, p. 196.

Tourist Offices

Cadillac: ☎ 05 56 62 12 92
Podensac: ☎ 05 56 27 17 54

panel enables you to admire the almost military organisation of the worker bees. Taste the results of their arduous labour. Acacia honey 54 F for 2lb 4oz (1 kg), Melva (honey, hazelnuts, sesame), 25 F for a 9 oz (250 g) pot.

Sainte-Croix-du-Mont
The oyster cliff

☎ 05 56 62 01 54
Open Easter–mid-Oct., Sat., Sun. and public holidays, 10am–noon and 2.30–8pm; Mon., Tues., Thurs., Fri., 2.30–6.30pm; July–Aug., Tues.–Fri., 2.30–7pm.
Admission charge.
The village is built on a cliff made from fossilised oysters (from the end of the Tertiary Era). The château and church offer a bird's eye view of the vineyards and the wine is stored in spectacular cellars. Under the gateway to the château, there's a cellar where local wines can be tasted.

Château de Malromé

Saint-André-du-Bois
Château de Malromé

4 miles (6 km) NE of Saint-Macaire

☎ 05 56 76 44 92

Open daily 15 June–15 Sept., 10am–noon and 2–7pm (Easter and All Saints Day, afternoons only); Sun., and Jan., Feb., Apr.–14 June and 16 Sept.–Nov., 2–6pm *Admission charge.*

This château, built by the counts of Béarn in the 14th C., was bought, together with its vineyards, in 1883 by the mother of painter Henri de Toulouse-Lautrec. The artist was then 19 years old and he returned every summer, painting incessantly. He died here on 9 September 1901 and was buried in the Verdelais cemetery, 2 miles (3km) from the château. After you've admired the luxurious apartments, still imbued with the spirit of its famous owner, you'll be invited to taste the château wines.

Cadillac
Château of the dukes of Epernon

☎ 05 56 62 69 58

Open daily July–Aug., 9.30am–7pm; phone for opening times out of season. *Admission charge.* If you're following the wine route, stop off at the *bastide* of Cadillac, seven centuries

old, which has retained two fortified gateways, the **Porte de la Mer** and the **Porte de l'Horloge**. The château of the dukes of Epernon has eight **monumental fireplaces** and original painted ceilings. The **Maison du Vin** offers information and wine tastings (☎ 05 57 98 19 20. Open daily.

Loupiac
A Gallo-Roman villa

2 miles (3 km) S of Cadillac

☎ 05 56 62 93 82

Phone for an appointment. *Free admission.* The remains of a luxurious Gallo-Roman villa were unearthed in the 19th C., containing a *frigidarium* (cold bath), a *caldarium*

(hot bath) and a *tepidarium* (warm bath), and even a swimming-pool decorated with beautiful mosaics. After the visit, the owner, Jean-Pierre Bernède, offers tastings of **Loupiac** wine.

On the water
The *Ville de Bordeaux*, boarding opposite the Place des Quinconces, in Bordeaux.

☎ 05 56 52 88 88

Admission charge. The only problem with this river cruise is that it depends on the tides – the boat can only pass under the stone bridge at low tide. Departure is around noon and the boat reaches Cadillac, Blaye or Pauillac at 2.30pm. After a two-hour stopover, you complete your journey by returning to Bordeaux. Dinner trips can be arranged. It is worth the trip for the scenery alone and you may be lucky enough to see the Mascaret, the tidal wave which sweeps up the Garonne as well as up the Dordogne (p. 185).

Podensac
Apéritif of the aristocrats

4 miles (6 km) from Cadillac, on the RN 113
Lillet Frères

☎ 05 56 27 41 41

Open 15 June–15 Sept., 8.30am–7pm;

Château de Cadillac

By appointment for the rest of the year.

Cross the Garonne and try an apéritif at Podensac. This is where Lillet, apéritif of the aristocrats, is made. It is a mixture of wine, fruit liqueur and quinine and was created in 1872 by the Lillet brothers. Try it frappé, with canapés, blue cheese, foie gras, smoked breast of duck or soft fruits.

73.90 F a bottle.

THE LOUPIAC WINE HARVEST

Loupiac is famous for its white wines which are similar to those of Sainte-Croix-du-Mont. The climate favours the growth of a microscopic fungus, *Botrytis cinerea*. This 'noble rot' softens the grapes and concentrates their sugar content, which is what makes Loupiac so special. The grapes are picked in successive selections of bunches after attack by the fungus. Seventy vine-growers cultivate the 988 acres (400 ha) of the appellation.

Rions

An ancient walled town

3 miles (4½ km) from Cadillac

Rions, beside the Garonne, is worth a detour. The city has retained its old defences and gates. The market-hall, old houses, remains of the citadel, cave and the 12th-C. church of Saint-Seurin are all interesting places for you to visit.

Langoiran

Frescoes and wine cellars

7 miles (11 km) from Cadillac
☎ 05 56 67 12 00
Open daily, July–Aug., 11am-noon and 2–8pm; out of season, weekends, afternoons only.
Admission charge.

The imposing ruins of a fortified castle demonstrate the power of the lord of Langoiran in the Middle Ages. You can visit the 14th-C. castle keep, which contains frescoes, and the

SHAD FISHING

Latresne, 5 miles (8 km) from Bordeaux. Latresne owes its name to the ancient tradition of shad fishing in the Garonne. The *traisne* was a type of net used to catch and land the fish. Shad is a traditional delicacy often served in restaurants along the river bank. It's grilled over freshly-cut vine tendrils and its roe is pan-fried and served as part of a sauce with a

base of oil, vinegar and shallots. Shad is the name given to several kinds of meaty fish which swim upriver to spawn.

wine-cellars beneath the fortress. The Cave Coopérative (☎ 05 56 67 41 50) on the Créon road sells the wines of several châteaux (open daily).

Sauternes

Langon, a port on the Garonne 28 miles (45 km) from Bordeaux, is the white wine capital of the Bordeaux district and the meeting-point for three prestigious vineyards: Sauternes, Graves and Bordeaux. The town faces south, overlooking the 12,355 acres (5,000 ha) of Sauternes and Graves vineyards. There's a lot for the wine connoisseur to see and do as the slopes of Sauternais are covered with historic vineyards and châteaux.

Barsac
Preignac
La Brède
Château de Malle
Château-Yquem
Langon
Roquetaillade
Sauternes

Château-Yquem
Sauternes
☎ **05 57 98 07 07**
Tour of the *chais*: daily,
2.30–4pm except
Sat.–Sun., closed in
August. Apply 3 weeks
in advance.
Free admission.
Unfortunately the château
that belongs to this world
famous vineyard, synonymous
with wine of the highest quality cannot actually be visited.
However, you can discover its
superb wine-cellars (*chais*).
This *1er grand cru classé* of
Sauternes remains the undisputed leader of the appellation (since 1855). No wine is
sold at the château.

✿ Château de Malle
Preignac
☎ **05 56 62 36 86**
Open daily Apr.–Oct.,
10am–noon and

2–6.30pm.
Admission charge.
This magnificent 17th-C.
historical residence has been
in the same family for three
generations. The visit is followed by a **wine-tasting** (fee
charged),and an optional
walk through the Italianate
gardens, with their handsome
statues. A bottle of Sauternes
(*2e cru classé*) costs from 100

to 200 F, a bottle of Graves
(white or red) costs from 40 F
to 60 F.

Clogs
**Rue de Lur-Saluces,
Preignac**
☎ **06 56 63 27 51**
The Sauternes wine-growers
still have their traditional
clog maker, Jean-Luc Claverie,
who makes clogs in the old-

LA BRÈDE ORCHARD

**Feyteau,
Chemin de Mons,
La Brède
☎ 05 56 20 22 29**
Tour by appointment.
The fruit from this orchard is bottled and preserved in extraordinary combinations. Catherine Bernhard mixes raspberries with Bordeaux wine, pears with spices and oranges with whisky... The various concoctions owe nothing to tradition. Many of the mixtures are the products of her 17 acre (7 ha) orchard. A jar of of jam weighing 10 oz (320 g) costs between 22 F and 25 F.

fashioned way. The clogs, carved from elder or laburnum wood, are made to measure. There's a wide range of sizes and a pair costs around 100 F.

✿ Roquetaillade
5 miles (8 km) S of Langon
☎ 05 56 76 14 16

Open daily, July–Aug., 10.30am–7pm; in the afternoons from Easter to All Saints Day; the rest of the year, school holidays, Sun. and public holidays.
Admission charge.
Not one, but two, fortified châteaux (12th and 14th C.), are hidden behind the walls of this huge fortress. Viollet-le-Duc created the interior and transformed the citadel into a wonderful medieval palace. It was used as a location for several scenes in the films *Fantômas* and *Highlander*. If the weather is fine, follow

the 'Les paloumayres' yellow **signposted paths**, through the vineyard and the woods.

Riding through vineyards
Discover the forest and the Sauternes district on horseback by day, and spend the nights in a *gîte*. The **circuit équestre du Sud-Gironde** is a memorable trek (from 2,000 to 6,000 F for a week, inclusive). You can also take a two-day trek through the vineyards, which are especially lovely in early autumn. Information: A.D.E.L. (Assoc. de Développement de l'Equitation de Loisir) Maison du Tourisme de la Gironde, 21, Cours de l'Intendance, 33000 Bordeaux, ☎ 05 56 51 05 62.

Spotcheck
C3-C4-D4

Gironde

Things to do
Meeting a craftsman
Ride through the vineyards
Orchard of La Brède

Within easy reach
*Entre-deux-Mers, p. 184,
The slopes of the Garonne,
p. 188.*

Tourist Office
**Sauternes:
☎ 05 56 76 69 13**

Château de La Brède
13 miles (21 km) S of Bordeaux
☎ 05 56 20 20 49
Open daily except Tues., 2–6pm, 1 July–30 Sept.; Sat.–Sun. and public holidays, Easter–30 June, 2–6pm and 1 Oct.– 11 Nov, 2–5.30pm.
Admission charge.
This elegant 14th-C. fortified château, surrounded by wide moats, has a lovely landscaped park. This was the birthplace of the philosopher Montesquieu, who produced most of his writings here. On the ground floor **the philosopher's bedroom** has been left as it was in his lifetime, as has the 7,000-volume **library** upstairs.

Bazas and the Bazadais

beef cattle country

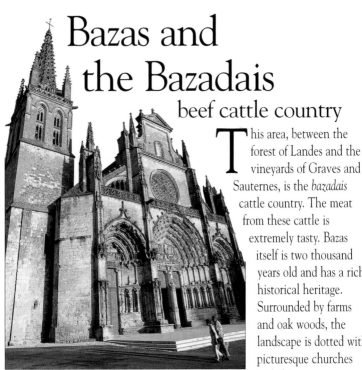

Cathedral of Saint-Jean-Baptiste, Bazas

This area, between the forest of Landes and the vineyards of Graves and Sauternes, is the *bazadais* cattle country. The meat from these cattle is extremely tasty. Bazas itself is two thousand years old and has a rich historical heritage. Surrounded by farms and oak woods, the landscape is dotted with picturesque churches and châteaux.

Bazas

The old city of Aquitaine

Apothecary
☎ 05 56 25 25 84
(Tourist Office)
Tour daily by appointment.
Admission charge.
Bazas was built on a spur of rock 25 centuries ago, and is one of the oldest cities in Aquitaine. Its Gothic cathedral, dedicated to John the Baptist (with superb 13th-C. triple portico), and chapter-house garden, are evidence of a glorious past. The lovely **Promenade** de la Brèche at the foot of the city walls (Allée Clemenceau) leads to the 17th-C. apothecary which houses a collection of glassware and pottery.

Food market

Pl. de la Cathédrale
Sat. morning.
The arcaded medieval square, in the heart of the town, is surrounded by 16th-C. houses

(no. 33, the house of the Astronomer, has astronomical symbols). The typical **market** sells ceps, capons and other local produce, as well as the local steak delicacy, *entrecôte bazadaise*, all brought together in a colourful atmosphere.

Gorges du Ciron

Trip in a rowing-boat or canoe
☎ 05 56 25 38 65 or
☎ 05 56 25 86 13
Open daily exc. 18 Dec.–9 Jan. In season, 9am–noon and 1.30–7pm; out of season, 10am–noon and 2–5.30pm.
West of Bazas, the Ciron flows from the mighty Garonne and winds along beside the Haute Lande under a luxurious canopy of **forest trees.** You can row a family-sized boat or paddle along more than 19 miles (30 km) of waterways (2-pers. canoe or 1-pers. kayak 60 to 110 F each depending

FÊTE DES BOEUFS GRAS

Bazas cattle are celebrated every year at this big fair. On the Thursday before Shrove Tuesday the most impressive animals are groomed to a spectacular shine. Their bone structure should be delicate, but muscled and the rump short and wide. The red meat must be marbled with tiny white spots of fat which melt during cooking, giving the flavour and finesse considered exceptional by connoisseurs.

(☎ 05 56 25 35 67. Open daily Jul.–Aug., 9am–6pm and Sat.–Sun. only 15 Apr.–15 Oct., 3–6pm, guided tours. Free admission.) The **Festival d'Uzeste**, *la Hestejada de las Arts*, is held here in the second fortnight of August.

Château de Cazeneuve
6½ miles (10 km) SW of Bazas
☎ 05 56 25 48 16
Open daily June–Sept., 2–6.30pm; July–Aug., 10.30am–6.30pm; Sat.–Sun., public holidays and Easter–All Saints Day, 2–6pm. *Admission charge.*
It was here that Henri IV abandoned his wife, Queen Margot, when they separated. The **royal apartments**, period furniture and the Cave of the Queen are worth a visit. A **wooded park** overlooks the gorges of the Ciron.

Spotcheck
D4

Gironde

Things to do
Visit the apothecary
Food market
Gorges du Ciron
Festival d'Uzeste

With children
Visit to an angora goat farm

Within easy reach
Slopes of the Garonne approx. 12½ miles (20 km) NW, p. 188.

Tourist Office
Bazas:
☎ 05 56 25 25 84

Aquitaine mohair
1½ miles (2km) from Bazas on the Auros road
Ferme de Gipon
☎ 05 56 25 15 11
Tours March-Oct., daily exc. Wed., 3pm; by appointment all year round. *Admission charge.*
This typical Landaise farm is actually a goat farm, where angora and dairy goats are reared. You can visit the goat-shed, and watch demonstrations of how mohair wool is processed and enjoy a country tea (booking necessary). At the shop you can buy mohair products and goats' cheese.

on the distance). You can also ride on horse-back, go rambling, mountain biking, or try archery or Landaise skittles.

In the footsteps of a pope at Château de Villandraut
9 miles (14 km) W of Bazas
☎ 05 56 25 87 57
Open daily, 1 June–30 Sept., 10am–12.30pm and 2–7pm; July–Aug., 10am–7pm; Oct.–May, 2–4.45pm. Closed 25 Dec.–1 Jan. *Admission charge.*
The Bazas district 'supplied' a pope for Avignon. Clement V set up his court in 1305 in the château of Villandraut, his native village. He is buried at Uzeste (3 miles/ 5 km from Bazas), in the superb collegiate-church.

Château de Cazeneuve

Bordeaux, capital of light

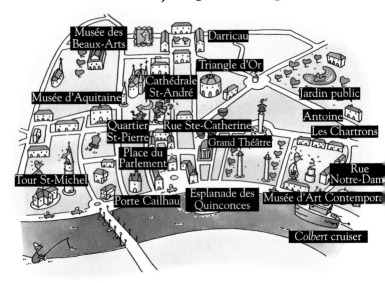

S tendhal considered Bordeaux to be 'the most beautiful city in France'.
Once a thriving sea and river port, it's now a European metropolis.
Its best ambassadors are its wines, appreciated the world over. The city
combines past and present with ease, massive modern buildings blending with
18th C. façades. Although large, Bordeaux is built on a fairly simple plan.
The northern district is centred around the Place des Quinconces, and the
old town huddles around the cathedral. Both districts provide opportunities
for leisurely walks.

The Esplanade des Quinconces

This huge esplanade is the rallying point for tourists and the very lungs of the city. In the centre, there is a huge

area of 30 acres (12 ha) where the **Bordeaux fairs**, such as the antiques fair and the pleasure fair, are held.

Le Triangle d'Or

Tourist Office
☎ 05 56 00 66 00
Guided tour (2 hours) by appointment.
The Golden Triangle is also known as the District of Great Men. It faces the Grand-Théâtre, and is bordered by

THE MIDNIGHT EDITION

The *Sud-Ouest*
Book 15 days in advance, free tour
☎ 05 56 00 33 90 or
☎ 05 56 00 33 33
From 10.30pm to midnight, watch the first edition of *Sud-Ouest*, one of the most important regional dailies, being put to bed. Follow the production line to the rotary presses and despatches and leave with the morning edition under your arm (from 1 Oct. to 30 June, except Sat., Sun. and holidays).

the Allée de Tourny, the Cours Clemenceau and the Cours de l'Intendance. It has a large number of 18th-C. mansions and many elegant shops. The church of Notre-Dame, with its beautiful baroque façade, is all that remains from the 17th C. The Place des Grands-Hommes has a **market-hall** with a glass dome. Its 30 stalls are a Mecca for shoppers.

The wine circuit
Maison du Vin
3, Cours du 30-Juillet
☎ 05 56 00 22 66
Open Mon.–Thurs., 8.30am–6pm; Fri., 8.30am–5.30pm.
Free admission.
If you want to learn everything you can about Bordeaux wines, the Maison du Vin will guide you through the labyrinth of regional appellations. It provides information and advice from wine makers. At **Vinorama**, a historical tour with 75 wax figures ends with a most unusual three-fold **tasting**, involving a 'Roman' wine, reconstituted according to an ancient method, a type of wine popular in 1850, and a modern wine for comparison.

Spotcheck
C3

Things to do

Guided tour of the Golden Triangle
The wine circuit
Boat trips
The parc de Bourran
Visit to the cruiser *Colbert*
Musée d'Aquitaine

With children

Parc du Moulineau
Cadaujac exotic farm
Zoo de Bordeaux-Pessac

Within easy reach

Blaye and Bourg, p. 114,
Libourne, p. 116,
Slopes of the Garonne,
p. 188.

Tourist Office

Bordeaux:
☎ 05 56 00 66 00

Vinorama
12, Cours du Médoc
☎ 05 56 39 39 20
Open daily except Mon., 1 June–30 Sept., 10.30am–12.30pm and 2.30–6.30pm, Sun., 2–6.30pm; Oct.–May, 2–6.30pm, Tues.–Sat.
Free admission.
To start your own wine-cellar, visit **L'Intendant** (2, Allée de Tourny ☎ 05 56 48 01 29, specialist shop) or go to the **Vinothèque** (8, Cours du 30-Juillet ☎ 05 56 52 32 05).

Boat trips
Quai Louis-XVIII
☎ 05 56 51 27 90
Explore Bordeaux and district by boat, cruising the waters of the vast river Garonne. **Pleasure boats** leave from the Embarcadère des Quinconces, and sail up the Gironde estuary, north to Bourg, Blaye and Pauillac (capital of Médoc), and south to

Cadaujac, Langoiran and Cadillac. If you prefer a shorter boat trip, there's an excursion that only visits the port area of Bordeaux in a motor-launch.

Le Quartier des Chartrons

This rejuvenated district situated beside the Garonne is where the wealthy wine merchants used to live. Wharfs are being turned into cultural venues or museums, and the 18th C. mansions built by the high society of Bordeaux are now occupied by antique shops. The feverish activity of the past has gone, and this is now somewhere to take a quiet stroll far from the bustle of the city centre.

❀ Musée des Chartrons

41, Rue Borie
☎ 05 57 87 50 60
Open Mon.–Fri., 2–6pm (Sat., May–Oct., 9am–noon).
Admission charge.
Visit the house of an 18th-C. wine merchant. Inside there's

a handsome wrought iron staircase leading to the rooms in which the great vintages were packed. There are bottles and rare labels tracing the history of packaging and shipping of wine. The wine was aged in the basement, in vaults built in 1720.

The Rue Notre-Dame

Behind the Cité Mondiale du Vin, village Notre-Dame
☎ 05 56 52 66 13
Open daily, 10am–noon and 2–7pm (Sun., Oct.–Apr., 2–7pm).

The Rue Notre-Dame now consists entirely of **antique shops** installed in the mansions that once belonged to wine merchants. Wander through this veritable Ali

Baba's cave where you'll find furniture and artefacts, porcelain, dolls, sculpture, old watches, tapestries, and more.

The Parc de Bourran

2½ miles (4 km) W of the Grand-Théâtre, access via Rue A.-de-Musset and Av. de la Marne
33700 Mérignac
Open daily, 8am–6.30pm; Apr.–Sept., 7.30pm.
Free admission.
This park occupies an exceptionally large space in the middle of an urban setting. The 42 acres (17 ha) of **greenery** and former farmland contain meadows, groves, bridges and waterfalls. The Devèze, a tiny tributary of the Garonne, runs through the park and a pond mirrors the reflections of a 19th-C. château. Its ancient trees are labelled.

Musée d'Art Contemporain de Bordeaux (CAPC)

7, Rue Ferrère
☎ 05 56 00 81 50
Open daily except Mon., 11am–6pm (8pm on Wed.). Guided tour: Sat.
Admission charge.
The former Lainé warehouses no longer store spices from the colonies, and they have since been replaced by a collection of contemporary art.

The vast central hall, reminiscent of a cathedral, has retained its original features and is used to display over-sized modern works. The art collection housed here is internationally famous.

When you're older...

Parc du Moulineau, 53, Rue du Moulineau, Gradignan
Daily from 7am till dusk.
Free admission.
If you've got children who hate being told they're too young when you're enjoying the wine tasting at the **Maison du Vin**, then this park, and the following three entries, are excellent places to pacify them. Start by taking them south, to the very edge of Bordeaux (in the direction of Bayonne), where there are 5 acres (8 ha) of greenery and around 50 animals living in this delightful park with its own zoo.

CADIOT-BADIE

26, Allée de Tourny
☎ 05 56 44 24 22
Open daily, Mon., 9am–noon and 2–7pm; Tuies.–Sat., 9am–7pm.
The chocolate-coloured wooden shopfront has not changed for over a century. M. Landry took over the firm of Cadiot-Badie, which has been a famous confectionery brand since 1826. Come and taste his Bordeaux chocolate truffles, with raisins soaked in brandy, his *guinettes*, succulent cherries in kirsch (36 F for 3 1/2 oz/100 g), or his *fanchonnettes bordelaises* in beautiful, old-fashioned boxes. All the chocolates are hand-made.

Cadaujac Exotic Farm

S of Bordeaux, towards Toulouse
Domaine de la Roussie, Cadaujac
☎ 05 56 30 94 80
Daily from 10am to 8pm
Admission charge.
The farm has 1,000 exotic animals to see, not to mention life-size reconstructions of dinosaurs and **camel rides**.

Zoo de Bordeaux-Pessac

S of Bordeaux, bypass exit no 12
3, Chemin du Transvaal
☎ 05 56 36 46 28
Daily from 8am–7pm.
Admission charge.
Animals, a flume, roundabouts – who could ask for more? A paradise for kids.

La Base Sous-marine

Bd. Alfred-Daney
☎ 05 56 11 11 50
Open Wed., Thurs., Sat. and Sun., 2–8pm. Closed in Sept. and Apr.
This German-built submarine base has been imaginatively converted into a **nautical museum**. Here, 70 yachts and motor boats tell the story of pleasure boating since the beginning of the 19th C. You can see, for example, the prototype of the *Ville-de-Paris* which competed in the 1992 Americas Cup.

Antoine

19, Cours Portal
☎ 05 56 81 43 19
Open daily, 7.30am–8pm (7pm Sun.).
This creative chocolate maker invented a *jupette*, for the benefit of the Mayor. It's a delicious chocolate containing cherries stuffed with truffle paste (100 F for 9 oz/250 g). His other speciality, the *Mascaron de Bordeaux* combines wine, grapes and chocolate paste.
(42 F a dozen).

Rue Sainte-Catherine

This is the street on which to go window-shopping. From the Place de la Comédie to the Place de la Victoire, it's the most densely populated shopping street in France with more than 250 shops, department stores and street-sellers. The people of Bordeaux can always be found here, their arms full of packages and bags. Avoid Saturday afternoons, unless you don't mind battling through the crowds.

Exotic chocolates

**Maison Darricau,
7, Place Gambetta**
☎ 05 56 44 21 49
Open Mon.–Fri., 10am–
7pm; Sat., 2–7pm.
At Darricau, the chocolate
maker's art and imagination
knows no bounds! There
are chocolates for the most
unusual tastes, flavoured
with ginger, cinnamon, curry
and tobacco, and sprinkled
with cocoa (350 F for 2 lb
4 oz/1 kg).

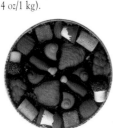

Le Musée des Beaux-Arts

20, Cours d'Albret
☎ 05 56 10 20 56
Open daily exc. Tues.
and public holidays,
11am–6pm.
Admission charge.
The museum is housed in a
wing of the magnificent
Hôtel de Rohan, the former
seat of the archbishop of
Bordeaux, which now serves
as the town hall. The
collection includes Italian

GALERIE DES BEAUX-ARTS

Renaissance paintings,
17th-C. Dutch and Flemish
masterpieces and paintings
by artists from Bordeaux,
including Redon, Marquet
and Lhote. Don't miss the
famous canvas by Delacroix:
*Greece on the Ruins of
Missolonghi* (1826).

Musée des Arts Décoratifs

39, Rue Bouffard
☎ 05 56 00 72 50
Open daily except Tues.
and public holidays,
2–6pm. Guided tours,
Wed. and Thurs.
Admission charge.
The 18th-C. Hôtel de
Lalande is a lovely setting
for this museum of applied
arts. The interesting displays
include furniture, pottery
and metalwork. In summer,
you can drink tea, eat
brunch or lunch in the
courtyard. After your visit,
take a wander through
the **pedestrianised streets**
nearby where you can go
shopping and discover the
magnificent mansions in
the Rue Judaïque, Porte
Dijeaux and the Rue du
Loup (the Hôtel Ragueneau
is at no. 71). The Rue
Bouffard and Rue des
Remparts contain a number
of antique shops.

Le Musée d'Aquitaine

20, Cours Pasteur
☎ 05 56 01 51 00
Open daily except Mon.
and public holidays,
11am–6pm. Guided
tours, Tues., 10am–noon.
Admission charge.
This historic and ethnographic museum portrays life in

THE BATTLE CRUISER *COLBERT*

Opposite 60, Quai des Chartrons
☎ 05 56 44 96 11
Open daily, 1 Apr.–30 Sept.,
10am–6pm (7pm Sat. Sun. and
public holidays); July–Aug., 10am–
7pm. Oct.–March, open daily exc.
Mon., 10am–7pm.
Admission charge.
A famous old warship, the
Colbert, is now enjoying her
retirement. A former missile-
launcher, she was decommissioned in 1993, and
is now open to the public. You can visit the boiler
room, kitchens, the admiral's stateroom, sick bay,
arsenal, and crew quarters. Explore the amazing
world of the battle cruisers, and get some exercise in the process (steep companionways).

Aquitaine from prehistoric times to the present. There are displays showing life in the country, at sea or on the river, and the wine trade and its contacts abroad. The displays are well conceived and the models and tableaux are precise reconstructions that will be of interest to young and old alike. It's a fascinating museum depicting local life.

The cathedral of Saint-André

This lovely combination of Romanesque and Gothic styles was built in the 11th and 12th C. The walls were strengthened in the 13th C. and in 1440 the separate bell-tower (166½ feet; 50 m high) was added by Archbishop Pey Berland.

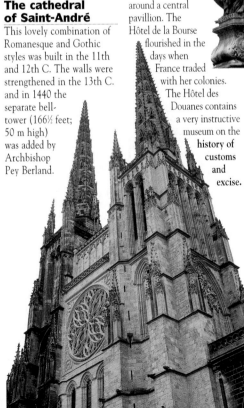

La Place de la Bourse

You'll have a good view of the square from the stone bridge. The former Place Royale was built in the 18th C. The Hôtel de la Bourse and the Hôtel de la Douane form a semi-circle around a central pavillion. The Hôtel de la Bourse flourished in the days when France traded with her colonies. The Hôtel des Douanes contains a very instructive museum on the **history of customs and excise.**

The streets of the Quartier Saint-Pierre

This medieval district is bounded by the Place de la Bourse and the Place du Parlement. This is the artisans' quarter, as indicated by the names of the streets: Rue des Argentiers (silversmiths), Rue des Bahutiers (cabinet-makers), Rue du Chai-des-Farines (flour store), etc. They are reminders of what a bustling city Bordeaux has been over the centuries. Rue Ferdinand-Phillipart, leading to the Place du Parlement, is lined with handsome Louis XV residences with grotesque masks and wrought iron.

Place de la Victoire, the student quarter

The square is dominated by the monumental Aquitaine Gate 36 ft (11 m) high. The number of bars is also impressive! If you want to see young people in action, come here on a Thursday night when students from all over France, who have come to study in Bordeaux, go out late at night before going home to their families. Some addresses popular with the student community are: Le Bœuf sur le Toit, Rue de Candale, Le Plana, and Place de la Victoire.

Place du Parlement

In the 18th C., the Marquis de Tourny demolished the walls that enclosed the Quartier Saint-Pierre and built new roads and squares in an urban masterpiece. The quarter changed completely and became the showplace of the period. The best example of this transformation is the Place du Parlement. It's paved with Italian-style cobbles and with elegant Louis XV façades and an Empire fountain. It's now surrounded by elegant shops and café **terraces**.

From the Place Saint-Pierre to the Porte Cailhau

Ecologists patronise the **organic food market** on Thursday morning, buying

vegetables, jams and beauty products. Bordeaux is a trading city at all times of the year.

The Cannelé de Bordeaux

This delicious cake is a speciality of the town. It looks something like a miniature caramelised rum baba. Its origins are in a little stick-

shaped sweet called a **cannelat** (little cane) made by nuns. However, the fluted baking mould may also have inspired the name. You will find them in all the best bakeries and they are especially good at Baillardran (Galerie des Grands-Hommes, ☎ 05 56 79 05 89 and 90, Rue Porte-Dijeaux, ☎ 05 56 51 02 09. 8.80 F each). To release the flavour, warm them in the oven for four or five minutes.

Bordeluche

Bordeluche is the local dialect and a sign of recognition for expatriate Bordelais. It originates from Gascon, with a dose of patois, and other additions thrown in. It's the language used in the markets and the poorer quarters. Words such as *baraganes* (leeks) and *tricandilles* (pork tripe), are not words you will have learnt in French at school, but this ancient language is being kept alive in the performances at the Café-théâtre de l'Onyx, so if you want to really impress the folks back home, learn a little *Bordeluche*.

The city gates

Only two gates are left, the **Porte Cailhau** (116 ft/35 m high) and the **Porte de la Grosse-Cloche**. The former is in the Place du Palais, and was rebuilt in 1495 in honour of Charles VIII. It is now a tourist information centre. The Porte de la Grosse-Cloche is older, dating from the 13th and 15th C., and is more unusual. It served both as the city belfry and the gate through which pilgrims passed on their way to the tomb of St James (Santiago de Compostela).

From La Rousselle to Saint-Michel

Don't miss the house with the medieval gable at 49, Rue des Bahutiers, and no. 12, Rue Pilet which has retained its half-timbering. The Rue de la Rousselle, between the two is where the mother of Michel de Montaigne was born. The oldest house in Bordeaux, dat-

ing from the 14th C. and the home of Jeanne Lartigue, Montesquieu's wife, are both in the Rue-Neuve.

Tour Saint-Michel

This is the tallest tower in southern France (380 feet (114 m). Come and browse in its **flea market** (2nd Sun. in March, June, Sept. and Dec.). Saint-Michel is still a busy place, as it was when the barges unloaded wood, iron and salt for small industries and workshops (coopers in the Rue Fusterie, armourers in the Rue des Faures etc). Tourny chose this district in which to build the Hôtel de la Monnaie (the mint) next to the Sainte-Croix church which has a beautiful Romanesque façade.

Jardin Public

Entrance in the Cours de Verdun
Open daily, 7am–6,30pm (Feb.), 7pm (March), 8pm (Apr–May), 9pm (July–Aug.), 8pm (Sept.), 7.30pm (beginning of Oct.), 6pm (end of Oct.–Jan.).
Free admission.

This 18th-C. park consists of 24.7 acres (10 ha) of landscape garden in the city centre. There are banks of flowers, ancient trees and a fine botanical garden, containing 3,000 species of plants in an area of 1¼ acres (0.5 ha) and in the Muséum d'Histoire Naturelle. There's a lake with ducks and swans, and you can take a mini-cruise on the *Petit-Mousse*.

Médoc
home of the great vintages

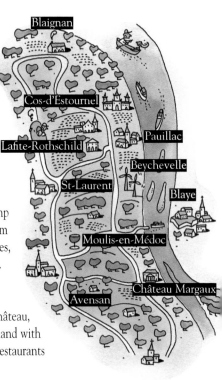

Blaignan

Cos-d'Estournel

Lafite-Rothschild

Pauillac

Beychevelle

St-Laurent

Blaye

Moulis-en-Médoc

Château Margaux

Avensan

T he Latin source of the name 'Médoc' (*in medio aquae*, 'in the middle of the waters') summarises the geography of this district. Bordered by the Atlantic ocean in the west and by the river Gironde in the east, it has a damp but sunny climate, protected from sea breezes by the forest of Landes, which is ideal for grape-growing. Médoc is the home of the great clarets. You can follow the great vintage route from château to château, and as great food goes hand in hand with great wine, try out some of the restaurants beside the Gironde estuary.

Château Margaux
Margaux
☎ 05 57 88 83 93
Free tour of the chais *only by appointment, during the week.*
This ancient fortified castle in the south of Haut Médoc is a masterpiece of early 19th-C. neo-Classical style. Its vast *chais* (wine-stores), with their Doric columns, have set the tone for all modern wine storage facilities. The handsome architecture is particularly suited to a *1er grand cru classé* which some people consider to be a work of genius. Château Margaux wine is not for sale at the château.

Musée des Arts et Métiers de la Vigne et du Vin
Moulis-en-Médoc, opposite the station
☎ 05 56 58 01 23
Open daily (public holidays included),10am–6pm.
Admission charge.
This wine museum, housed in the cellars of the Château de Maucaillou, explains all there

is to know about grape-growing and wine-making, as well as the skills of making barrels, the work of the *maître de chais*, who stores the wine, and the making of glass bottles. There is a tasting at the end.

Château de Beychevelle
Saint-Julien-Beychevelle
☎ 05 56 73 20 70
Open 9.30am–noon, 1.30–5pm, Mon.–Sat., June–Sept.; Mon.–Fri., Oct.–May.
Free tour of the chais.
Visit the lovely *chais* of this *4e grand cru classé* and explore its gardens and terraces which lead down to the Gironde. The vineyards contain heaters which waft warm air through the vines whenever the weather turns too cold. A bottle of 1995 or 1996 vintage costs 270 F, 1997: 195 F (1999 prices).

Château du Cos-d'Estournel: oriental fantasy
☎ 05 56 73 15 55
Free tour Mon.–Fri. by written request sent two days in advance.
Louis-Gaspard d'Estournel, who lived in the 19th C., was fond of all things oriental as well as the wines of Médoc, so he built an exotic wine palace. The château, setting for a *2e grand cru classé*, is next door to Château-Lafite. It's a mix of Chinese and Indian styles. The heavily carved door and copper turrets were inspired by the architecture of the royal palace in Zanzibar.

Le Petit Musée d'Automates
3, Rue Aristide Briand, Pauillac
☎ 05 56 59 02 45
Open daily, June–Sept., 10.30am–7pm; the rest of the year, w/ends and public hols by appointment.

Château du Cos-d'Estournel

Spotcheck
B1-B2-C2

Gironde

Things to do
The *grands crus* circuit
The Pauillac district by bike
Golfing in Médoc
The Bordeaux school
Excursions on the Gironde

With children
Petit Musée d'Automates

Tourist Offices
Lesparre-Médoc:
☎ 05 56 41 21 96
Pauillac: ☎ 05 56 59 03 08

Admission charge
The museum is the guardian of an old French tradition: the making of automata. It's presented like a little theatre of mechanical arts, where tableaux of animals such as cats, frogs or rabbits perform with great imagination and humour. Thanks to

A LITTLE WATER
Excursions on the Gironde
Tourist Office of Pauillac
☎ 05 56 59 03 08
Médoc lies along the Gironde estuary. From Pauillac, you can take a barge to explore this regional artery. As the gateway to the sea, the river is busy with the comings and goings of fishermen and lighters. The slopes are covered with the legendary vineyards and on the banks there are oyster and prawn farms. Local eateries feature the finest home-grown delicacies (lamprey, shad, elvers and other freshwater and sea fish).

artistry and mechanical precision, a fantasy world has been created, where animals have replaced human beings.

Pauillac
Bichettes and lamb

Pauillac is the historic capital of Médoc and centre of the wine trade. It's here that you will find the largest number of *grands crus classés* of Bordeaux, including three of the five most prestigious. This city has more to offer than just wine, however. There's a lovely **marina** which is shared by yachts and fishing vessels. From this port, passengers once

AGNEAU DE PAUILLAC

Pauillac lamb has been a trade mark of the region since 1995. The lambs are exclusively milk-fed. Since they live among vineyards, they never get to feed on grass. In the spring, as soon as the shoots begin to appear on the vines, the ewes are brought back to the herd. The lambs never eat anything other than their mother's milk, hence the delicacy of their meat, which now has the coveted red label. The sheep are reared exclusively in herds. The price of a leg of Pauillac milk-fed lamb is about 120 F for 2 lb 4 oz (1 kg).

Château Pichon-Longueville-Baron

embarked on transatlantic liners en route for South America. The local delicacy is the **bichette**, the white shrimp which lives in the estuary. They can be eaten with a little water flavoured with aniseed liqueur, and followed by *agneau de Pauillac* (see box on left). To admire the lovely countryside, rent a **bicycle** from the Maison du Tourisme et du Vin (La Verrerie, Pauillac, ☎ 05 56 59 03 08, open daily all year round).

Château Mouton-Rothschild

☎ 05 56 73 21 29
Tour of the *chais*, by appointment only, daily except 1 May, Apr.–Oct.; out of season, Mon.–Fri. A landscaped park surrounds the huge winestore (open to visitors) in which the oak barrels are stored in rows. A collection of wine labels designed by Picasso, Dali and Soulages are the centrepiece of the museum devoted to works of art related to the vine and to wine. This

vineyard is located on a hillside called a *mothon* and yields wine of the highest quality (known as *premier cru*).

Château Pichon-Longueville-Baron

☎ 05 56 73 17 17
Winestore open daily in season, 9am–noon and 2–6.30pm (5.30pm on Fri.). Out of season, open daily 9am–noon and 1.30–6pm (5pm on Fri.). By appointment.
Free admission.
This château, with its slender turrets, could almost be Sleeping Beauty's magic castle. It produces good quality wine (*deuxième cru*). The ultramodern winestores were remodelled in 1992. There's a specially designed area for visitors with a rotunda overlooking the work-rooms and vats. A 1993 vintage costs 270 F.

The Bordeaux school

Cordeillan-Bages (Pauillac)
☎ 05 56 59 24 24
Open Feb.–Nov., (book one month in advance). *Admission charge.*
This is the ideal place to improve your knowledge and become a wine-buff. In this *relais-château* (hôtel château), you can try to detect the 59 aromas that go to make up the bouquet

---

...ation of one of the finest, greatest and most classic of all the wines of Médoc.

of the wines of Bordeaux. If you want to learn more, there are four guided visits to the prestigious châteaux which

Blaignan
Les noisettines du Médoc
N of Pauillac
☎ 05 56 09 03 09
Workshop open 15 June–

been established for over three centuries. They dip large hazelnuts in a special syrup and coat them with hot caramel. Noisettines can only be eaten in the master's workshop in the summer. For the occasion, the confectioners don 17th-C. costumes. Pay 29 F for 5¹/₂ oz (150 g) of pure pleasure!

will definitely turn you into something of an expert.

Château Latour
☎ 05 56 73 19 80
Free tour of the winestore by appointment only. The round tower of this ancient fortified château faithfully guards the vineyard. It's here that stainless steel vats were used for the first time in the 1960s. This revolution did not, however, put an end to oak vats, since these are indispensable for the cre-

15 Sept., daily, exc. Sun. and public holidays, 2.30–6.30pm (by appointment June and Sept.). Out of season: sampling and sales, Mon.–Sat., 9am–noon and 2.30–5.30pm (closed for Feb. school holidays).
This confectionery company has

Louens
Golf in the Médoc
Bordeaux bypass, exit no. 7, towards Le Verdon
Le Pian-Médoc
☎ 05 56 70 11 90
Open daily, all year round.
This is one of the loveliest golf courses in Europe, with two links between the vines and the châteaux. Players can take lessons from the pro on greens which have been used by the greatest of the world's players (indiv. green fee: weekdays, 250 F; weekends, 300 F).

Château Latour

The Landes Girondines coast
kingdom of cyclists

This beach stretches all the way from the Pointe de Grave to the Bassin d'Arcachon. The sand is held in place by dunes, the oldest of which have disappeared under the pine forest of the nearby Grande Lande. The Côte d'Argent offers a glorious vista of ocean on one side and pine forest on the other, while inland the lakes of Hourtin-Carcans and Lacanau provide further ecological riches.

Cordouan
The lighthouse
5½ miles (9 km) off the pointe de Grave
Departure for a trip from the Pointe de Grave (port-bloc),
La Bohème II launch.
☎ **05 56 09 62 93** or
☎ **06 09 73 30 84**
Admission charge.
This lighthouse, built in the late 16th C. to help sailors find their way through the capricious sea lanes of the estuary, is a real maritime palace. There's a surrounding wall as well as a monumental portico, royal apartments and a lovely chapel with a vaulted ceiling and pretty stained glass windows. The **trip** to and from the lighthouse (4 hours) is worth making for its own sake.

Soulac-sur-Mer
Dune d'Amélie
☎ **05 56 09 86 61**
(Tourist Office).
15 June–15 Sept.
Guided tours.
Why not begin by visiting the basilica of Notre-Dame-de-la-Fin-des-Terres, which was covered by sand in the late 18th C. Of additional interest are **500 neo-colonial villas** which are a reminder of how the middle classes of Bordeaux enjoyed themselves here at the seaside in the late 19th C. The Dune d'Amélie (½ mile (1 km) south) is a classified nature reserve.

SOULAC
SUR MER

Contaut
The footbridge
Access from the D 101E or by cycle track
☎ **05 56 09 19 00**
End of June–15 Sept.,
Wed.–Sun.
Paid guided tours.
Free admission.
No dogs allowed.

An unusual walk over a 2,000 ft (600 m) long footbridge, 10 ft (3 m) above the ground, which crosses the Contant lagoon. The lagoon harbours rare animals and some species of plants dating back thousands of years.

Lacanau
The lake
On the Lacanau lake you can **sail yachts** or **catamarans**, go **windsurfing** or **water skiing**. The lake is surrounded by pines and in the south-east corner, its wild shores are home to a variety of birds. The best way to see these is to approach quietly in a canoe.

Surfers' rendez-vous
The Lacanau-Océan beach is the ideal place to learn to surf and several clubs offer **lessons**. One of these is the Lacanau Surf Club (Maison de la Glisse, Boulevard de la Plage, ☎ 05 56 26 38 84). The **Jardin des Vagues** offers courses perfect for 5-10 year olds if your children are keen to learn. Don't miss the heats for the Lacanau Pro championship in

GETTING AROUND THE GIRONDE COAST

Little train: departure from La Pointe de Grave, Le Verdon
☎ 05 56 09 61 78
(Tourist Office)
Open daily, July–Aug:
Sat.–Sun., Easter–
mid-Oct. Runs in both
directions, the return
journey lasts 1 hour.
Admission charge.

The 56 miles (90 km) of the Gironde coast are largely suitable only for walkers, horse-riders or cyclists. There are many well-signposted paths

and cycling tracks between the beach and the pine forest (especially around the lakes). The less energetic, or families with young children can take the little tourist train which runs along beside the beach between Soulac and the Pointe de Grave.

Spotcheck
B2-B3

Gironde

Things to do

The Cordouan lighthouse
Dune d'Amélie
The Contaut footbridge
Water sports at Lacanau
Surfing lessons
Visit to a windmill
Walking, riding or cycling along the coast

With children

The wave garden
The little tourist train

Tourist Offices

Soulac-sur-Mer:
☎ 05 56 09 86 61
Lacanau: ☎ 05 56 03 21 01

mill produced quality flour. It has been painstakingly restored by the son and grandson of the last miller. Its huge oak gearwheel still works and during your visit

you'll learn about the production of flour. The first movement of the sails in the morning, when they try to find the wind, is spectacular.

the second fortnight in August, which attracts professionals from all over the world.

Vensac

The windmill

*10 miles (16 km)
S of Soulac*
☎ 05 56 09 45 00
Open daily, 1 July–31
Aug., 10am–noon and
2.30–6.30pm; June and
Sept., weekends, 10am–
noon and 2.30–6.30pm,
Apr.–May and Oct., Sun.
afternoons, 2.30–6.30pm.
Admission charge.
For two centuries the Vensac

Arcachon and its basin
sun, sea and sand

Arcachon is a town built in three periods over four seasons. At first it was a summer holiday seaside resort before becoming famous as a winter retreat because of its mild climate. Later, the resort began to attract autumn and spring holidaymakers. The beach, the fishing, amusements and the pine forest are all important assets.

The triangular Arcachon basin, a deep bay, contains an inland sea where oysters are farmed and has several good swimming sites.

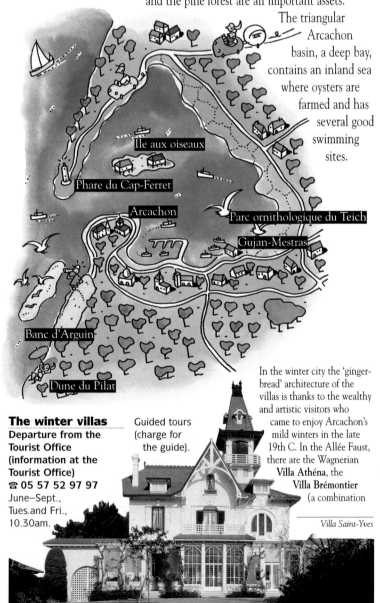

Ile aux oiseaux

Phare du Cap-Ferret

Arcachon

Parc ornithologique du Teich

Gujan-Mestras

Banc d'Arguin

Dune du Pilat

The winter villas
Departure from the Tourist Office (information at the Tourist Office)
☎ 05 57 52 97 97
June–Sept.,
Tues. and Fri.,
10.30am.

Guided tours (charge for the guide).

In the winter city the 'gingerbread' architecture of the villas is thanks to the wealthy and artistic visitors who came to enjoy Arcachon's mild winters in the late 19th C. In the Allée Faust, there are the Wagnerian **Villa Athéna**, the **Villa Brémontier** (a combination

Villa Saint-Yves

of a pagoda and a castle) and the **Villa Graigortan**, in French Compagnie des Indes style. Many of these ornate residences are haunted by memories of the celebrities who once lived in them.

International Women's Film Festival

☎ 05 56 22 47 25
18–24 Sept.

Each year, Arcachon celebrates the women who have contributed to the film industry. Actresses and directors, script-writers and producers from all over the world are given due recognition. Films are shown every day at the Palais des Congrès and the Olympia, to select

the winner of the Festival Prize. Animated discussions take place between the film teams, the jury, and the public who all participate in the vote. Booking for seats starts at the beginning of August (information and programmes are available at the Tourist Office).

LA DUNE DU PILAT

12 miles (7½ km) S of Arcachon, on the D218
At 390 ft (117 m) this is the highest dune in Europe. This living mountain is as disturbing as it is fascinating. Because no vegetation has taken root on it, it moves freely and continues to grow, having tripled in size over the last century! You can climb the north-east face, up a flight of wooden steps, and get a magnificent view. Since 1978 it has been a listed site. The sand mountain is 1½ miles (2½ km) long and moves 13 ft (4 m) every year.

Big game fishing

Seegritt, Cap-Ferret
☎ 05 56 60 66 61
8 May–15 Nov.
If there's something of the Hemingway about you, you'll enjoy the excitement of fishing for shark. You're taken out into the open sea in a powerful launch (400 F per

Spotcheck
B3

Gironde

Things to do
Circuit of the winter villas
Big game fishing
The Casino park
Climbing the dune du Pilat
Women's Film Festival
Bird island
The lighthouse of Cap-Ferret
House of the oyster
Bird sanctuary
Picnic on the Banc d'Arguin
Canoeing or kayaking

With children
Bassin d'Arcachon Zoo

Within easy reach
*Pays de Born, p. 214,
Parc Régional des Landes de Gascogne, p. 218.*

Tourist Offices
Arcachon:
☎ 05 57 52 97 97
Lège-Cap-Ferret:
☎ 05 56 03 94 49

fisherman; 200 F for an accompanying guest, who is allowed to fish, but not for shark). Other addresses can be had from the Tourist Office of Lège-Cap-Ferret.

The Parc du Casino

Avenue Victor-Hugo, Ville d'Hiver
☎ 05 57 52 98 98
Open daily all day long.
Free admission.
This pleasant park was created during the Second Empire and has hardly changed at all over the years, with its curving avenues, lawns, flowerbeds and waterfalls. It has an arboretum planted with more than 60 rare species of tree. It overlooks the town and has a **splendid view** of the whole Arcachon basin.

The Arcachon basin

The basin is like an **inland sea** which breaks up the uninterrupted sweep of the Côte d'Argent. It opens onto the Atlantic through a narrow passage which is particularly vulnerable to damage from the elements. Water rushes through it so violently that you have to be a very experienced sailor to be able to navigate its narrow channels. There's a complete calm at low tide, but wind and sand particles whip up again as soon as the tide rises. Inside the basin, the exceptionally mild

climate is an ideal breeding ground for oysters and a home to many sea-birds.

Île aux Oiseaux

Tour of the island, departure from Arcachon, Thiers pier
☎ 05 56 54 60 32
Departures daily.
Admission charge.
The island, a paradise for birdlife, is right in the centre of the basin. Horses once grazed here, swimming out to the island to enjoy its sweet grass. Today, only oyster-farmers land here to supervise their oyster-beds, which are marked out with wooden stakes. Their huts on wooden stilts at the southern end of the island welcome the brave souls who try and land here by sea-kayak.

The Cap-Ferret lighthouse

☎ 05 56 03 94 49
Open July–Aug., 10am–noon and 3–6pm, Tues., Wed., Sat., Sun., June and Sept.,

3–5.15pm (departures every 45 minutes).
Admission charge.
The viewing platform is reached by climbing 258 steps and offers a **magnificent view** of the Arcachon area – the ocean, dune du Pilat, oyster-beds, the Île aux Oiseaux and the sea lanes. While you are there, visit the pretty **seaside resort** of Cap-Ferret.

Gujan-Mestras

Maison de l'Huître
☎ 05 56 66 23 71
Open daily, Apr., Sept., 10am–noon and 2–6.30pm; Mon.–Sat., Oct.–March, 10am–12.30pm and 2.30–6pm; Sun. by appointment for groups.
Admission charge.
This is the oyster-farming capital of the basin. Gujan-Mestras is busy with the constant traffic of *pinasses* (oyster boats) entering and leaving the seven ports (La Barbotière being the most lively). At La Maison de l'Huître (Port de Larros), former oyster farmers may be available to explain all the secrets of their craft (see pp. 24 and 25).

Bird sanctuary

Le Teich
☎ 05 56 22 80 93
Open daily, July–Aug., 10am–8pm; Sept.–mid-Apr., 10am–6pm (7pm beginning of Sept.); mid-Apr.–June, 10am–7pm.
Admission charge.
This is like an international airport for birds. Hundreds of thousands of migrating birds

stop here every year. The signposted routes and guided tours led by an expert will help you to identify some of the 300 species flying overhead. Don't forget to bring your binoculars to get the maximum benefit from this wonderful display of aerial acrobatics.

Banc d'Arguin
Crossing from Arcachon, Thiers pier.
☎ 05 56 54 60 32
Only in July–Aug.
This sandbank at the mouth of the basin is a living sculpture. The rising and falling tides change its contours on a daily basis. Tufts of grass act as a landmark for the sea-swallows which reproduce in large numbers here (4,000 breeding pairs). This islet is a bird sanctuary but you can also try a windy (and sandy!) picnic with a guide (day tours with picnics leave from the oyster-farming port of Arès, ☎ 05 56 60 18 07).

Caviar from the basin
Moulin de la Cassadotte Biganos
☎ 05 56 82 64 42
Closed Dec.–Jan.
Real sturgeon caviar is produced at this former mill,

A TRIP ROUND THE BASIN

Centre Nautique
☎ 05 56 22 36 83
Union des Bateliers
☎ 05 56 54 60 32
You may understandably be satisfied with the wonderful spectacle of the sun setting over the coast, but the best view of the Arcachon basin is actually from the water. There are many monitored trips and excursions available. The Centre Nautique offers a great choice of sporting activities: canoe-kayaking, rowing, sailing or scuba-diving. The Union des Bateliers organises tours of an oyster-farm, under the guidance of a professional who will teach you all you want to know about breeding, farming and harvesting oysters. (Guided tours last 1 1/4 hours, by appointment from May to October.)

now a fish-farm. The breeding-ground can be visited and you can leave with a pot of caviar: it's delicious for breakfast (580 F for $3^1/_2$ oz; 100 g).

Zoo du Bassin d'Arcachon
Near the Lac de Cazaux
La Teste
☎ 05 56 54 71 44
Apr.–Sept., daily, 10am–7pm; Oct.–March, open Wed., Sat., Sun. and public holidays, 2–6pm.
Admission charge.
This is one of the largest zoos in France, with fifty wild animals, a bear enclosure and a 25 acre (10 ha) amusement park. It has everything to satisfy even the most demanding child (or adult!).

Banc d'Arguin

The Born district
black gold

This is where the long string of lakes of Landes begins. It runs parallel to the Côte d'Argent, between the Arcachon basin and Bayonne. This chain of water is where the old *landes* (heath) once stood. Between Sanguinet and the seaside resort of Mimizan, the Born district has exhumed traces of its past; among the treasures discovered was a source of oil. It's a lovely area of ocean, lakes and forests.

Lac de Parentis

Sanguinet
The lake

Musée des Sites Lacustres,
Place de la Mairie
☎ 05 58 82 13 32
Open daily, July–Aug., 10am–noon and 2.30–7pm; out of season, only by appointment.
Admission charge.

Once upon a time, the Lac de Sanguinet was covered by an oak forest inhabited by pre-historic man. Archaeologists have recently unearthed many artefacts, including Iron Age vases, canoes carved out of pine trees as well as Gallo-Roman artefacts and jewellery, all beautifully preserved. On the lake there are **water sport** facilities.

Le Club de Voile
☎ 05 58 78 64 30
Here you have a choice of trying your hand at wind-surfing (100 F for two hours) or hiring a catamaran. Enjoy the water!

Parentis-en-Born
Musée du Pétrole
Route du Lac
☎ 05 58 78 43 60
Open daily July–Aug., guided tours at 11am or 3pm.
Admission charge.
Since 1954, oil has been pumped from the Lac de Parentis via underground pipelines 7,330 ft (2,200 m) below the surface. This municipal museum traces the

history and uses of oil in the Landes (it is even used to make chewing-gum!).

THE HEALING WATERS

The little hamlet of Bouricos, between Pontenx and Labouheyre, has a famous fountain that has a reputation for curing skin diseases and epilepsy. It can be found near the sanctuary of the chapel (access via the D 626). Further south, the village of Escource has six springs whose sources all rise here. They are harder to find but are supposed to help cure eye and skin diseases. Beware of traffic jams on well-known pilgrimage days, especially on St. John's Day (midsummer).

Biscarosse

Musée de l'Hydraviation
332, Avenue L.-Bréguet
☎ 05 58 78 00 65 and
☎ 05 58 78 03 03
Open daily, 10am–7pm in July–Aug.;
3–7pm Apr.–Sept.;
2–6pm Oct.–Mar.
Admission charge.
In the early 20th C., Pierre Latécoère tested hydroplanes on the Lac de Parentis.

Pioneers of the airmail service all landed here and Jean Mermoz, the French aviator, left from here for Santiago in Chile on 13 May 1930. This former airbase with a prestigious past is now a museum celebrating early aeronautical adventures.

Mios

Jardin des Papillons Exotiques
1748, Rte de Bordeaux
☎ 05 58 78 67 42
Open May, June, Sept., daily, 2–6pm; July–Aug., daily, 10.30am–6.30pm.
Admission charge.
If the weather's bad, take shelter between Mios and Sanguinet in this **indoor garden** filled with exotic and tropical butterflies which fly freely in their hundreds.

Spotcheck
B4

Landes

Things to do

Water sports
Petroleum of Parentis museum
Hydro-aviation museum
Visit to the paper-mills of Gascony

With children

Exotic butterfly garden

Within easy reach

Arcachon, p. 210.

Tourist Office

Mimizan: ☎ 05 58 09 11 20

Mimizan

Gascony paper-mill
☎ 05 58 09 19 01
Tours daily by appointment; in July, Thurs. only (book at the Tourist Office)
Free admission.
This is one of the oldest paper-mills in Landes. All the stages of papermaking are explained, from shredding the pulp to laminating it into sheets. The pine needles removed from the logs are used to make a **'needle ski-slope'** and you can rent skis here (in summer only).

La Grande Lande
European champion of forests

This is a huge evergreen forest of pine trees, with an undergrowth of heather and gorse and clearings in which maize is grown. Low houses with large windows and wooden frames contribute a melancholy charm this area which was a putrid bog 150 years ago. Now it's the largest forest in western Europe and beneath its sleepy canopy is a world in constant movement.

Belin-Béliet
The abandoned churches

Access via the D 110 (Saint-Michel) and D 110/E1 (Saint-Pierre)

Churches in the Landes forest can often be found lying abandoned. Whole villages have had to pack up and leave their churches behind because they were invaded by sand and water. Such churches include Saint-Michel-de-Vieux-Lugo (11th–15th C.), a stop for pilgrims on their way to Compostela, and the Romanesque church of Saint-Pierre-de-Mons.

Hostens
The lagoons of Gat-Mort

Access via the D 110 E6, between Louchats and Saint-Magne
☎ 05 56 88 53 44
Free guided tours, 15 June–15 Sept., Thurs., Fri. and Sat.

These little stretches of water are what remains of the boggy heathland. They escaped being drained in the 19th C. and retain the wildlife they had before the pine forests were planted. Follow the signposted path to see the dragonflies, insects and carnivorous plants which

inhabit this completely natural bog which has been open to the public since 1997.

WALKING ON STILTS

Nouvelles Echasses, Moulin de Jammine, 44, Chemin des Meuniers, Belin-Béliet ☎ 05 56 88 80 58
Patrick Hausséguy makes the traditional Landes stilts in his workshop. Furthermore, he is reviving the ancient art of stilt-walking once used by the shepherds of the region, and he regularly organises walks on the moors. It's best to learn to manipulate these wooden legs – which make you 3 ft (1m) or more taller – before venturing on one of the rambles!

The lakeland
☎ 05 56 88 53 44
Closed 15 Dec.–15 Jan.
Free admission.
In the middle of the moors there is a huge leisure centre surrounding the **six lakes**. There are two **large sandy bathing beaches**, a **bird sanctuary**, a botanical garden, and a **climbing-wall**. **Mountain bikes** can be rented so you can explore the forest paths, with their wonderful scent of pine resin at your own pace.

Le Barp
An ultra-modern research centre
15½ miles (25 km) SW of Bordeaux
C.E.S.T.A.
☎ 0810 555 222 (low-cost call)
Guided tour, one day a month, by appointment. This ultra-modern centre is equipped with computers, a centrifuge for testing satellites, and rooms for testing the flight patterns of the 'secret' stealth missiles. The **Centre d'Études Scientifiques et Techniques d'Aquitaine** produces the flying machines of tomorrow using computer-aided design.

Pissos
L'Arial Artisanal
16½ miles (26 km) E of Parentis
La Maison des Artisans, Route de Sore
☎ 05 58 08 97 42
Open daily, Apr.–14 June, 3–6pm; 15 June–15 Sept., 10am–noon and 3–7pm; Wed.–Sun., 16 Sept.–March, 3–6 pm. Closed 15 Jan. and 1–15 Oct.
This old landaise farm, or *arial*, houses an art gallery, a craft exhibition and a display of antique glass. In the adjoining workshop you can watch Alain Jame making earthenware pottery, while close by, you will find Carlos Vieira, master glass blower, in the process of transforming red-hot molten glass into works of art.

Spotcheck
C3-C4

Landes

Things to do
Visiting the lagoons of Gat-Mort
Exploring C.E.S.T.A.
Bathing, biking, rambles
Canoeing and kayaking
L'Arial Artisanal
Rambling on stilts

Within easy reach
*Sauternes, p. 192,
Bazas, p. 194,
Bordeaux, p. 196,
Arcachon, p. 212,
The Albret district, p. 226.*

Tourist Offices
Dax: ☎ 05 58 56 86 86
Mont-de-Marsan:
☎ 05 58 05 87 37

On the waters of the Grande Leyre
☎ 05 58 07 73 01
Open May–mid-Oct., 9am–6pm; out of season, call first.
Rental: canoe 200 F or kayak 100 F for the day.
The gentle lapping of the water and the birdsong are all that break the silence of a trip on the Leyre river. The Leyre flows through the Haute Lande into the Arcachon basin. Beneath the forest canopy, you can enjoy a wonderful journey and you can easily cover 12½ miles (20 km) or more in a day. There are great places to stop off along the way. In summer, canoes (2 pers.) and kayaks (1 pers.) can be hired from Pissos, Saugnac, Belin-Béliet, Salles, Mios or Trensacq.

Natural Regional Park of Landes de Gascogne

the lore of the forest

L andes de Gascogne, the moorland of Gascony, has changed completely since the early 19th C. What was once a huge area of bog and moor, inhabited only by a few shepherds who crossed it on stilts, has been transformed into a vast pine forest, giving rise to a new ecosystem along with new economic and social conditions. This regional nature park and ecological museum of the Grande Lande was founded in 1970, to ensure that the ongoing transition is a smooth one.

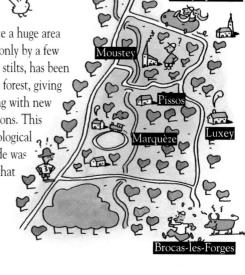

Cap-Ferret

Biganos

St-Symphorien

Moustey

Pissos

Marquèze

Luxey

Brocas-les-Forges

Ygos
Le Sandalier
9½ miles (15 km)
S of Sabres
Route de Morcenx
☎ 05 58 51 73 68
Open daily, 9am–noon, 2.30–7pm
Before walking through the forest, buy some suitable footwear in Ygos from René Dauba, who makes rope sandals and espadrilles by hand.

Sabres
Écomusée de Marquèze
☎ 05 58 08 31 31
Open daily, June–Sept., 10am–noon and 2–6pm; July–Aug., 2–7pm; Apr., May, Oct.–5 Nov., Mon–Sat., 2–6pm; Sun. and public holidays, 10am–noon and 2–6pm.
Admission charge.
Are you prepared to travel back in time? At Marquèze life is as it was in Landes in the 19th C. The houses in the oak forest clearing (*arial*) are those of artisans, tenant-farmers, and metalworkers. You can wander around finding out how life was lived, what tools were used and what clothes were worn. Even the chickens are fed in the old fashioned way, and the mill grinds rye flour for bread. Access is via the little forest train from Sabres which sets the tone for this journey into country life. An ideal outing for children.

Luxey
Pine resin factory
14½ miles (23 km)
NE of Sabres
☎ **05 58 08 01 39**
Open daily, June–Sept.,
10am–noon and 2–6pm;
July–Aug., daily, 2–7pm;
Apr–May, Oct.–5 Nov.,
phone for opening times.
Admission charge.
In an abandoned industrial
site, which is remarkably well
preserved, resin is distilled
just as it was in 1954. The
pine sap is processed in the
traditonal manner. It is
collected by tapping the
bark, transported in wooden
barrels, boiled in a still, then
turned into turpentine or
black resin.

Mousjey
Musée des Croyances Populaires
15½ miles (25 km)
N of Sabres
Church of Notre-Dame
☎ **05 58 07 70 01**
Open daily, July–Sept.,
10am–noon and 2–7pm.

Admission charge.
Here you'll learn how hiccups
were traditionally cured. This
museum of folk medicine in
the heart of the Haute Lande
surveys the supernatural and
the local religious heritage of
healing fountains, sacred
stones and fires.

Brocas-les-Forges
The *ganaderia* de Malabat
9½ miles (15 km)
N of Mont-de-Marsan
☎ **05 58 51 64 01**
Guided tour by the
ganadero (1½ hours), all
year round, book first.
This is where the cows and
bulls are bred for the bull-
running and fighting events
in the summer, known as *La
Course Landaise* (p. 72 and
73). In his *ganaderia*, Pascal
Fasolo will explain all the
subtleties of raising cattle
and the rules of this popular
Gascon pastime. Although
the cows are gentle with their
owner, they are aggressive in
the ring. Don't look them
straight in the eye!

Spotcheck
C4

Landes

Things to do
The Ecomusée de Marquèze
Pine resin factory
Museum of popular beliefs
Visit to a fighting
cattle-breeder
A craft paper-mill

Within easy reach
*Sauternes, p. 192,
Bazas, p. 194,
Bordeaux, p. 196,
Arcachon, p. 210.*

Tourist Office
Sabres: ☎ 05 58 07 52 79

FROM PINE TO PAPER
Smurfit, Cellulose du Pin, Biganos
☎ **05 56 03 88 94**
Tours by appointment.
(groups). Children
under 14 not admitted.
This huge factory near
the Arcachon basin is a
temple to craft paper.
At Biganos, 1,200 tons
of strong brown wrap-
ping paper are pro-
duced every day. From
stripping the pine trees
to despatch-
ing the
paper rolls,
you'll see all
the manu-
facturing
processes,
and you'll
discover
that,
amongst
other things, wood is
used to make beauty
products! The paper
industry is a sustain-
able business and helps
the forests here to
thrive. (pp. 78 and 79).

Marensin
the land of currents

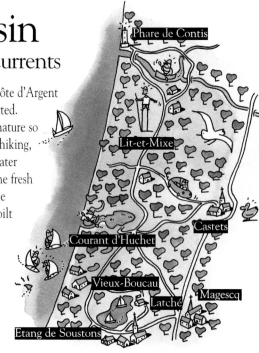

This part of the Côte d'Argent is the most deserted. It's been left to nature so it's perfect for walking, hiking, mountain-biking and water sports. Currents carry the fresh water of the rivers to the ocean through an unspoilt landscape. By the sea, Vieux-Boucau and the marine lake of Port-d'Albret attract those who prefer marine water-sports.

The Huchet current

Departure from the SW bank of the Lac Léon.
Booking required,
☎ **05 58 48 75 39**
Excursions in a small boat, Apr.–Oct., departures 10am and 2.30pm.
Admission charge.
This is an extraordinary experience. A boatman takes you on a **galupe** (a flat-bottomed boat without an engine) from Lac Léon towards the ocean, through luxuriant vegetation, which makes you feel as if you were exploring the Amazon. After 5 miles (8 km), the boat turns around as it approaches the ocean and returns upstream. In summer, it's best to take the three to four hour trip in the afternoon.

Soustons-Port-d'Albret

Étang de Soustons

Centre nautique
☎ **05 58 48 06 80**
(Base de Port-d'Albret)
☎ **05 58 41 32 23**
(Base de Soustons)
If you like calm waters, come to this lovely lagoon. If you want a bit more action how-ever, try the **beach** at Port-d'Albret (5 miles/8 km away), and practise bodyboarding, surfing and skimboarding.
On rainy days, shelter in the **Musée des Automates** and enjoy the mechanical dolls (Soustons, ☎ 05 58 41 31 22, open daily, 11am–8pm, closed from 11 Nov.–Feb. school

holidays, admission charge) or be transported to an Asian village, with tiny animals, in the **Tropica Parc** near Azur (☎ 05 58 48 04 99, open daily, Apr.–Oct., admission charge).

Cork
Magescq

6¹/₂ miles (10 km)
E of Soustons
Atelier Bertails
☎ 05 58 47 70 07
Open during the week
(Sat.–Sun. In summer),
9am–noon and 2–7pm.
The cork-oaks of Marensin
have made cork bottle-
stoppers and cork shoe-soles
into local exports. New uses
for cork have been found
by Patrick Bertails,
including bread-bins,
fruit-baskets, candle-
holders, picture frames,
etc. – all guaranteed
not to sink!

The lighthouse and the Contis current
Contis-plage

9¹/₄ miles (15 km) S of
Mimizan, via the D 41
☎ 05 58 72 12 19
Open daily in summer:
10am-noon, 3-6pm. Out
of season, by appointment.
The Contis lighthouse is 127 ft
(38 m) high and it dominates
the surrounding landscape.
In this valley, only one water
source, the Contis, has
survived and still runs through
to the sea. This waterway is
popular with canoeists. The
river is full of pools and edged
with oak and pines. There are
some difficult descents as the
gradient to the ocean is quite
steep. Always take a guide
(to find out prices and to book
☎ 05 58 42 47 38).

Musée des Vieilles-Landes
Lit-et-Mixe

12¹/₂ miles (20 km)
S of Mimizan
☎ 05 58 42 72 47
Open daily, 10am–noon
and 4–6.30pm, July–
Aug. Guided tour by
appointment exc. Sun.
Free admission.
Guaranteed to be 100 %
authentic. The villagers of
Lit-et-Mixe created this
museum to keep
the tradition of
the old crafts
going, and they
have assem-
bled objects
bequeathed
to them by their
ancestors. There are shepherds' stilts, tools for tapping
pine-resin and implements
used for cork-making, wood-
cutting, clog-making, sawing
and smithery.

The Landes duck
Castets

By the RN 10, 10 miles
(16 km) NW of Dax
Chanchon
☎ 05 58 89 40 63
Free tours, 15 June–15
Sept., Tues.
and Thurs.
at 5pm.
The
increase
in maize
cultivation
has brought
farmyard animals
into the
clearings of the
great pine forests. Here the
duck, bred for its liver, breast
and legs, lives in the forests
and swims on the lakes in
the forest clearings. At the
Chanchon farm, Philippe and
Josiane Lataste offer a complete range of **succulent duck
products,** typical of Landes,
and processed in their family
cannery (sales all year round).

Spotcheck
B4-B5

Landes

Things to do
Excursions in a rowing-boat
Cork factory
The Contis lighthouse
Musée des Vieilles-Landes
Watersports at the beach

With children
Automata museum
Tropica Parc

Within easy reach
*Dax, p. 236
South coast of Landes,
p. 240.*

Tourist Offices
Contis:
☎ 05 58 42 88 65
Vieux-Boucau:
☎ 05 58 48 13 47

THE PRESIDENT'S SHEEP FARM
12¹/₂ miles (20 km)
NW of Dax
No guided tour.
Private property.
Latché, birthplace of
President of François
Mitterrand, is a typical
Marensin farmhouse
with half-timbering
and red bricks. It's 2
miles (3 km) NW of
Soustons, and you'll
find it if you follow
the road which leads
to the little village of
Azur. Soustons has a
monument to François
Mitterrand, a statue
of the President with
his famous
labrador.

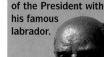

Mont-de-Marsan
the bullring of Landes

A small town at the confluence of the Midou and the Douze, Mont-de-Marsan has been the capital of Landes since the French Revolution. Its administrative and military functions (air base 118 was opened in 1945) has given it no time to beautify itself. As they say round here, it doesn't reveal its charms to a visitor in too much of a hurry. Yet there's a lot to see and do, especially at the Grandes Fêtes de la Madeleine in July.

Despiau-Wlérick museum

6, Place Marguerite-de-Navarre
☎ 05 58 75 00 45
Open daily except Tues. and public holidays., 10am–noon and 2–6pm.
Admission charge except Mon.
The museum is dedicated to early 20th-C. French sculpture. It's housed in a 14th C.

castle keep and specialises mainly in figurative work by two local artists of the 1930s, Charles Despiau and Robert Wlérick. There's a lovely **view** from the terrace.

Jean-Rameau Park

Place Francis-Planté
Free admission.
This park covers 4 acres (6 ha) beside the river Douze. This former garden of the prefecture is planted with plane trees and magnolias. It contains sculptures by Charles Despiau which are surrounded by flowers, greenhouses, ponds and avenues of greenery. This haven of peace is dedicated to Jean Rameau, a local poet and novelist.

Markets

The **Saturday morning market** is held near the Place Saint-Roch. It's a traditional farmers' market where local farmers sell their produce from folding tables. There are chickens, a few *broutes* (turnip greens or cabbage used to make the local soup known as *garbure*), *pastis* (a traditional local

cake), apple pie and *cruchade* (pieces of polenta fried in goose fat). If you are looking for eggs, they're as fresh as they come. An **antiques market** is held in the same place on the 1st Wednesday of every month.

Fiesta flamenca

Festival of flamenco art
2nd week of July
☎ 05 58 06 86 86
Free admission (except to certain concerts).
Although you may associate flamenco with Spain, for one week a year Andalusia comes to Mont-de-Marsan. The greatest exponents of Flamenco art visit the town and enliven it with their music, song and dances. There's a bonus in the shape of dancing classes for those who are fascinated by this form of artistic expression (beginners to advanced, from 1,000 to 3,000 F).

Musée de la Course Landaise

6½ miles (10 km) SE of Mont-de-Marsan
Bascons
☎ 05 58 52 91 76
Open May–Oct., 2.30–7pm; out of season, booking only.
Admission charge.
This 13th-C. chapel has been dedicated to Notre-Dame-de-la-Course-Landaise since 1970 (*see photo above*), and a pilgrimage is made here on Ascension Thursday

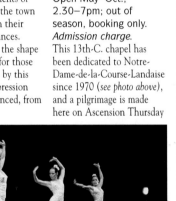

Golf Mont-de-Marsan

4½ miles (7 km) from Mont-de-Marsan
Route de Périgueux
☎ 05 58 75 63 05
This 18-hole golf course surrounded by pine trees is hardly ever crowded. You can play a round at your own pace. Clubs can be rented from the pro shop.

(see the Madonna protecting an *écarteur*). The museum next door contains many trophies, costumes and objects connected with the *Course Landaise* and its subtle rules (see pp. 72 and 73).

The perilous jump

(see pp. 72 and 73).

Spotcheck

C5

Landes

Things to do

Jean-Rameau park
Antique and farmers' markets
Fiesta flamenca
Mont-de-Marsan golf course
Musée de la Course Landaise
Despiau-Wlérick museum

Within easy reach

Bas-Armagnac, p. 228, Tursan, p. 230, Chalosse, p. 232.

Tourist Office

Mont-de-Marsan:
☎ 05 58 05 87 37

LES FÊTES DE LA MADELEINE

Visit Mont-de-Marsan during the second fortnight of July and you'll get caught up in the fever of the Fêtes de la Madeleine. They attract thousands of *hestayres* who come from both sides of the Pyrenees to take part in the parades and folklore events and to hear the *bandas*. For five days, the *bodegas y casetas* (Spanish inns) overflow, and the Plumaçon bullring (8,000 seats) applauds great toreadors from Spain. (Reservations from the Comité des Fêtes ☎ 05 58 75 39 08).

Nérac and the Albret district

a land of plenty

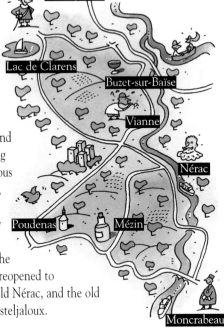

The land of Henri IV, at the frontier between the Landes forest and Gascony, has a rich heritage. There are châteaux, churches and dovecotes in a gently undulating landscape. This is a region famous for its melons, wild mushrooms, asparagus and foie gras, where every village seems pervaded by savoury aroma of pigeon stew. The main tourist attraction is the River Baïse that has now been reopened to shipping. Don't forget to visit old Nérac, and the old walled towns of Vianne and Casteljaloux.

A walk around the Garenne

Nérac, the intellectual capital of the region in the 16th C., was home to many scholars. It became the political capital thanks to Henri de Navarre who became King Henri IV of France. Stroll in the Parc de la Garenne (a former royal park laid out by Queen Margot) beneath the **ancient oaks**. The park follows the River Baïse for 1¼ miles (2 km). Petit Nérac contains the oldest houses on the Rue Séderie, Rue Sully, Rue Bourges and Rue de l'École.

✿ The château
Rue Henri-IV
☎ 05 53 65 21 11
Open daily except Mon., Tues, Oct.–Mar., 10am–noon and 2–5pm; daily Apr.–Sept. Closed in Jan.

Admission charge.
Of the four original wings, only the elegant north wing, its colonnaded gallery and turret remain. Jeanne d'Albret lived in the Château d'Albret, where her son Henry IV sheltered after the St. Bartholomew's Day Massacre. The museum contains 16th- and 17th-C. paintings, modern works, furniture and archaeological finds.

The Pont-Vieux and abandoned quays

Boat trip on the River Baïse on board the *Prince-Henry*.
☎ 05 53 84 72 50
July–Aug., departures at 11am, 3pm, 4.15pm and 5.30pm. One hour guided tours.
Admission charge.

Tobacco bales, corks, wine barrels and flour no longer leave from here for the French West Indies. The River Baïse was made navigable from the 13th C. and had up to 14 dams over a 52 mile (84 km) stretch. Nowadays, only tourists navigate this old route.

La Cigale Chocolate factory

2, Rue Calvin
☎ 05 53 65 15 73
Open daily except Sun., 9am–12.15pm and 2.30–6.30pm. Closed one month in summer. Guided tours by appointment for groups.
Free admission.

du 15 juillet au 25 août
pour CAUSE de CHALEUR et CONGÉS
la CHOCOLATERIE
sera **OUVERTE**
le MERCREDI UNIQUEMENT
*de 9ʰ30 à 12ʰ00
un seul exposé
le même jour à 10ʰ30*

If you're a chocolate addict, this might not be the place for you – the tour is an invitation to temptation. You'll learn about the history of cocoa, from the Aztecs in Peru to the court of the Sun King. Three tastings (yes!) punctuate the slide show, which is followed by a visit to the laboratories. Where's the shop?

Barbaste

Henri IV's mill

*4 miles (6 km)
N of Nérac*
☎ 05 53 65 27 81 or
☎ 05 53 65 09 37
The four unequal towers of the 14th-C. Barbaste mill are famous throughout the region. According to legend, they represented different heights of the miller's four daughters. The 10-arched Romanesque bridge (late 12th C.) linking the mill to the village is magnificent.

Vianne

Glass-blowing

6 miles (10 km) N Nérac
Vianne glass factory
☎ 05 53 97 65 65
Open Mon.–Fri., 9am–noon and 2–6pm; Sat., 2.30–6.30pm.
This beautiful 13th-C. walled town takes its name from Vianne de Gontaud, a woman who inspired the founder. It has retained its four towers, city walls and grid-pattern layout. Visit the Vianne glassworks where glassblowers use traditional techniques. In the exhibition and shop, you'll find lamps (around 300 F), and vases (around 150 F).

Spotcheck
D4

Lot-et-Garonne

Things to do

Boat trip on the River Baïse
Cruise on the canal
Ganaderia of Buros
Swimming and water-sports
Walking, rambling and mountain-biking

With children

Discovering the forest

Within easy reach

Agen, p. 174,
Aiguillon, p. 178,
Marmande, p. 180,
Grande Lande, 216.

Tourist Office

Nérac:
☎ 05 53 65 27 75

ASPARAGUS COUNTRY

A tasty vegetable lies buried in that uninteresting field! White asparagus is completely covered, the purple variety barely emerges.

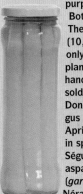

Both grow well in Aquitaine. The plant produces its best crop (10,000 plants per ha; 2½ acres) only after three years. Asparagus planted in March–April is picked by hand, then graded before being sold for 20-25 F for 2½ lb (1 kg)). Don't consider looking for asparagus at any time other than March, April and May as it's only in season in spring. (Caldralbret SCA, Séguinot, Nérac, ☎ 05 53 97 66 50: asparagus, wild strawberries (*gariguettes*) and the renowned Nérac melon.)

Buzet-sur-Baïse
A compulsory stop for wine lovers
12½ miles (20 km) NW Nérac

The region produces an excellent local wine, the Côtes-de-Buzet, which is just as good as any claret. The rich, mellow, ruby-coloured wine improves with age. Visit the **Cave des Vignerons de Buzet** (tastings): Le Bourg, (☎ 05 53 84 74 30. Prices per bottle range from 25 F to 130 F. **Château Pierron** (1 mile; 1½ km from Nérac), (☎ 05 53 65 05 52) visit the *chai* in which Armagnacs are aged. Its specialities include Buzet Rouge, Buzet Rosé and the Floc de Gascogne liqueur.

A long voyage
Aquitaine Navigation
☎ 05 53 84 72 50
Apr.–1 Nov.

Leave Buzet and spend a few days steering a pleasure boat along the canal that runs alongside the Garonne and the river Baïze. Even land-lubbers will enjoy it. You don't need a permit and the conditions are excellent. The weekly cost for four people in high season comes to 6,000 F.

Escalans
Ganaderia de Buros
1½ miles (2 km) from Gabarret, D 656 towards Mont-de-Marsan
☎ 05 58 44 36 57
Open May–Oct., every Thursday, 2.15pm; Any other day by appointment.
Admission charge.

The *Course Landaise* is explained on pp. 72 and 73. Jean Barrère, whose family members have always been picadors, welcomes you to visit his cattle stud. After showing you some of the jewels of his collection, including a short film made in 1938, you'll visit the breeding arenas, see the wild bulls and watch – without being at any risk– the *écarteurs* perform leaps and jumps as in the ring. The whole beautiful estate covers 321 acres (130 ha).

Casteljaloux
The Clarens lake
In direction of Mont-de-Marsan.

This magnificent leisure centre lies at the edge of the Landes forest. The 42 acre (17 ha) lake offers all the facilities of the beach, with its fine sand, flume, pedalos and surfing. The best way to enjoy and explore the forest is on foot or by mountain-bike. Visit the pigeon-lofts, the plains and the slopes. The local farmhouses will sell you **all the local delicacies.** Golfers can test their swing or play a round at the 18-hole golf course. ☎ 05 53 93 51 60.

Caubeyres
The stag and the herbarium
7 miles (11 km) E of Casteljaloux
P.A.R.L.E. Association Exhibition Centre
☎ 05 53 84 00 28
Open Mon.–Fri., 9am–noon and 2–6 pm; Sat. and Sun. upon reservation.

Discovering nature, recognising animal tracks, creating an herbarium, watching stags, having lunch in a pigeon-loft and taking a guided tour through the forest – these are just some of the activities which this association organises for children and adults alike. All are traditional and nature-oriented and are a good introduction to the region.

Poudenas

The château

9½ miles (5 km)
S from Nérac
☎ 05 53 65 78 86
Open daily except Mon.
14 July–31 Aug., 3–6pm,
by appointment for
groups; Whit Sun.–All
Saints Day, 3–6pm.
Free admission.
Poudenas is a lovely village
(*see photo above*), whose steep
streets are dominated by the
château (*see photo below*).
This beautiful castle, rebuilt
over the centuries, dominates

the Landes forest and the
Gélise valley. The main
attractions are the 18th-C.
Italian furniture, the
monumental staircase and the
18th-C. vaulted stables.

Floc de Gascogne liqueur

Floc de Gascogne is a locally-
produced liqueur, made on all
the farms in the area from a
16th-C. Gascon recipe. It's a
blend of grape juice and
Armagnac, made during the
grape harvest, and is aged in
barrels for seven months.
Drink it chilled as an apéritif

in a melon, with foie gras or
served with a *croustade* (an
apple tart). At the **Domaine
de Cazeaux** (6½ miles/10 km
SE of Poudenas) you can visit
the *chai*. The estate has its own
distillery and a lovely copper
still. Local wines, Armagnac,
prunes in Armagnac and
Floc are sold. The **Ferme de
Gagnet** (near Mézin, 3 miles/
5 km E of Poudenas) sells
goose and duck preserves, foie
gras and Floc (44 F for a bottle
which recently won the gold
medal at the regional show in
Toulouse).

TAKING IT WITH A PINCH OF SALT

On the first Sunday
of August, the 40
members of the
Académie des Menteurs
(liars' academy) from
the small village of
Moncrabeau elect their
king. The candidate is
seated on the liars'
throne and tells a
story combining truth
and lies. The members
of the jury then award
candidates in mea-
sures of salt. At the
end the mounds of salt
are weighed and the
person who has the
most is deemed to be
the 'best corrector of
any truth'. Make sure
you don't miss this
delightful contest.

Lower Armagnac

and its famous brandy

The vineyards of Lower Armagnac are at the eastern extremity of the Landes forest (see p. 42), surrounded by 13th- and 14th-C. *bastides*. This is where the oldest and best-known French brandies are produced. With its gentle green rolling hills, the region is a favourite with cyclists, hunters, naturalists, those interested in medieval history and, of course, brandy connoisseurs from all over the world.

Labastide-d'Armagnac
Typical *bastides*

*11½ miles (18 km)
E of Mont-de-Marsan*
☎ 05 58 44 81 42
Museum open daily in season, 10am–noon and 2.30–6.30pm.
Admission charge.
Walking around this 13th-C. *bastide*, you might feel you're back in the Middle Ages. Come and browse around the antiques fair on the 4th Sunday of every month. Follow in the footsteps of the so-called *embarrats* from the Protestant temple (and its **museum** about the *bastides*) to the 14th-C. wash-house, passing the Château du Prada. A plan of the *bastide*

is available at the Tourist Office, Place Royale,
☎ 05 58 44 67 56.

Notre-Dame des Cyclistes

*2 miles (3 km) SE of
Labastide (D 626)*
☎ 05 58 44 80 52
Open daily, Apr.–Sept., 2–6pm; July–Aug., 10am–noon and 2–6pm.
Free admission.

Thanks to a cycle-loving priest, this 11th-C. chapel became a shrine to cycling in 1959. The Luis Ocaña bicycle museum traces the history of the bicycle and its sport and contains many **old bicycles from the Tour de France** as well as the shirts worn by the great champions.

Cyclists assemble here on Whit Monday (☎ 05 58 44 68 78, closed Dec.–Jan.).

Poudesseaux
Museum of nature and hunting

*4½ miles (7 km)
W of Labastide*
☎ 05 58 93 92 33
Open daily, July–Aug., 10am–6pm.
Admission charge.
This museum will teach you about the history of traditional hunting practices in France, especially the wood pigeon-shooting and trapping that takes place in the autumn. There are slide shows and tableaux of hunting scenes. In the garden, there's a genuine dove-cote of the type used here as a decoy.

Jean-Rostand centre

☎ 05 58 93 92 43
Open daily, Easter–late Oct. (except Sat. and Sun. morning, 9am–noon and 2–6pm.
Admission charge.
Here you'll learn all about the life of this famous biologist, who chose this area as an ideal site for the pursuit of his research on flora. The significance and importance of the centre lies in the diversity of natural environments found here.
A signposted path takes you on a walk past streams, ponds, peat-bogs, through a forest rich in birch and other leafy trees. Breathe in the sweet fragrance of nature and let your 'ecological conscience' mature, as the great scientist would have wished.

Perquie

Château de Ravignan

2½ miles (4 km) SE of Villeneuve-de-Marsan
☎ 05 58 45 26 44
Open Sat.–Sun. July–Sept., 3–7pm; out of season, by appointment.
Admission charge.
This elegant Louis XIII château is magnificent. Its rooms house dramatic high mantelpieces and 17th- and 18th-C. furniture, paintings and costumes as well as a collection of 500 engravings relating to Henri IV. If

THE ÉCOMUSÉE DE L'ARMAGNAC

2 miles (3 km) SW of Labastide-d'Armagnac
☎ 05 58 44 84 35
Open 1 Apr.–1 Nov., Mon.–Fri., 9am–noon and 2–6.30pm; Sat. 2–6.30pm; Sun. and public holidays, 3–6.30pm. Out of season, daily exc. w/ends and public holidays, 9am–noon and 2–6pm.
Admission charge.
This 198 acre (80 ha) estate has three important sites dedicated to Armagnac, the regional nectar. There is a history of grape-growing techniques, secrets of the distillation and ancient wine-stores (*chais*). At the Auberge de l'Armagnac, taste the Floc de Gascogne, a delicious apéritif and take a walk in the bird sanctuary.

you're lucky, a member of the Ravignan family will show you around and introduce you to the estate's wine-stores (*chais*).

Spotcheck
C5-D5

Landes

Things to do

Écomusée de l'Armagnac
Notre-Dame des Cyclistes
Visiting the *chais*

Within easy reach

Grande Lande, p. 216,
Mont-de-Marsan,
p. 222,
Tursan, p. 230.

Tourist Office

Labastide-d'Armagnac:
☎ 05 58 44 67 56

Arthez-d'Armagnac

Visit to the *chais*

Domaine d'Ognoas

2 miles (3 km)
E of Villeneuve
☎ 05 58 45 22 11
Open daily, 1 May–30 Sept., Mon.–Fri., 8.30am–noon and 1.30–5.30pm; Sat.–Sun. and public holidays 2–6pm. From 1 Oct. to 30 Apr., same opening hours, Mon.–Fri.
Free admission.
This former barony is a lovely estate, crossed by the Cours du Midou. It now belongs to the Département. The oldest still in Gascony (1804) remains in operation here and distills a brandy in which you can discern the fragrances of vanilla and prunes.
A farm, an old mill and the deer who wander through the estate complete the charm of this 'site of remarkable taste'. Local Armagnac is on sale and the prices of the flagons vary according to age. Remember that brandy doesn't age once it's in the bottle, so don't expect a younger brandy to improve.

Tursan, the yellow district

Aire-sur-l'Adour

W here the river Adour enters Landes, it crosses Aire-sur-l'Adour. To the west, between the pine forests and the Pyrenees, lie the vineyards and maize fields of Tursan. The area's rich historical heritage dates from Roman times; more recently Tursan boasts a great gastronomic tradition of foie gras and local wines.

Aire-sur-l'Adour

Church of Sainte-Quitterie-du-Mas

31 miles (50 km) N of Pau
At the top of the Rue F.-Despagnet
☎ **05 58 71 79 78**
(M. Labadie)
Tours daily exc. Thurs., 2–6pm.
You'll need to take a torch with you if you visit this church. This is the last resting-place of Gascony's patron saint, Sainte Quitterie, a 4th-C. martyr. She lies in a magnificent marble sarcophagus at the far end of a dark crypt. Try out the unusual acoustic phenomenon produced in front of the little altar facing her tomb. You'll also be impressed by the purity of the water which flows through the crypt. It is reputed to cure headaches.

Trips on the Adour
Canoë-kayak Club, Boulevard Lamothe
☎ **05 58 71 67 88**
(M. Bourrec)
The Adour rushes down from the mountains and still has considerable impetus when it reaches Landes. It's a waterway with capricious bends and curves but which lends itself perfectly to canoeing

and kayaking. Leave from Aire-sur-l'Adour in a one- or two-person craft, and enjoy a delightful, calm and restful trip. The only essentials are to be able to swim and to wear a life-jacket. You can go alone (60 F per pers.) or be accompanied (beginners).

Landscape of Les Landes

Eugénie-les-Bains
Cooking courses with Michel Guérard

5 miles (8 km) E of Aire-sur-l'Adour
Les Prés d'Eugénie
☎ 05 58 05 06 07
Michel Guérard, renowned guru of not only *cuisine minceur* (low-fat cooking), but also rich gourmet cuisine, reveals his secrets twice a year in the first week of November and the second week in March. If you get close enough to the master, you may just discover why your soufflés always collapse! He'll teach you the ABC of the kitchen by way of ten recipes: A is for aromatics,

B is for bouillons and C is for cooking etc. There are six courses, two of which are about wine, and each individually costs around 650 F, or 3,000 F for all six. It's best to book well in advance.

Geaune
Tursan wine

8½ miles (13 km) SE of Aire-sur-l'Adour
Coopérative des Vignerons du Tursan
☎ 05 58 44 51 25
Shop open daily, 9am–noon and 2–5pm. Guided tour of the cellar by appointment, Tues.–Fri., 8am–noon and 2–5.30pm; Sat., 9am–noon.
Free admission.
The 250 winemakers here produce the only wine with the appellation of Landes. The fairly harsh climate of the foothills, with sun on the slopes and the mildness of the Atlantic combine to create a strong, fruity wine. White Tursan goes very well with fish, the rosé with white meat and mild cheeses, and the red with *confits* and game. Every year a million bottles leave this ultra-modern cellar. A red, rosé or '*haute carte*' white wine costs around 21.50 F.

Samadet
Samadet porcelain

7 miles (11km) E of Geaune
5, Rue de l'Église
☎ 05 558 79 13 54
By appointment all year round
Free admission

THE FOIE GRAS MARKET

Rue Gambetta, Aire-sur-l'Adour.
Covered market.
The cultivation of maize in the area has encouraged the rearing of farmyard animals. Try Landes duck which is fattened for its liver (Landes is now the biggest foie gras producing département in France). Every Tuesday, from November to February, the foie gras market is held here in front of the cathedral. Local breeders display the full range of their products – livers, preserves, rillettes, terrines, duck breasts and cooked dishes.

Spotcheck
C5

Landes

Things to do

Church of Sainte-Quitterie-du-Mas
Cookery lessons
Tursan wine
Trip on the Adour
The foie gras market

Within easy reach

Mont-de-Marsan, p. 222,
Bas-Armagnac, p. 228.

Tourist Office

Aire-sur-l'Adour:
☎ 05 58 71 64 70

Annick de Sansonetti opened her workshop in 1982, in the very village where, in 1840, the old Manufacture Royale de Faïence (which rivalled all the greatest 18th-C. European potteries) closed its doors. Annick herself works with clay, adopting the traditional methods used in Samadet in the 18th C. You may catch her in the delicate act of decorating a piece, which she executes completely by hand. All her pieces are unique and sold exclusively in her workshop.

Piece from the porcelain museum in Samadet, at present closed for repairs

Chalosse
the cornucopia of Landes

Chalosse is a district between two waterways, the Gave de Pau and the Adour. It's a region of rolling hills, sand dunes and pine forests, at the gateway to the Pyrenees. This region is truly a land of plenty. There are cattle, geese, ducks, chickens and bees, all of which help to produce some of the best food in Landes. Montfort-en-Chalosse is famous for the largest goose and duck market in Europe.

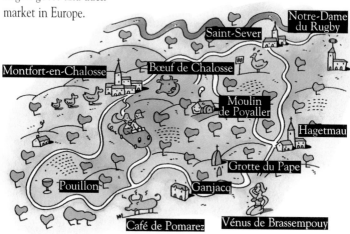

Notre-Dame du Rugby
Saint-Sever
Montfort-en-Chalosse
Bœuf de Chalosse
Moulin de Poyaller
Hagetmau
Grotte du Pape
Pouillon
Ganjacq
Café de Pomarez
Vénus de Brassempouy

Saint-Sever
The Benedictine abbey
9 miles (14 km)
S of Mont-de-Marsan
Place du Tour-du-Sol
Rue du Général-Lamarque
☎ 05 58 76 01 38.
Open daily. 1 July–30 Sept., 2.30–6pm. Out of season, by appointment. Free admission.

The abbey church, founded in 988 AD, is evidence of a prestigious past. There are some magnificent remains in the museum of the Jacobin convent: the *Apocalypse de Saint Sever*, a powerful medieval

frieze, is analysed in a slide show. On the way to the abbey, you can admire the lovely **18th-C. mansions** in the Rue du Général-Lamarque (nos. 6, 11, 21 and 26).

Old Landes porcelain
La Porcelaine des Pins, 10, Place Léon Dufour
☎ 05 58 76 13 65

Open all year round, Tues.–Sat., 9am–noon, 2–7pm.

If you find this old Landes porcelain charming (p. 231), then choose your favourite design for a dish or plate and have it fired as you watch. The designs are all traditional.

The yellow chicken of Landes

This chicken has a bare neck and lives for 81 days (not a day longer). Its food is 100% natural as this king of free-range chickens lives out in the fresh air and scratches for worms to complement its diet, 80% of which is cereals. At Saint-Sever, the breeders have banded together to market its yellow, fragrant flesh, under the Saint-Sever label. It costs around 40 F for 2lb 4oz (1 kg) (available in super-markets).

Foie gras from Landes

Maison Dubernet,
31, Rue Lafayette
☎ 05 58 76 01 20
Open Tues.–Sun. morning, 8am–12.30pm and 2.30–7pm.
Michel Dubernet's family have been selling foie gras since the French Revolution.

The family shop sells over 200 products, either fresh or canned, all of which have the **taste of Gascony**. Try the whole canned duck foie gras (160 F for 7oz/195 g) or the goose foie gras (413 F for 14oz/400 g). Top of the range is the Chancelier duck foie gras (1,010 F for 2lb 4oz/1kg).

Brassempouy

Musée de la Préhistoire

6½ miles (10 km) SE of Hagetmau
Rue Principale
☎ 05 58 89 21 73
Open daily, July–Aug., 3–6.30pm; Apr.–Oct., 3–6pm; Nov.–March, 2.30–5.30pm.
Closed Mon. out of season.
Admission charge.
You'll recognise her despite her age. The Venus of Brassempouy, also known as 'the woman in a hood', is known throughout the world. She is 23,000 years old, and is the oldest human representation known. Visit the museum of the excavations, which are still taking place at the caves of the Pope and the Hyenas (open in summer), and don't miss the 15th-C. romano-gothic village church.

Spotcheck
C5

Landes

Things to do

Visit to a Benedictine Abbey
The foie gras auction
Course Landaise
Samadet porcelain

Within easy reach

*La Grande Lande, p. 216,
Mont-de-Marsan, p. 222.*

Tourist Office

Saint-Sever:
☎ 05 58 76 34 64

NOTRE-DAME-DU-RUGBY
Grenade-sur-l'Adour
11½ miles (18 km) NW of Aire-sur-l'Adour

If you're a fan of the oval ball, say a prayer in the chapel of Notre-Dame-du-Rugby, on the south bank of the river Adour. Before Grenade, a road climbs up to this little chapel, which is lined with rugby shirts and decorated with stained glass windows. Look closely: in one of the windows Jesus is passing the ball to the Virgin Mary! To make sure your prayers are answered write in the golden book.

Gaujacq
Château and Plantarium
3½ miles (5 km) N of Amou, by the D 58
☎ 05 58 89 24 61
Open daily, July–Aug., tours at 11am, 2pm, 3pm, 4pm, 5pm and 6pm. daily exc. Wed., 15 Feb.–June and Sept.–15 Nov., tours at 3pm, 4pm and 5pm.
Admission charge.
The Marquis de Montespan came here to forget the infidelities committed by his wife with the king, Louis XIV. This large château looks more like a Gallo-Roman villa, but the 17th- and 18th-C. apartments are still intact and are lived in to this day. Before you leave, take a look at the splendid collection of plants in the botanical garden, which has a wonderful view of the Pyrenees.

Mugron
Moulin de Poyaller
Towards Hagetmau
☎ 05 58 97 95 72
Guided tours of the mill and the farm (1½ hours), daily except Sat. 19 Mar.–11 Nov., 2.30–6.45pm. In July–Aug., daily, 2–7.45pm.
Admission charge.
The water-mill still turns as it always has in this little hamlet dominated by the ruins of the feudal dungeon. Find out how it works and watch the traditional milling of flour. In the surrounding area, bucks and does are bred for venison in open farms which can be visited. Extend your visit by taking out a **rowing-boat**. Open in the afternoon only (picnics possible from 12.30pm).

which four rooms are devoted to the art of bull-fighting. He is such an enthusiast that he films all the local *Courses*. Pictures, photos, documents, memorabilia and costumes decorate this shrine to the art of fighting cows. Nearby, the covered **ring** presents the most handsome animals in the region (in summer only).

Pouillon
Chalosse wines
7½ miles (12 km) S of Dax
Domaine du Tastet
☎ 05 58 98 28 27
Open daily except Sun. afternoon, 8am–noon and 2–7pm.
Jean-Claude Romain opens his cellar and his *chai* to enable you to taste the rare wines from the slopes of Chalosse. There's the syrupy white Gros-Manseng, the dry whites Arriloba and Baroque, the Cabernet rosé or the red Tannat. These wines

Pomarez
Mecca of the Course Landaise
7 miles (11 km) S of Montfort
☎ 05 58 89 87 42
By appointment.
Admission free.
The *Course Landaise* is very popular here. Visit Alain Laborde, who has turned his café into a unique museum in

come from the remnants of the vineyards that once covered part of the region. They used to be exported to England via the river Adour. They have recently been revived and their quality is constantly improving. Price of a bottle: 16 F (dry rosé and white) 17 F (red), 20 F (sweet white).

Montfort-en-Chalosse

Fountain of the 100 steps

10½ miles (17 km) W of Saint-Sever

This old *bastide* was built on a hillside at a height of 361 ft (110 m). At the end of the 19th C. steps were built to make the fountain below easier to reach. As you climb, you pass through a jungle of bamboo and come across forty or so different kinds of plants, before arriving at an old restored wash-house. This is a lovely walk, which will make you forget to count the 100 steps!

COURSE LANDAISE

The real centre of the Course Landaise is in Chalosse. This is nothing like the *corrida*. The aim is to provoke the cow to charge in the ring and to avoid it at the very last moment, either by stepping aside or by leaping over it. The cow is not killed at the end (see pp. 72 and 73). It's important that a rope-holder keeps the animal on a lasso to avoid any accidents, since the taut rope prevents the animal from tossing its head. But if the rope is pulled too tight it may pull the cow too far from the *écarteur*, which is not considered fair play. Watch the public lessons at the École Taurine every Saturday afternoon in Pomarez.

Skittles

Skittles is another favourite pastime in Chalosse (p. 289). It became unpopular but now skittle alleys are opening up again in the villages (such as Castelnau, at the exit from Montfort). They are usually well signposted. Try your hand at a game; you'll be welcomed and be able to compete for the prize, generally a round of white wine.

Musée de la Chalosse

Domaine de Carcher
☎ 05 58 98 69 27

Open daily, March–Nov., 2–7pm.
Admission charge.

This museum is a reconstruction of 19th-C. life. On your visit you'll see the house and garden of two tenant farmers with numerous outbuildings, including the *chai*, wine-press and bread oven. You can find out about the environment, lifestyle and traditions of Chalosse which seem as lively as Yoan and Martin, the two Chalosse oxen who are symbols of the region.

Lourquen

Chalosse cattle

3½ miles (5 km) NE of Montfort
Association Bœuf de Chalosse
☎ 05 58 97 93 31

This tasty, tender meat gets its flavour from the way the cattle are reared. The animals (Limousine or Aquitaine breeds) are fattened in the fresh air for four years, feeding exclusively on maize for their last six months. Ask for Chalosse beef in butcher's shops which display a special red and green sign (120 F for 2lb 4oz (1 kg) of sirloin).

Dax, spas and bullfights

'Run everywhere and drink hot water'. This health resort, the former capital of Landes, attracts thousands of people who come to take the waters: spa water is to be had in abundance! But there is more than just spa water on offer here– it's also a place for bull-fighting *afficionados*.

day. Before succumbing to the temptation of the food in the market, admire the 13th-C. apostle portico, whose tympanum depicts a theme very popular in the Middle Ages: the weighing of souls.

The Dax madeleine

Maison Cazelle, 6, Rue de la Fontaine-Chaude
☎ **05 58 74 26 25**
Open daily except Sun., 8.30am–12.15pm and 2–7.30pm.
This little cake is never more than 24 hours old. Philippe Cazelle replaces his entire stock of madeleines every morning in the small shop that has been in the family since 1906. Flour, butter, eggs, sugar but, of course, no preservatives; the recipe is unchanging and always successful. These plump little cakes are eaten by the plateful (45.60 F for a dozen).

Hot water spa

Place de la Fontaine-Chaude. Free.
Flow: 84,760 cu ft (2,400 cu m) a day.
The water pours out from the bowels of the earth at 147°F (64°C)! You can drink it directly from the taps which continuously pour the steaming water into the basin. The waters take several thousand years to push their way up 6,670 ft (2,000 m) to the surface, where temperatures of 176°F (80°C) have been recorded. They are ideal for soothing the joints and alleviating rheumatism, and are so hot they were once used for boiling eggs.

The cathedral of Sainte-Marie

Access from the Rue Saint-Vincent or Rue de l'Évêché
Open daily, from 3pm.
The best time to visit is on Saturday morning, **market**

DAX CELEBRATES

The biggest festival is the August féria (around the 15th). There are 5 days (and 5 nights!) of merrymaking and corridas. If you want to see a bullfight, you'll have to book well in advance on ☎ 05 58 90 99 09. If you come back in the second weekend of September, there'll be bull-fights as well as three days (Fri., Sat, and Sun.) of free salsa during the *Toros y Salsa* festival.

The *Ophioglossum* of the Azores

Parc du Sarrat,
Rue du Sel-Gemme
Open Tues., Thurs., Sat., at 3.30pm (guided tour, 1½ hours). Closed Dec. and Jan.
Admission charge.
The *Ophioglossum* of the Azores is a fern, and just one of the rare species in this 7½ acre (3 ha) botanical garden. There are winding paths, a stream which ripples over stones and through the undergrowth, and over a

thousand trees which provide shade in this refreshing garden.

Military aviation

58, Ave. de l'Aérodrome
☎ 05 58 74 66 19
Open daily except Sun. and public holidays., 2.30–5.30pm. Guided tours, Tues. and Fri.
Admission charge.
For those who have a passion for flying machines, this museum, in the grounds of the Ecole Militaire d'Aviation Légère (ESALAT), has around 20 decommissioned planes and combat helicopters, all of which help to tell the story of light aviation in the French army.

Les Barthes de l'Adour

Pey

9½ miles (15 km) SW of Dax
☎ 05 58 72 65 40
(booking between 8.30 and 9.30pm)

Open daily, Apr.–Oct.; Sat.–Sun. the rest of the year.
Around Dax, the river Adour widens into several *barthes* (flood plains), favoured by many wading birds and other aquatic species. The *barthes* can be visited by **canoe**, with a guide (120 F per adult, 90 F per child). The trip lasts for two hours and you'll discover a natural park, and learn about its history and the life of its wild birds. Pay careful attention as you pass a natural heronry on your trip.

Spotcheck
B5

Landes

Things to do

Visiting the *barthes*
Museum of Light Aviation
Hot-water spa
Festivals and corridas

Within easy reach

Grande Lande, p. 216, Marensin approx. 18¾ miles (30 km) W, p. 220.

Tourist Office

Dax: ☎ 05 58 56 86 86

WATER TREATMENTS

Dax is France's leading spa resort, so take advantage of it and take the cure for half a day. There are hydrojets, warm and cold showers, bubbling water-beds, and all the arts of water massage to rid your muscles of any knots. (Calicea, water exercise centre, Saint-Paul-lès-Dax, opposite the Lac de Christus, ☎ 05 58 90 66 66, open daily, adults and children over three years, two-hour all-in treatment, 55 F.)

The Orthe district
crossroads of the mountain streams

The Orthe district is the southernmost point of Les Landes, and is at the confluence of the mountain streams (*gaves*) of Pau and Oloron. It's the gateway to the Basque country, Béarn and the Landes forest. Consequently it

has a varied past, beginning in prehistory and continuing through the Gallo-Roman period to its conquest by the English, who built the *bastide* at Hastingues, and crossed by pilgrims making their way to Santiago de Compostela.

take advantage of the wonderful choice of pieces on offer at the big ceramics market.

Hastingues

Ceramics Festival at Arthous abbey
☎ 05 58 05 40 40
10 and 11 June
70 ceramists from all over Europe gather in the gardens of this 12th-C. abbey to honour the Dogon women potters. In Mali these women fashion the ochre clay into *hérés*, *jamas* or *nidéis* – round pots decorated with imprints of ropes, nets or ears of corn. This festival is an opportunity to see artists at work, and

Sorde-l'Abbaye

The pilgrim monastery
2½ miles (4 km) SE of Peyrehorade
☎ 05 58 73 04 83
(Town Hall).
Guided tours (20 min.), daily Apr.–Sept., 10.30am–noon and 2.30–7pm; Oct.–March, Mon.–Fri. by appointment. *Admission charge.*
Before they reached the river Adour, pilgrims on their way to Compostela would stop at this monastery, much of

which dates from the 17th C. There are also remains of Gallo-Roman baths in the abbot's residence. By the stream, there's a subterranean boathouse which is unique in France.

Nuits d'Été en Pays d'Orthe
Second fortnight in August.
☎ 05 58 73 00 52
This is a small and original festival because the concerts are given by local bands and ensembles, and the music is also composed in Landes. You can learn a lot about the area through this music.

Peyrehorade

Trips on the *gaves*
Club des Gaves
☎ 05 58 73 60 03 or 05 58 73 16 08
Open Mon.–Fri., 8.30am–noon and 1.30–5pm. By appointment 24 hours in advance.
Take a family trip on the *gaves* in a **couralin**, a small traditional motor boat used

for fishing. You can take a fisherman as a guide who will talk about his trade and point out the villages that lie along the river from Peyrehorade to where the *gave* meets the Adour (200 F for 1 hour, 300 F for 2 hours).

Saint-Étienne-d'Orthe
The clog-maker
5 miles (8 km)
NW of Peyrehorade
Le Sabot des Landes
☎ **05 58 89 16 81**
Open daily except Sun.

Claude Labarthe's family have been making Landes clogs for six generations. Visit his workshop any afternoon and watch him carving the wood to make the clogs (ready-to-wear from 140 F to 180 F a pair). Decorative clogs are also available from about 20 to 200 F, and can be used as wall decorations to hold flowers or clothes-brushes.

Port-de-Lanne
Country church and antiques market
2½ miles (4 km) NW of Peyrehorade
The 13th-C. church of Sainte-Madeleine, just before the confluence of the river Adour and the *gaves*, is a rare example of rural gothic architecture. Its high roof and bell-tower entrance were added in the 17th C. as were the triumphal arch and the little columns with carved capitals.

PEYREHORADE MARKET
Grandes Halles
17½ miles (28 km)
S of Dax.
Wed. mornings.
Peyrehorade is one of the oldest market towns in Aquitaine. Permission to hold a market here was first granted in1357 – by the king of England! In the shadow

Spotcheck
B5

Landes

Things to do
Ceramics festival
Landes music festival
Visiting a clog-maker
A trip on a *couralin* down the *gaves*

Within easy reach
Bayonne approx. 19 miles (30 km) W, p. 242,
Orthez approx. 19 miles (30 km) E, p. 278,
Salies-de-Béarn approx. 12½ miles (20 km) SE, p. 276.

Tourist Office
Peyrehorade:
☎ **05 58 73 00 52**

There's a lovely 18th-C. statue of the Virgin and Child above the south altar. On 14 and 15 August, an **antiques market** is held here.

of the château of the viscounts of Orthe (now the Town Hall), duck and goose breeders and shad and salmon fishermen sell their wares. Traditional produce is displayed alongside more recently introduced fruits, such as the Asian pear (nashi), kiwi fruit and tamarillo, which flourish here in the mild climate.

The south coast of Landes
at the edge of the 'gouf'

The south coast of Landes lies at the end of the chain of lagoons, where the pine forest stretches right to the outskirts of Bayonne. In the middle, Capbreton, a former liner port, and Hossegor, a seaside resort with pretty Art Deco villas, lie opposite the 'gouf'; a trench 11,330 ft (3,400 m) deep in the sea just off the coast. In the second week of August, these peaceful resorts are transformed for the world surfing championships.

Capbreton
Écomusée de la Pêche et de la Mer
Casino Municipal, top floor
☎ 05 58 72 40 50
Open daily, June-Aug., 9.30am–noon and 2.30–7pm; Apr.–May and Sept., daily, 2–6pm; Oct.–March, Sun., public and school holidays, 2–6pm.
Admission charge.
Thanks to a reconstruction of the captain's bridge, you can imagine yourself at the helm of a trawler at sea. Eleven aquariums contain every species of fish in the region. There are models and maps of the 'gouf' – a deep sea trench which lies only 1,330 ft (400 m) from the beach.

Fishing on board a catamaran
The *Jean B*, in the port (Av. Pompidou)
☎ 05 58 72 33 36
Sail out on a large catamaran and go **deep-sea fishing**. The *Jean B* and her crew will take you out in the early hours to put down the trawl-lines for catching shark and will teach you all the tricks of the trade. The tackle and bait are supplied

(200 F per person). In the afternoon, you take a one-hour walk (40 F) along the Landes coast. On **15 August**, there are spectacular and traditional Biarritz fireworks (200 F per person).

The master story-tellers
Festival du Conte
☎ 05 58 06 86 86 or 05 58 72 21 81
The fraternity of storytellers, who call themselves *Les Maîtres Rêveurs* (the master dreamers), organises the Festival du Conte in the second fortnight of July at

THE SOUTH COAST OF LANDES • 241

FORBIDDEN DELIGHT

The ortolan, a small brownish bunting native to southern Landes, is still eaten secretly. Its capture is now forbidden but locally it's a gourmet delicacy. This bird was netted in the autumn and fattened on millet seed for a month. To prepare it for cooking, it was smothered in a glass of Armagnac and braised. The few mouthfuls it yielded were subjected to an elaborate ritual. The gourmets would wrap their heads in a white napkin to inhale the fragrance of the cooked bird before eating the flesh – a pleasure enhanced by the excitement of breaking the law.

Capbreton. There are children's stories in the morning and stories for grownups in the evening. The festival lasts for five days.

Seignosse
L'Étang Noir
Access via the D 89, at the entrance to Seignosse-bourg (Av. du Hall-des-Sports)
Maison de la Réserve
☎ 05 58 72 85 76
July–early Sept., guided tours Mon.–Fri., at 10.30am, 3pm and 5pm.

Out of season, free visit (without tour) daily, 9.30am– 6pm.
Free admission exc. guided tours.
This 128 acre (52 ha) nature reserve has examples of all the wildlife of the wooded marshes and moors of Landes. Sturdy footwear and binoculars are essential.

Hossegor
Beach sports
This family seaside resort is only separated from neighbouring Capbreton by the canal du Boudigau.

Spotcheck
B5

Landes

Things to do

Fishing and boat trips
Visiting a nature reserve
Learning to surf

With children

Storytelling festival

Within easy reach

*Grande Lande, p. 216,
Marensin approx. 12½
miles 12½ miles (20 km)
N, p. 220,
Bayonne 10 miles (16 km)
S, p. 242,
Biarritz, p. 246.*

Tourist Offices

Hossegor: ☎ 05 58 41 79 00
Capbreton: ☎ 05 58 72 12 11

Young people come here from all over the world for the **Rip Curl Pro** professional surfing championships. The town is invaded by so many surfers

that you might think you're in California! If you want to join them, there are plenty of places to learn surfing here. They include the Hossegor Surf Club which organises courses (☎ 05 58 43 80 52). The Basco-Landais style of architecture, which flourished in the 1920s and 1930s (p. 51), can be seen in the villas that surround the golf course and along the seafront.

Bayonne
gateway to the Basque country

Bayonne stands at the confluence of the rivers Nive and Adour. Its old quayside is lined with half-timbered houses which the residents paint with oxblood to protect them from bad weather. The city is divided into three districts and has been fought over by successive invading armies, from the Visigoths, Arabs, Normans to the English. The invasions lasted for three centuries! But the results haven't been too bad: the town is known for the most famous ham in the world and a party spirit that exists nowhere else, which peaks at the Fêtes de Bayonne street festival.

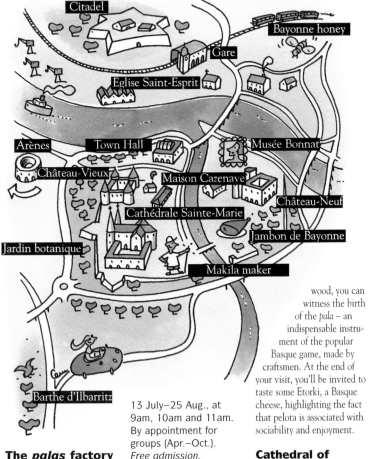

wood, you can witness the birth of the *pala* – an indispensable instrument of the popular Basque game, made by craftsmen. At the end of your visit, you'll be invited to taste some Etorki, a Basque cheese, highlighting the fact that pelota is associated with sociability and enjoyment.

The *palas* factory
Fabrique Alza, Zone Artisanale Saint-Frédéric
☎ 05 59 55 95 08
Tours Thurs. and Fri.,
13 July–25 Aug., at 9am, 10am and 11am. By appointment for groups (Apr.–Oct.).
Free admission.
This factory is well-known to all the pelota professionals, as far afield as Spain and South America. In the workshop, permeated with the scents of

Cathedral of Sainte-Marie
Grand Bayonne
Open Mon.-Sat., 7am–12.30pm and 3–7.30pm; Sun., 3.30–8pm.

Free admission.
The 13th–16th C. cathedral has two spires nearly 300 ft (90 m) high and a Gothic apse. Inside, the keystones of the vaulted ceilings are painted and gilded with armorial shields, a reminder of the medieval English past of the city. All around the cathedral you can walk through the **old lanes** that lead to the ramparts of Vauban.

The cloister
Next to the cathedral.
Open daily 16 Oct.–Easter, 9.30am–12.30pm and 2–5pm; from Easter to 16 Oct., 9am–12.30pm and 2–6pm.
Free admission.
The cloister is so huge that in the Middle Ages it was used for public debates and general meetings. Only three sides of the 14th-C. structure have survived. On the east side you'll find the tombstone of Léopoldine de Lorraine, who was lady-in-waiting to the Queen of Spain.

Guided tour of Bayonne
Tourist Office,
Place des Basques
☎ 05 59 46 01 46
By appointment only.
Admission charge.
The tourist office can provide you with an approved guide and lecturer who will take you on a tour of old Bayonne, and illustrate specific features of life in the area. Learn more about the rich past of the city in this delightful way.

Musée Bonnat
5, Rue Laffitte,
Petit Bayonne
☎ 05 59 59 08 52
Open daily except Tues., and public holidays, 10am–12.30pm and 2–6pm.
Admission charge.
This is **one of the most prestigious museums in**

Spotcheck
A6

Pyrénées-Atlantiques

Things to do
Tour of a *palas* factory
Guided tour of Bayonne
Fêtes, fairs, ferias and festivals
Botanical garden

Within easy reach
Valley of the Nivelle,
p. 256,
Lower valley of the Nive,
p. 258,
Hasparren district, p. 260.

Tourist Office
Bayonne: ☎ 05 59 46 01 46

France, containing works by Rubens, El Greco, Murillo, Goya, Ingres and Degas. Most of the treasures were donated by Léon Bonnat, a generous collector who lived in the city. The building dates from the early 20th C. Don't miss the Rubens room (second floor) and the exceptional cabinet of 1,800 drawings on the ground floor) which is internationally renowned.

Jambon de Bayonne
41, Rue des Cordeliers,
Petit Bayonne
☎ 05 59 25 65 30
Open Mon.–Sat., 20 Apr. –10 July, 9am–noon and 2–6pm; Mon.–Sat., 12 July–28 Aug., 10am–1pm

and 2–7pm (6pm Sat.);
Aug.–Easter, open daily
exc. Sun., Mon. and Sat.
afternoons, 9am–
12.30pm and 2–6pm.
Free admission.
Pierre Ibaïalde
knows Bayonne's
best-kept secret – how
to salt a ham (p. 26).
This craftsman preserv-
er and salter will tell you the
story of how a wounded wild
boar was found completely
preserved in a salt marsh in
the 15th C. Then he'll reveal

the regional ingredients
essential for his art. These are
Espelette red pepper (to spice
and redden the ham) and
Salies salt. There's a **tasting**
at the end of the visit, in the
huge drying room where the
hams are hung. The price for
2lb 4oz (1 kg) of ham on the
bone is 79 F, off the bone,
95 F. You can also try it in the
local *pintxos* (tapas) bars such
as **Ibala**, on the banks of the
Nive and **Trinquet Moderne**.

Chocolate heaven

**Maison Cazenave,
19, Arceaux du
Port-Neuf**
☎ 05 59 59 03 16
Open Tues.–Sat.,
9am–noon and 2–7pm;
Aug., 9am–noon; school
holidays, Mon.–Sat.,
9am–noon and 2–7pm.
Bayonne was the first city in
France in which chocolate
was made. As early as 1496,
Jews expelled from Portugal
brought the knowledge from
the New World and choco-
late-making has remained a
lively tradition ever since.
If you need any convincing,
try the drinking chocolate at
Cazenave. This is nothing like

a normal
hot chocolate
drink; it's foaming,
thick and unequalled since it
was first perfected in 1854.
The master chocolate-maker
also makes chocolate bars
flavoured with orange, coffee,
cinnamon, vanilla, almonds
etc. (9oz; 250 g bar costs 28 F).

The Bayonne calendar

Arènes, Av. des Fleurs
☎ 05 59 25 48 19
Guided tours daily exc.
w/ends, 8am–noon
and 1.30–6pm. Closed
for a month around the
end of Sept.
Free admission.
Ham, pelota, jazz and bull-
fighting are all on the agenda
in a typical Bayonne calendar
of events. The **Foire au
Jambon de Bayonne** (ham
fair) is held on the Esplanade
du Réduit and the Carreau
des Halles in the week before
Easter (Thurs., Fr., Sat.). From
the first Wednesday in August,
the **Fêtes de Bayonne** is a
thriving day- and night-time

street festival (from Wed.
evening to Sun. evening),
with a unique atmosphere.

Around
15 August,
the great **Feria
de l'Assomption** is
celebrated with bullfights in
the oldest bullfighting town
in France. Every Thursday at

4pm, from October to June,
barehanded **pelota** is played at
the Trinquet Saint-André,
Rue du Jeu-de-Paume
(☎ 05 59 59 18 69, admission
charge). In July, the **Jazz
aux Remparts festival** lasts
six days and six nights. In
Bayonne, during summer
festivals, people tend not to
bother too much with sleep!

❀ **Bayonne honey**

Loreztia,
8, Av. des Prés
☎ **05 59 55 49 14**
Open Mon.–Fri. and Sat.
morning, 9am–noon
and 2–6pm.
The bee-keeper Jacques Salles
is also a confectioner. His
bees fly all over the region; to
the heather of Landes in the
north, to the mountainous
Basque country in the south
as well as to the local acacia
and other flowers. The harvest is worth the journey and
these regional flavours can be
savoured in the delicious pots
of honey (from 11 F to 16 F
for 9 oz; 250 g). His straw-
berry, plum and berry jams
are equally delicious. (23 F
for 11½ oz; 340 g).

Botanical
garden

Allée des Tarides,
near the war
memorial, Nouveau
Bayonne
Open daily,
15 Apr.–15 Oct.,
9am–noon and 2–6pm.
Free admission.
In this garden over 1,000
species and varieties of
plants cover an area of
32,290 sq ft (3,000 sq m)
along the city walls. All of
them are meticulously

The botanical garden

labelled so you'll know what
you're looking at. When you
leave, take a look at the
Château-Vieux, where Du
Guesclin was imprisoned
(go into the inner courtyard).

The *makila* maker

37, Rue Vieille-Boucherie,
Grand Bayonne
☎ **05 59 59 18 20**
Open daily, 4–6.30pm;
Sat., 10am–noon;
closed on Sun.
Free admission.
M. Léoncini is one of the
last remaining craftsmen to
continue the tradition of
making the *makila*, the
Basque walking-stick. It was
used not only for walking but
also for defence and is made
from the wood of the medlar
tree. Come and see
how he carefully
carves the stick with
a sharp blade, then
burnishes it. You can
see the elegant tradi-
tional Basque patterns
with which he decorates
each unique walking-
stick. *Makilas* are not
mere souvenirs, they
are real works of
art, produced in a
picturesque
workshop,
custom-made
and strictly
to order.

BARTHE D'ILBARITZ

Av. d'Ilbaritz
☎ **05 59 46 60 68**
Free tours daily;
guided tours from
June–Sept., Mon.–Fri.
at 4pm and 6pm
(by appointment
for groups)
Free admission.
The Adour river has
taken centuries to find
its definitive course. It
finally fixed on the
upper Bayonne, but
only because man
helped it to do so.
The *barthes* (flood
plains) along its banks
show just how unstable
this waterway can be.
However, it's a haven
for wildlife, and the
warm, humid atmo-
sphere allows many
unusual plants and
creatures to flourish.
Take a walk along the
1,666 yd (1,500 m) path
from Ilbaritz, on the
outskirts of the town.

Biarritz – surfing capital

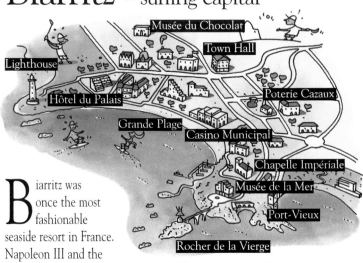

B iarritz was once the most fashionable seaside resort in France. Napoleon III and the Empress Eugénie built a villa here and between the world wars it was patronised by such world-famous names as Coco Chanel, Sacha Guitry and Charlie Chaplin. In the 1950s, the Duke of Windsor, Luis Mariano and Frank Sinatra came here to enjoy themselves. There has recently been a new influx: the surfers. Although things have changed, traces of the glorious past can be seen, like leafing through the pages of an old photo album, at this resort which marks the start of the Basque coast.

Villas of the 'Belle Epoque'

Start at the Hôtel du Palais, built on the site of the Villa Eugénie. The splendid residences on the Avenue de l'Impératrice show how high society was attracted to this 'queen of beaches' right up until the seaside resort lost its exclusivity. La Roche-Ronde, at no. 15, is a baronial castle, with turrets, watch-towers and crenellations (Mata Hari, the famous spy, stayed here). The Villa Paz at no. 58, is an example of 1930s Basque style and the Villa Mirasol at no. 13 has a lovely stained glass window facing towards the outside! Visit the Avenue Edouard VII and the Avenue de la Reine-Victoria and see why the resort was popular with the British aristocracy.

The beaches

Despite the stories, the Grande Plage is not dangerous, although it was once called *la plage des fous* (madmen's beach). It's ideal for strong swimmers and surfers and is also the most fashionable of the beaches as the

Spotcheck
A6

Pyrénées-Atlantiques

Things to do

Swimming and surfing
The festivals
Musée de la Mer
Fast-thalasso
The chocolate museum

With children

Eldora Parc

Within easy reach

*South coast of the Landes,
p. 240,
Valley of the Nivelle,
p. 256,
Hasparren district,
p. 260.*

Tourist Office

Biarritz: ☎ 05 59 22 37 10

casino is right on the seafront. The Côte des Basques beach to the south is even livelier. This is where *surf biarrot* was born. From the overhanging cliff (the villas teeter on the edge) there's a **wonderful view** of the mountains and on a clear day you can see San Sebastian.

are dedicated to the Iberian-American world. With retrospectives and new features, they provide a window on the art world on the other side of the Atlantic.

Musée de la Mer

Plateau de l'Atalaye
☎ 05 59 22 33 34
Open daily, 9.30am-12.30pm and 2–6pm; 9.30am–midnight in July–Aug.; Easter school hols, w/ends and public hols in May, June, Sept., 9.30am–7pm; school hols in Feb. and at Christmas, 9.30am–6pm.
Admission charge.
Seals swim freely in the huge tank at this sea museum. Don't miss their feeding times at 10.30am and 5pm. The **shark**

Biarritz Latino
Franco-Iberian and Latin-American theatre and Latin American cinema and culture festivals.
Late Sept.–Oct
Most Basques claim to have an uncle in America; and it's more than likely he's in South America rather than the US. With so much Basque emigration, it's important to keep up contacts. The theatre festival (organised in mid-Oct. along with the city of Bayonne) and the cinema festival (end of Sept. to the beginning of Oct.)

(Information available at the Tourist Office or Biarritz Festival Office ☎ 05 59 22 37 00).

Musée de la Mer

CHIPIRON AND COJONES

In Biarritz, fresh squid are cooked in their own juices. The local dish, called *chipiron*, combines the subtle flavour of the squid with the sharpness of its ink. This is only one of the unusual dishes of the region. Even stranger are the *cojones*, stuffed bull's testicles. The dish is cooked at the time of the *temperadas*, the gelding, when bulls lose their male organs for the bullring. Gourmets eat the tender meat stuffed with a savoury meat mixture.

cave will give you goose-pimples and you'll also see the underwater world and the flora and fauna of the Gulf of Gascony. From the esplanade opposite there's a lovely ocean view.

Fast-thalasso

**Thermes marins,
80, Rue de Madrid
☎ 05 59 23 01 22**
Take advantage of your stay to lose a few pounds or recharge your batteries. The Thalassotherapy (sea water treatment) centres have recently introduced short treatment packages called 'fast-thalasso' which allow you to try a range of à la carte treatments, as long as you book in advance. Try the seawater steam jet or the seaweed baths. The Thermes Marins even have a special treatment for fat thighs.

The Imperial chapel
Rue Pellot
Open Thurs., 3–5pm.
This chapel is surprisingly bright and colourful and full of Napoleonic insignia (*see below*). The chapel was built in 1864, on the orders of the Empress Eugénie, in the former imperial park of the Villa Eugénie (now the Hôtel du Parc). Four masses a year are held here to pray for the souls of the French Imperial family.

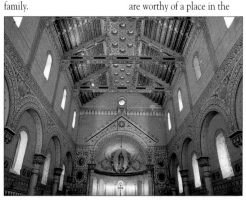

Poterie Cazeaux
**15, Rue Larreguy
☎ 05 59 23 15 01**
Open daily except Sun., 10am–12.30pm and 3–7pm.
Free admission.
The firm of Cazaux has been making Basque pottery entirely by hand for

four generations. The clay is turned on a wheel and pieces are modelled to order. They include decorative tableware and even wall-tiles for the kitchen or bathroom. In the shop (10, Rue Broquedis, ☎ 05 59 22 36 03), you'll find knife-rests at 25 F each, coasters at 290 F or a handsome glazed jar 25½ in high (64 cm) from 4,800 F.

The chocolate museum
**14-16, Av. Beaurivage
☎ 05 59 24 50 50**
Open daily exc. Sun., 10am–noon and 2.30–6pm (7pm in summer).
Admission charge.
Serge Couzigou, master chocolatier, has found his way into the record books after making the largest Easter bell out of chocolate. The museum displays 50 of his amazing chocolate sculptures, which are worthy of a place in the

Louvre itself. The remainder of the 3,230 sq ft (300 sq m) of museum space is devoted to tools, artefacts and posters all relating to chocolate and its manufacture. If all this gives you a taste for chocolate, there's a convenient shop!

Anglet
The 'love room'
N of the Biarritz lighthouse
Plage de la Chambre d'amour
Never shelter in this cave at the foot of the Cap Saint-Martin cliffs, especially if you're with your sweetheart. Two local lovers paid with their lives in the *chambre d'amour* because they were too engrossed to notice the rising tide. Visit the cave on foot from the beach of the same name (the path is signposted).

Chisteras makers
6, Allée des Liserons
☎ 05 59 03 85 04
Open daily except Sat. afternoon, Sun. and public holidays. Tours at 5pm.
Admission charge.
A *chistera* is a woven willow glove or mitt used to throw the ball in pelota (see pp. 74 and 75). Jean-Louis Gonzales and his brother Pierre are the last craftsmen in France still making this strange device, said to be based on a fruit basket. You can watch them at work showing their skills, both in basketry and woodwork, which enable them to get the perfect curve for throwing and catching the ball. Each mitt costs between 1,000 and 1,800 F.

Bidart
Eldora Parc
RN 10
☎ 05 59 47 71 72
Open daily, Apr.–30 Sept. 2–7pm. July–Aug. and school holidays, 10am–9pm.
Admission charge.
This is another link with South America, but this time for the youngsters. There's a hacienda and gardens, plus a farm, where llamas and alpacas can be petted. There's a whole South American world in a very pleasant leisure park. There are also interesting exhibitions about South America and its links with the Basques.

SURFING
Biarritz is the French capital of surfing, and headquarters of the National Federation. It attracts all the great champions thanks to its excellent waves. The Biarritz Surf Festival, held in July, is one of the high points in the surfing year. The *long board* legends come here to defend their titles against the young lions of the surfboard and a Hawaiian Aloha contributes music and festivities. The Basque coast is the ideal surfing spot. Its rocky sea bottom and high winds encourage the formation of rollers and makes them last a long time before they break. Surfers swim out to the wave and leap up on the board, standing upright and ensuring they stay as close as possible to the hollow part of the wave, the curl. Then they ride the wave for several hundred yards, performing special moves by jumping, turning on the breaker or by altering the position of their feet (see pp. 96 and 97).

The Basque coast
a favourite with artists

The Basque coast stretches from Biarritz to Hendaye, and over the years has attracted many artists and celebrities. Its rocky cliffs are topped with villas, chapels, châteaux and Basque houses. Here and there the sheer cliffs are broken up by little beaches. Guéthary and Hendaye are popular seaside resorts which attract the crowds in high summer.

Bidart and Guéthary

Musée de Guéthary
Parc Saraleguinea
☎ 05 59 54 86 37
Open daily except Tues.,
Apr.–Sept., 2.30–6.30pm;
July–Aug., 3–7pm
Admission charge.
Bidart and Guéthary are
two former whaling ports
that stand side-by-side facing
the sea. Among the luxury
villas in Guéthary, the villa
Saraleguinea contains the
remains of the only Roman
villa discovered in the
Basque country.

Antiques and golfing
From July to September, you
can hunt for antiquesall along
the Basque coast. The fun
starts on Saturday mornings
in Guéthary at the flea
market at the *fronton*. In
Hendaye, the market is held
on the fourth Sunday of the
month throughout the year.
As for golfing there are eight
courses in the Basque country
and you can take book lessons
through the Centre d'Entraîn-
ement d'Ilbaritz at Bidart.
You'll be put in touch with
several pro teachers and be
offered a selection of course
packages. (☎ 05 59 43 81 30).

Espadrilles made to measure
Maison Garcia, RN 10, Bidart
☎ 05 59 26 51 27
Open daily except Sun.,
in season, 8am–8pm;
out of season, Thurs.
and Fri., 9–11am and
2–6pm.

Maison Garcia makes the
traditional Basque espadrille
with rope and natural rubber
soles to your exact measurements and taste. You can
choose the fabric or bring
your own to be 'espadrilled'.
You can even request person-
alised designs. The price
ranges from 50 F to 300 F,
depending on the complexity
of your requirements. They
take a week
to make.

THE BEST SURFING SPOT ON THE COAST

The Parlementia beach, north of Guéthary, boasts a monster wave, the biggest in France. It reaches at least 3 ft (1 m) in height but can grow to as much as 20 ft (6 m)! This very high, straight and powerful wave attracts experienced surfers from all over the world. Local surfers handle it with skill because they know the sea-bed is rocky here. Bring your binoculars to watch the big waves and to admire the skill of the surfers, as the action takes place quite a long way from shore.

Ciboure and Socoa
Ravel's house

Ciboure, located opposite Saint-Jean, was the birthplace of the composer Maurice Ravel, born here in 1875. His house is in the port (12, Quai Maurice-Ravel), next to other period houses. The 16th-C. fort de Socoa, built by Henri IV to protect the coast from attack by sea, dominates the whole bay. It's the starting point for the scenic Corniche road.

The Corniche
D 912, 3½ miles (6 km)
Between Socoa and Hendaye, follow the extraordinary **rocky coast** overlooking the ocean. You'll find yourself constantly stopping the car to look at the view, especially along the route of the old railway line. You can also enjoy a walk along the foot of cliffs.

Château d'Abbadie
Route de la Corniche
☎ 05 59 20 04 51
Open Mon.–Fri., Feb.–May and Oct.–15 Dec., 11am–noon and 2–4.30pm; Mon.–Sat., June–Sept., 10am–2pm (free tours) and 3–5.30pm (guided tours). *Admission charge.*
The rotunda on the top of this edifice constructed by Viollet-le-Duc was used as an observatory. The interior is lavishly decorated in an oriental style, reflecting the passion of the cartographer who owned it. Overlooking the sea, it has one of the most beautiful locations on the coast, and the huge grounds are a favourite with birds.

Spotcheck
A6

Pyrénées-Atlantiques

Things to do
Shopping for antiques
Golf

Within easy reach
Valley of the Nivelle, p. 256.

Tourist Office
Hendaye: ☎ 05 59 20 00 34

Hendaye
Last beach before Spain

This resort has a **magnificent beach** and lovely villas standing amid exotic plants. On the right bank of the Bidassoa the town faces Spain, and its Île aux Faisans was the setting for numerous treaties between France and Spain (the island is now jointly owned by both countries).

Urrugne
❀ Château d'Urtubie
☎ 05 59 54 31 15
Open daily except Tues. Apr.–Oct., tours at 11am and from 2–7pm (every half-hour). *Admission charge.*
Its stones tell the stories of six centuries of history in the Basque country. Louis XI, then Marshall Soult and the Duke of Wellington stopped here (the latter during the Napoleonic Wars).

Saint-Jean-de-Luz
city of Louis XIV

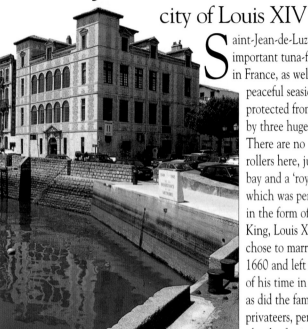

Saint-Jean-de-Luz is the most important tuna-fishing port in France, as well as being a peaceful seaside resort, protected from the swell by three huge sea-walls. There are no breakers or rollers here, just a calm bay and a 'royal sun' – which was personified in the form of the Sun King, Louis XIV. He chose to marry here in 1660 and left many traces of his time in the town, as did the famous Basque privateers, permitted to plunder foreign ships on behalf of the monarch. You can take walks here, swim, see the huge cliffs along the coast and taste the *ttoro*.

Louis XIV's house
Pl. Louis-XIV
☎ **05 59 26 01 56**
Guided tour daily, exc. Sun. morning, July–Aug., 10.30am–12.30pm and 2.30–6.30pm (5.30pm June–mid-Oct.); Mid-Oct.–May, by appointment for groups.
Admission charge.
This is where Louis XIV stayed at the time of his marriage to the Spanish Infanta Maria Teresa. The Sun King, accompanied by Cardinal Mazarin, used to throw gold pieces to the crowds from the balcony. Inside, a handsome Basque staircase leads to the green-panelled dining room; the vermillion tableware decorated with enamel was a gift from Louis XIV to his hosts.

The Church of Saint-Jean-Baptiste, scene of Louis XIV's wedding

The secrets of pelota

Information at the Tourist Office
☎ 05 59 26 03 16
or at the Club Luzean, Fronton Municipal
☎ 05 59 26 13 93

Saint-Jean-de-Luz, like any self-respecting Basque town, has its *fronton* and its *jaï-alaï* where international competitions are held. If you're keen learn pelota, this is where to come. You'll be taught a little theory about *pala* with the naked hand, or *chistera* with the basket, then have practical lessons, after which you'll be ready for a game (adults and children aged 8 and over, individual lessons: adults 50 F; children 30 F).

Musée Grévin

Pavillon de l'Infante, 7, Rue Mazarin, in the port.
☎ 05 59 51 24 88
Open daily, Apr.–Oct., 10am–noon and 2–6.30pm (7pm in July–Aug.); school holidays, open daily 2–6pm. Groups by appointment

all year round.
Admission charge.

At this waxwork museum you can attend the royal wedding (and even enter the nuptial bedchamber!), relive some pages of Basque history, such as the signing of the Treaty of the Pyrenees with Spain, or even ride in the whaling ships of the Basque privateers.

Saint-Jean-de-Luz macaroons

Maison Adam, 6, Pl. Louis-XIV
☎ 05 59 26 03 54
Open daily exc. Mon. 8am–12.30pm and 2–7pm; Sun., 7am–1pm and 2–7pm. Closed 4 weeks in Feb.

Since 1660, the firm of Adam has kept the secret of manufacturing these little almond cakes which the Sun King reputedly enjoyed. The shop is right opposite the house where Louis XIV stayed, where they continue to combine sugar, Valencia almonds and egg whites to make these delicious treats. (around 50F a dozen). While you're there, try the Touron Basque (soft nougat).

Studded handbags

Sellerie Laffargue, 25, Rue Gambetta
☎ 05 59 26 11 38
Open Tues.–Sat., 9.30am–12.30pm and 3–7.15pm.
It was cattle collars that gave M. Laffargue, the saddle-maker, the idea for his famous studded Basque handbags.

Spotcheck
A6

Pyrénées-Atlantiques

Things to do

Learn how to play pelota
Ecomusée de la Tradition Basque
Take a sea trip
Fishing and scuba-diving
'Wellbeing and health' day

Within easy reach

Valley of the Nivelle, p. 256,
Lower Valley of the Nive, p. 258.

Tourist Office

Saint-Jean-de-Luz:
☎ 05 59 26 03 16

THE PRIVATEERS OF SAINT-JEAN-DE-LUZ

A local fraternity still perpetuates the memory of these Basque privateers. In the late 17th C., Louis XIV authorised all the fishermen to plunder foreign ships for the benefit of the state. This profitable business soon became a major activity in the gulf, employing 7,000 men as late as 1794. Every year in mid-September, the order of the Corsaires de Saint-Jean-de-Luz dons the ceremonial dress of its heroes – the plumed tricorn hat and a black and red cape.

His workshop is now famous and the handbags (from 290 F), belts (280 F) and wallets (180 F) are very popular and are sold in a lovely wooden Basque shop with an oak staircase and gallery.

Basque fabrics

**Maison Charles Larre,
4, Pl. Louis-XIV
☎ 05 59 26 02 13
Open daily,
9.30am–12.30pm
and 2.30–7.30pm.**
This lovely linen was originally woven to make blankets for cattle, as proved by the photo displayed in the shop. It's now made into tablecloths and napkins, and is sold by the metre. There's even an embroidered version. It costs between 98 F for 39 in (1 m) (cotton) and 130 F (linen and cotton) for the greater widths. From 36 F for 39 in (1 m) in the narrower widths..

Ecomusée de la Tradition Basque

**Ferme Berrain, R.N.10
☎ 05 59 51 06 06
Open daily, July-Aug.,
9am-8pm; the rest of the
year, daily, 10am-7pm.**
Admission charge.
This museum embraces all the features of the Basque identity: gastronomy, regional dress, crafts, linen weaving etc. The Izarra distillery has recently been included. This Basque liqueur, created in 1903, is a subtle mixture of aniseed, cinnamon, and around 20 different herbs and spices. A tasting session will allow you to compare the different versions: yellow, with the flavour of bitter almonds; green, enhanced by peppermint, or the slightly acid white.

Tuna and sardines

These fish contribute to the popularity of Saint-Jean-de-Luz. Every day in the early morning, the fishermen return in their wooden boats with their catch of tuna and sardines from the gulf. While the fishermen start repair work on their nets, loud bidding fixes the price of the fish for that day. If you can't attend the auction sale (restricted to fishmongers), try not to miss the **tuna festival (Fête du Thon)** at the beginning of July.

The cliffs along the coast

Walk northwards or drive southwards, D 912.
The folds in the cliffs around the bay are exposed layers of rock eroded by the action of the waves. Walking along the north-east coast, from the Sainte-Barbe lighthouse to the Erromadie beach, you get an even better view of these strange cliffs. The wild landscape looks as if it has been compressed in the south-west. From the fort of Socoa to Hendaye, there's a wonderful view from the Corniche over the bay and the gulf.

Off to sea on the *Marie-Rose*

Departure opposite the town hall.
**Cruises (Apr–Sept.):
daily 2pm, 4pm and
5pm (25 to 70 F).
Sea fishing: 8am to
noon (150 F). Scuba-
diving on request
☎ 05 59 26 39 84**
The *Marie-Rose*, a former pilot ship, is also used as a symbol of Saint-Jean-de-Luz, where it has been working for many years. You can take a trip on the boat (lasting from half an hour to two hours) either to admire the landscape, especially the shale cliffs, or to fish in the open sea.

The surfing beaches
NE coast, Erromadie and Lafitenia. SW coast., La Pergola and La Bougie

You can relax by watching the surfers catching the waves. At Saint-Jean-de-Luz, Lafitenia has the best waves. They can reach from 5 to 13 ft (1.5 m to 4 m) high and are the delight of experienced surfers. Excitement is guaranteed at Erromadie, where the rocky headland makes the waves very dangerous due to rocks barely concealed under the water. Nearer the bay, the sea-wall reduces the size of the swell, making it possible for beginners to take the plunge. Seize your first small rollers at Bougie (Socoa) or at La Pergola (Ciboure).

Ttoro
This typical dish is the subject of local cult to such an extent that it has its own festival in September. This dish used to be made from whatever was left over from the fish auction. To serve 8, you need: a gurnard, 1lb 2oz (500 g) conger eel, 1lb 2oz (500 g) monkfish, 8 langoustines, head of a hake and a scorpion fish. Sauté the hake with a chopped onion, a garlic clove, and 2 tbsp olive oil for 10 min. Add a large dash of white wine, 18 fl oz (50 cl) of water, a chopped tomato, and season with salt and pepper.

Simmer for 1 hour. Cut the fish into slices, sprinkle them with flour, then fry them. Pour the strained soup over them. Bring the soup back to the boil, then add 1lb 2oz (500 g) mussels and simmer for another 30 minutes. Delicious!

Marine massage
**Institut de Thalassothérapie Helianthal,
Place Maurice-Ravel
☎ 05 59 51 51 51**

Open daily except 3 weeks from the end of Nov. to the beginning of Dec.
After a short medical examination, you're free to pamper yourself with a day of bio-marine treatments at this seawater treatment centre. There are relaxing massages, tonic showers, mud treatments and seawater cascades. Everything to make you feel good. To end your day on a note of perfect relaxation there's a Turkish bath. You can then go out into the bracing sea air and feel revitalised and replenished ('wellbeing and health' day from 450 F).

THE BASQUE WHALING SHIPS
Before they became privateers, the Basque fishermen were whalers. In the early 17th C., they had to pursue whales as far as Greenland, as they became so rare on the Basque coast. The hunt for blubber and whalebone (sought after for corsets and helmet plumes) was so successful that the Basques became expert harpooners. However, unable to keep their sources a secret, they soon lost out to the Dutch.

Nivelle valley

Sheltered by Rhune point, the highest peak of Labourd, the climate of the green hills of the Basque hinterland is exceptionally mild. Along the Nivelle valley, there are moors, and hills, all bathed in the gentle light that also illuminates the white walls of the houses.

dominated by the Rhune

St-Jean-de-Luz

Ascain

St-Pée-sur-Nivelle

La Rhune

Sare

Ainhoa

La Palombière

Grottes de Sare

The little train of the Rhune

Departure from the Col de Saint-Ignace, Sare, every 35 min.
☎ 05 59 54 20 26
Open daily, 19 March–11 Nov., from 9am (8.30am in summer).
Admission charge.
You'll get magnificent views of the Basque country as you travel along at 5 mph (8 km/h) on this little railway to the summit of the Rhune. You'll pass fields grazed by sheep and wild horses as you climb to an altitude of 3,000 ft (900 m)

where the pagan cult of the heights is still celebrated. Even at this height there are *ventas* (shops) offering local specialities (*tapas*) and **Basque crafts**.

Saint-Pée-sur-Nivelle
Witches and pelota
8½ miles (14 km) E of Saint-Jean-de-Luz
The ancient feudal château, with only one tower, is known as 'the witches' château', as witch trials were once held here. Inside the church, there is a beautiful scallop-shaped ceiling. Here, the *chistera* (the willow mitt used for playing pelota) is an object of pride. It was a boy from this village who first had the idea of catching the ball in a fruit basket in 1856. In summer,

watch the **demonstration game of pelota** every Friday at 9.30pm, the game for professionals on Wednesday afternoons and the **Force Basque** trials every Thursday at the *fronton* (9.30pm). The nearby lake has a beach, **water sports**, picnic grounds and exercise equipment.

Ascain and Sare
Where *Ramuntcho* was born

The two villages sit beside the Nivelle on the steep slopes of the Rhune. Ascain has a pretty square and a medieval church which inspired Pierre Loti's novel *Ramuntcho*. In Sare, the 17th- and 18th-C. houses were once used by smugglers and resistance fighters against the Spanish. There's an inscription to that effect on the Town Hall (the house with arches).

The caves of Sare
☎ 05 59 54 21 88
Open daily, Easter–Sept., 10am–6pm; July–Aug., 9.30–8pm; Oct.–11 Nov., 11am–5pm, 12 Nov.– Dec. and 7 March– Easter, 2–5pm;2 Jan.– 7 March, 2–4pm.
Admission charge.
An illuminated blue path guides you through the twists and turns of this prehistoric world. From gallery to gallery, the light, images and sounds recreate the atmosphere of the caves lived in by early man and his contemporary, the cave-bear.

La Palombière
4 miles (6 km) S of Sare, on the D 306
Col de Lizarrietta
On this Pyrenean peak, at an altitude of 1,470 ft (440 m) large nets called *pantières* are spread to catch wood pigeons.

Special corridors have been created in the oak forest through which the wood pigeons fly so that they are lured into the nets which then collapse on them. To learn more about this sport visit the watchtowers with a scout who will explain it all to you. This all springs into action during the hunting season from 1 October to 20 November, (pp. 86 and 87). Wonderful views.

Ainhoa
This 12th-C. *bastide* is one of the loveliest Basque villages (the whole *bastide* is a listed site.) The main street is lined with large red-and-green half-timbered houses whose upper floors are corbelled (see the Gorritia house and its lintel). There are lovely walks around it, offering the opportunity to contemplate the magic greenery of the Basque country.

Spotcheck
A6

Pyrénées-Atlantiques

Things to do
Taking the little train up the Rhune
Watching pelota games and *Force Basque* trials
The caves of Sare

Within easy reach
Biarritz, p. 246, Basque coast, p. 250, Saint-Jean-de-Luz, p. 252.

Tourist Office
Saint-Pée-sur-Nivelle:
☎ 05 59 54 11 69

BASQUE SAVOURY PRESERVES
Road from Saint-Jean-de-Luz, Ascain
☎ 05 59 54 08 67
Open daily except Sun., 9am–7.15pm.
Do you fancy trying *Axoa;* a dish of slices of veal cooked with hot red Espelette pepper? Or perhaps *piperade*, with green chilli peppers, tomatoes and eggs, or stewed wood pigeon preserved in its own gravy? You can try these delights and take some home with you, so you can still savour Basque cuisine

after your holiday. At this small cannery, the best local foods are prepared and preserved in jars. If you want to do the tour (free), call 48 hours in advance.

The lower Nive valley

T he Nive is the main river of Labourd, the eastern, inland part of the Basque country. It flows gently down the mountain to Bayonne where it joins the Adour.

On either side of its course, villages are dotted in a luscious green landscape. Woods and fields, some of them terraced, alternate in the picturesque valleys and the alluvial plain. There's plenty of history, as well as delicious local food to be sampled here.

Cambo-les-Bains
Hot springs
19 miles (30 km) E of Saint-Jean-de-Luz
Thermes (Chaîne Thermale du Soleil)
☎ 05 59 29 39 39
The Honorine spring is rich in sulphur compounds and can help to alleviate the pain of those suffering from rheumatism and respiratory infections. If you want to feel its benefits, try the **Therm' découverte** package, which allows you four treatments in a single day. On Wednesdays, an antique market is held in the Parc Saint-Joseph and there are also guided walks

(☎ 05 59 29 70 25, departure from the Laborde car park, 9am in season, 1.45pm out of season; also on Sundays, free).

Arnaga, Edmond Rostand's house
☎ 05 59 29 70 57
Open daily, Apr.–Sept., 10am–12.30pm and 2.30–7pm; Oct.–All Saints Day and Christmas holidays, every day, 2.30–6pm; Feb.–March, Sat.–Sun., 2.30–6pm. *Admission charge.*
This house is as huge as Cyrano de Bergerac's nose! Inside are memorabilia of the great writer, including the

César award given to Gérard Depardieu for his interpretation of Rostand's most famous hero, Cyrano. The house and gardens are classic examples of Basque turn-of-the-century architecture.

Itxassou
Cherry-picking time
2 miles (3 km) S of Cambo-les-Bains
The black cherry festival is celebrated in May or June in this lovely setting. The cherry is the local symbol and forms the basis of a Basque cake. In the church beside the Nive, engraved on a little plaque, is the Charte d'Itxassou. This charter affirms the rights of the Basque nation, as claimed a the nationalist movement dissolved in 1974.

Le Pas de Roland
1 mile (1½ km) S of Itxassou, left bank of the river Nive
Roland, the hornblower of Roncevaux, passed through here. A kick from his horse is

said to have made the famous pass now known as the Pas de Roland. Leaving the church at Itxassou, a narrow scenic road leads to the mythical spot above the Nive.

Riding a mule
All year round
☎ 05 59 29 78 00
Half a mile (1 km) past the Pas de Roland, towards the Saint-Pierre restaurant, you can hire mules at Mandozaina. A mule is the ideal mount – the smugglers' choice – for exploring the Basque mountains. Its surefootedness is legendary (half a day or several days will cost 400 F a day). Children under the age of 10 will ride donkeys.

Espelette
The capital of the chilli pepper
2 miles (3 km) E of Cambo-les-Bains
This village, typical of the

Labourd area, is the capital of chilli peppers, which are bought and sold here every Wednesday morning in the indoor market. Take a look at the feudal château and the galleries in the church. Celebrate the pepper festival here, the last Sunday in October.

THE LITTLE TRAIN OF THE NIVE
Departures from Bayonne station
☎ 05 59 37 03 57
Booking only on Fri., July–Aug.
Admission charge.
Ride right up the Nive valley on a charming little train. On your arrival at Saint-Jean-Pied-de-Port, another little train will take you through the old town and will stop for a typical Basque lunch and a game of pelota. The guided commentary on this tour will allow you to discover about the Adour, Labourd and the ancient capital of Lower Navarre, all in a single day.

Larressore
The *makila* maker
2 miles (3 km) N of Cambo-les-Bains
Atelier Ainciart-Bergara
☎ 05 59 93 03 05
Open daily except Sun. and public holidays, 9am–noon and 2–6pm.
The Bergara family has been making *makilas*, the Basque sword-stick, for more than 200 years. By tradition, the name and arms of the owner are engraved on

Spotcheck
A6-B6

Pyrénées-Atlantiques

Things to do
Hot springs
Rambling and hiking
Riding a mule
The little train of the Nive

Within easy reach
*Biarritz, p. 246,
Saint-Jean-de-Luz,
p. 252.*

Tourist Office
Combo-les-Bains:
☎ 05 59 29 70 25

the stick. The cost of this unique item ranges from 1,400 and 3,300 F (you'll have to wait a few days for the order to be finished).

Arcangues
Luis Mariano's grave
6½ miles (10 km) NW of Ustaritz
Luis Mariano, a French operetta singer, died in 1970 and is buried here in a cemetery with a magnificent view of the Pyrenees. His house can be viewed and there is a bust of him by the sculptor Paul Belmondo.

Hasparren
sanctuary of the Basque country

The Hasparren district is squeezed between two Basque provinces; Labourd and Lower Navarre. It's a land of change, whose peaceful hills and valleys suddenly change to sharp rocky escarpments, honeycombed with caves which were inhabited by early man. In this region of varied landscapes, there are few monuments to visit but the country cottages are most attractive.

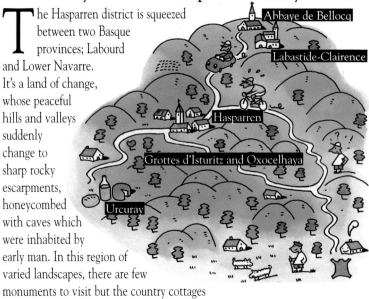

Hasparren
Francis Jammes's house
15½ miles (25 km) SE of Bayonne
Eyhatzea house, where the famous Basque writer Francis Jammes lived, stands at the edge of the town on the road to Bayonne. He died here in 1938 and is buried in the village cemetery. The poet's house itself cannot be visited but admission to the grounds is free. It's pleasant to stroll among the old trees and rare plants, to recapture the inspiration that the bard of the

Basque country found here. An archeological centre was recently established in the property (information at the Tourist Office.)

Saint-Martin-d'Arbéroue
The caves of Isturitz and Oxocelhaya
D 14 S of Hasparren
☎ 05 59 29 64 72
Open daily, 15 March–15 Nov., 10am–noon and 2–6pm (departure for the last tour), except Mon. and Tues. morning 15 March–31 May and 1 Oct.–15 Nov. In July–Aug., 10am–6pm.
Admission charge.
A prehistoric musical instrument carved out of bone was found here. Plunge back into the past

and find out what life was like 40,000 years ago. You can see paintings, tools as well as wonderful rock formations in these extraordinary caves.

Labastide-Clairence
Visit a *bastide*
5 miles (8 km) NE of Hasparren
Information
☎ 05 59 29 65 05
Guided tours all year round.
Admission charge.
Although this village is in the Basque country, Gascon is spoken here. The 14th-C. *bastide* has all the ingredients of a typical Basque village with half-timbered

THE TRADITIONAL COUNTRY HOUSE

GOIZEKO IZARRA

This type of house can be seen everywhere in Arbéroue. The *etxe* (pronounced 'etcheh') is like an extension of the caves of prehistoric man, in the rituals attached to it and in its protective function. It's almost always oriented to face the rising sun and the lime-washed façade with red half-timbering is wide and open. The name of the owner is always written on the lintel over the door. The porch leads into a large workroom which serves as a living room. The cowshed is behind the house and leans against the back wall which never has much decoration.

houses and a galleried church. Many craftsmen exhibit their work in the main square. The Tourist Office arranges a guided tour of the village.

Bonloc
Boncolac factory

3½ miles (5 km) SE of Hasparren
☎ 05 59 29 54 08
Guided tours July–Aug., from Tuesday to Friday, 10am–noon and 2–6pm. Out of season, by appointment only.
Free sampling at the shop all year round, Fri. and Sat.
This factory lies in the countryside and millions of chocolates, sweets, desserts and ice creams are manufactured here. You can visit the chocolate workshop and see

the huge oven which holds several thousand cakes. And, of course, there's a shop where you can taste the Basque cakes and the chocolates.

Mendionde
Paragliding, walking and cycling

Road from Louhossoa to Helette
Baigura Leisure Centre
☎ 05 59 37 69 05
Seeing the Basque country from above is a wonderful introduction to paragliding (300 F). At Baigura, the sports are always based around nature, and include paragliding, hiking, mountain-biking and horse-riding. If you don't feel energetic,

Spotcheck
B6

Pyrénées-Atlantiques

Things to do
The caves of Isturitz
Guided tour of a *bastide*
Visit a chocolate factory
Paragliding, walking, cycling

Within easy reach
Bayonne approx. 15½ miles (25 km) NW, p. 242, Biarritz approx. 18¾ miles (30 km) NW, p. 246.

Tourist Office
Hasparren:
☎ 05 59 29 62 02

a small railway will take you to the top of Mont Baiguria.

Belloc
Local cheese

2 miles (3 km) N of Labastide-Clairence
Abbaye de Belloc
☎ 05 59 29 65 55
Open daily, Tues.–Sun. morning, 10–11.45am and 2.30–6pm.
In the Benedictine monastery of Belloc, the monks sell their own cheese,

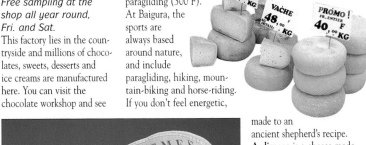

made to an ancient shepherd's recipe. **Ardigasna** is a cheese made from raw ewe's milk, heated very slowly, and always has a soft texture (around 87 F for 2lb 4oz; 1 kg). It's sold on the spot, outside the times of the church services, or it can be sent by mail order. The monks also recently began weaving carpets from Basque wool.

The Ossès valley
birthplace of the Basque horse

The Ossès valley in Lower Navarre is a small circular plain surrounded by the foothills of the Pyrenees, which rise to 2,670 ft (800 m). The bridge over the Nive at Bidarray, was once used by pilgrims bound for the tomb of St James at Santiago de Compostela, and is said to have been built by *laminaks*, the Basque equivalent of leprechauns. The vulture, however, is an ever-present reality, and it hovers menacingly over this prosperous and beautiful region.

The church of Saint-Julien at Ossès

Ossès

A beautiful altar screen

8½ miles (13 km) N of Saint-Jean-Pied-de-Port

The altar screen in the 16th-C. church of Saint-Julien is the most beautiful in the Basque country. The **Maison Sastriarena** (1628) was once the residence of the bishops of Bayonne, and the Maison Harizmendi, 250 yards (200 m) further on, served as a lodging for the prelate who married Louis XIV to Maria-Theresa in 1660 in Saint-Jean-de-Luz (p. 252).

Recipe for Basque cake

Restaurant Mendi Alde
☎ 05 59 37 71 78

You can learn how to make a Basque cake at any time of year, as long as you book two or three days in advance. The three-hour course costs 140 F and you will not only learn how to make the cake but also how to bake bread.

Bidarray

The pottok nature reserve

4½ miles (7 km) W of Ossès. Signposted route from the village.
☎ 05 59 52 21 14
Open daily, Jun.–Sept., 11am–6pm. Out of season, by appointment
Admission charge.

The Maison du Pottok (pronounced 'pottok'), on the heights of Bidarray, is a rest home for the little thick-maned Basque horse. On a 1¼ mile (2 km) hike through the mountains, you can

CAVE OF 'THE SWEATING SAINT'

Take a handkerchief (essential), and rub 'the sweating saint'. The water on this stalactite, which looks strangely human in form, is applied to a diseased part of the body and allegedly has instant curative powers. In the cave of Arperkosaindua, there are rags all over the ground, left (along with the disease) by the pilgrims who have been visiting this magical site for centuries. To get there, leave from Bidarray and take the little road beside the river Bastan (D 349) to the Bernaténêa farm and then continue on foot along the GR 10 (half an hour's walk). If this gives you blisters, you can cure them when you get there!

learn about the history of this Pyrenean breed, which was a favourite with smugglers (see pp. 82 and 83). It was once on the verge of extinction but its representatives now live among Pyrenean goats and a prehistoric breed of cow which were also nearly wiped out.

The smokehouse in the valley
☎ 05 59 37 74 41
Open daily,
9am–7.30pm.
Guided tour.
Free admission.

Jérôme and Marisa de Joantho smoke trout, salmon and eels. The fish can be salted, smoked over beechwood or simply cooked. All the fish comes from the waters of the Bastan, a local mountain stream.

Whitewater sports
By the D 918, towards Saint-Jean-Pied-de-Port
Base Eaux Vives
☎ 05 59 37 72 37
Open daily, Apr.–Sept., 9am–7pm; Nov.–Mar., 10am–6pm.
Lower Navarre is full of rushing mountain streams and rivers which are perfect for whitewater sports. At Bidarray, on the Nive, the watersports centre offers safe, introductory courses in canoeing, kayaking

and canyoning. There are also one- or two-day treks, always with a guide. For children, 6 to 12 years old, there's a chance to try whitewater rafting with the family in a safe environment. Rates per person: 150 F a trip (children: 75 F, rafting only) or 250 F a day (two types of activity).

Bird watching excursion
Comité Ispégi, Dimitri Marguerat
☎ 05 59 37 77 20
Group excursions by appointment.
You can watch vultures hovering over the mountains of Lower Navarre in the company of a state-approved

Spotcheck
B6

Pyrénées-Atlantiques

Things to do

Hiking through the mountains
Whitewater sports
Bird watching

With children

Whitewater rafting

Tourist Office

Ossès: ☎ 05 59 37 74 62

guide. Dimitri Marguerat will take you into the world of birds of prey where you'll be enthralled by their aerial acrobatics and grace. He'll lend you binoculars so you can see better and he'll point out any treasures on the ground whether flowers or plants, animals or insects. This wonderful and extremely informative experience costs 900 F for a group.

The Aldudes valley
the power of tradition

The Aldudes valley, around Saint-Étienne-de-Baïgorris, is a green meadowland surrounded by hills covered with chestnut groves. It has served as a niche for the most ancient Basque customs. The houses are all unique, of pink or red sandstone, the typical building stone in this incredibly lovely valley.

Saint-Étienne-de-Baïgorry

7 miles (11 km) W of Saint-Jean-Pied-de-Port
The lovely bridge spaning the Nive was built in 1661. Nearby, in the church of Saint-Étienne, a baroque altar screen dominates the nave and its three storeys of wooden galleries. The small door to the right of the porch was once reserved for **cagots**, people who were regarded locally as 'untouchables'. Don't miss the Basque language services held on Saturday evenings and Sunday mornings at 10.30am.

The Château d'Étxauz

☎ 05 59 37 48 58 or ☎ 05 59 22 55 20
Open daily except Mon., 10am–noon and 2–5.30pm. Closed Jan.–Feb. Guided tour. *Admission charge.*
The château of the viscounts of Baïgorry was burned down during the Wars of Religion but was restored in the 16th C. One of its owners, Bishop Bertrand d'Etxauz, became famous at the time of the witchcraft trials (1609). He saved four members of the Basque clergy who had been sentenced to be burned at the stake, by taking over the ecclesiastical court hearings himself.

THE QUINT DISTRICT

Deep in the Baïgorry Valley, eight French families live on 6,177 acres (2,500 ha) of land rented from Spain by France and known as the Pays Quint. The rent is 400,000 F a year. This political and legal anomaly is a legacy from the 16th C., when the division of Navarre divided a pasture which shared both sides of the mountain. In 1856, a treaty permitted this piece of Spanish territory to be used by France. However, the tenants were so neglected that the telephone and electricity were only installed in 1979 and 1983 respectively! You can visit the *kintoars* by taking the road through Urepel.

Basque games

Tourist Office
☎ 05 59 37 47 28
July–Aug.
Saint-Étienne-de-Baïgorry regularly hosts local championships in the ancient games of *Force Basque*. Twelve competitors from each village vie with each other in amazing feats of strength such as lifting logs, sacks of wheat, boulders, anvils and even a cart! Don't miss these Basque games, which are not just a show for tourists (p. 75).

A 1900 Basque wedding

Even-numbered years only, on 14 July and 15 August
Every other year, Saint-Étienne-de-Baïgorry plunges itself into wedding fever by re-enacting a typical Basque marriage of 1900. At 4pm, the villagers don native costume and travel back in time. Even years only, at the end of July, there's another collective celebration, **Life in 1900**. 150 costumed players demonstrate wheat threshing with a steam engine, old-fashioned crafts and, of course, a magnificent country feast.

Irouléguy wine

Cave d'Irouléguy
☎ 05 59 37 41 33
Open daily, 9am–noon and 2–6.30pm. Closed on Sun. Oct.–March. Guided tours (vineyard and wine and spirit store (*chai*) at 10am and 4.30pm daily (except Sun.), 15 June–15 Sept.; out of season, by appointment for groups.
Admission charge.
The little vineyard of Irouléguy clings to the steep mountainside between Saint-Jean-Pied-de-Port and Saint-Étienne-de-Baïgorry. The wine has had an Appellation d'Origine Contrôlée (AOC) since 1954. Its 494 acres (200 ha) produce 107,800 gallons (4,900 hl) of wine (red, rosé or white) which benefit from the local microclimate of very mild autumns and a southern prevailing wind. The wine costs between 26 and 45 F a bottle.

Les Aldudes

Basque pork

9½ miles (15 km) S of Saint-Étienne-de-Baïgorry
Pierre Oteiza, Urepel Rd
☎ 05 59 37 56 11
Shop open daily, 8am–7pm.

Spotcheck
B6-B7

Pyrenees-Atlantiques

Things to do
Basque games
'Life in 1900'
Irouléguy wine

Tourist Office
Saint-Étienne-de-Baïgorry:
☎ 05 59 37 47 28

Pierre Oteiza has reintroduced the rustic *pie-noir*, the Basque country pig. These free-range pigs feed exclusively on corn and chestnuts. Their meat is of exceptional quality and is sold by Fauchon in Paris. They yield a variety of products, including ham on the bone (130 F for 2 lb 4 oz: 1 kg) and sausages (42 F for 9 oz; 250 g). The factory can be visited at weekends by request.

The Cize district
the heart of the Basque mountains

Around Saint-Jean-Pied-de-Port, the hills of Lower Navarre are occupied by flocks of sheep (and, allegedly, the ghosts of the pilgrims on their way to the shrine of St James at Santiago de Compostela). This pastoral district cherishes the traces of its ancient history, but in modern times it's famous for the delicious ewe's milk cheese which shepherds still make in their huts.

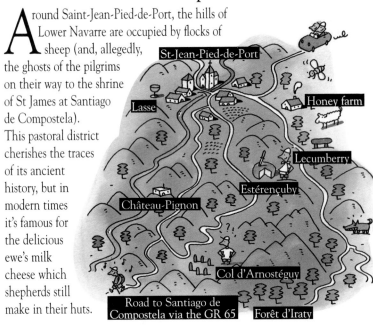

St-Jean-Pied-de-Port

Lasse

Honey farm

Lecumberry

Estérençuby

Château-Pignon

Col d'Arnostéguy

Road to Santiago de Compostela via the GR 65

Forêt d'Iraty

Fôret d'Iraty
Iraty
12½ miles (20 km) SE of Saint-Jean-le-Vieux by the D 18
Departure from the Chalet de Cize, by the lake. For a guide, contact the ONF, Henri Laquet-Fiau
☎ **05 59 37 02 39**
Charge payable for tour.

Take a short journey through the heart of the Basque mountains on this wonderful excursion. The guide stops many times on the 1½ mile (2.6 km), walk to talk about the fauna, flora, and prehistoric monuments in this lovely beech wood. The ideal period for this walk is from May to the end of October. In winter, hikes in snowshoes are organised.

La Miellerie
Xumilenia, Ahaxe
☎ **05 59 37 19 79**
Open daily, July.–Aug., 10am–7pm; out of season, it's best to telephone ahead, daily exc. Mon. and Wed.

The local bees just follow the Laurhibar valley to the trees of the Iraty forest in order to produce their range of deliciously-flavoured honeys. Learn all about them at this exhibition, which explains in detail how the worker bees gather the nectar to make the honey, before tasting a few of them! Chestnut honey costs 26 F a 1 lb 2 oz (500 g) pot, mountain heather honey 35 F .

THE HISTORIC ROAD TO SANTIAGO DE COMPOSTELA

If you want to follow in the footsteps of the medieval pilgrims, take the GR 65. At the southern exit from Saint-Jean-Pied-de-Port, on the D 428, drive to the ruins of the Château-Pignon. Then 1½ miles (2½ km) further on the GR turns off the main road to the right. This historic path runs over the peaks and leads to Spain via the Bentarte Pass. It even crosses the battlefield of Roncevaux (August 778), where Roland fought the Basques, and the views are magnificent.

Urkulu

Le Tropée

12½ miles (20 km) S of Saint-Jean-Pied-de-Port, by the D 301 and the D 428

Col d'Arnostéguy. Leave your car at the pass beside frontier post no. 205 and continue on foot towards the Urkulu. This strange monument was erected 2,000 years ago at an altitude of 4,730 ft (1,419 m). It's a perfect circle of megaliths 10 ft (3 m) high, right by the Spanish frontier. On your way down stop at the post-medieval village of Estérençuby, where the Nive rises.

Estérençuby

Ossau-Iraty cheese

Ferme Xaltoinia
☎ 05 59 37 02 87

Sales all year round. By appointment Jan.–May. Jean-Michel Maïtia is an expert at making this cheese, which is symbolic of the Pyrenees. You'll probably find him hard at work on his farm. If not, he'll explain the cheese-making process; how milk is curdled, and how the curd is cut, stirred, moulded and aged for at least three months. This all results in a cheese with

a unique character (85 to 90 F for 2 lb 4 oz/1 kg), which the shepherds eat as a snack with wine from neighbouring Irou.légy. The cheese is made between January and May.

Lecumberry

The dolmen tour

6½ miles (11 km) SE of Saint-Jean-Pied-de-Port

These dolmens are 6,000 years old. The best are found near Lecumberry (D 18). 1¼ miles (1.8 km) in the direction of Saint-Sauveur, take the little road to the right (marked with an iron cross) which leads to the Maison Gaxteenia,

Spotcheck
B7

Pyrenees-Atlantiques

Things to do

Hiking excursions
The dolmen tour
The road to Santiago de Compostela

Tourist Office

Saint-Jean-Pied-de-Port:
☎ 05 59 37 03 57

and ask permission to see the dolmen. At the Bilgossa pass on the road that leads off to the right (after the Lecumberry fronton), walk eastwards over the peaks. One mile (1½ km) on, after a little pass, you'll see the Buluntza dolmen in a field.

Lasse

Basque cider

1½ miles (2 km) SW of Saint-Jean-Pied-de-Port, by the D 403

Auberge l'Aldakurria, near Ithurraldéa
☎ 05 59 37 04 94

Pierre and Ginette Iribarne have revived the Basque cider-making tradition which disappeared in the 19th C. Made from the fruit of 1,700 apple trees in their orchards, 4,850 gallons (22,000 l) of cider are sold at their inn. Try the dry or sweet cider (15 F a 1¼ pint (75 cl) bottle), just like the pilgrims bound for Compostela. In this restaurant, you can help yourself to as much cider as you want, directly from the cask (included in the price of your meal).

Saint-Jean-Pied-de-Port
at the foot of Roncevaux

How could one not succumb to the charm of Saint-Jean-Pied-de-Port? The former capital of Lower Navarre, situated beside the Nive with its characteristic red sandstone houses, has guarded the foot of the Roncevaux Pass since the 12th C. Ancient ramparts and a citadel built by Vauban protect this pretty little town, unspoilt by tourism. It's a good place to go for a walk and the local market on a Monday morning is definitely worth a visit.

The old town

After the Notre-Dame gate, the Notre-Dame-du-Bout-du-Pont church and the bridge over the Nive, visit the Rue d'Espagne with its row of medieval houses of pink or grey sandstone which bear the signs of old crafts. There's even a bakery with the price of wheat – in 1789 – written over the door! The Porte d'Espagne, at the end of the street, is the best preserved part of the city walls.

The Monday market

From the Place de Gaulle to the Place du Trinquet

From dawn, cattle and sheep invade the main street and

remain until it's time for the collective pelota game, an old tradition, played in the bare-handed manner. At 5pm, the inhabitants meet at the fronton in the Place du Trinquet, where the betting is fast and furious.

A load of hot air

☎ 05 59 37 24 18
All year round

This is just the place to take a hot air balloon trip, floating over the hills and the farms. Take off from near Saint-Jean-Pied-de-Port with Jean-Pierre Jacques, an expert balloonist. On landing, crack open a bottle of champagne to celebrate this exhilarating flight. (Min. 2 passengers, adults 1150 F, accompanied children under 10 free.)

THE CHEESE OF OSSAU-IRATY

Uhaldia, Arnéguy,
5 miles (8 km) S of Saint-Jean-Pied-de-Port, D 933
☎ **05 59 37 06 98**
Open daily, best to phone before visiting. Another delicacy from this region. Not far from the Spanish border, Martin Harriet makes cheese from his manech ewes which have red and black heads. If you meet him, he'll explain how he works to obtain the 'refined hardness' by aging the cheese for three months, and why the Basques eat it as a dessert with cherry jam. Between May and October, he's alone with his flock high in the mountains and his wife is left in charge. If you want to buy some cheese, expect to pay about 80 F for 2 lb 4 oz (1 kg).

Basque linen

Maison Cherbacho Inchauspé,
16, Rue d'Espagne
☎ **05 59 37 18 84**
This shop has old-fashioned wooden shelving and counters. The Inchauspé family have been supplying the region with Basque linen (p. 68) and other fabrics since 1848 (95 F to 149 F for 39 inches; 1 m), including table linen and teatowels. You can also have a tablecloth made to order (6 ft/1.80 m wide) or order a dressing gown in Pyrenean wool (around 1,000 F).

The pilgrims' way

Walk in the footsteps of the pilgrims bound for Compostela. Many of them stopped at Saint-Jean-Pied-de-Port, and could be identified by the scallop-shell attached to their bags or hat. This symbol also decorated the places that welcomed them. Take the cobbled path to the citadel and admire the view over the whole of the Cize district from the top. Then, if you have the stamina, carry on walking towards the Spanish border, taking the road from Arnéguy which will bring you to site of the battle of Roncevaux (778), where the Basques defeated the Frankish army led by the heroic Roland.

Ispoure
The liqueurs of Saint-Jean

Domaine Brana,
3 bis, Av. du Jaï-Alaï
☎ **05 59 37 00 44**
Open daily July-Aug., 10am–noon and 2.30–6.30pm; the rest of the year, by appointment for groups.
Since 1897, the Brana distillery has specialised in making liqueurs. The favourite is made from the Williams pear that is grown here. This delicious pear brandy goes well with the typical wine of the region, the Irouléguy appellation, aged in a *chai* built in typical Navarre style – an old tower at the foot of the steep terraces. A visit to the *chai* includes a slide-show and tastings. Sales on the spot.

Pyrenees-Atlantiques

Things to do

Playing pelota in the market
Taking a ride in a hot-air balloon

Tourist Office

Saint-Jean-Pied-de-Port:
☎ **05 59 37 03 57**

The Mixe district
crossroad of the pilgrims

Bidouze in northern Lower Navarre, links the plain of the *gaves* (streams) with the first of the Basque foothills. The Gascon influence disappears, giving way to the Basque identity which is felt strongly at Saint-Palais, once capital of Navarre. This is the Mixe district which was once was the main resting-stop for pilgrims on their way to Santiago de Compostela. Ostabat remains the point at which the three main pilgrim routes converge.

Bidache
City of eagles
12¹/₂ miles (20 km)
N of Saint-Palais
Château of the Dukes of Gramont
☎ 05 59 56 08 79
Open daily 15 Apr.–30 Sept., 2.30–6.30pm (show at 3.30pm). 2nd show at 5pm at w/ends and public holidays, as well as 15 June–15 Sept. *Admission charge.*
Although the château was burned down during the Revolution in 1796, this residence of the Dukes of Gramont retains much of its former pride. Its ruins deserve to be seen. Inside,

the building is used for breeding 70 birds of prey of 25 different species, from the South American condor to the Egyptian vulture. Every day they perform an impressive aerial ballet,

just as in the Middle Ages when falconry was a regular practise.

The chair-makers' village
2¹/₂ miles (4 km)
SE of Bidache
Came
☎ 05 59 56 02 72
Workshop open daily (Sat.–Sun. only in the afternoon), 8am–noon and 2–7pm. *Free admission.*
In this village, all the craftsmen make chairs. In his workshop-museum, Pierre Lataillade will tell you the history of this local craft, and show you the complete range

of chairs in all their styles (regional, Louis-XVI, Directoire, etc.) which he and his seven fellow chair-makers produce. The chairs are made of cherrywood, walnut or oak (from 1,100 to 4,500 F).

Saint-Palais

✿ Musée de Basse-Navarre
☎ 05 59 65 71 78 (Tourist Office)
Open daily except Sun.; in season, 9.30am–12.30pm and 2–7pm; out of season, 9.30am–12.30pm and 2.30–6.30pm.
Admission charge.

THE *FORCE BASQUE* FESTIVAL
Saint-Palais Tourist Office
☎ 05 59 65 71 78
The Sunday after 15 Aug. in the afternoon. **Twenty strapping men fighting over a rope. This is the *soka tira*, Basque tug-of-war, the highlight of the *Force Basque* games held every year at the Saint-Palais fronton (p. 75). No-one misses these ritual games which were inspired by work on the land – lifting boulders is like removing stones from fields, lifting the cart, like dragging a wagon that had become stuck in mud.**

In this museum, Saint-Palais retains the remnants of its past as the administrative capital of French Navarre in the 16th C. Furniture, sculpture and Navarre coinage (minted in the city), are displayed alongside exhibits relating to the three pilgrim routes to Compostela which join up 6¼ miles (10 km) from here, at Ostabat. Nearby, opposite the church of Saint-Paul, there's a house decorated with carved heads of the last kings of Navarre. Saint-Palais comes alive every Friday morning for a **market**, and in summer a big game of pelota is held on Wednesdays at around 4pm at the fronton.

Linen weaving
Ona Tiss, 23, Rue de la Bidouze
☎ 05 59 65 71 84

Open Mon.–Thurs., 9am–noon and 2–6pm; July and Aug., open Mon.–Sat. *Free admission.*
Michel Hourcade follows the age-old rules of Basque weaving (p. 68). He operates two old wooden looms and the thread is twisted to make it stronger. He employs traditional patterns on his fabrics as well as colours that are fast at 194F (90°C). The strict attention to tradition is impressive. In the shop, you can buy

Spotcheck
B6

Pyrenees-Atlantiques

Things to do
City of eagles
Force Basque festival
Musée de la Basse-Navarre

Within easy reach
Salies-de-Béarn, p. 276, Gave d'Oloron, p. 280.

Tourist Office
Saint-Palais:
☎ 05 59 65 71 78

cotton fabric (116 F for 39 in/1 m, 6 ft/1.7 m wide, with the traditional seven bands of colour) or a tablecloth and set of six napkins (400 F).

The pilgrims' meeting place
2 miles (3 km) S of Saint-Palais, by the D 302, take the road on the left.
The Gibraltar plaque on Mont Saint-Sauveur, marks the exact spot at which the three pilgrimage routes to the tomb of St James at Santiago de Compostela converge. From here, walk along the GR 65, until you reach the chapel at Harambels, then continue to Ostabat, which had more than 14 hostels in the 14th C. You'll be travelling the sacred path (6½ miles (10 km) round trip), trodden by thousands of pilgrims for centuries.

Mauléon-Licharre

capital of the espadrille

Mauléon is not only the capital of the Soule district, but also the capital of the espadrille, as nearly 70% of French espadrilles are made here. The 3,800 inhabitants enjoy an exceptional medieval heritage and are Basque through and through. Here, as elsewhere in this Basque province, the *pastorales* are performed, a form of popular theatre in which everyone in the village takes part (even the youngest.)

A medieval fortress

Tourist Office
☎ **05 59 28 02 37**
Open daily 15 June–
15 Sept., 11am–1.30pm
and 3–7.30pm; from
Easter to 15 June and
15–30 Sept., w/ends only.
Admission charge.
This medieval château
(12th C.) is a real fortress.
Its massive structure and
thick walls resisted many
assaults during the battles
between the kings of Navarre
and of England. It has a
lovely view of the town and
the whole valley beyond.
The ancient castle is also
noted for the depth of its
wells and vaulted cellars.

The Château d'Andurain

**Hôtel de Maytie,
Place du Fronton**
☎**05 59 28 00 18**
Open daily except Thurs.
and Sun. morning, July–
20 Sept., 11am–noon
and 3–6pm; out of
season, groups by
appointment.
Admission charge.
This splendid 16th-C.
residence was home to the
Bishop of Oloron, Arnaud de
Maytie, a local champion in
the fight against the Protestants. It has handsome carved
fireplaces, a Renaissance staircase and a roof structure like
an upturned triple keel, as
well as a library of very old,

rare books. The nearby Hôtel
de Montréal (17th C.), is now
the Town Hall.

The espadrille factory

**Prodiso,
Zone Artisanale**
☎ **05 59 28 28 48**

Château d'Andurain

THE SOULETINE PASTORALE

Performed annually in the village of Soule, July–Aug.

This is an ancient and popular tradition which brings the inhabitants of the village together around a story taken from local life. It's rehearsed for several months then performed in costume, always featuring the same characters. There are the goodies (the Christians), the baddies (the Turks) and the supernatural world (the angels). For three hours, battle scenes, choirs and musical interludes are performed in the Souletine language, a variation of Basque.

Guided tours Mon.–Fri., 8am–noon and 2–6pm. Feb.–Sept. by appointment. *Admission charge.*

Mauléon has been making espadrilles for 150 years. At Prodiso, several hundred are made every day, with genuine rope soles covered with rubber. The tour explains the origin of the shoe, once the sandal of poor people. Manufacture is now semi-automatic.

A river runs through it

2½ miles (4 km) E of Tardets
**Fly-fishing courses
Jean-Pierre Ruata,
Montory
☎ 05 59 28 59 69**

If you saw the film starring Robert Redford, you'll remember the beauty of casting with a fly-fishing rod. You can learn how to do it in the *gaves* (mountain streams) of the Soule, which are just as lovely as the torrents of Montana. So hire the tackle (waders not included), take a quick lesson and soon you'll be catching your very first

trout (300 F for half a day, 500 F for a day).

The local markets

Every Tuesday morning in the upper town from 8am to noon

and Saturday mornings in the lower town from 6 to 11am, local producers and craftsmen display their

Spotcheck
B6

Pyrenees-Atlantiques

Things to do
Visit to an espadrille factory
Fly-fishing courses
Local markets
A Souletine Pastorale

Within easy reach
*Gave d'Oloron, p. 280,
Oloron-Sainte-Marie,
p. 282,
Valley of the Barétous,
p. 284.*

Tourist Office
Mauléon:
☎ 05 59 28 02 37

best wares. Don't miss the famous ewe's milk cheese (*ardigasna*), made by the shepherds in their *cayolars* (mountain huts). It takes six months to age and in the great Basque tradition it's eaten with redcurrant or quince jelly.

The Osquich pass

9½ miles (15 km) W of Mauléon, by the D 918.
This strategic site is on the look out every autumn when the wood pigeons migrate. The pass, north of the forest of Arbailles, has an excellent view of the birds. You can watch the nets collapse as the wood pigeons pass through. Netting is a traditional form of catching the birds (p. 86). While here, visit the 14th-C. chapel of Saint-Antoine 1,000 ft (300 m) up (the road branches off towards Mauléon after 550 yds; 500 m).

Haute Soule
canyon country

This is the most secret and unspoilt part of the region, the heart of the Basque country. Here, nature is king. The peaks rise as high as 6,670 ft (2,000 m), and the valleys of the Gave de Larrau and the Gave de l'Uhaïtxa lead to the huge forest of Iraty and deep canyons cut into the

limestone. The slate-roofed houses and flocks of sheep tended by shepherds are typical of the Basque mountain country.

Sainte-Engrâce

Deep in the valley
D 113 S of Tardets
This typical village lies at an altitude of 2,100 ft (630 m), at the edge of a rock formation known as a *cirque*. The 12th-C. church clings to the slope. It has lovely colourful capitals and an asymmetrical roof. Outside, the cemetery has some interesting round Basque headstones, and the surrounding area is perfect for exploring on foot.

The gorges of Kakouetta
☎ 05 59 28 73 44
Open daily, 8am–8pm,
15 March–15 Nov.
Admission charge.
This is certainly a memorable trip, right in the heart of the Basque mountains. The walk takes one or two hours, along specially-made paths and over little footbridges through a natural canyon, with water trickling or rushing down the sides. In some places the sides of the gorge

are only a few yards apart and you'll come across a waterfall and a cave containing giant stalactites.

The Souletine springs
Around Tardets, W of the D 918 and of the D 26.
Bring jerrycans and water-bottles with you. The springs of the Haute Soule produce pure, sparkling water, which is not only refreshing, but also good for your health! Sample the waters of Licq-Athérey (4$\frac{1}{4}$ miles (7 km) S of Tardets), a crystal-clear stream in the hamlet of Teintuaborde. For a last glass, the cave of Camou has twin springs, one hot (100°F/38°C) and salty, the other icy cold. Take your pick or choose them both! They are said to do wonders for rheumatism. To find out how to get to these springs, ask the way at the nearby inn, l'Auberge d'Aguer.

The crevasses of Holzarté

Access via the D 26, from Larrau. In the locality of Logibar, take the GR 10.
Tourist Office of Tardets
☎ 05 59 28 51 28
Free admission.

You cross this extraordinary crevasse by means of a footbridge suspended 500 ft (150 m) above the void. Right down at the bottom of the ravine is the torrent which has cut

through the limestone over time as if were a piece of cheese. Visiting this amazing natural phenomenon is an unforgettable experience. However, you should allow for a two hour walk there and back, so wear appropriate footwear.

Spotcheck

B7

Pyrenees-Atlantiques

Things to do

The gorges of Kakouetta
The crevasses of Holzarté
Kayaking and canoeing

Within easy reach

Valley of the Barétous, p. 284.

Tourist Office

Tardets: ☎ 05 59 28 51 28

buzzards, eagles and harriers), wood pigeons in October and grey cranes in November. Around the 20 October, 100,000 wood pigeons fly through the pass in less than two days!

SHEPHERD'S DAY

Cheeses at the market in Tardets
On Monday morning (Place Centrale), from 1 July to 31 August. Every other Monday out of season.
The shepherds begin their day at dawn, milking the ewes who have been kept overnight in a *koralian*, a stone sheepfold. They are milked again in the evening. The milk is filtered for cheese-making. In mid-July, the sheep cease to give milk. In November, the shepherd brings them back to the valley, only to return to the pastures again next May (p. 84).

The Orgambidexka pass

8¹/₂ miles (13 km) W of Larrau, by the D 19
☎ 05 59 25 62 03
Bird-watching
daily 15 July–15 Nov.
Binoculars are for hire.
Free admission.

At an altitude of 4,280 ft (1,284 m), this is one of the most important places for migrating birds in Europe. There's a constant procession: swifts in July, birds of prey in August and September (kites, honey-

Gave le Saison

Tourist Office
☎ 05 59 28 51 28
Kayaking down the Gave le Saison is a popular summer pastime. If you've never paddled a kayak, you'll get two hours' training to bring you up to speed. (You leave from Tardets either alone or in a group of 10 maximum.) Other more turbulent local rivers are accessible if you like excitement. Individual lessons are 50 F for two hours, 70 F to kayak down the river.

Salies-de-Béarn
deposits of white gold

This city is rich in deposits of 'white gold': salt. Its waters are seven times saltier than the Atlantic Ocean. Salt is honoured every year on the third weekend of September. Salies salt is used as a seasoning and is also said to be good for rheumatism. The old town has many picturesque houses and also hides a gastronomic rarity, in the form of *mêture*, a cornbread traditional to Béarn which is now made only by one bakery (Place d'Albret, Thursday in winter).

Place du Bayaà
Musée des Arts et Traditions Béarnais
Open Tues.–Sat.,
15 May–15 Oct., 3–6pm.
☎ 05 59 38 00 33
Admission charge.
The salty spring emerges from here in a basement. It was once open to the skies but was covered over for protection. Salt water also springs from the Fontaine du Sanglier, in a corner of the main square. The Renaissance house next door houses a museum of Béarnaise traditions, including many artefacts once used for producing salt.

Musée du Sel
Rue des Puits-Salants
Information at the Tourist Office.
Open Tues.–Sat.,
15 May–15 Oct., 3–6pm.
Admission charge.
This museum details the complete history of salt extraction, from the Bronze Age to the present day. Since 1992, the museum has been housed in the 17th-C. Maison Darrémoudine. There's a salt-maker's workshop and an explanation of the privileges (which still exist) of the *part-prenants*, who have had the hereditary right since 1587 to draw salt water from the spring.

The wines of Salies
Domaine Lapeyre-Guilhemas,
52, Av. des Pyrénées
☎ 05 59 38 10 02
Open daily except Sun. and public hols, 8.30am–12.30pm and 2–7.30pm; in summer, Sun. morning. The Lapeyre family has been making wine since 1900. The rosé, a dry fruity wine grown on the slopes of the salt city, is drunk in summer with Béarnaise charcuterie. The red and the dry white wines are also considered high quality. Judge for yourself after a visit to the *chai*. Prices per bottle are 28 F (Guilhemas white), 39 F (Lapeyre white), 28 to 32 F (rosé), 35 to 45 F (red).

Spotcheck

B6

Pyrenees-Atlantiques

Things to do

The salt museum
The wines of Salies
The antique fair
The salt festival

Within easy reach

Orthe District, 12½ miles
(20 km) NW, p. 238,
Mixe District approx. 15½
miles (25 km) S, p. 270.

Tourist Office

Salies-de-Béarn:
☎ 05 59 38 00 33

A town of fêtes and fairs

Each year, around 14 July, artists and sculptors flock to Salies to compete for the coveted prize awarded for the best picture of the town. **Salies à Peindre** lasts for three days, during which the streets are dotted with easels. Easter and early August are reserved for the antiques fair and on the second weekend in September, the Heste de la Saü, the salt festival, is celebrated.

Bellocq
Rosé of Béarn

4½ miles (7 km)
N of Salies
Les Vignerons de Bellocq
☎ 05 59 65 10 71
Open Mon.–Sat., 9am–noon and 2–6.30pm, in summer.
Free admission.
Béarn-Bellocq has been an Appellation d'Origine Contrôlée (AOC) since 1975, and is the result of collective activity by 15 enthusiastic wine-makers since 1944. The wine is the colour of rosewood and has a fragrance of berries.

The pilgrim's staff

**Espace Athanor,
Chemin du Marais**
☎ **05 59 37 92 41**
No pilgrim would ever have thought of leaving for Compostela without his staff. He needed it to defend him-

WHITE GOLD

Thermes, Pl. du Jardin-Public
☎ **05 59 38 10 11**
According to legend, salt was discovered here thanks to a wild boar. A hunter was chasing his prey in the Middle Ages when he discovered the animal had drowned in a salty spring. Today, the salt of Salies-de-Béarn is used to season food and to treat lumbago, rheumatism and muscular spasms. Patients are plunged into the water but are so buoyant they have to be strapped down! You can buy bath salts or kitchen salt, a five-bath pack or 2 lb 4 oz (1 kg) of kitchen salt costs 65 F.

self, and used it to hang a gourd on. This staff (*bourdon*) is now manufactured in Bellocq, on the road to Santiago de Compostela. You can choose boxwood, olive wood or oak, unless you prefer ash, from which lances for tourneys were made. The staff is made to suit the height of the owner; it should reach the chin (from 650 F).

Orthez

Orthez, capital of the Béarn region in the 13th C., was a Protestant stronghold in the 16th C. On the pilgrim route to the tomb of St James at Santiago de Compostela, its historic past is still alive in the medieval old town. As an intellectual centre of Protestantism, it was responsible for its own massacre in 1569, when Catholics were thrown off the old bridge. Today, Orthez has abandoned religious wars in favour of basketball –the town's proud motto being 'touches-y si tu l'oses!' (touch me if you dare!).

Le Pont-Vieux

This old bridge is topped with a gateway-cum-castle-keep. It was the work of Gaston Fébus, Prince of Béarn in the 14th C. The bridge withstood the Wars of Religion and the battles against the Duke of Wellington in 1814. There's a mystery attached to it, as no one knows which window was the Capérans window, through which the Protestant soldiers threw the Catholic priests into the river during the massacre of 1569.

Jeanne d'Albret's house

Rue du Bourg-Vieux
☎ 05 59 69 14 03
Open Mon.–Sat.,
10am–noon and 2–6pm
Admission charge.

It's not absolutely certain that Jeanne d'Albret, mother of Henri IV of Navarre, lived in this 15th-C. house, but she would have found it to her liking, with its half-timbering and pretty garden. It now houses the Tourist Office and a little museum of Protestantism, which ably reconstructs the past of Orthez, a stronghold of Calvinism.

Fêtes d'Orthez

Béarn is an area that likes to celebrate, and the Orthez festivals are among the liveliest. There are *bandas*, bull-fights, *Courses Landaises* and much rejoicing in the streets. The biggest celebration is at the end of July, but the dates vary (Tourist Office
☎ 05 59 69 02 75).

Lac d'Orthez

Open-air leisure centre, Route de Biron
☎ 05 59 67 08 31
Open daily, all year round.
Admission charge from Easter to Sept..
Here walkers, anglers and

BIRD SANCTUARY
Biron
2 miles (3 km) SE of Orthez
☎ 05 59 67 14 22
Open daily in summer, 10am–7pm; Wed.–Sun. in winter, 10am–6pm. Guided or free tour (1½ hours).
Admission charge.

This 32 acre (13 ha) area of swamp and lagoons beside the Gave de Pau is home to 50 different species of birds. Walk in this natural setting dotted with hides, and you won't miss a thing because the park even has its own

video-cameras which capture anything you miss, and show it to you on the big screen in the museum. In addition to birds, there are Camargue horses.

bathers can enjoy relaxing on, in and around the lake. On the main beach, in July and August, there's a lifeguard.

Water-skiing on the lake
☎ 05 59 69 17 28
Open daily, Apr.–Oct., 9am–noon and 2–6pm
If you prefer action to lying all day on the beach, try the new sensations that Lake Orthez has to offer. The spot is well-known to afficionados of water-skiing. If you're not afraid to get your feet wet, just jump right in! Regardless of age or ability, there's a course for everyone and you can feel perfectly safe as all courses are supervised by state-approved instructors.

Weaving Basque linen
Établissements Moutet, Route de Biron
☎ 05 59 69 14 33
Open all year round, Mon.–Fri., 9am–6pm.
In this little family workshop, which was converted into a factory in the early 20th C., blankets for oxen were still being woven by hand until recently. Today, every type of Basque linen is made here (p. 68), in front of your eyes, on very efficient machines which produce an amazing range of products. All items are available for purchase in the shop. Table linen (tablecloth, 64 in (160 cm) square: 190 to 300 F), or kitchen cloths (an

Spotcheck
C6

Pyrenees-Atlantiques

Things to do
The Fêtes d'Orthez
Leisure centre at the lake
Bird sanctuary

Within easy reach
Pays d'Orthe approx. 19 miles (30 km) NW, p. 238.

Tourist Office
Orthez: ☎ 05 59 69 02 75

embroidered tea-towel from 45 to 60 F), damask, embroidery and gifts.

The poet's house
7, Avenue Francis-Jammes
☎ 05 59 69 11 24
Open Mon.–Fri., 8.45am–12.45pm; in season, 10am–noon and 8–6pm.
Free admission.
Francis Jammes (1868–1938), a famous Basque poet and novelist, lived in Orthez for 33 years (1897–1907) during which time he published a dozen books, including *Clara d'Ellébeuse*, *Le Roman du Lièvre* and *Pomme d'Anis*. His 18th-C. house, called Chrestia, typical of the local style, is open to the public.

Gave d'Oloron

N avarrenx and Sauveterre-de-Béarn both span the Gave d'Oloron just before it flows into the Gave de Pau. These are ancient stop-overs on the road to Compostela, and were involved in the 16th-C. Wars of Religion. Navarrenx was more heavily fortified and eclipsed Sauveterre. Nowadays, they have a shared history and their medieval streets are a delight. The *gaves* district all around them is the heart of lower Béarn.

Sauveterre-de-Béarn

The bastion of the Gave

Five round trips around the town; one cultural walk signposted in the medieval city.

Above the Gave d'Oloron, the town perches on a limestone cliff. Facing it, there's a fortified bridge which features in the legend of the 'judgement of God'. This is a terrible family story of a countess who was suspected of infanticide, and was thrown into the water, from which she was miraculously saved. Take in the view over the medieval town and the 13th-C. Tour Montréal.

The *palas* maker

Jean Araspin,
Rue du Temple
☎ 05 59 38 55 05
This little wooden bat, or racquet, used to play the local game of pelota, is slightly bigger than a table-tennis or Jokari bat (p. 74). You can watch as Jean Araspin makes them in his workshop, a few miles from the Basque frontier (35 to 68 F).

Laàs

Maize Museum of Domaine de Laàs

6¼ miles (10 km) E of Sauveterre-de-Béarn, by D 27
☎ 05 59 38 91 53
Open daily Easter to All Saints Day, 10am–7pm.
Admission charge.
This late-18th-C. nobleman's residence contains some important collections including relics of Napoleon. In the stables there's a fascinating maize museum which tells, in a very scientific manner, the eventful history of this plant, which is the symbol of Béarn. You can take a walk in the beautiful grounds among ancient trees which run down to the banks of the Gave de Pau and lunch in the picnic area.

RAFTING ON THE GAVE

Information: Centre
Nautique (Soeix)
☎ 05 59 39 61 00
Eaux Vives (Navarrenx)
☎ 05 59 66 04 05
Open May–Sept.
This is a paradise for
lovers of whitewater
sports. Descend the
rapids of the *gave* in a
huge boat holding 20
people: terrific fun!
Cover the 15¹⁄₂ miles
(25 km) from Navarrenx
to Sauveterre with a
pilot, it's quite safe for
a family outing (costing
from 140 to 200 F a
day). A coach brings you
back from Sauveterre.

Spotcheck

C6

Pyrenees-Atlantiques

Things to do

Rafting on the Gave

Within easy reach

*Mixe district, p. 270,
Mauléon-Licharre,
p. 272.*

Tourist Office

Sauveterre:
☎ 05 59 38 58 65

Charre

Château de Mongaston

*7¹⁄₂ miles (12 km) SE of
Sauveterre-de-Béarn, by
the D 343*
☎ 05 59 38 65 92

Open daily except Tues.,
1 May–31 Oct., 2.30–
6pm; out of season by
appointment.
Admission charge.
This medieval fortress served
as a hostel for pilgrims on
their way to the tomb of
St James at Compostela
in the 16th C. The hilltop
château houses a museum of
lifesize historic figures which
tell the story of Béarn.

Navarrenx

The salmon kingdom

*12 miles (19 km)
SE of Sauveterre*
Because the grandfather of
Henri IV considered himself
to be 'stuck here like a louse',
Navarrenx became an important fortified city. You can
discover some of the remains
on foot, from the great gateway of Saint-Antoine to the
16th-C. church of Saint-
Germain, not forgetting the
arsenal and the town hall
square. The Gothic **ramparts**
and the houses along the walk
date from the same period
and are worth a visit.

Salmon fishing

Town Hall
☎ 05 59 66 14 93
From March to July, you
can watch the skills of the
salmon fishermen. Down-
stream of the weir with its
remarkable 'salmon ladder',
anglers compete in the
world championship every
year. The holder of the
record for the largest salmon
(43 lb; 19¹⁄₂ kg) caught it on
a line in 1948. The Gave
d'Oloron at Navarrenx is
easy for the fish to navigate,
thanks to the short distance
between the ocean and the
snow-capped peaks of the
Pyrenees.

Aren

Château d'Aren

*7¹⁄₂ miles (12 km)
SE of Navarrenx,
by the D 936*
☎ 05 59 88 01 91
Open daily 1 July–
30 Sept., 3–7pm.
Private property.
Admission charge.
This château contains a
wonderful wall painting
(1450) representing a scene
of courtly love, and the lady
and her knight are in court
dress. The château has
recently been restored.

Salmon-ladder at Navarrenx

Oloron-Sainte-Marie
capital of the beret

Two famous mountain streams meet at Oloron, the Gave d'Aspe and the Gave d'Ossau. Oloron is the capital of Upper Béarn and has some historic sites. The beret and weaving industries remain prosperous, and

M. Lindt's chocolate is carted away by the truck-load! A recent artistic initiative based on the pilgrimage to the tomb of St James at Santiago de Compostela is worth following.

The 12th-C. Romanesque church of Sainte-Croix

The cathedral of Sainte-Marie

Carvings in white Pyrenean marble on the tympanum of this cathedral depict scenes of daily life such as hams being smoked and salmon-fishing.

Inside, on the first column on the left of the entrance, there's an unusual holy water stoup reserved for lepers.

Jazz and *garbure*

These are the two celebrated favourites at Oloron. The Oloron Jazz Festival, which focuses on modern jazz, is held at the end of June to early July (☎ 05 59 39 98 00). Garbure soup is enjoyed, tasted, and overflows all the soup-tureens, on the first Saturday in September, during the Foire du Terroir.

Lindt chocolate factory
Av. de Lattre-de-Tassigny
☎ 05 59 88 88 88
Open daily except Sat.–Sun., 8.30–11.30am and 2.30–5.30pm (Fri. 4.30pm).

Free admission.
Stock up for Easter and Christmas at factory prices. Lindt chocolates are sold at normal prices elsewhere. Don't leave without tasting the famous *Pyrénéens* chocolates, which are eaten iced here.

The 'art road' to Compostela
☎ 05 59 39 79 18
Stages: Parc Pommé, Pl. Saint-Pierre, Promenade Bellevue, Rue Barthou, footbridge over the Gave d'Aspe, Rue des Barats, Rue Labarraque, etc. Since 1990, Oloron has paid homage to the modern pilgrim to Santiago de Compostela with new works of art to celebrate the famous pilgrims' way. In the Parc Pommé, a huge bed

Spotcheck

C6

Pyrenees-Atlantiques

Things to do

Jazz Festival
Foire du terroir
Soeix water sports centre

With children

Faget water sports park

Within easy reach

*Mauléon-Licharre, p. 272,
Vallée du Barétous,
p. 284.*

Tourist Office

Oloron-Sainte-Marie:
☎ 05 59 39 98 00

commemorates their journeys and their nights spent under the stars. In the Place Saint-Pierre, a large rock evokes the spirit of nature and outside the town, Agnos celebrates the *Cantate* by Gérard Koch, a hymn to spirituality. It's planned that one day this extraordinary art tour will extend to the town of Santiago de Compostela itself.

Soeix
Water sports centre

1¹/₂ miles (3 km) S of Oloron
☎ 05 59 39 61 00
Open all year round.
There are great facilities for water sports all along the Gave d'Aspes, a fast-flowing mountain stream. These range from the joys of **family rafting** (200 F per day), to **swimming in whitewater** and **canoeing and kayaking** (110 F for two hours) or hydrospeed. There are classes for beginners and the more advanced.

Faget
Water sports park

4¹/₂ miles (7 km) N of Oloron
Lac du Faget
☎ 05 59 39 20 75
15 June–mid-Sept.
10.30am–9pm
Admission charge.
For those who prefer calmer waters, this aquatic park has flumes, bubble rivers, currents and waterfalls, so there's no danger of being bored! The park is open to anglers all year round, Wednesdays, Saturdays and Sundays, as well as during school and public holidays.

Ogeu-les-Bains
The weavers of Béarn

*7¹/₂ miles (12 km)
SE of Oloron*
Atelier Mayalen
☎ 05 59 34 90 87
Open daily, 2–7pm.
In this pretty village, with its 17th-C. château, Mayalen and Daniel Valotteau welcome you to their cosy workshop. Here they hand-weave plaid shawls, (600 to 1,300 F), cushion covers (150 to 250 F), scarves in alpaca (260 F), wool, mohair or cotton, and make waistcoats, (from 1,000 F). (Sundays, phone first.)

THE BÉATEX BERET FACTORY

**Rue de Rocgrand,
Oloron-Sainte-Marie**
☎ 05 59 39 12 07
Guided tour by arrangement in July. Register at the Tourist Office

☎ 05 59 39 98 00.
Free admission.
Thirteen operations are involved in making the real Basque beret. The most spectacular is the felting; you'll see 600 berets immersed in a bath of soapy water and clubbed with wooden mallets to make them thicker! (No sales at the factory.)

The Barétous valley
home of the musketeers

The Barétous Valley is at the western end of Béarn; and is as mild in climate as Soule. Although the people in this gentle landscape are renowned for their fiery temperament (two of Alexandre Dumas' three musketeers –Porthos and Aramis – were from here), they also have a more peaceful side to them. Every year the area celebrates an ancestral ritual at the bottom of La Pierre-Saint-Martin: the *Junte de Roncal*.

Arette
Earthquakes
12 miles (19 km) SW of Oloron-Sainte-Marie
On 13 August 1967, an earth-quake which measured 5-6 on the Richter scale almost wiped out the village. The houses have been rebuilt to withstand another earth-quake, the possibility of which cannot be completely ruled out by the experts.

Maison du Barétous
☎ 05 59 88 95 38
Open daily except Sun., July–Aug., 9am–noon and 2–6pm; out of season, 9.30am–noon and 2–5.30pm.
Admission charge.
This museum will enlighten you on the Barétous charac-ter: fiery and secretive, but gentle as a lamb. They are also loyal, as demonstrated by

the undertakings they made in a peace treaty in 1375 with their Spanish neighbours, by which they still abide.

The botanical path
La Pierre-Saint-Martin Tourist Office
☎ 05 59 66 20 09 and
☎ 05 59 88 95 38
July–Aug.
At an altitude of 5,500 ft (1,650 m), in this desert-like landscape, more than 60 varieties of flowers bloom in

summer. You can admire them during a walk on the largest *lapiaz* (limestone pavement dissected by rivulets of water) in Europe. You can make your own way with information and maps from the Tourist Office at La Pierre-Saint-Martin.

The caverns of La Pierre-Saint-Martin
Tourist Office
☎ 05 59 66 20 09
Daily in summer.
Departure from the Sainte-Engrâce church.
Interior temperature: 41 °F (5 °C).
Admission charge.
At the bottom of a vertical shaft, 1,000 ft (300 m) deep, there are 18$^{1}/_{4}$ miles (30 km) of underground caverns linking huge chambers which extend as much as 4,510 ft

POTHOLING
Pyrénées Aventures Nouvelles, Aramits
☎ 05 59 34 10 70
This is a gentle introduction to potholing. You'll learn how to use the ropes, about mouseholes, clefts and laminations. An extraordinary world reveals itself in the light of your lamp. Time is a wonderful sculptor of the depths (adults and children from 8 years old; adult 240 F per day). Great fun unless you prefer something gentler like rock-climbing or paragliding!

LA PIERRE SᵗMARTIN
COL de SOUDET
Alt. 1540 m

(1,375 m) underground! The Salle de la Verna, which is big enough to contain Notre-Dame-de-Paris one and a half times, is particularly impressive. You reach it through a tunnel dug in 1960 to remove river water. You're in total darkness and you have to walk for an hour to get there. Make sure you wear warm clothing.

La Junte de Roncal
Au col de la Pierre-Saint-Martin,
16¹/₂ miles (26 km) S of Arette.
Come and celebrate the eternal peace between the shepherds from France and Spain every 13 July, at 11am.

The tradition dates back to 1375, the year a treaty was signed which ended the bloody battles between the inhabitants on opposite sides of the mountain. The ritual is unchanging. At milestone 262 of the D 132, the French mayors of the valley, in traditional dress, hand over three blond heifers to the Spanish mayors and once again promise 'peace from now on'.

Lanne-en-Barétous
The giant nets
3¹/₂ miles (5 km) NW of Arette, via the D 919
Wood pigeon hunting is at its height in mid-October (p. 86). At the Ayduc hides, giant nets called *pantières* await the 7,000 birds which are caught here each year by beaters rattling their *chatars* (feather-covered objects). To reach the site, turn left at the entrance to the village (coming from Arette), towards the Auberge des Chasseurs, then go the last 1,670 ft (500 m) on foot.

Aramits
The sheepdog village
2¹/₂ miles (4 km) N of Arette, by the D 133
One of the three musketeers in

Spotcheck
C7

Pyrenees-Atlantiques

Things to do
The botanical path
The caverns of
Pierre-Saint-Martin
Introduction to potholing

Within easy reach
*Mauléon-Licharre, p. 272,
Haute Soule, p. 274,
Oloron-Saintes-Marie,
p. 282.*

Tourist Office
Arette:
☎ 05 59 88 95 38

Alexandre Dumas' tale lived here before taking up the sword. Aramis lived in the old lay abbey, whose handsome portico is still visible to the left of the church. Every year on the third weekend of September, there is a shepherds' festival with sheepdog trials. You can watch the skills of shepherd and sheepdog working together.

Gave de Pau

furrow of the Béarn

B efore it reaches Béarn, the Gave de Pau is just a mountain stream. The edges of the river along the route to Bétharram are bordered with an unbroken line of trees. It then runs through Nay, a 14th-C. *bastide*, and Pau before flowing through the elegant vineyards of the Jurançon and eventually reaching Lacq and Orthez. Throughout its journey through Béarn, the stream leaves behind pebbles which are used to pave the village streets.

Lestelle-Bétharram

Musée du Patrimoine

15½ miles (25 km) SE of Pau
☎ 05 59 71 92 30
Open daily in summer, 2–5.30pm; Sat. and Sun. out of season, 2–5pm.
Admission charge.
This 14th-C. *bastide* has an ancient pilgrimage site – the sanctuary of Bétharram (open daily in season, 8am–noon and 2–6.30pm; out of season, 9–11am and 2–5pm, free admission). Visit the chapel, which is full of paintings, and stop at the unusual museum.

The caves of Bétharram

2½ miles (4 km) S of Pau
☎ 05 62 41 80 04
Open daily, 25 March–25 Oct., 8.30am–noon and 1.30–5.30pm; the rest of the year, Mon.–Fri. by appointment.
Admission charge.
Your journey through these magnificent caves is partly by boat, but you reach them by cablecar and leave on a little train! These different modes

of transport will enable you to discover amazing natural phenomena – stone waterfalls, 'chandelier rooms', stalagmites and stalactites. Wear warm clothes.

Asson

❀ The kangaroo park

3½ miles (6 km) from Nay.
☎ 05 59 71 03 34
Daily, from 8am till dusk.
Admission charge.
Most meetings with Australians in this region take place on a rugby pitch. Here, however, there's a population of around 70 kangaroos and wallabies who are quite tame.

You'll also find Patagonian maras, monkeys, antelope, exotic birds, marmosets and lemurs in this little zoo at the foot of the Pyrenees.

Nay

The market and the beret

10½ miles (17 km) SE of Pau
Musée du Béret, Place Saint-Roch
☎ 05 59 61 01 32
Open Apr.–11 Nov. and school holidays, daily exc. Mon., 10am–noon and 2–6pm; the rest of the year, by appointment.
Admission charge.
You'll see berets here everywhere on Tuesday, the day of

MAKER OF SHEEP-BELLS

Établissement Daban, 24, Rue des Pyrénées, Nay
☎ 05 59 61 00 41
Open Tues.–Fri., 8am–noon and 1–6pm; Sat., 8am–noon.
Tours Mon. and Sat. afternoons.
Maurice Daban is a master craftsmen, and his workshop constantly rings to the sound of different shaped and sized sheep bells. The sheep bell indicates the age, size and sex of the animal that wears it. In his workshop you can watch as he transforms sheets of iron, coated with copper and brass, into a melodious instruments. You can choose from 35 F for a 5½ in (14 cm) bell to 1,600 F for the biggest, 15½ in (40cm), perhaps in the company of a local shepherdwho is tuning his ear to this pastoral symphony.

the picturesque **Nay market** (there's also an evening market every Monday in summer). Here the 'Basque' beret is in its rightful place and if you visit the museum you'll learn all about this regional head-gear, which originated in Béarn. The original shape was wider and had a little tail, the *lou cabillou*, hanging from the

centre. When it was hand-knitted it was called *bounet*, and it was worn set at an angle on the head.

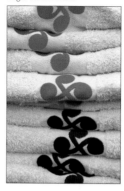

Coarraze
Weaving workshop
2½ miles (4 km) from Nay
Créations Sylvie Thiriez, 6, Avenue de la Gare
☎ 05 59 61 19 98
Factory shop open daily except Sun. and Mon. morning, 9am–noon and 2–6.30pm. Tour of the factory on request.

Spotcheck
C6

Pyrenees-Atlantiques

Things to do
The caves of Bétharram
The Beret Museum

With children
The kangaroo park

Tourist Office
Pau: ☎ 05 59 27 27 08

Free admission.
The best Basque tablecloths are made here. Bring your table measurements, choose your fabric, and the workshop will get to work and have it ready in 15 minutes! You can watch as the 4,000 threads are aligned on a drum, operated by means of a punched card. Be sure to allow for the cloth shrinking slightly after the first wash! (p. 68).

Pau, city of Henri IV

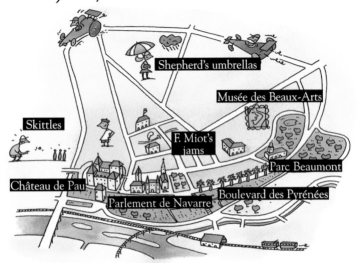

Shepherd's umbrellas

Musée des Beaux-Arts

Skittles

F. Miot's jams

Parc Beaumont

Château de Pau

Boulevard des Pyrénées

Parlement de Navarre

The capital of the département of Pyrenees-Atlantiques is a green city. Facing the Pyrenees, it has gardens designed by the English who adopted and embellished it until 1914. It's also, above all, the birthplace of Henri IV, the Vert-Galant. From the château to the old town, the future king has left many traces. Today, at Whitsun, the modern capital of the Béarn throbs to the sound of motor-racing engines during its annual fixture.

National museum of Château de Pau
☎ 05 59 82 38 19
Open daily, 15 June–15 Sept., 9.30am–12.15pm and 1.30–5.45pm; phone for information out of season.
Admission charge.
This château, birthplace of Henri IV, was heavily restored in the 19th C. by Louis-Philippe and Napoleon III. After visiting the elegant 16th-C. kitchen, the dining room with space for 100 place settings, the large reception room and the apartments of the Empress Eugénie, you can marvel at the tortoise shell which served little Henri de Navarre as a cradle. There are also some lovely 16th- and 18th-C. Gobelin tapestries to admire.

The Boulevard des Pyrénées
Between the château and the Parc Beaumont, this 2,000 yd (1,800 m) boulevard has an **exceptional view** of the Pyrenees. On a clear day you can see more than 62½ miles (100 km) of the mountain range, from the Basque country to the Central Pyrenees. Lamartine was moved to remark 'It's the

most beautiful view of land, just as Naples has the most beautiful view of the sea'.

Francis Miot's jams
48, Rue Maréchal-Joffre, 120 yds (100 m) from the château

☎ 05 59 27 69 51
Open daily except Sun. and Mon. morning, 10am–noon and 2.15–7pm.
This jam-maker is known the world over. You can taste the delicious classic flavours of his brilliant creations. These jams are said to have various effects – to calm, relax, and, it's claimed, restore youthful potency (the 'Vert-Galant' is supposed to be an aphrodisiac). Three jars (9 oz; 250 g) will cost you 65 F; one jar 24 F each.

The Musée des Beaux-Arts
Rue Mathieu-Lalanne
☎ 05 59 27 33 02
Open daily except Tues., 10am–noon and 2–6pm.
Admission charge.
All the European Schools are represented here: Spanish, Italian, Dutch, Flemish, French and English, from the 15th to the 20th C. Wander through this very rich collection and stop to admire

the two masterpieces, Rubens' *The Last Judgement* and *The Cotton Exchange in New Orleans* by Edgar Degas.

The public gardens
Pau holds the national record for green space with 1,853 acres (750 ha) per 88,000 inhabitants; 915 sq ft (85 sq m) for each person! Pau has an exceptional number of open spaces which all deserve a visit. There's a wood in the Royal Park, kitchen gardens in the grounds of the château, trees in the Boulevard des Pyrénées, the footpaths of the king, the Lawrence Park,

Spotcheck
C6

Pyrenees-Atlantiques

Things to do
The public gardens
Play skittles
The Musée National des Parachutistes
Visit to the Gelos stud farm

Tourist Office
Pau: ☎ 05 59 27 27 08

and above all the **Parc Beaumont** with its Allée Anne-de-Noailles.

SKITTLES
5, Allée du Grand-Tour (nine-pin skittles)
☎ 05 59 62 37 96
Daily, but especially on Saturdays in summer. Skittles have become once more very fashionable. Try following the Béarnais version, much enjoyed by Henri IV. It's played in an arena, and the very complex rules are reminiscent of those of billiards. A spectacular game, punctuated with excitement, skittles is once more producing young champions who play the 6- or 9-nine pin version. Each skittle weighs 6 lb 8 oz (3 kg) and measures 37½ in (96 cm).

AN OVERWHELMING LOVE

The city of Pau had a great love for Henri IV and he always expressed his attachment to it. On the day he was assassinated, it's said that thunder 'broke the King's arms on the gates of the château' and that 'in the royal herd, cows fell to their knees', while 'the bull threw itself into the moat'. When Louis XIV succeeded him, the inhabitants proudly inscribed on their statue of the Sun King in the Place Royale: 'This is the grandson of our great Henri' – in Béarnais of course.

Bernadotte's house
Musée Bernadotte,
8, Rue Tran
☎ 05 59 27 48 42
Guided tour daily except Mon., 10am–noon and 2–6pm.
Admission charge.
Bernadotte, Marshal of France, had an amazing career and you can learn more about this little-known Gascon by visiting his birthplace. He was a private soldier and became a companion of Bonaparte, who made him a Prince of the Empire. He fell out with the Emperor and joined Charles XII, King of Sweden and Norway, succeeding him to the throne in 1818! The city of Pau has thus given birth to two founders of dynasties,

Henri IV and Bernadotte (p. 59). The current Swedish Royal family still bears the surname of Bernadotte.

The Ravine of Hédas
From the Place Reine-Marguerite, which until the 16th C. was the gateway to the city, follow the Rue René-Fournets to the Ravine of Hédas. A covered river once flowed here and was the city's only water supply. The fountain and wash-house are remnants of this once busy district. The bed of the former water-course is now a narrow path, lined with trees, houses and unkempt gardens. You can stroll along it before climbing the steps of the Pont des Cordeliers.

Le Musée National des Parachutistes
École des Troupes Aéroportées
☎ 05 59 72 52 18
Tours Mon., Wed., Thurs. and Fri. at 1.30pm, 2.30pm, 3.30pm

and 4.30pm (by appointment in the morning); w/ends and public holidays by appointment.
Free admission
Parachuting is said to have originated with Leonardo da Vinci and his flying machine. It has been closely associated with French history for over half a century, and today has its own museum. From its early forerunners to the present day, the story of parachuting is presented here, with archives that provide the documentary evidence.

The château district
The palaces along the Boulevard du Midi, near the château, used to welcome important visitors in the 19th C., including kings of Spain, England and Sweden. In the heart of the city (Rue Henri-IV), the Parlement

de Navarre, once the court-house, is now home to the local authority. The neighbouring half-timbered houses which straddle the Gave de Pau overlook the Place de la Monnaie opposite what was, until the Revolution, the only other mint in France.

A real shepherd's umbrella

**Aux Parapluies
des Pyrénées,
1, Rue de Laussat**
☎ **05 59 27 53 66**
Open daily except Sat. afternoon and Sun., 8am–noon and 2–7pm. This umbrella enables the shepherd to stay dry in the mountain rains and never be struck by lightning (its ribs are made of cane). Christophe Pando is the only traditional maker left. He'll help you to withstand the 'downpours' of the Béarn (from 480 to 660 F).

The pebbles of the Gave

**Verdier S. A.,
6, Rue des Druides**
☎ **05 59 32 14 38**
Open daily Mon.–Sat. morning, 9am–noon and 2–6pm. Guided tour by appointment.
Free admission.

This workshop makes 400 sweets a minute, including the famous *gave* pebbles, coloured grey. Verdier is the town's greatest confectioner. He knows how to get the best out of chocolate and moulds it into interesting and appetising shapes. Prices are 30 F for 10½ oz (300 g), nougatine, 34 F for 10 oz (280 g).

Gelos national stud farm

*S of Pau, towards
Oloron*
☎ **05 59 06 60 57**
Guided tours Tues. and Thurs., 2.30pm. Groups by appointment (provisional timetables).
Admission charge.
You can see the horses being worked, before visiting the stables, saddlery, forge and insemination laboratory. This handsome set of classic buildings is where the Anglo-Arab horse was born, and many of the 80 stallions here belong to this breed. There are also carthorses and the rare Landes pony. In early July you can witness the Anglo-Arab horse trials, and in early November, it's the turn of the carthorses.

Jurançon
the royal vineyard

The wine of Jurançon is the emblem of this corner of Béarn. The Jurançon lies between the Gave de Pau and the Gave d'Oloron, and its vineyards are surrounded by slate-roofed Béarnaise houses, facing the mountains. The area is littered with Roman and medieval remains, and inspired Colette to write: 'As an adolescent I met a passionate, imperious prince, a traitor like all the great seducers, the Jurançon'.

Gan

La Cave des Producteurs de Jurançon

5 miles (8 km) S of Pau
53, Avenue Henri-IV and 24, Rue des Pyrénées
☎ **05 59 21 57 03**
Guided tour:
Mon.–Sat., 8am–noon and 2–6pm, by appointment.
Free admission.
A few drops of the famous syrupy wine, the colour of maize, were used for the baptism of Henri IV in 1553. The South Béarn vineyard is now much bigger, covering 1,235 acres (500 ha) and producing 2.8 million bottles

of the yellow wine. When you visit this vineyard, follow the complete route of the royal grape from the vine to the *chai* (wine-store), and taste at least two of the 15 vintages which the 300 wine-makers produce here (from 26 F a bottle for a wine that is harvested early, to 150 F for a wine made from a late harvest).

Artiguelouve

The Domaine du Cinquau

6½ miles (10 km) E of Pau
☎ **05 59 83 10 41**
Guided tours of the wine and spirit store daily by appointment.
Free admission.
This is an archetypal small estate in the Jurançon.

JURANÇON ON HORSEBACK
7½ miles (12 km) NW of Pau
La Forge, Route des Bois, Arbus
☎ 05 59 83 13 87
Cover the road and pathways of Jurançon on horseback.
You can rent a mount either for an hour's wander through the vineyards or for a one week's pony-trek into

the peaks of the Pyrenees. The Béarn looks wonderful from the peaks and, in the undergrowth, the animals will take no notice of you. The Valleys of the Aspe and the Ossau also wait to be explored.
One hour: 60 F, Six-hour day: 300 F, Weekend with full board: 900 F. Week: 3,500 F.

Pierre Saubot, the wine-maker, will welcome you under the porch which overlooks 17½ acres (7 ha) of vines and will take you into the *chai* where you can see the grape-sorting machine, the wine-press, the barrels and the cellar with its oak casks. Even before you taste it, you'll understand why the Jurançon is famous for this wine, which has a taste of toasted almonds.

Saint-Girons-de-Monein
The church
12½ miles (20 km) N of Oloron-Sainte-Marie by the D 9.
☎ 05 59 21 29 28
In July–Aug., guided tour, Mon.–Sat., at 11am,

3pm, 4pm, 5pm; Sun. at 4pm and 5pm. Out of season, daily except Sat. at 4pm and 5pm.
Admission charge.
A bell-tower 133 ft (40 m) high dominates the 'Paris of Béarn', as Henri IV called it. Saint-Giron has the largest Gothic church in Béarn, the size of a cathedral. Admire the porch, the nave, the monumental altar screen and climb the spiral staircase in the bell-tower to see the oak timbers of the **completely restored roof** in the shape of an upturned keel.

Sauvelade
The abbey
11½ miles (18 km) NW of Monein. Open daily. Free admission.
The village is tiny but its

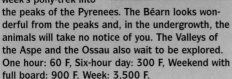

position on the route to Compostela has left a legacy in the shape of this 12th-C. abbey, as beautiful outside as it is inside. Built in

the shape of a Greek cross, it has a cylindrically vaulted nave and a concave ceiling (at the crossing of the transept under the belfry). The exterior of golden sandstone has a pigeon-loft belltower.

Saint-Faust
City of bees
7½ miles (12 km) W of Jurançon
Chemin des Crêtes
☎ 05 59 83 10 31 and
☎ 05 59 83 04 60
Open daily,
1 Apr.–15 Oct., 2–6pm.
Admission charge.
If you look closely you'll see the queen laying her brood and the worker bees going about their daily tasks. From capturing a swarm to collecting the honey, everything is explained. A computerised observation post makes it possible to analyse the social organisation of the colonies. A 1 lb 2 oz (500 g) pot of acacia honey is 30 F, mountain honey 27 F and a 9 oz (250 g) pot of pollen, 35 F.

Spotcheck
C6

Pyrénées-Atlantiques

Things to do
The wine of Jurançon
City of bees
Jurançon on horseback

Tourist Office
Pau: ☎ 05 59 27 27 08

Saubestre gateway to Béarn

This area, north-west of Pau, was once heavily wooded. Its rolling hills lie parallel to the Gave de Pau, and from the top of them you can see the Pyrenees. The woods have now largely disappeared to be replaced by maize cultivation, producing a green and golden landscape. Saubestre is divided in two by the Luy-de-France, a river which once separated the Kingdom of France from the Kingdom of Navarre.

Lescar

Ethnological museum

6¹⁄₂ miles (10 km) NW of Pau.
Tourist Office
☎ 05 59 81 15 98
Lescar, at the western exit of Pau, was the first capital of Béarn. It's a lovely old town whose 12th-C. cathedral is full of reminders of the district's illustrious past. Enter through the fortified entrance and see its treasures. There are wonderful capitals in the choir and the floor is covered with a mosaic including a hunter with a wooden leg! Beside the cathedral, the former cellars of the bishop's palace contain an ethnological museum. Lower down in the town, the church of Saint-Julien has a lovely 16th-C. altar screen.

Morlanne

Château de Morlanne

15¹⁄₂ miles (25 km) NW of Lescar, via the D 945
☎ 05 59 81 60 27
Open, 1 Apr.–31 Oct.
Tour of the château: daily exc. Tues. 2.30–6.30pm.
Tour of the park: daily exc. Tues., 10.30am–6.30pm.
Admission charge.
An important defence post in the Middle Ages, this brick fortress was completely restored in 1971. Opposite, the village church and Maison Domecq (once a lay abbey) form an attractive group with the château and

offer a lovely view of the Pyrenees. You can picnic in the château **grounds**.

Momas
Rare vegetables of Momas
12½ miles (20 km) NW of Pau, by the D 945
☎ 05 59 77 14 71
Open Sat.–Sun. and public holidays, afternoons, 1 Apr.–1 Nov. Other days on request. *Admission charge.*
Discover 'everlasting spinach', imported by the Roman legions, and 'poor man's ham', a sort of salsify whose flavour is reminiscent of ham. You can combine a visit to this

garden, which contains 1,000 varieties of rare plants, with a visit to the château (14th–18th C.), which has lovely wood panelling and views of the Pyrenees.

Arzacq
Musée de la Faune et des Traditions du Béarn
☎ 05 59 04 54 03
Open July–Aug., 2–7pm.

Admission charge.
Here you can stroke one of the loveliest animals from Latin America, a type of beaver known as myocastor which is a protected rodent. There are also chinchillas from the Andes, and some of the animals and birds that are native to Béarn itself.

Sault-de-Navailles
Wooden toys
6½ miles (10 km) N of Orthez
☎ 05 59 67 52 05
Open daily except Sat.–Sun., 9am–noon and 2–7pm.
Bernard Pourtau's workshop is a must for children and game-players alike. He carves, saws, sands and polishes many different games and toys, including decorated *palas* bats for playing pelota (from 55 to 75 F), Béarn skittles (600 F for 6, with traps), and

Spotcheck
C6
Pyrénées-Atlantiques

Things to do
The rare vegetables of Momas
Lac de Thèze leisure centre

With children
Visit a wooden toy workshop

Tourist Office
Lescar:
☎ 05 59 81 15 98

LAC DE THÈZE
9½ miles (15 km) N of Pau, by N 134 Free admission all year round.
On the shores of the lake, follow the paths leading to the banks of the Luy-de-France. At the leisure centre, you can learn to play six-pin skittles, a popular game in the region (p. 289) and have a go at steering remote-controlled model ships. Fishing is also permitted here.

some lovely Chinese-checkers boards (160 F) or game tables (350 F). His favourite wood is that of the plane tree.

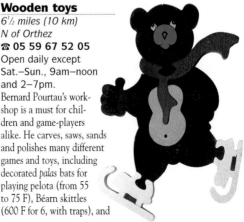

Vic-Bilh
In the country

The name Vic-Bilh means 'old country' in Béarnais. Vic-Bilh, with its hills, its many waterways, its umbrella pines and cypresses, in many ways resembles Tuscany, and yet it's in the Pyrenees. Thanks to its turbulent past, there are many medieval fortresses and châteaux amidst the vineyards of the famous wines of Madiran.

Morlaàs
The former capital
5 miles (8 km) NE of Pau
Morlaàs was the capital of Béarn from the 9th to the 12th C., but all that remains of its glorious past is the church of Sainte-Foy, with its beautiful Roman portal. Several old houses surround the church, including no. 1, the house of Jeanne d'Albret (15th C.) and the arcaded former town hall. The Tourist Office houses a small museum which exhibits several old stones from the church and part of the monument of Morlaàs, which is no longer standing.

Garlin
Château de Mascaraas-Haron
3¹⁄₂ miles (6 km) SE of Pau
☎ 05 59 04 92 60
Open daily except Tues., 15 May–15 Sept.; Sat. Sun. and public holidays, all year round, 10am–noon and 3–6pm.

Admission charge.
The 16th–17th-C. Château of Mascaraas-Haron stands on a road which crosses the peaks, overlooking the Madiran vineyards and facing the Pyrenees. Still inhabited to this day, it's prettily furnished and contains a wonderful collection of works of art and Flemish furniture from the 14th to 18th C. The grounds of the château are beautifully **landscaped**.

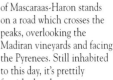

Cannery on a farm
8 miles (13 km) NE of Thèze
Castetpugon
☎ 05 59 04 74 06
Free guided tour daily, by appointment.
The rule here is simple – each bird must eat 26 lb (12 kg) of maize a fortnight. This strict

regime is said to make their meat very tasty. After the ducks are fattened and killed, the liver, thighs and breast are sent to the processing rooms to be prepared and cooked. Have a taste, but don't eat it all at once – the tins can be kept for three years (foie gras: 39 F for 2¹/₄ oz; 60 g, breast: 42 F for 14 oz; 400 g).

Montaner
Château de Montaner
21¹/₂ miles (35 km) E of Pau, by the D 7
☎ 05 59 81 98 29
Open daily, except Tues., 1 Apr.–31 Oct., 10am–noon and 2–7pm. *Admission charge.*
This red-brick 14th-C. fortress has a certain presence: at one time it controlled Béarn, Armagnac and Bigorre. From its massive 140 ft (42 m) high keep, Gaston Fébus, the illustrious Prince of Béarn, defended France when threatened by

English Gascony, and within its walls he dreamed of a great Pyrenean state. Facing the château, the village

Spotcheck
C6

Pyrénées-Atlantiques

Things to do
Visit a cannery
Fishing and windsurfing
Madiran wine

With children
The Lac de Bassillon

Tourist Office
Morlaàs: ☎ 05 59 33 62 25

MADIRAN WINE
9¹/₂ miles (15 km) N of Lembeye
Château de Crouseilles
☎ 05 59 68 10 93
Open Mon.–Sat., 1 Oct.–14 May, 9.30am–12.30pm and 2–6pm; 15 May–30 Sept., 9am–1pm and 2–7pm; open Sun., June–Sept., 2–6pm.
This red wine (A.O.C.) is very powerful. All producers are obliged to store it for one year before it's marketed. It accumulates its wonderful energy from growing at an altitude of 1,000 ft (300 m), on the sunny slopes of Béarn and Bigorre. The dry white of Pacherenc (the only white wine of Madiran) has a strange flinty taste, while the sweet whites taste of honey. Try these, and all the other varieties, at the Château de Crouseilles, an attractive 18th-C. building, which contains the Cooperative Regional cellar. (Madiran: 23 to 54.50 F a bottle, Pacherenc: sweet, 35 to 80 F a bottle; winter sweet, 195 to 390 F a 50cl bottle; dry, 19 to 33 F a bottle).

church has one of the finest collections of 15th- and 16th-C. **frescoes** in the area.

Cadillon and Bassillon
The lakes
Respectively at 6¹/₂ miles (10 km) NW and at 4¹/₂ miles (7 km) E of Lembeye
The Lac de Cadillon in the Madiran vineyard is an excellent spot for **fishing**. Spend the day there, enjoying the **playgrounds**, picnic areas, tennis, basketball and other games. Further south, the Lac de Bassillon, without amenities, is nevertheless an interesting nature reserve for birds and a paradise for anglers. Swimming is forbidden, but you can cool off in the swimming pool, filled with water from the lake.

The Aspe valley
deep in the mountains of Béarn

This is the most unspoiled of the three valleys of the Béarn mountains. It's the natural route to Spain via the Somport pass. The countryside is still wild and you may even see a bear washing itself in the mountain streams. The pilgrims bound for the tomb of St James at Santiago de Compostela, and many wars, have left their mark, but the lily of the Pyrenees still survives in the lush meadows.

Asasp

Sarrance

Lourdios-Ichère

Accous

Moulin d'Orcun

Etsaut

Osse-en-Aspe

Lescun

Chemin de la Mâture

Fort du Portalet

Sarrance

Musée Notre-Dame-de-la-Pierre

11½ miles (19 km)
S of Oloron
☎ 05 59 34 55 51 and
☎ 05 59 34 54 61
Open daily, 1 July–Sept.,
10am–noon and 2–7pm;
out of season, Sat.–Sun.,
school and public
holidays, 2–6pm.

Admission charge.
This tiny village has been an important shrine since the 14th C. Take the historic route, from the church to the museum. It reconstructs the traditional pilgrimage of the 1930s, passing through the 17th-C. cloister, inhabited by three monks who run a guest-house (*gîte d'étape*). Ask them to tell you the legend of the Virgin of Sarrance, who was bathing in the nearby river…

Lourdios-Ichère

The Écomusée

4½ miles (7 km) E of
Sarrance
☎ 05 59 34 44 84
Open daily, 15 June–
15 Sept., 10am–noon
and 2–7pm; out of
season, Sat.–Sun. and
school holidays, 2–6pm.

Admission charge.
You'll find everything from a Béarnaise mountain village here: mill, fountain, garden, fern plantation, orchard, and church – thirty-two authentic sites, all central to traditional life. This living museum changes with the seasons and has a permanent exhibition of agricultural and pastoral life, today and yesterday.

Spotcheck
C7

Pyrénées-Atlantiques

Things to do
Écomusée de Lourdios-Ichère
Mountain biking
Hiking and walking
Paragliding and hang-gliding

Tourist Office
Bedous: ☎ 05 59 34 71 48

waters of the mountain was harnessed to provide power. Before visiting the mill, contact the miller, Jean-Jacques Bellegarde.

GARBURE

This dish, typical of the Valley of the Aspe, is a vegetable soup which changes according to what is in season. To make it, put slices of potato into boiling water along with seasonal vegetables. Season with salt, pepper, chilli pepper, garlic, thyme and parsley. Simmer until the vegetables are soft, add some shredded green cabbage and bring back to the boil. Half an hour before serving, add a piece of preserved pork, along with its fat, and a tablespoon of goose or duck fat. Arrange thin slices of day-old bread in a dish and pour the soup over them. Serve piping hot.

Accous
Basco-Béarnais farmers
*6½ miles (10km)
S of Sarrance*
Open daily, July–15 Sept., 9.30am–1pm and 2–7.30pm; rest of the year, Mon.–Fri., 9.30am–noon and 2–6pm, Sat.–Sun., 2–6pm.
One of three museums which together constitute the Écomusée of the Aspe Valley. They feature the shepherds of the Béarn and their mountain life: the *estive* (moving sheep to summer pastures), the flora, the herds, cheese-making. The exhibitions, audio-visual shows and tastes and flavours of the region will help you to understand the bond between the Béarnais and their mountain.

Route d'Aydius
☎ 05 59 34 74 91
Open all year round by appointment.
Admission charge.
This is the only working mill left in the valley and it's the site of a living museum. From the grain to the baking, learn how old-fashioned bread was made and what life was like at the mill. A guide will take you on a tour of the area in a carriage, and tell the story of how the gushing

Bedous
The Orcun mill
*1½ miles (2½ km)
N of Accous*

Mountain-biking through the Pyrenees

**VTT Nature,
Route d'Espagne**
☎ 05 59 34 75 25

Explore the Aspe Valley on a mountain bike. You can rent one from Louis Gandon (60 F for half a day) and he will suggest a route for you to take. All you have to do is find the right path and you're off – excitement guaranteed. The rides down the mountain are organised into different levels: 'degustation' ('tasting') for beginners, and 'dégringolades' ('tumble down') for the more reckless. A word of warning to the brave; you'll have to climb up on foot or opt for the lift!

Osse-en-Aspe

Ferme-auberge et Bergerie Pimparela

½ mile (1 km) from Bedous
Quartier Ipère
☎ 05 59 34 52 23
Open daily for sales, tours by appointment.

Take a look around before you try the produce here. The sheep, cows and goats grazing on the rich pastures around this farm are responsible for the cheeses maturing in the dairy. Visit the workshops and take away some of the best produce of Upper Béarn: cheeses of Ossau-Iraty and home-made pork specialities, lamb's liver pâté, lamb stew with prunes, etc.

Lescun

Refuge de L'Arbérouat

NW of Lescun
☎ 05 59 34 50 43
Open Jan.–Sept.

This village, whose houses all date from the 15th and 16th C., nestles in the green Cirque de Lescun. Visit the church of Sainte-Eulalie and see the lovely altar and the wooden galleries. The GR 10 will lead you to the Pic d'Anie (8,346 ft; 2,504 m), a round trip of eight hours on foot. First take the car to the Refuge de l'Arbérouat (4,833 ft; 1,450 m), the departure point for this excursion, which is signposted from beginning to end.

Etsaut

On foot

☎ 05 59 34 86 15
(Eric Corno)

Eric Corno will be your personal mountain guide and will take you wherever you want, depending on the amount of energy you have and what you want to see;

including flora, fauna and interesting sights in the valley. If you're brave, he'll even take you to climb a peak. One or more days (140 F per day, 1,000 F for 12 pers.).

Maison d'Ulysse
☎ 05 59 34 87 78
Shop open daily May–Sept., 10am–1pm and 3–8pm; out of season, telephone first.

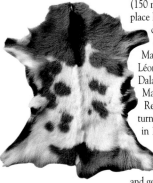

All that's missing is a bearskin. In this workshop, all the skins in the region end up as waistcoats, throws, slippers or decorative skins. Didier and Catherine Sorli, traditional skinners, tan and stretch the skins of rabbits, goats and lambs, keeping the fur and hair intact. There's little 'mouse' made of rabbit skin (25 F), a goatskin purse (50 F), or a big teddy bear (350 F), and lambskins for decoration (150 F).

Le Chemin de la Mâture
1½ miles (2 km) S of Etsaut (after the right turn, take the GR 10 towards the left).
This narrow path was cut directly out of the marble cliff by man and was used to bring down tree trunks in the 18th C. to be made into ship's timbers. The run is only 13 ft (4 m) wide and overlooks a 670 ft (200 m) drop yet it was once used by horses harnessed

to a cart! Take the round trip on foot or on horseback, following the white and red signs of the GR 10., but only if you're not afraid of heights.

Fort du Portalet
1½ miles (3 km) S of Etsaut, overhanging the N 134
A bottomless ravine surrounds this fortress, which clings to the rock 500 ft (150 m) above the *gave* at a place known as Gorges d'Enfer – the gorges of hell. This is where Marshal Pétain imprisoned Léon Blum, Édouard Daladier, Georges Mandel, Maurice Gamelin and Paul Reynaud… but it was his turn to be incarcerated here in 1945! It's not open to the public, but just seeing it is a lesson in history, architecture and geography.

Borce
The bear enclosure
6½ miles (10 km) S of Accous
☎ 05 59 34 88 88 and 05 59 34 71 48
Open daily, June–mid-Sept., 10am–noon and 2–7pm; all year round, groups by appointment. *Admission charge.*
Antoine, Ségolène and Myrtille live here but they are not native. They were bought from a bankrupt circus and symbolise the beast of the Pyrenees – the bear. This is about as close as you'll get to the real thing, as you're unlikely to encounter the last remaining authentic specimens of these magnificent animals that once freely roamed the Pyrenees.

❀ PARAGLIDING AND HANG-GLIDING

Hang-gliding: Virvolta, Boulevard Leclercq, Accous
☎ **05 59 34 50 30**
Paragliding: Abelio,
☎ **05 59 34 58 07**
Open all year round. See the valley spread out at your feet by paragliding or hang-gliding. Take your first leap into the air with a qualified instructor in a two-person hang-glider. Aged from 5 to 77, all you need is a pair of trainers and half a day to feel like a bird-man challenging the mountains. The 15-minute flight costs 380 F per adult, 350 F for children under 16. A 15-minute paraglide costs 350 F.

The Ossau valley
refuge of vultures

In its descent down the mountain facing Pau, the Gave d'Ossau has carved a valley through the cold Arudy marble and the hot waters of Laruns. The traditions of the hot springs, stone-quarrying and the movement of the shepherds and their flocks animate a landscape dominated by the Pic du Midi d'Ossau (9,613 ft/ 2,884 m), which everyone here calls 'Jean-Pierre', in homage to the stone giant that dominates the whole of Béarn.

Sévignac-Meyracq

Louvie-Juzon

Arudy

Plateau de Bénou

Aste-Béon

Laruns

Col d'Aubisque

Gourette

Eaux-Bonnes and Eaux-Chaudes

Ossau cheese

Lac de Bious-Artigues

Lac d'Artouste

Sévignacq-Meyracq
Château
*1½ miles (2 km)
NE of Arudy*
☎ 05 59 05 72 36
Open daily except Wed.,
1 July–15 Aug., 1–7pm.
Admission charge.
The little château, the church
and, in the background, the
Pic du Midi d'Ossau make a
perfect composition. The
16th-C. church has one of
the loveliest porticos in
Aquitaine as well as a very
ornate Gothic throne. The
Renaissance château is
private property and cannot
be visited but you can look
at it from outside. The church
of Sainte-Colome, 1½ miles
(2 km) further south, is
worth seeing.

Arudy
La Maison d'Ossau
*16½ miles (26 km)
S of Pau*
Place de l'Église
☎ 05 59 05 61 71
Open daily, July–Aug.,
10am–noon and
3–6pm; Jan.–
June, and Sept.,
Tues.–Fri.,
2–6pm,
Sun., 3–6pm;
school hols,
winter and
spring (zones
A, B, C),
Tues.–Fri., 2–
6pm, w/ends
3–6pm.
If want to get
to know the
Ossau valley,

you should take a visit to this museum. Housed in a 17th-C. mansion, it displays the prehistoric past of the region, as well as the traditional life – everything is here, from worship of the Sun god to ewe's milk cheese. The Pyrenees National Park lies 12½ miles (20 km) to the south.

Plateau de Bénou
6½ miles (10 km) SW of Arudy, by the D 294
Climb up to the Plateau de Bénou

(2,900 ft; 870 m) where the flocks gather in summer. In this huge area, there are blocks of stone more than 39 in (1 m) in diameter, arranged in circles from 10 to 27 ft (3 to 8 m) across. They mark tombs of the first communities to live here nearly 10,000 years ago. It's an ideal spot for a picnic.

The vulture observation ground
Just before the Plateau de Benou, from Arudy.

Spotcheck
C7

Pyrénées-Atlantiques

Things to do
Rafting and canoeing
The vulture cliff
Walking and hiking
Moving the flock
Petit train d'Artouste
The Gourette cablecar

Tourist Office
Laruns:
☎ 05 59 05 31 41

Leave your car at the chapel of Notre-Dame-de-Houndaas, and take the wide path that turns off to the right. Half an hour later, on a little ledge overlooking the valley, you'll have reached the observation ground. If you're quiet you may be lucky enough to see a marie-blanque, a little vulture with a yellow head, enjoying a meal.

MARBLE FROM THE VALLEY
Arudy, Route du Bager, towards Saint-Christau.
Large blocks of Arudy marble are still cut from the open quarry. Marble has been extracted for centuries and used to decorate châteaux and buildings throughout the world – even the Empire State Building in New York. The cheapest variety is the grey-blue stone and the most desirable is red-veined or polychrome.

to a wide screen. You'll feel a bit like a peeping Tom, watching the chicks being fed, or even born! There's a small exhibition next door about the countryside and animals of the Pyrenees.

Laruns

Walking and hiking

8½ miles (14 km) S of Arudy

Maison de la Vallée-d'Ossau
☎ 05 59 05 33 04

Five guides are available to take you for a hike through the major sites of the Ossau valley. Walks usually last three to eight hours, at heights between 1,330 and 4,330 ft (400 and 1,300 m). The guides will adapt the walks to suit your abilities and to allow you to discover the treasures of the surrounding area, including fauna, flora, heritage etc. Individual rate: from 110 F per day (around 1,400 F for 12 pers.).

Louvie-Juzon

Mountain sports

1½ miles (2 km) S of Arudy

C.P.L., Place Camps
☎ 05 59 05 82 28

Mountain sports can be summed up as either going up or coming down. For going up, try the training-rocks of Arudy and Bouvier (from 140 F for half a day). For going down, the wild canyons of the Ossau valley are perfect for **canyoning** (from 170 F) and the *gaves* of the high Béarn are ideal for **whitewater rafting** or canoeing and kayaking (from 150 F). Mountain-biking, quad-biking and potholing are also available in this area.

Aste-Béon

The vulture cliff

☎ 05 59 82 65 49
Open daily exc. Sat., 6 Feb.–5 March and All Saints day school hols, 3–6pm. Daily, 2 Apr.–28 Apr. and July–Aug., 10am–1pm and 2–7pm; 29 Apr.–May and Sept., 2.30–6.30pm.
Admission charge.
Video cameras on top of the cliff transmit everything that happens in the vultures' nest

Taking the flock to the mountains

For three days and two nights, the Ossau valley resounds to the sound of bells and bleating. The sheep are being moved to the high summer pastures on the Spanish border, one of the major events in the life of the shepherds and the villagers. As the flocks pass through, late into the night, each village (Iseste, Bielle, Béost, Laruns) becomes

OSSAU CHEESE
**Joseph Paroix,
Bilhères-en-Ossau
☎ 05 59 82 64 24**
In his hut on the Cap
de Point in summer,
and on the Bénou
plateau in winter,
Joseph Paroix will show
you how he makes the
famous Ossau cheese.
He heats the milk from
his ewes to 86°F/30°C
(12½ pints (7 l) are
needed for 2 lb 4 oz
(1 kg) of cheese). He
then leaves the milk to
curdle and after cutting
the curd with a whisk,
he heats it again to
100°F (38°C), pours it
into moulds, pierces it
with needles and drains
off the whey. He rubs it
with salt and turns the
cheeses every 4 or 5
days for 4 months. The
cheese can be bought
on the spot (80 F for 2
lb 4 oz/1 kg), and also
at the Laruns market
on Saturday mornings
(and Thursday evenings,
in summer), or from
M. Casabonne, Route
des Cols, Laruns,
☎ 05 59 05 35 11.

stop for a few moments'
enjoyment. Don't miss this
event (usually the second
week in July, dates at the
Tourist Office Vallée-d'Ossau,
☎ 05 59 05 31 41). The
mountain tradition also

inspires the Fête de Laruns
(15 Aug.) and a **Cheese fair**,
a feature of the old-style market (first weekend in Oct.).

Eaux-Bonnes and Eaux-Chaudes
The virtues of sulphur
The hot water springs
(55°–95°F; 13°–35°C) have
been used since the 16th C.
to treat a variety of ills and
you can take advantage of
their virtues, à la carte. At
Eaux-Bonnes, a bubbling bath
(60 F) or jet shower (50 F)
are good for pain and arthritis
(**Eurothermes ☎** 05 59 05
34 02, open May–Oct., daily
except Sun. and public hols,
8am–noon). At Eaux-Chaudes,
a combination of relaxing
bath, sulphurous bath and
drink will make you feel rejuvenated in just 40 minutes;
the treatment must be booked
and costs 100 F (**Complexe
Thermal ☎** 05 59 05 31 55,
open May–Oct., daily except
Sun. and public hols, 2–6pm).

Fabrèges-village
Petit train d'Artouste
SE of Gabas
Access by cable-car.
☎ 05 59 05 36 99
Open end of May–Sept.,
daily; w/ends in Oct.
This railway, once used to
repair flood barriers, winds for
6½ miles (10 km) across the
peaks at an altitude of 6,600 ft

(1,980 m) to the overspill at
the Lac d'Artouste. The trip
takes an hour but you'll then
have to walk for 15 minutes

to get to the lake. Panoramic
views all the way.

Gourette
The Gourette cablecar
7½ miles (12 km)
E of Laruns
Tourist Office
☎ **05 59 05 12 17/60**
Open daily July–Aug.,
9am–5pm; open during
the skiing season.
Admission charge.
Take the easy way up 8,000 ft
(2,400 m) for the extraordinary view of the Cirque de
Gourette. You can then walk
the 4½ miles (7 km) to the ski
resort. The ascent is via two
cable-cars, Les Bosses (4,670
to 6,000 ft/1,400 to 1,800 m),
then Pène-Blanque (4 places,
up to 8,000 ft/2,400 m).

The Pyrenees National Park

The Pyrenees National Park was created in 1967, and is uninhabited, except for the birds and animals that flourish here. In these mountains, where the natural heritage is jealously preserved, only shepherds and woodcutters are tolerated. This world without fences or enclosures covers the upper part of the valleys of the Aspe and Ossau, and can only be crossed on foot.

Etsaut

Maison d'Etsaut
☎ 05 59 34 88 30 and
☎ 05 59 34 70 87
Open daily
1 May–15 Sept.,
9.30am–
12.30pm and
2–6.30pm.
Free admission.
This information centre is housed in the former SNCF railway station of Etsaut. The flora and fauna of the National Park are all detailed, and there's a lot of information about its most famous inhabitant, the bear. You're most unlikely to see one, though, as they hide from humans. However, the birds of prey, izards (mountain goats) and marmots are very tame. Find out where to see them and what excursions are possible in the Aspe and Ossau valleys (also Maison de Gabas, ☎ 05 59 05 32 13).

Vallée d'Aspe

The Saoubathou pass
Beyond Lhers, SE of Lescun
Departure: from the Aoumet car park.

THE LEGENDARY GYPAETE

If you spot this bird of prey you're very fortunate indeed. It has a wingspan of up to 10 ft (3 m) and is extremely rare. Only 17 breeding pairs have been counted throughout the Pyrenees. Their eyes are yellow circled with a pinky-red ring, the face and ruff are black the long wings are dark grey, and look as if they're shot with fire. The bird lives at low altitude in the cliffs and 90% of its diet is carrion bones (so you're not at risk!). It's protective and guarded, and only produces one chick a year.

This circular walk will take about 6 hours. After Lhers, make for the car park at Aoumet, and take the path to the Caillau hut. Climb to the Souperet pass at the Pic de Labigouer, where you'll see izards (mountain goats). Further on, marmots will accompany you on your way to Saoubathou Pass while large birds of prey fly overhead. The route brings you back to where you started.

Vallée d'Ossau

Tour of the Lacs d'Ayous

½ mile (1 km) S of Gabas, by the D 231, to the right.

Four hours' walking for a fantastic view! Take the car to the Lac de Bious-Artigues, via the D 231, then take the GR 10 on foot to the refuge

of the Lacs d'Ayous (1,870 ft/ 560 m high, two and a half hours). At 6,600 ft (1,980 m), the view, in good weather, is sublime. The Pic du Midi d'Ossau (which is 3,330 ft/ 1,000 m higher still) is reflected in the Lac Gentau, at your feet. Take your time to savour these unique moments because going down is quicker than going up (an hour and a half).

The tour of the Pic du Midi d'Ossau

½ miles (1 km) S of Gabas, by the D 231, towards the right.
Time: 7 hours

This is the most dramatic hike in the Pyrenees National Park. At the refuge of the Lac

de Bious-Artigues, follow the path to the Suzon Pass. Less than 5 hours later, at 7,670 ft (2,300 m), you'll reach your goal. The Peyreget Pass overlooks a unique landscape that embraces all the large peaks east of the valley. Just above, the Pic du Midi d'Ossau is amazingly close. Leave early in the morning and you'll also see izards (mountain goats) on your trip. A truly wonderful excursion.

Spotcheck
C7-D7

Pyrénées-Atlantiques

Things to do
Maison d'Etsaut
Hiking and walking
Excursions on a theme

Tourist Office
Etsaut: ☎ 05 59 34 88 30

Excursions on a theme
Gabas, vallée d'Ossau
☎ 05 59 05 32 13
or Etsaut, Vallée d'Aspe
☎ 05 59 34 88 30
In summer only.

The wardens of the National Park regularly organise walking-tours with a **naturalist** theme. They include an introduction to botany, nocturnal life, reading the landscape, watching birds of prey, animals, etc. They are open to all, are quite easy to understand (children are welcome) and last the maximum of one day. The only requirement is very basic – that you have suitable shoes and clothes.
Price for the day: adults, 100 F, children under 12 years, 20 F.

Z

PHOTO CREDITS

Inside pages:

The photographs in this book were all taken by **Alex Chollet**, with the following exceptions:
J. Debru: p. 7 (t., b.); p. 12 (b.r.); p. 14 (t.l., c.r.); p. 19 (b.l.); p. 24 (c.); p. 25 (t., b.); p. 36 (c.l.); p. 40 (t.); p. 85 (t.); p. 92 (b.r.); p. 95 (t.l.); p. 106 (t.); p. 107 (t.); p. 115 (t.); p. 120 (b.r.); p. 122 (b.l.); p. 125 (c.r., b.c.); p. 142 (c.r.); p. 143 (t.r.); p. 145 (c.r.); p. 147 (c.l.); p. 160 (c.l.); p. 163 (b.r.); p. 165 (c.r.); p. 166 (t.c.); p. 170 (b.); p. 189 (c.l.), p. 191 (c.l., b.l.); p. 194 (b.); p. 199 (t.); p. 207 (t.l.); p. 213 (t.); p. 234 (b.l.); p. 240 (b.l.); p. 251 (t.c.); p. 255 (t.r., c.r.); p. 264 (c.c.); p. 266 (b.c.); p. 269 (b.r.); p. 275 (c.l.); p. 284 (c.r.); p. 301 (b.); p. 307 (b.r.).

Follet Visuels/E. Follet: p. 7 (c.); p. 12 (t.); p. 36 (b.); p. 37 (t.l.); p. 38 (t.); p. 39 (t.l., b.r.); p. 82 (t.l., c.r.); p. 92 (c.l.); p. 198 (c.l.); p. 223 (t.); p. 243 (b.l., b.r.); p. 244 (b.); p. 247 (b.); p. 251 (b.); p. 254 (t.); p. 259 (b.l.); p. 263 (t.); p. 275 (b.l.); p. 281 (t., c.); p. 286 (t.); p. 288 (t.); p. 292 (c.); p. 293 (t.); p. 305 (t., b.).

Alence Tour Béarn, Follet: p. 299.

Philippe Barret/Éditions Philippe Lamboley: p. 9 (t.); p. 11 (c.c.); p. 14 (b.l.); p. 19 (t.r.); p. 21 (b.l.); p. 30; p. 31; p. 32; p. 33 (b.); p. 42; p. 43; p. 62 (b.r.); p. 155 (c.c.); p. 166 (c.l.); p. 171 (c.r., b.c.); p. 174 (b.r.); p. 181 (b.l.); p. 239 (b.r.).

Hémisphères Imales: S. Frances, p. 8 (t.), p. 204 (b.l.); **L. Sassi,** p. 73 (t., c.l., b.); **P. Wysocki,** p. 196 (t.).

Hachette Livre: p. 110 (t.l.); p. 58; p. 59; p. 85 (c.r.); p. 279 (b.r.); p. 290 (t.l.).

L. Parrault: p. 176 (b.r.); p. 182 (b.r.); p. 265 (b.r.).

P. Sordoillet: p. 144 (b.); p. 153 (t.); p. 187 (b.r.).

C. Sarramon: p. 257 (c.l.).

Phare de Cordouan: p. 12 (c.l.), p. 208 (t.l.). **La Maison de la Truffe:** p. 19 (b.r.). **C.D.T. de la Dordogne:** p. 20 (b.r.); **Grelet,** p. 137 (t.l.). **Burdin:** p. 41 (t.). **Grottes de Villars:** p. 54 (b.l.), p. 137 (c.). **Grottes d'Isturitz:** p. 55. **Noak/Le bar Floréal:** p. 62 (c.c.). **Ganaderia de Buros:** p. 72 (b.); **Jean-Bernard Lafitte,** p. 226 (t.c.). **Force basque:** p. 75 (c.r.), p. 271 (b.l.). **A.F.P.T.O.:** p. 83 (t., b.). **Château d'Urtubie:** p. 111 (c.r.). **Lambert Voyages :** p. 116 (c.r.). **G. d'Auzac:** p. 121 (c.c.). **Issigeac:** p. 129 (b.r.). **Seita:** p. 130 (c.l.). **Anitta:** p. 131 (c.l.), p. 178 (c.r.). **Château de Lanquais:** p. 133 (t.l.). **Château de Mareuil:** p. 135 (b.r.). **Ville de Périgueux:** p. 138 (b.r.). **Château de Hautefort :** p. 142 (t.). **Château de Varaignes:** p. 145 (b.). **Mine d'or:** p. 147 (b.l.). **Château de Castelnaud :** p. 159 (c.r.). **Parc archéologique de Beynac:** p. 160 (c.c.). **O.T. de Monpazier:** p. 162 (t.). **O.T.S.I. de Monflanquin, Didier Veysset:** p. 166 (c.r.). **Haras National de Villeneuve-sur-Lot, Olivier Houdart:** p. 168 (b.r.). **O.T. de Villeneuve-sur-Lot:** p. 169 (c.). **Grottes de Lastournelle:** p. 171 (t.). **Walibi:** p. 175 (t.). **Conservatoire végétal régional d'Aquitaine:** p. 177 (t.r., c.r.). **Festival lyrique de Marmande:** p. 180 (c.c.). **Fleurs séchées, La Chèvre:** p. 187 (b.). **Château de Malle:** p. 192. **Roquetaillade:** p. 193 (t.r.). **Les noisettines du Médoc:** p. 207 (c.l.). **Ville de Soulac-sur-Mer:** p. 208 (c.c.), p. 209 (t.l., c.l.). **Moulin de Vensac:** p. 209 (b.). **O. T. d'Arcachon, Ducléon:** p. 210. **Les amis du Musée de l'Hydraviation:** p. 215 (c.l.). **Conseil Général des Landes, Gouyou:** p. 223 (c.l.). **O.T. de Casteljaloux:** p. 226 (t.r.). **Faïencerie de Samadet:** p. 232 (b.r.). **O. T. et ville de Dax :** p. 237 (c.l.). **Mairie de Bayonne:** p. 243 (t.l.), p. 244 (t.l.), p. 245 (t.r., b.). **Maison Cazenave:** p. 244 (t.r.). **O.T. de Bayonne :** p. 244 (c.r.). **Biarritz Tourisme, J. Pavlosky:** p. 246 (t.l.), p. 247 (t.). **Eldora Parc:** p. 249 (b.r.). **O. T. de Hendaye:** p. 250 (t.). **Château d'Abbadie:** p. 251 (t.r.). **O.T. de Saint-Jean-de-Luz:** p. 252 (b.). **Mandozaina, Itxassou:** p. 259 (c.l.). **Base de Loisirs Baigura:** p. 261 (b.). **Agence Photo Aquitaine:** p. 265 (c.r.). **Les Chemins de Garazi:** p. 268 (b.r.). **Domaine Brana:** p. 269 (c.r.). **Château d'Andurain:** p. 272 (b.). **J. et J.-P. Ruata, Montory:** p. 273 (b.l.). **O.T. de Salies-de-Béarn:** p. 276 (b.l.), p. 277 (c.r., b.r.). **Office Municipal de Pau:** p. 288 (b.), p. 289 (t.c., c.r., b.r.), p. 290 (b.), p. 291 (t.). **Haras National de Pau-Gélos, Robert Polin:** p. 291 (b.). **Maison de la vallée d'Ossau, Laruns:** p. 304 (b.r.).

Front cover:

Background © **L. Parrault; Alex Cholet** (t., c.); **Tony Stone Images** (b.); © **Jaques Debru** (peppers)

This guide was created by Olivier Cabiro, Pascal de Cugnac and Laure de Vandiére, with the assistance of Marie Barbelet, Denis Hil, Muriel Lucas, Frédéric Olivier, Françoise Picon and Irène Tsuji

Illustrations: François Lachèze

Illustrated maps: Philippe Doro

Cartography: © Idé Infographie (Thomas Grollier)

Translation and adaptation: Chanterelle Translations, London

Additional design and editorial assistance: Christine Bell, Eleanor Stillwell, Mary Sandys and Cecilia Walters

Project manager: Liz Coghill

We have done our best to ensure the accuracy of the information contained in this guide. However, addresses, telephone numbers, opening times etc. inevitably do change from time to time, so if you find a discrepancy please do let us know. You can contact us at: hachetteuk@orionbooks.co.uk or write to us at Hachette UK, address below.

Hachette UK guides provide independent advice. The authors and compilers do not accept any remuneration for the inclusion of any addresses in these guides.

Please note that we cannot accept any responsibility for any loss, injury or inconvenience sustained by anyone as a result of any information or advice contained in this guide.

First published in the United Kingdom in 2000 by Hachette UK

© English translation and adaptation, Hachette UK 2000

© Hachette Livre (Hachette Tourisme) 2000

All rights reserved. No part of this publication may be reproduced in any material form (including photocopying or storing it in any medium by electronic means and whether or not transiently or incidentally to some other use of this publication) without the written permission of the copyright owner, except in accordance with the provisions of the Copyright, Designs and Patents Act 1988 or under the terms of a licence issued by the Copyright Licensing Agency, 90 Tottenham Court Road, London W1P 9HE. Application for the copyright holder's permission to reproduce any part of this publication should be addressed to the publisher.

Distributed in the United States of America by Sterling Publishing Co., Inc. 387 Park Avenue South, New York, NY 10016-8810

A CIP catalogue for this book is available from the British Library

ISBN 1 84202 014 5

Hachette UK, Cassell & Co., The Orion Publishing Group, Wellington House, 125 Strand, London WC2R 0BB

Printed in Spain by Graficas Estella

Voucher section

Wherever you see this symbol ❀ in the guide, you will find a voucher in this section which will entitle you to a discount or special offer. If you find a voucher here you want to use, the corresponding page number in the guide is there for your reference.

On presentation of this Vacances guide

L'Écomusée du Libournais

(history museum)

p. 123

Buy two entry tickets and get one free

Offre une entrée gratuite pour deux entrées achetées

Écomusée du Libournais

45, Le Bourg

33570 MONTAGNE

☎ 05 57 74 56 89

On presentation of this Vacances guide

Le Musée des Arts et Traditions Populaires

(museum of arts and traditions)

p. 125

Individual entry tickets for 10 F and free entry for children under 13

Propose l'entrée individuelle à 10 F et l'entrée gratuite pour les enfants de moins de 13 ans

Musée des Arts et Traditions Populaires

2, Rue Raoul-Grassin

24400 MUSSIDAN

☎ 05 53 81 23 55

Le Château de Lanquais

p. 133

Group rates for one individual entry ticket

Propose une entrée au tarif de groupe

Château de Lanquais
24150 LANQUAIS
☎ 05 53 61 24 24

Le Musée Municipal du Cognac

(cognac and wine museum)
p.135

Reduced price entry tickets

Propose l'entrée au tarif réduit

Musée Municipal du Cognac, du Pineau et du Vin
Rue du Docteur-Lacroix
24410 SAINT-AULAYE
☎ 05 53 90 81 33

La Maison des Tourbières

(tour of the peat bogs)

p. 135

Half-price entry

Offer valid for guided tours of the Maison des Tourbières and tour of the surrounding paths by a nature guide

Propose l'entrée à demi-tarif

Offre valable pour la visite guidée de la maison de la tourbe et des sentiers par un animateur naturaliste

Maison des Tourbiéres

Le Petit Lyon
24320 VENDOIRE
☎ 05 53 90 79 56

Le Village du Bournat

(19th C. village)

p. 149

Free poster of the 'Village du Bournat'

Offre un poster du 'Village du Bournat'

Village du Bournat

Le Bournat
24260 LE BUGUE
☎ 05 53 08 41 99

On presentation of this Vacances guide

Le Château de Fénelon

p. 161

Group rates for individual entry tickets

Propose l'entrée au tarif de groupe

Château de Fénelon

24370 SAINTE-MONDANE

☎ 05 53 29 81 45

On presentation of this Vacances guide

Le Musée du Pruneau Gourmand

(prune museum)

p. 171

A free small bottle of prune liqueur

Offre un bocal de crème de pruneau

Musée du Pruneau Gourmand

47320 LAFITTE-SUR-LOT

☎ 05 53 84 00 69

On presentation of this Vacances guide

Le Musée des Conserves Gourmandes

(museum of food preserving)

p.181

Free visit to the museum and a free tasting

Offre la visite du Musée et une dégustation gratuite

Musée des Conserves Gourmandes
Ferme Mauvezin
47200 MARMANDE
☎ 05 53 94 20 48

On presentation of this Vacances guide

Le Château des Ducs de Duras

p.182

Group rates for individual entry tickets

Propose l'entrée au tarif de groupe

Château des Ducs de Duras
Place du Château
47120 DURAS
☎ 05 53 83 77 32

Les Musées de La Réole

(automobile, agricultural, railway and military museums)

p.186

25% discount on adult entry tickets and 15% discount on child entry tickets

Offrent 25% de réduction sur les entrées adultes et 15% sur les entrées enfants

Musées de La Réole
19, Avenue Gabriel-Chaine
33190 LA RÉOLE
☎ 05 56 61 29 25

Les Cycles Garbay

(bike hire)

p.189

10% discount on all mountain bike hire

Offrent 10% de réduction sur la location de VTT ou VTC

Cycles Garbay
1, Cours de la République
33490 SAINT-MACAIRE
☎ 05 56 63 28 08

Le Château de Malle

p.192

10% discount on entry tickets

Offre 10% de réduction sur le billet d'entrée

Château de Malle

33210 PREIGNAC
☎ 05 56 62 36 86

Le Château de Roquetaillade

p.193

One free entry ticket
Offer valid once only

Offre une entrée gratuite
Offre valable une fois

Château de Roquetaillade

Roquetaillade
33210 MAZÈRES
☎ 05 56 76 14 16

Le Musée des Chartrons

(wine history museum)

p.198

25% discount on entry tickets

Offre 25% de réduction sur le billet d'entrée

Musée des Chartrons

41, Rue Borie
33300 BORDEAUX
☎ 05 57 87 50 60

Le Château de Nérac

p. 224

25% discount on the price of entry tickets for you and your family

Offre 25% de réduction sur le billet d'entrée pour vous et votre famille

Château de Nérac

Rue Henri-IV
47600 NÉRAC
☎ 05 53 65 21 11

Loreztia

(apiary)

p.245

10% discount, and a free gift

Propose 10% de réduction et vous offre un cadeau

Loreztia

8, Avenue des Prés

64100 BAYONNE

☎ 05 59 55 49 14

Le Château d'Urtubie

p.251

One free child entry ticket
Offer valid for families (minimum 4 people)
visiting the château

Offre une entrée enfant gratuite
Offre valable pour toute famille de 4 personnes minimum
visitant le château.

Château d'Urtubie

RN 10

64122 URRUGNE

☎ 05 59 54 31 15

On presentation of this Vacances guide

Le Musée de Basse-Navarre

(history museum)

p.271

Group rates for individual entry tickets

Propose l'entrée au tarif de groupe

Musée de Basse Navarre et de Saint-Jacques

Place Charles-de-Gaulle
64120 SAINT-PALAIS
☎ 05 59 65 71 78

On presentation of this Vacances guide

Le Parc aux Kangourous

(kangaroo park)

p.286

Group rates for individual entry tickets

Propose l'entrée au tarif de groupe

Parcs Zoologiques Parc aux Kangourous

Saint-Pie
64800 ASSON
☎ 05 59 71 03 34

On presentation of this Vacances guide

Abelio

(hangliding centre)

p. 301

10% discount on all their products

Offre 10% de réduction sur tous les produits

Abelio

64490 ACCOUS
☎ 05 59 34 58 07

All these promotional offers are exclusive to our readers, and are valid until 31st March 2002

Ces offres promotionelles sont reservées à nos lecteurs, et sont valables jusqu'au 31 mars 2002

NOTES

NOTES

HACHETTE TRAVEL GUIDES

Titles available in this series:
PROVENCE & THE COTE D'AZUR (ISBN: 1 84202 006 4)
BRITTANY (ISBN: 1 84202 007 2)
LANGUEDOC-ROUSSILLON (ISBN: 1 84202 008 0)
POITOU-CHARENTES (ISBN: 1 84202 009 9)
SOUTH-WEST FRANCE (ISBN: 1 84202 014 5)
PYRENEES & GASCONY (ISBN: 1 84202 015 3)

A GREAT WEEKEND IN . . .
*Focusing on the limited amount of time available on a weekend break,
these guides suggest the most entertaining and interesting ways
of getting to know the city in just a few days.*

A GREAT WEEKEND IN PARIS (ISBN: 1 84202 001 3)
A GREAT WEEKEND IN AMSTERDAM (ISBN: 1 84202 002 1)
A GREAT WEEKEND IN ROME (ISBN: 1 84202 003 X)
A GREAT WEEKEND IN NEW YORK (ISBN: 1 84202 004 8)
A GREAT WEEKEND IN BARCELONA (ISBN: 1 84202 005 6)
A GREAT WEEKEND IN PRAGUE (ISBN: 1 84202 000 5)
A GREAT WEEKEND IN FLORENCE (ISBN: 1 84202 010 2)
A GREAT WEEKEND IN NAPLES (ISBN: 1 84202 016 1)
A GREAT WEEKEND IN LONDON (ISBN: 1 84202 013 7)
A GREAT WEEKEND IN VIENNA (ISBN: 1 84202 026 9)

Also to be published in 2000
A GREAT WEEKEND IN BERLIN (ISBN: 1 84202 061 7)
A GREAT WEEKEND IN BRUSSELS (ISBN: 1 84202 017 X)
A GREAT WEEKEND IN VENICE (ISBN: 1 84202 018 8)

ROUTARD
*Comprehensive and reliable guides offering insider advice
for the independent traveller.*

To be published from Autumn 2000
PARIS (ISBN: 1 84202 027 7)
PROVENCE & THE COTE D'AZUR (ISBN: 1 84202 019 6)
BRITTANY (ISBN: 1 84202 020 X)
ANDALUCIA (ISBN: 1 84202 028 5)
SOUTHERN ITALY, ROME & SICILY (ISBN: 1 84202 021 8)
GREEK ISLANDS & ATHENS (ISBN: 1 84202 023 4)
IRELAND (ISBN: 1 84202 024 2)
CALIFORNIA, NEVADA & ARIZONA (ISBN: 1 84202 025 0)
BELGIUM (ISBN: 1 84202 022 6)
THAILAND (ISBN: 1 84202 029 3)
CUBA (ISBN: 1 84202 062 5)
WEST CANADA & ONTARIO (ISBN: 1 84202 031 5)